THE 50 GREATEST RANGERS GAMES

MARTYN RAMSAY

THE 50 GREATEST RANGERS GAMES

FOREWORDS BY
RICHARD GOUGH AND **DAVID EDGAR**

To Allan, my Dad, who first introduced me to Rangers, for better and for worse,

To Graeme, Walter, Ally, Brian and Paul, my heroes, who lit up one childhood with enough euphoria to fill thousands more,

And to Helen, my partner, who provided the belief and patience that helped me realise a life-long ambition.

First Published in Great Britain in 2020 by DB Publishing,
an imprint of JMD Media Ltd

ISBN 9781780915982

CONTENTS

INTRODUCTION

By the time you open this book I dearly hope that it is out of date, that more great European nights and Old Firm victories have been experienced or you have even seen some trophies won. That would be absolutely fine with me because, after all, these lists – be they greatest football games, albums or movies – are only ever just a snapshot of opinion at a certain point in time and are always destined to change soon afterwards, such is the fickle nature of fandom. They are historical documents in themselves in that they gauge what mattered most to people at a particular juncture of history, in this case the May of 2019 when the listeners of *Heart and Hand* voted for their greatest Rangers games of all time.[1] Recency bias is naturally an inherent factor, but these polls can also demonstrate the capricious nature of fashion, with some games, music or movies once perhaps out of favour now making a comeback. That, ultimately, is the result of historians doing their job well: constantly bringing moments of the past out from the shadows and back into the spotlight.

The purpose of writing the book, on the back of the podcast series of the same name, was to further explore the question of 'What *does* make a Rangers game great?' In addition to that, why do some games resonate strongly and others not at all? Why are some eras being re-discovered with vigour and others being seemingly lost to time? Is Europe more important than being top dogs in Scotland? Why are there 18 Old Firm games in the top 50 but only four in the top 20? Simply put, why have the Rangers fans voted in the way that they did and what does that say about the way we cultivate our past? In doing so, this book can be critical of games that are overrated as well as flying a flag for those deserving of more attention. There are notes of recrimination and regret at what might have been in amongst the many love letters to the club and its heroes.

This is not really a collection of 50 match reports, although the detail of the chosen games is still contained within the chapters. This is, hopefully, more a collection of retrospectives, some being more like essays than anything else. Some of the games selected just stand alone and they provide enough interest from the field of play to fill a whole discussion. Other chapters focus more on the context in which the matches were set and what impact the game had on history. In other instances there are occasions when an obvious individual bursts out, demanding to be talked about in more depth. Often, however, the games chosen are connected to wider questions and that is where

---

1 Listeners were asked to submit their ten greatest Rangers games in order of preference, with the top place getting ten points, the second nine points and so on down to one point for tenth place. The list was therefore compiled on that basis. When matches were tied on the same number of total points, they would be separated on the basis of how many different people voted for each game. There were over 170 games chosen in total.

my interest has been regularly diverted. Among the broader themes covered are the addiction of being a football fan, the illusion of the inevitable in history, the denial of our heroes' darker weaknesses, the close relationship between hubris and nemesis and that special bond we have with those who first introduced us to this sport and, in particular, this great club.

Insight from players and managers, both contemporaneous and reflective, has been included where relevant; however, this is ultimately, and unashamedly, a book from the perspective of the Rangers fan. My podcast on the *Heart and Hand* network, *The Time Capsule*, re-evaluates games from our past, but in doing so always includes the view from a fan who experienced it live. We like to think of these events as some kind of shared collective memory, which of course doesn't wholly exist. There were thousands of sets of eyes at these fixtures, all with their own stories to tell. It was therefore important to me that I included those memories and reflections, where I had already done a show on the game in question, or to seek those voices out in the cases where I hadn't. I am therefore extremely grateful to Ian Hogg, Andy McGowan, Adam Thornton, Cameron Bell, Stuart McColl, Steven Harrigan, David Marshall, James Forrest, Marina Bannatyne, Caroline Morrison, Scot Van Den Akker, Iain McColl, Iain MacLennan, John Cowden, Steven Campbell, Alan Marshall, Jeff Holmes, John Kennedy, Ross Hendry, Allan Ramsay, Barry McNeil, Graeme Harvey, David Fleming, Graeme Macdonald and Hamish Tindall for their invaluable input. Lastly, of course, my thanks must go to David Edgar, not only for his contributions throughout this book but his support throughout the project and for letting me do these shows in the first place.

There are other voices that come to the fore. Football commentators, the voices that shape the game early in our life, are often inextricably linked to the games and those memories. One could always hazard an educated guess about what teams Scotland's triumvirate of Archie Macpherson, Jock Brown and Gerry McNee favoured, but their general love for the game was never really in doubt. Sky's famous duo of Martin Tyler and Andy Gray gave some gravitas to some of the 90s Old Firm clashes somewhat in contrast to Ian Crocker's contrived staccato in the 21st-century era, whereas Peter Drury's sublime way with words wedded poetry to that unforgettable UEFA Cup run in 2008. Voices from the arts, popular culture and philosophy, mostly heroes of mine, make an appearance now and again to remind us that sport has its own place within the humanities.

The Rangers games that didn't make the list are of nearly as much interest as the ones that did. There is no room for Jock Wallace's two treble-winning sides of the late 1970s and, indeed, it would appear that 'The Treble' itself may well not be as great an achievement as we seem to believe, with only two domestic matches from seven of those seasons featured. Bill Struth's leviathan term in office only produced one game and the same number can be attributed to the classic Scot Symon side of Baxter, Ritchie, Caldow, Millar, Brand *et al.* The famous European triumphs over

Bayer Leverkusen in 1998 and Wolverhampton Wanderers in 1961 weren't famous enough to push them into contention, and the iconic Scottish Cup Final replay of 1981 against Dundee United and the 1998 semi-final against Celtic could only make the top 75. Recent memory and the advantage of glorious technicolour are significant factors, of course, but when the very first game in 1872 and the 1928 Scottish Cup Final make the list, it is not enough to explain why scores of famous matches since then haven't impacted enough. Notwithstanding the emotional resonance of 2012, the fact that Ally McCoist features in this list as a manager as often as Struth and Symon combined is an alarming one.

Both the club and the fans can do history better. The official stadium tour is a true gem and the guides are expertly able to eke out the magic from the bricks and mortar, bringing some old stories to life. When they can't, it is because they don't need to, as some rooms simply speak to us themselves. Yet, it is the *football* that is being lost. The games, the action, the narratives and the lived experiences of those victories and defeats are slipping further and further into sepia. As the club heads towards its 150th anniversary in 2022, it would do well to collate a vast bank of oral history, capturing the recollections of those who were there and lived every moment, both the agony and ecstasy. For this is what it is really all about.

Perhaps I am being a little too critical. The greatest challenge for those voting is rooted in the fact that Rangers is such a successful club. So many painful decisions had to be made when leaving out notable occasions from each individual top ten. Games that would make the summit of similar polls for most clubs – cup finals that completed trebles, league-winning games, European semi-finals – didn't even make the 100 greatest Rangers games. When so spoiled for choice, it is unsurprising that some big moments slipped through the net.

It is important, however, for me at least, that this kind of history continues to be improved and that the matches of yesteryear maintain some sense of vibrancy. Not that we should judge the quality of older matches by today's standards of conditioning, technique and organisation, more that the achievements of the day should not be forgotten. When young fans are introduced to Rangers, they shouldn't just be handed something to keep them occupied on a weekend afternoon. Instead, it should be clear to them that they are continuing something special that goes back a century and more. The same streets walked, the same songs sung, the same passion expressed. When there is little connection to the past, the dangers of lean years or even healthy years in an increasingly globalised sport become acute because there is little to cling onto or worth fighting to preserve. Without the historical context, the here and now can easily feel trivial and meaningless to youngsters who have the global superstars of elite football to take up their dreams. This is the result of history done badly – dry, dull and irrelevant. When history is done well, however, it can be a fuel that creates the necessary energy, on and off the park, that can drive future success. The club's identity and purpose becomes more vivid and, therefore, so does the need to find ways of keeping it that way.

It is only when we truly understand the mistakes of the past that we can negate their reoccurrence in the future. It is only when we truly connect with the successes of the past that we have the hunger to keep producing more of them and it is *this* that separates the greatest from the rest: an insatiable yearning for glory. As you will soon see, it is exactly this that has defined the most successful club in world football and I hope continues to do so for many decades to come.

Here's to 50 more.

Martyn Ramsay,

Sydney, 2020

FOREWORD

I find it amazing and a genuine privilege, that so many games during my time at Rangers Football Club are still considered by you to be great. That word means different things to each and every one of us in a footballing context. Games with lots of goals and action can be instant classics and some can be ground out but are thought of as great because of what they mean. For example, I didn't play at Tannadice that night in May 1997, but I was still honoured to go up and lift that ninth league trophy in a row and I fully understand why it remains so symbolic even now.

In my opinion, for a Rangers game to be great, there had to be something on the line. I remember we were going for the treble in the Scottish Cup Final of 1993 and the feeling that day was in sharp contrast to how we felt a year later, when we lost the chance to make it a double-treble against Dundee United at Hampden. The stakes matter.

European football naturally raises the significance, and the matches home and away against Leeds United in 1992/93 were so special because they hadn't been beaten down there for so long. Similarly, the match away to Marseilles later that season, where both sides needed a win to reach the first-ever Champions League Final, stands out even now. They were a first-class team, possibly the best I've ever played against, but we handled it with strength, quality and dignity.

Ultimately, the games against Celtic are always the most important games I always find. They're your greatest rivals and those games always seem to come up when I talk to supporters. We look at those games as defining moments in players' careers. To score against them will always be remembered. During my career I scored four times in an Old Firm game and they always come up in discussion. One of those games was my debut at Ibrox, the 2-2 draw in October 1987 that had everything, and another was my first as captain, where I popped up to score the winner in a cup final. European games, finals and league deciders meant a lot, but you always remember the Rangers players who do well against Celtic. It's how you all judge us!

The 5-1 victory at Ibrox in August 1988 was a strange one because the Rangers supporters wanted eight! We were excellent, one of our strongest teams was 1988/89; very physical and very strong. We turned up at Parkhead in the November thinking we had their number and they beat us 3-1. It taught me never to take anything for granted again. More than any, however, it is the four Old Firm games when we were going for nine-in-a-row that stand out the most in my mind. Those games around that time were what it's all about. They tooled up with Di Canio and van Hooijdonk, but they couldn't stop us. We were so good defensively with an outstanding goalkeeper and players on the break that could really hurt them. I loved going there. We had a team of winners and it was the test of that. We were a true team and it was when things were against us that we showed our true mettle.

It is very important for the club to cultivate that history. It's our 150th anniversary soon and we will be one of the first to celebrate such a feat. It's vital, therefore, that Martyn and people like him, keep that flame burning. When I played, I played in a golden era and when my father was growing up he also had a golden era to enjoy in the late 50s and early 60s. He would tell me stories of going to White Hart Lane to see Rangers. Those stories should be passed down and treasured for as long as possible. Generations are sometimes lucky and sometimes not. Martyn grew up watching my team deliver 18 trophies in 11 years but kids growing up in the last decade have been less fortunate. It *will* come, however, and when it does it will be very special indeed. It wouldn't surprise me if that match topped this list in 20 years' time.

You knew that it was different in the build-up to a big game, a potentially 'great' game. When I was filling my car up people would say, 'make sure you get it right on Saturday' or 'don't let us down Goughie, we really want this!' So you knew that you were part of a big family and how important we were to so many in the city. It was always on my mind that you would either let a lot of people down or make them happy.

Hopefully during my time, we made a lot of supporters very happy.

Richard Gough

FOREWORD

It all sounded so simple.

As a Rangers fan of nearly 40 years, the invitation to select the ten greatest games in the club's storied history initially seemed so straightforward. After all, I have attended hundreds of matches in person, watched a similar amount on television (or, in the days before saturation TV coverage, listened on the radio) and read copious amounts of print about the legendary fixtures from before my birth.

And then I tried to do it.

Oh, some classics leapt to mind immediately – about 25 of them. Then I began to think about criteria. Did they have to be trophy wins? Did they have to lead to something? Did I have to have been there? Could I pick games from before I was even a glimmer in my dad's eye? It got complex, and it got complex *fast*. My 'shortlist' – it makes me laugh to think I ever thought of it as that – touched three figures at one point. Some of the choices were agonising. I honestly think I spent more time on this decision than I did on proposing to my wife.

I strongly suspect I'm not alone in this and that everyone who accepted Martyn Ramsay's challenge to help him compile the 50 greatest games Rangers Football Club have participated in found themselves similarly wracked by doubt. You see, Rangers are unique in world football. We have more trophy victories than anyone else to choose from for one thing. We have witnessed countless epic battles in our own city and all the way across Europe. We've watched some of the greatest players ever to grace a football pitch in these isles. Triumph, tragedy, revolution, evolution – Rangers story is unrivalled in its drama and scope.

It was an epic undertaking worthy of this legacy that Martyn set off on and the result is the wonderful book currently in your hands. Martyn is as committed and passionate a Rangers fan as you will ever meet. I have sat with him in stadiums watching the Gers play and marvelled at the transformation of this urbane modern gentleman into a whirling firestorm of raw emotion as he was put through the wringer by our team's display. After a particularly memorable Old Firm goal, he once picked me up and hugged me so hard I feared he'd broken a rib. We often joke about the slightly ridiculous level of importance Rangers and their results have on our lives. Yet knowing the foolhardy nature of the decision to place so much of our identity in the hands of 11 strangers playing football doesn't make that hold any less strong; as long as we draw breath, we'll continue to obsess, marvel and howl at what happens when those players take to the field. Like me, Martyn is a lifer. He is, as Andy Cameron so sagely noted, a teddy bear till the day he dies.

The games included in this list are, of course, the reason we do it. For every cold, freezing and frustrating afternoon spent cheering the side on, every so often comes a match where Ibrox feels like the centre of the world. Everybody becomes gripped with the sure and certain knowledge that this is where they belong. Every supporter becomes part of a blue wall dedicated to helping the team to victory and this, to put it simply, *matters*. Sport offers up drama and emotion that even art, no matter how great, can engender. It is immediate, it is ferocious, and it is real. You feel blessed to have witnessed it, you feel part of something larger than yourself and, in all honesty, there's no feeling like it.

This list is not definitive – how could it be? By the time you come to read it, other matches will have taken place which (hopefully) will be challenging for a place in the pantheon. If the same poll was conducted in a few years, some matches would move up, others down and still more drop out altogether. History is, of course, fluid.

What Martyn has done in this book is take a representative sample of votes from the listeners of *Heart and Hand – The Rangers Podcast* and tried to place them in context. There will be choices you disagree with – there are choices *he* disagrees with – but the debate over them will continue to provide entertainment for many years to come. What is certain is you will enjoy this witty, insightful and passionate book from a real and proper Ranger I'm proud to call my friend. This is his love letter to our club. I hope you enjoy it as much as I did.

David Edgar
January 2020

50

Aberdeen 2 Rangers 3

Skol League Cup Final
Sunday 23 October 1988

'I hope the wee man was watching. We've won for him.'
(Graeme Souness, post-match)

In a sense the Skol League Cup Final of 1988 was best defined by a player who didn't participate at all. He couldn't, of course. Two weeks previously Rangers and Aberdeen faced off for the first time that term in a league match at Pittodrie. Rangers suffered their first defeat of the season; however, much worse to befall Ian Durrant, whose right knee ligaments were left in much the same state as his career. The assault by Neil Simpson was the worst, but not the only violent incident in an encounter that left referee Louis Thow's door unhinged following a meeting with Terry Butcher's foot and the Scottish football press in a state of deep soul-searching. 'When players of the limitless ability of Durrant are so severely damaged,' wrote Alan Davidson in the *Evening Times*, 'it becomes time to ask serious questions of the morality of the game and it is legitimate, too, to wonder if it is indeed worth the candle.'

The Simpson tackle was arguably the apotheosis of what was becoming the dominant rivalry in Scottish football. A violent undertone was never far away from the surface of the fixture since Aberdeen's resurgence, as the 1970s gave way to the 1980s, ran in stark contrast to Rangers' decline. However, this had taken that tension to a new level and all the build-up to the final, so soon after this dark episode, was dominated by fears of a Hampden battlefield. The BBC, as part of their studio guest line up, had former grade one referee Alan Ferguson in to speculate on the job that the match referee George Smith had in store. He wasn't ambiguous in his thoughts on Simpson's selection for the final. 'I'm absolutely astonished at the naivety of the Aberdeen management and Aberdeen as a club, that Simpson is actually on the park today. I think that if you're trying to stop vendettas happening then you have to remove the source of that vendetta in the first place.'

The game was marked by Durrant's absence too. This was the third final in a row for Rangers and the success of the previous two was in no small part down to the young midfielder. His capacity for running into space at the right time opened the scoring in the Old Firm final of 1986 and his ability to drive fearlessly at the heart of a defence put Rangers into a 2-1 lead in the classic final against Aberdeen the year before. Without this, Rangers would have to rely more on width, most notably that of Mark Walters, to try and open a famously stubborn defence.

Rangers started with Woods; Stevens, Butcher, Gough, Brown; Walters, Wilkins, Ian Ferguson and Neale Cooper, with Kevin Drinkell partnering Ally McCoist up front. It would very much be a tight midfield three of Cooper, Ferguson and Wilkins with Walters roaming on whatever flank he felt would be more fruitful. When on the left wing, Rangers were well served by Gary Stevens, who at the time was arguably the finest right back in British football. The issue was more acute when he exposed John Brown on the other side. Aberdeen, under the management of Alex Smith, adopted a standard 4-4-2 with Snelders in goal behind a back four of McKimmie, McLeish, Miller and Robertson, a midfield four of Connor, Simpson, Bett and Hewitt with the contrasting partnership of Charlie Nicholas and Davie Dodds in attack.

This final, for the first hour at least, lacked anywhere near the same level of flair and technical assurance of the 1987 epic. Much of the play, mostly from Aberdeen, was extremely direct and the only two goals of the first half both came from defensive errors. Rangers were ahead before 15 minutes had been played. David Robertson, still three years before his move to Ibrox, gave Snelders a weak throw to deal with and Kevin Drinkell pounced. Snelders was beaten in no man's land and could only pull the Englishman to the floor inches inside the box. He guessed the right way for the penalty but he wouldn't have saved McCoist's spot kick in ten attempts. The delight was short-lived, as Aberdeen drew level on 19 minutes with a goal that typified a scrappy opening period. John Hewitt delivered a second corner in quick succession and it was missed by all of Woods, Butcher, Gough and McLeish before being diverted into the net via the thigh of Dodds. Drinkell, Stevens and Walters all went close, but Aberdeen were comfortable and kept Rangers to the periphery.

Rangers had a sharper focus at the start of the second half. Drinkell and McCoist were carving out half chances as Gough and Brown were encouraged to roam forward and draw the opposition out. However, half chances were all they were getting as Aberdeen began to swamp Ray Wilkins in midfield and keep the attacks at bay. His partner Ian Ferguson was having a quiet game until the 56th minute. Walters won a throw down by the right-hand corner flag which Stevens launched into the Aberdeen box, where it was nudged away from the unlucky Drinkell by Willie Miller but right into the traction engine that was Ferguson's right foot. A bicycle kick from 14 yards in a cup final as the Rangers fans were already deep into a rendition of 'God Save The Queen'. Fergie was already a cup-final hero, scoring the winner in the 1987 Scottish Cup Final for St Mirren, but even he would have struggled to script that moment any better.

It was a volley that ignited a dramatic final third. Rangers, now with the space on the counter, looked as if they would wrap it all up. Walters went inches over with a rasping drive before McCoist hit the bar with a cross-cum-shot. However, like in the first half, Aberdeen were soon back level and it was in no small part down to a Rangers mistake. Terry Butcher was dispossessed by Charlie Nicholas in midfield with a weak tackle that was not exactly in keeping with the captain's reputation. He immediately released Bett in space down the Rangers left and his deep cross was met by a looping header from Dodds, which Woods could only watch sail over him and into the net. A second goal for Dodds, much maligned and underrated as a player, but it was not one that would leave Woods and Butcher, the bedrock of the Souness revolution, looking too pretty.

'It was totally against the run of play,' recalled Andy McGowan, standing behind the Aberdeen goal at the time. 'It shook us out of any feeling that this was going to be a procession. Somehow everything was all back on the line.'

The final 20 minutes typified an old-fashioned cup final of the time. Woods would atone from a similar position as he prevented the worst possible pre-match scenario any Rangers fan could have envisaged. Aberdeen took a quick free kick around 30 yards from goal and Neil Simpson, the pantomime villain, attempted a chip that was heading for the top left-hand corner before the England goalkeeper managed to scramble back to tip over, smashing his back against the goalpost in doing so. The cup could have gone to either side in the last four minutes of the match. Aberdeen walked through an exhausted Rangers midfield and Jim Bett found himself in acres of space behind John Brown at left-back. Woods did his job in narrowing the angles but Bett, such a composed and accomplished player, snatched at the shot and the ball was dragged harmlessly wide. 'The chance to win the cup if ever there was one,' screamed Archie McPherson on commentary. There would be more.

At last McCoist began to find space in the penalty area as Rangers bounded straight back up the field but he blazed over. Miller and McLeish, now very much in the autumn years of a fruitful partnership, had kept him smothered but the cracks were starting to appear as fatigue kicked in. Eventually McCoist would get a final opportunity which he didn't pass up. Once more it came from an aerial cross ball that was headed back and nudged away from its target (Drinkell again) before finding Ally seven yards out to sweep the ball home though the legs of Snelders. 'Classic McCoist,' recalls Andy McGowan, 'the right place at the right time. Bett was half-marking him and for some inexplicable reason, he moved out and left McCoist with space. We thought that was it, the game was won.'

Not quite yet. There was one further chance for Aberdeen to take the final into extra time for a second year on the spin and again it came from errors down our left-hand side. This time Butcher couldn't make a simple clearance on the bye line and Woods spilled the cross into the path of Dodds, who was denied a dramatic hat-trick by the diving Gary Stevens. Finally, time was up.

One of the most striking things about this game to the modern eye is the lack of squad rotation used by Souness. 86 minutes on the clock, Aberdeen nearly breaking down the door to snatch the cup and he hadn't used a single substitute. It's therefore no real surprise that Rangers would lose in Cologne a few days later in the UEFA Cup or that Ally McCoist would pick up a hamstring injury at Love St the following weekend. It was full throttle, very much in the manager's image.

This match may lack the overall quality of the previous two finals and that is why they feature further up this list. However, it does resonate with fans for a few reasons, besides the drama of a late cup winner by a club legend. Rangers were now in a blood duel with Aberdeen that would last for the next five years in any meaningful footballing sense. For fans of a certain generation, during that period, namely mine, this was a fixture that invoked more excitement and trepidation than any Old Firm match. Secondly, it was yet more evidence in the memory bank that Rangers, despite losing such an exceptional talent so cruelly, would adapt their approach and find a way to win trophies. Aberdeen would finally beat Rangers in the 1989 final and would add the Scottish Cup at the end of that season; however, more often than not over the coming seasons, when the time came they were posted missing. Whilst Rangers fans savoured the accumulation of titles, their Grampian counterparts would celebrate Simpson's brutality with more pride than any scarce Hampden triumph. More 'Rent Free' than 'Stand Free'.

In the end it was just very typical of the Souness conveyor belt that churned throughout the era, that when one piece of midfield dynamite was taken away another explosive hero would pop up with a bicycle kick that even Her Majesty would enjoy.

49

Rangers 0 Fiorentina 2

European Cup Winners' Cup Final, First Leg
Wednesday 17 April 1961

'He was a wise man who said that to stand still was to go backwards. In this age of progress, an age of remarkable changes in the very framework of the game, none can stand still – and survive ... Our young men are poised to give battle with the eagerness and enthusiasm that took them into the last stage. I am sure they will bring further dignity to our colours, no matter the actual score.'

(John F. Wilson OBE, Rangers Chairman, Matchday Programme Message)

Not all of the selections on this list made it due to the content of the 90 minutes. There are arguably four matches that resonated not for the quality of the action nor the importance of the outcome, but purely for the symbolic significance of the game being played at all. It jars somewhat, given that the very identity of the club is based on the accumulation of trophies, for two defeats to be considered amongst the greatest 50 matches in its history; however, it is correct to acknowledge the Rangers side that took to the field as the last Scottish side in a European final as well as the team that stepped out at Ibrox as the first British side to take part in one. New ground had been broken beyond the parish walls.

The competition itself was new ground. So new, in fact, that no one appeared to know for sure what it was actually called! The official match programme proclaimed it the 'European Cup Winners' Tournament', on the match ticket it states 'European Cup Winners Competition' whereas on the same page of the *Evening Times* the day before the game two different articles called it the 'National Cup Winners Cup' and the 'European Cup Holders Final'. The uncertainty surrounding it can be explained by the fact that it was something of a prototype and not a UEFA one. It was the brainchild of the Mitropa Cup Committee, organisers of a competition between clubs from Central European countries since 1927, and featured teams from only ten countries. Not every nation had a national cup competition at the time and France and Spain declined the invitation for their clubs to participate. European football's governing body would take up the idea the following season but only officially recognised this match in 1963 following intensive lobbying by the Italian Football Federation.[2]

There are some understandable reasons why this campaign as a whole should be fondly remembered generations later. Having been humbled in a European Cup semi-final the previous season by German opposition in Eintracht Frankfurt (who of course were similarly crushed by Real Madrid in the final at Hampden), Rangers gained some degree of revenge and reputational renovation with an 11-0 aggregate hammering of Borussia Mönchengladbach in the quarter-final. The 8-0 second-leg victory would naturally catch the eye, but the damage was done with an outstanding 3-0 win away from home with some sensational goals such as the third from Ian McMillan. This set up the game that fans still sing about, the first 'Battle of Britain' in European competition, where the Rangers came to Wolverhampton town with a two-goal lead and an enormous travelling support to book their place in the final.

The build-up in the press was one of excitement at this new frontier couched in the context of an insecurity about Scotland's place in the global game. Rangers at this time were a canvass upon which dreams could be projected. 'At international level,' wrote Peter Hendry in the *Evening Times*, 'Scotland is undoubtedly considered amongst the "also rans". But at club level Glasgow Rangers are rated in the top bracket.' Incredibly, this first leg was played four days after Scotland were soundly beaten 4-0 away from home by Czechoslovakia in a qualifier for the 1962 World Cup (the Czechs would reach the final only to be defeated by Garrincha's Brazil) with five Rangers players *and* the cup final referee involved. *La Viola* were not the reigning Coppa Italia winners and started a succession of clubs, including Rangers in 1972, who would win this tournament only after being entered because they lost out in the cup final to the league winners. They had won a *Scudetto* in 1956 and would be runners up for the next four years, boasting a team with Kurt Hamrin, the star of Sweden's World Cup in 1958, who remains the seventh highest scorer in the history of Serie A with 190 goals, two ahead of Giuseppe Signori and Alessandro Del Piero. Rangers had just secured another league title, however, so Fiorentina were respected in Glasgow but not feared.

Sadly there was little, if anything, for Rangers fans to savour about the match itself. Both on and off the pitch, it was not exactly an advert for the beautiful game. Fiorentina produced a showcase of gamesmanship and what is sometimes now romantically described as the 'dark arts'. There was nothing romantic about how it was received by the Scottish press at the time, however. 'The men from Foulorence!' boomed the *Times*. 'Fiorentina are the dirtiest, most unscrupulous, and most ruthless Continental team ever to disgrace Ibrox Stadium. Just about one thing these unsporting Italians did not bring on to the Ibrox field was an atomic warhead,' wrote Gair Henderson, perhaps

---

2 https://www.uefa.com/MultimediaFiles/Download/EuroExperience/uefaorg/Publications/01/51/54/12/1515412_DOWNLOAD.pdf

mindful of the anti-Polaris demonstrations then underway at the Holy Loch. The *Glasgow Herald* were more understated but concurred that the Italians had a 'mastery of the arts of body checking, tripping and almost every other infringement of the football rule book'. Scot Symon was in no doubt. 'We were not beaten by a defensive system. Our boys built up attacks all right. As soon as danger threatened there was a body check, a push or a deliberate foul to keep them out.'

Not for the last time in a European contest, Rangers, in their blue and white vertical stripes, were beaten by themselves as much as the opposition. Both goals, scored by Luigi Milan, were close-range finishes following terrible errors in the Rangers defence. In the 12th minute, Harold Davis produced a calamitous attempt at a back pass to the goalkeeper Billy Ritchie which was pounced on by Petris and rolled into Milan's path for a simple finish. With seconds remaining, another poor Davis pass put Bobby Shearer under pressure when he was dispossessed by Milan, who received the ball back from Hamrin and swept it home. It could have been so different if Eric Caldow had converted a penalty only six minutes after the opening goal. It was dragged well wide of the left-hand post but pictures show the goalkeeper Albertosi almost at the six-yard line as he met the line of the ball. Rangers waited for a re-take but referee Steiner didn't oblige, perhaps having been so generous in awarding the spot kick in the first place following a tackle on Ian McMillan that was widely agreed to be fair.

The Italians punished Rangers for individual errors and the skill of Hamrin, Petris and Milan was undeniable. However, the newly crowned Scottish champions were blunt and never offered any real penetration, opting too often for high crosses that were dealt with easily by a towering defence and goalkeeper. It can't be stressed enough that this game was played at a time of very little cross pollination in footballing ideas, especially in north-western Europe. This was a Rangers side still developing into one of the best in the club's history, one where the creative influence of Jim Baxter and Willie Henderson was still to fully blossom. As a result, compared to the continent's best, they were honest and strong but arguably limited technically and certainly tactically. Rangers forward Jimmy Millar, who missed the first leg through injury, summed up the approach neatly in Tom Miller's Baxter biography. 'We had no master plan. We went into games in Europe against the likes of Real Madrid the way we would prepare for a game against Raith Rovers. Although it was around this time Scot Symon started to send us out with the simple instruction – *just give the ball to Jim … he'll make things happen.*'

Symon's opposite number that evening was a little more considered. Hungarian Nándor Hidegkuti was part of the 'Magical Magyars' who turned football on this island on its head with their sensational 6-3 defeat of England at Wembley in 1953. He scored a hat-trick and did so from a deep-lying centre-forward role that left the English defence unsure if they were still playing the same sport. It is no real surprise that as a manager he was able to approach these games in a way that still felt alien to British opponents. The Chairman's programme message could have been written with him in mind. '*None can stand still and survive.*' A lesson that would be learned and then forgotten at Ibrox many times over in the decades that were to follow but was delivered here at a time where it was more prescient than ever before.

Unsurprisingly, the ugly tension on the pitch was replicated on the terraces. The growing frustration in the Rangers support with on-field events reached its climax with 20 minutes remaining when Bobby Shearer was scythed down by Claudio Rimbaldo and this led to the first torrent of bottles and cans onto the park. As the Rangers players sportingly clapped their opponents off the pitch at full-time, Rangers fans were clambering to pull down the Italian flag from the top of the main enclosure. A policeman rescued it before it was ripped apart. Nine Rangers fans were charged with breach of the peace the following day.

A disappointing and frustrating night at Ibrox was followed by another close defeat in Italy ten days later; however, there is merit for the inclusion of this game, and not just because of the groundbreaking achievement inherent in the fixture itself. This collection of players, '*with men like Bobby Shearer*', arguably deserve a lot more love than they get in our modern-day appreciation and certainly more than one solitary entry in this poll. A legendary side in the early 60s that dominated Scottish football, culminating in a treble success in 1963/64, and could have fulfilled wider promise were it not blunted by Baxter's broken leg in Vienna the following season, took a big step on that road when they stood on the Ibrox turf that night.

A field so familiar and yet so unexplored.

48

Rangers 3 Celtic 1

Scottish Premier Division
Thursday 2 January 1997

'It ain't what you don't know that gets you into trouble, it's what you know for sure, that just ain't so.'
(Anon)

It certainly looks like something that Mark Twain would have said. That folksy charm belying a cold, cutting observation about human behaviour. The quote is attributed to him at the start of Adam McKay's Oscar-winning drama *The Big Short*. Ironic, perhaps deliberately, that a movie about deception and misinformation should start with such a falsehood. There are no records of Twain saying anything of the sort but it doesn't matter to the viewer, who can easily find a wry comfort in assuming that it is something that Twain would have surely quipped to someone at some point. It's the sentiment that matters, not the facts.

Eventually Scottish football historians will be able to establish the last time Rangers won an Old Firm game without decision-making by the match officials being reported as being the deciding factor. It certainly wasn't the New Year fixture of 1997, just as the nine-in-a-row epic was reaching its conclusion. With Rangers 2-1 ahead and only four minutes left on the clock, the ball was nodded down by Phil O'Donnell into the path of Jorge Cadete, who smashed it past a stationary Andy Goram. Sadly for him, Gordon McBride's flag was already up for offside and the goal never stood. Cue hysteria. 'WHY THE REFFIN HELL WAS THE GOAL DISALLOWED' bellowed *The Scottish Sun* the following morning, for some reason omitting the question mark. Phone-in shows were alive with complaints of bias, conscious or otherwise. Celtic had been denied a title because of this decision!

When this argument is brought up, as it regularly has been over the years, its advocates often choose to ignore the small problem of the big gap. Rangers went into this game 11 points ahead, although Celtic had two games in hand. Neither side were able to generate a large winning run during that pressure-cooker season. Rangers managed seven wins in a row twice (once at the very start and then a winter stronghold, of which this game was part) and Celtic's best effort was the six on the spin following this game, when the pressure had been somewhat lightened. Twice that season they were handed encouragement when Rangers dropped points before Celtic next played but couldn't capitalise on either occasion. It is a large assumption therefore that the games in hand would have been converted under that strain or that even if they were, that a five-point gap was manageable. Ultimately, Celtic came to Ibrox that night needing to win. A draw wasn't really good enough. Poor offside call or not, they needed more than Cadete's equaliser.

As is so often the case, these games are characterised more by the surrounding soap opera than the story of the match and how the result was ultimately achieved. Despite being close to the height of our riches (January 1997 saw Joe Lewis' ENIC buy 25 per cent of the club for £40m) Rangers were severely under-strength for the third Old Firm game of the season. Richard Gough and Brian Laudrup were out and Paul Gascoigne, Andy Goram, David Robertson and Erik Bo Andersen made themselves available despite being laid low with the flu. Alan McLaren and Joachim Björklund returned to the heart of the defence but neither had played a lot of football in recent weeks. Ally McCoist would captain the side. Celtic were at full strength but handicapped themselves by keeping Pierre van Hooijdonk on the bench as his contract dispute rumbled on.

The opening exchanges produced chances at both ends; however, unusually for an Old Firm game, the tempo was slow, with players perhaps suffering from their winter ailments. Then there was a gear change in the ninth minute when Robertson was fouled by Jackie McNamara just over 30 yards from goal. As the home crowd chanted 'Albertz! Albertz!' Martin Tyler noted on commentary that he was getting a 'genuine reputation as a set piece specialist'. One could criticise the gap in the wall or Stewart Kerr's positioning, but when a free kick nearly touches 80mph and is dead on target for the inside of the side netting, there is little more to do than shower the taker with all the praise. 'The Hammer has torn Celtic apart,' Tyler exclaimed. Jörg Albertz would go on to score eight times against Celtic. He had set the tone of this game, and his Rangers career, in thunderous fashion.

The game became more alive as the pace increased. Fouls mounted up which meant both sides could work each other from set pieces, Goram and McCoist blocking efforts from Di Canio and Stubbs whilst Petric and Ian Ferguson went close at the other end. Goram also found the target when he landed a ball right on Paulo Di Canio following a break in play. This led to the Italian wanting a piece of every Rangers player on the park and a simmering feud was born that boiled over in the final game between the two in March.

Tommy Burns relented and brought on van Hooijdonk to replace Simon Donnelly eight minutes into the second half and the impact was almost immediate as he forced another incredible stop from Goram to add to what was becoming a personal duel between the two stretching back to November 1995. He was needed again to make an even better close-range save from David Hannah six minutes later. Rangers were wobbling. Both wing-backs were making unforced errors and a shattered Gascoigne was lost with the pace in midfield. Smith eventually made a change when he replaced him with Charlie Miller on 66 minutes, but it didn't prevent the equaliser that all in the ground must have felt was becoming inevitable. Tom Boyd was able to run freely at the Rangers defence, Cadete and van Hooijdonk linked up nicely in the penalty area and Di Canio was left in space to fire home an effort that even Goram couldn't do much about.

'At that point you're taking a draw,' recalled Alan Marshall. 'Let's not kid ourselves. It was just wave after wave and we were fearing the worst. Everyone was getting tetchy from the start of the second half and now that had developed into something worse. Even though we had previous for "rope-a-dope", like in the November game, there just seemed no energy left in the tank.' The next ten minutes, however, perfectly encapsulated the major weakness in that Tommy Burns side. Celtic had most of the ball but, with Rangers reeling, couldn't produce a single chance during that dominant period. Dangerous and threatening when chasing a lost cause. Nervous and impotent when the chance to cut down their nemesis was begging.

Smith moved and Burns reacted. Off came McCoist and Craig Moore, on entered Peter van Vossen and Erik Bo Andersen, whilst Celtic brought on the attack-minded Andreas Thom to replace Alan Stubbs. Yet again in this match the impact of the substitutions didn't take long in coming. The newly formed Celtic defence, which now included midfielder David Hannah, engaged in a game of head-tennis on the edge of their own penalty area, and when McNamara couldn't gain control from a weak Brian O'Neill header, Albertz could and he slid in Bo Anderson. The Dane had work to do but kept his cool perfectly with a first-time finish to put Rangers into the lead.

If it was another 'cat and mouse' special from Smith then it was an opportunistic one. This was Celtic's own doing. They were in control of the game and responded to the Rangers substitutions by needlessly overloading in attack and sacrificing the shape when they needed it most. Cadete's 'goal' three minutes later was another example of piercing the lines when there was nothing to lose. After Paul McStay blasted an effort so high over the bar that it would have cleared two set of goals standing on top of one another, Rangers counter attacked in a very controlled and familiar fashion. It was Bo Andersen again who would show a calmness in front of goal so out of place in the middle of the mayhem, but it had the stamp of Albertz all over it from his punishing run and then a perfect pass.

There was an outpouring at Ibrox. A draw would have given fans great confidence in getting over the line to the nine. A win felt like it was a certainty. Sitting behind me that evening was Kai Johansen, another Dane who had experienced the feeling of scoring a winner against Celtic. He said there and then that the league was over. No one near him was arguing. Walter Smith would never utter it publicly; however, his charge down the trackside perhaps spoke more truth.

Despite trying to get the game postponed due to the worsening flu crisis, Rangers travelled to Easter Road two days later and won 2-1 – further evidence of a side that could still fall back on a steely resolve when on the ropes. This was the ninth Old Firm game in succession without defeat. It wasn't an accident, nor was it a conspiracy. Rangers generally had the correct shape, a game plan that was ideally suited for the opposition and players who would step up when the nettle needed to be grasped, whether they be Danish legends for life or just for one important night.

Celtic's analysis of the match seemed to focus less on poor managerial decisions, psychological frailties or defensive mishaps and more on private investigations into the ticket history of officials. '… *it's what you know for sure, that just ain't so*.' There were many perfect aphorisms accredited to Mark Twain without evidence of his authorship. Another one of those perhaps sums up this game, and the general narrative of the battle between the two sides during this period, better than any other.

History doesn't repeat itself but it often rhymes.

47

Rangers 3 Rapid Vienna 1

Europa League Group Stage
Thursday 4 October 2018

'That's a Rangers performance of old, a successful Rangers performance. It was an incredible night.'
(Steven Gerrard, post-match)

From the rubble of 2012, the road to that next destination was always going to be a longer one. As soon as the 54th league title was secured at Rugby Park on 15 May 2011, the 55th was already sharply in focus. It's how Rangers Football Club defines itself to the world after all: a league-title-winning machine. The fallout from the financial implosion a year later, however, blew that prize far into the distance. The journey has had its inevitable diversions but also its necessary landmarks. That first step at Brechin, the emotional first night back at Ibrox, the first triumph over Celtic, the return to the top flight. And Europe. Not the ignominy of a Luxembourg shrubbery. The return to a proper, lucrative platform with its own theme music and opponents with a similarly rich history.

The first sense of this return came in the previous game, an away trip to face Villareal on Spain's east coast. The opening group game of the Europa League in a recognisable stadium involving players fans didn't have to google. If Rangers were in awe by the shock of conceding so early, they were shaken from their slumber at half-time and engaged their top-class opponents in a swashbuckling final half hour which saw two equalisers in a pulsating 2-2 draw. For the thousands packed into the upper tier of the stand that shook behind those two Rangers goals, the feeling of rebirth will never be forgotten.

If truth be told, Rangers had absolutely no business being in this stage of the competition so early in their development under a new manager, coaching staff and an influx of fresh faces into the squad. The initial impact of Steven Gerrard's arrival was the formation of a resoluteness away from home in the four qualifying rounds which, when mixed with a bit of fortune at times both on the field and in the draw, as well as a scintillating second-half performance at home to Maribor, saw Rangers take their place in a European tournament proper for the first time in eight years.

Despite the overwhelming and understandable propensity to delight in a history of domestic dominance, European football still resonates strongly with the Rangers support. Seventeen of the 50 games chosen (almost exactly a third) come from European competition. When Rangers finally secured promotion back to the top tier of Scottish football with a 1-0 victory at home to Dumbarton in April 2016, much of the social media activity was the sharing of how other footballing nations were reporting it. In an increasingly globalised game, how we are seen around the world matters. There would be few better ways to demonstrate that renaissance to the watching world than by having another big European night under the Ibrox lights.

'The atmosphere was incredible,' remembers one of those fans packed in that night, James Forrest. 'The stand was bouncing up and down and I hadn't experienced the stadium move like that before. My father assured me that we would be in more trouble if it wasn't moving but it was still an insane feeling. This was the kind of night I was waiting to get back ever since 2012. A big European game under the floodlights and everything about it was just magical.' Rangers fans had been starved of that colour, noise and glamour and they showed the appreciation from the outset. Thankfully the team responded in turn.

This match was played during a time when they were coming thick and fast for Rangers and, therefore, due to injuries and conditioning, the team selection was often changeable. Joe Worrall, on loan from Nottingham Forest, had come in unexpectedly to start in Spain and kept his place for the visit of Rapid. He also started in the horrendous display at Livingston the previous weekend; however, Borna Barisic and Kyle Lafferty were replaced by Jon Flanagan and Ryan Kent by the Thursday night.

The first half had more than a few characteristics that would echo throughout the rest of the season. Rangers had possession and impetus, feeding off the excitement in the stands, but did not yet have the chemistry and connectivity in attack that could tease open well-drilled opposition. There would be danger on the counter as Andrija Pavlovic went close with a header after he ghosted in between the fledgling partnership of Connor Goldson and Worrall. Rapid's opener would come from a controversial decision and not the last that Rangers would suffer in this competition. With only five minutes remaining until half-time, Rapid scored from a neat, but clearly offside, passing move. Andrei Ivan was released whilst standing in a different shade of grass from any defender, directly in front of the assistant referee, and his low cross was diverted by Lassan Coulibaly into the path of the Norwegian Berisha, who kept his composure to slot home nicely.

Allan McGregor lost his temper with the match officials and was booked for the trouble; however, Rangers did not need to wait long before justice and parity were restored. Intelligent passing from Ryan Kent, a devilishly dangerous cross by James Tavernier and a poacher's finish from Alfredo Morelos. If ever a goal was typical of Rangers in 2018/19 it was this one, and the match was level at the interval.

Not for the first time in that season's Europa League campaign, it took until the second half before Rangers fully believed that they deserved to be there and, when they finally accepted their new standing in the game, could play with more freedom and expression. Both loanees, Kent and Ovie Ejaria, made the keeper work as, inevitably, did Morelos. The momentum was only going in the one direction, propelled by the symbiosis of the players and the fans. Any fears that the match would end in a familiar glorious failure were suppressed in the 83rd minute. Ejaria's control and pass into the box for Morelos was perfect and Mario Sonnleitner was given the impossible choice of allowing the Colombian a free hit on goal or committing a certain foul and giving up a penalty opportunity to Tavernier.

There wasn't even a hint of doubt from the Rangers captain at the penalty was converted with great technique and conviction into the top-right corner. Rapid threw everything at getting a late equaliser and upon their final foray into the Rangers box they were caught out. Worrall towered above the rest to clear the lines and Daniel Candeias then had three crucial touches inside 20 yards. The first was another looping clearance from Worrall's header, the second was a robbery of Potzmann on the halfway line and the final touch came from the back of his boot, saving time and momentum, to send Morelos clean through on goal to wrap up the points with ease.

The Rangers fans didn't see enough of that second-half courage and fluidity over the course of the season to ensure another of those landmarks, a trophy, would be reached. They had, however, seen enough to give them hope that this wouldn't be another long, difficult diversion away from where they desperately wanted to be. Regardless, that night in itself restored some pride. 'This game will go down as one of my all-time favourites because it had been so long since we had experienced such a night,' said James. 'Although the rest of our Europa League campaign would prove to be a disappointment, that night will be one I will never forget.'

This game may jar with older fans as it takes its place on such a pantheon. Compared to some of the other European victories still to come on this list, it may look a little down-market. However, the symbolism alone makes it a deserving entrant, before we even consider the fact that it was a fun match played in such a vibrant atmosphere. Football, like all sport, thrives on relevance. Achievements that go unnoticed by the watching world tend to ring hollow. 2012 and the subsequent years were so difficult because we were shut out from any relevant sporting contest. It had been like watching football in the dark. And now the lights were coming back on.

46

Dundee Utd 0 Rangers 3

Scottish Premier League
Sunday 24 May 2009

'I've never wanted anything more in my life than for those players to win that championship.'
(Ally McCoist, post-match)

It's not that Rangers fans have ever been blasé about winning the league championship, it's just that some have been celebrated with more exuberance than others. Further up this list lies the sheer drama of 2003 and the victorious climax to a bitter campaign in 2011. The gift from the heavens in 2005 and the night of historic destiny in 1997. And, in particular, the end of those long hungers in 1975 and 1987. Agonising barren droughts washed away in an afternoon.

Writing as I am in the summer of 2019, the reaction to the title win in 2009 (the first since 2005) seems ridiculously exaggerated. Ewan Murray, writing for *The Guardian*, started his match report by saying, 'Nobody who witnessed this epic outpouring of emotion could be left in any doubt as to how desperate Rangers had become to reclaim the title. Euphoric scenes, which absorbed four years of the Ibrox side's frustration, greeted this definitive victory. Rangers are champions again, for the 52nd time in their history; few of their previous triumphs can surely have prompted such visions of relief.' He ended the piece, which recognised the automatic qualification for the following season's Champions League, by saying, 'This was Rangers' day and, financially, their salvation.' Fair to say, that didn't age well.

At the time, however, it was bang on the money. For the post-Souness generation, three seasons without a title was something of a famine and, although nothing quite like the enmity that coloured the 2010/11 season, there was more than enough tumult in this campaign to ensure that the travelling support made their way to Dundee more desperate for success than many could remember.

The melodrama had started with the controversial return of Kenny Miller following a period at Celtic and continued in Kaunas, Lithuania. Less than three months on from the prestige of a UEFA Cup Final, Rangers had been dumped out of Europe at the first attempt before a league match had been played. All that had been forgotten by the end of August due to an unforgettable 4-2 victory at Parkhead, thanks in no small part to Miller; however, the league form would struggle to find consistency until the very final stretch, the notable low moments being a home defeat to Celtic, which left Rangers seven points behind at New Year and then a very sluggish spell in March. It was arguably an off-field issue that best allowed Walter Smith to sharpen the focus for the title run-in. Barry Ferguson and Alan McGregor were suspended by the club for two weeks without pay following a heavy drinking session whilst on international duty, which was compounded by childish behaviour on the bench at Hampden for a qualifier against Iceland. With both players out of the picture, the Rangers midfield looked more balanced with Davis, Edu and Mendes blending well, culminating in a 1-0 victory over Celtic at Ibrox where Davis scored the winner and Rangers were top of the table with only three games remaining.

It would never be as simple as that, of course. A midweek draw at Hibs handed the initiative back to Celtic who, thankfully, responded in turn by dropping two points at the very same ground the following weekend. This meant that, after so many twists and turns, for the first time since 1991 Rangers would go into the final game of the season knowing that a win would guarantee the title.

Stuart McColl was a 16-year-old at the time, just starting to follow Rangers all over the country. 'Manchester was one of the greatest days of my life, but losing the league so soon after was one of the worst. I couldn't concentrate on anything else the week before this game, which wasn't ideal as I was in the middle of exams! I got there 30 minutes before kick-off and the atmosphere was just unbelievable. I had been to Old Firm games and European games before but I had never experienced anything like that around the time that the teams were just warming up.'

If there were any nerves amongst the travelling numbers, they were misplaced. 'We met a journalist that was good friends with my dad,' Stuart recalls. 'He mentioned that he had bumped into Ally McCoist beforehand and he had said that it would all be over before half time.' It was clear from the off that this Rangers side were showing the same confidence as their assistant manager. The first goal took all of six minutes and it came from Northern Ireland. Kyle Lafferty, the media villain for play-acting in a spat with Aberdeen's Charlie Mulgrew the week before, was the hero as he adjusted his body well to divert Kris Boyd's cut back into the net. The chance was really born out of the driving run of Steve Davis, cutting in from the right-hand side with a skill and endeavour that had United on the back foot all afternoon and further evidence of how crucial the Ulsterman was in the second half of that season. Those early goal celebrations, the kind that would be replicated at Kilmarnock two years later, showed a side very much in sync with the support. Everyone desperately wanted this title.

Everyone with the exception of those at Parkhead, of course. Celtic were at home to Hearts, awaiting a slip up at Tannadice, and on 23 minutes the stadium was alive with excitement. It had nothing to do with the ponderous scoreless draw taking place in front of them but news of a Dundee Utd equaliser. Perhaps the tide was turning!

It was, however, a beautifully coordinated piece of fake news. 'Operation Tango' was a plan some days in the making, that involved Rangers fans texting some Celtic-supporting acquaintances at an agreed time with the 'bad' news. For those watching at home it was glorious piece of comedic theatre. Those in Dundee had no idea.

Those in Dundee didn't care. They were enjoying a party but were still aware that the mood could change at any time. Some clear water was required and every bear packed into the ground must have thought that Kris Boyd had created it when he found space in the box, steadied himself and unleashed one towards goal before being denied by a superb goal-line clearance by Kovacevic. 'This is where I start thinking that this is going to turn away from us because I wanted it that badly,' recalls Stuart. 'At the time I couldn't believe he had missed it. Harsh when I look back now but we just needed the second goal.'

That crucial goal came just before the interval and from the same devastating technique as the goal that arguably sparked the season into life in the first place. Pedro Mendes had stunned Celtic with a volley from outside the box back in August that sent Rangers into a deserved 3-1 lead. This goal was similar, although from his left foot, as he pierced a ruck of bodies in the box once a Sasa Papac free kick looped up after hitting the wall. Class and technique, allied with a cool and intelligent footballing brain, is always required when the stakes are so high.

The momentum was now unstoppable and a third goal six minutes into the second half finished the match as a contest. Fittingly, it came from Kris Boyd with his 31st strike of the season after some more good work by Davis and Mendes released Whittaker down the right, who managed to find Boyd inches onside to give Zaluska no chance from point-blank range. Boyd's future had been a hot topic of debate throughout the season, with his departure a real prospect during the January transfer window. A banner at the League Cup semi-final late that month read 'NO BOYD = NO GOALS = NO TITLE'. The volume of goals was never the issue, it was more where he produced them. Title-winning seasons for Rangers and Celtic are usually defined by their head-to-head record and away trips to the rest of the top six. Boyd's strike rate in those fixtures was relatively poor. The way Smith set up for those challenges didn't suit his natural game unless Rangers had built a comfortable position. There's a strong argument to be made that his goals set up a title charge but never made that crucial difference.

It wasn't an argument that many fans were having that afternoon as they partied hard at the return of the league championship. The rest of the game was a non-event. A light training session as the players awaited the helicopter carrying the trophy and some champagne. Ferguson got a cameo at the end and, upon the insistence of his new captain Davie Weir, they lifted the trophy together. Celtic's Georgios Samaras famously proclaimed in the build-up that Rangers wouldn't 'deserve' to be champions. Thousands at Tannadice loudly disagreed as the silverware was passed around with delight.

There were clouds in the background, however, and perhaps this is why this match, the first of the ten title-winning games on the list, is cast so far adrift from the next one (Game 18). Ewan Murray's final line about financial salvation was very wide of the mark; however, the economic concerns were starting to become acute. Even at the time of immediate celebration, Walter Smith's future was not clear, and if he had failed to get this over the line that day it could well have led to an early exit and not, as it turned out, the start of an incredible three-in-a-row in such trying circumstances.

Denial was still the preferred option, however. Football fans of all colours have a tendency to ignore the horizon and live in the moment instead. Barren spells do that to you because you just never know for sure when you will be able to dine out on that glory again.

45

Rangers 1 Celtic 0

Scottish Premier League
Sunday 28 February 2010

'Men who are desperate for a solution are easy to persuade because they wish desperately to be persuaded.'
(JK Galbraith, 'The Age of Uncertainty')

'Absolutely magic. Just won us the league. So it has. Superb!' Such was the expert analysis on *Sky Sports News* as Tottenham's Robbie Keane joined Celtic on loan for the remainder of the 2009/10 season. There was a time, before the impromptu introduction of sex toys, where the biannual 'Deadline Day' coverage was appointment viewing on Sky. Reporters would camp out in the close vicinity of football stadiums and training grounds where they would consume the minutiae of ongoing deals nearly as much as they did coffee. Inevitably, by lunchtime a crowd would gather. Children, whom for the most part should either have been in school or their bed, were surrounded by the ghosts of their Christmas future as the anticipation of season-defining signings would build before fizzling out in a depressing anti-climax.

Not so at Parkhead. It's easy, not to mention fun, to mock the hundreds who were huddled in a car park late into the February night to pay homage to the new messiah, the man who was going to claw back a ten-point deficit against a Rangers side that had lost only one league game all season. However many clubs Keane had turned up at, pleading his life-long love, he was still a dangerous player, even though he was coming to the end of his career. It was a good coup – he would finish the season as Celtic's top scorer – but there was a lack of realism in such pronouncements when one considers the battered and beleaguered state of Tony Mowbray's side as a whole. Rangers fans aren't exempt from this nonsense either, of course, especially since 2012. It is universal. Football fans across the world are all guilty of the same thing. We all wish desperately to be persuaded.

Keane's debut came the following night at Kilmarnock. Celtic lost 1-0. He did come up with a few goals in the next four games, but if he really was going to alter the direction of the league title then it would have to be at Ibrox on the final day of February. A Rangers win would give Walter Smith a ten-point gap with a game to spare and in effect the league would be all over. The scene was set for a hero after all.

The build-up to kick off had many familiar ingredients. The Celtic high command indulged in what had become a standard Machiavellian paranoia by leaking, in the week before the game, that they had complained to the SFA about the standard of refereeing in previous Old Firm encounters. This would lead ultimately to the prospect of a referee strike later in the year but was designed to put pressure on Dougie McDonald's handling of this match. The Rangers goalkeeper, Allan McGregor, had provided the tabloids with more salacious interest when he was injured in an incident in Glasgow the previous weekend, although he would be passed fit to take his place between the posts. It would be the day that Rangers paid their respects to one of McGregor's predecessors, Gerry Neef, the reserve goalkeeper in the 1972 Cup Winner's Cup squad, but the minute silence was again disrupted by the Celtic support in the Broomloan Road end.

'You're fucking getting it!' The tone of the match and the wider narrative was set in the first three minutes with two Kevin Thomson tackles on Keane in quick succession. Speaking to *Heart and Hand* in 2017, Thomson denies singling out the Irish international specifically. 'I never earmarked Robbie Keane, anyone was getting it. It just so happened to be him. He pulled my top and pulled me towards him. Called me a wee prick or something and as I ran back I told him he's fucking getting it again.' Careful design or happy happenstance, it was the perfect opening act in the latest episode of this saga of strife.

Keane was still busy in that first half though. He sailed a free kick over the bar from just outside the box and then was foiled by the other main character in that week's drama, McGregor, who saved brilliantly from his right-foot volley. Both sides had their chances in an open 45 minutes. Boyd and Miller should have done better for Rangers and Marc-Antoine Fortune certainly should have for Celtic right before the interval. Thomson did leave a game-changing mark on a player, but it was one of his own. An accidental collision with Lee McCulloch's heel necessitated a 27th-minute substitution and Maurice Edu had the ball in the net within a minute on the field, but it was ruled out for a handball from Miller on the way to his controlled right-foot shot.

If the media leak was engineered to put pressure on Dougie McDonald, the success of the plan was negligible to say the least. Madjid Bougherra was booked for a lunge on Keane after 12 minutes and there could have been a case made more than once that afternoon for a second yellow card. To no avail, however, and the image of 'Boogie' winking quickly developed into a favourite GIF on fan message boards everywhere. McDonald did show a red card midway through the second half, and it was for the new Celtic captain. Scott Brown and Kyle Lafferty got themselves into the inevitable midfield tussle, Brown's head landed in Lafferty's chest and the Ulsterman reacted as he was often prone to do, given half a chance. It put Celtic very much on the back foot and yet again gave them an out in the aftermath should the result go against them. Walter Smith was quick to shut that down post-match. 'The Old Firm games are always awkward, everybody comes under scrutiny. You always argue with the refereeing decisions, it doesn't matter what anybody says. It would be nice if they were going to criticise the referee, then they come out of the closet and do it, rather than do it in an anonymous manner. The referee's under enough pressure as it is. I thought the referee handled the game very well.'

As the second half developed, Rangers grew in strength. A draw would probably have been enough to see off the Celtic title challenge, but as time ticked away and pressure wasn't converted into a goal, it would have been a strangely deflating way to end such a game. One final corner in the 93rd minute was enough to break the resistance. It was swung in from Thomson on the left-half side and found Bougherra, who controlled well and tested Boruc with a right-foot drive. The Polish goalkeeper should have done better, as should Kris Boyd when it was spilled into his path. Edu didn't make any mistake from less than a yard out and sent Ibrox wild. 'I think we've just seen the goal that has won a championship,' said a deflated Davie Provan on co-commentary.

Every fan, regardless of age, enjoys a last-gasp winner against Celtic, but for a generation of Rangers fans – those who missed nine-in-a-row and were too young to appreciate the successes of the early 2000s – this was a period to properly savour. David Marshall was of that era and has fond memories of this moment in particular. 'Bedlam, utter bedlam. The reaction of Ibrox that day will live with me for the rest of my life. The whole stadium was a sea of limbs and bodies jumping through the air as Walter led the way running down the touchline like it was 1997 again. For my own part, I had to stop jumping about to prevent an asthma attack, seriously! However, as I paused for breath, I just took everything in around me and watched as friend and stranger alike embraced each other in a joy that is hard to describe if you haven't experienced it before. I have experienced "better" and bigger moments than the "Edu Game" following Rangers. However, for that moment of sheer ecstasy inside Ibrox and losing all your inhabitations, there are not many that can beat it.'

This is a surprise choice to be included in such company. A pretty scrappy game where Rangers toiled to overcome a poor Celtic team at home. There are perhaps two reasons to explain its lasting popularity with a younger generation. Firstly, it was the first, and to date only, time when they saw a Rangers side win a title in comfort, this match all but confirming that before March. Secondly, it had a 'moment'. The last-minute winner was aesthetically ugly but beautiful in its emotional impact. Moments matter. Whenever we watch them back, we are instantly re-connected with the exact same emotions that we had the first time.

It will be forever known as the "Edu Game". In his play *Life of Galileo*, Bertolt Brecht describes a scene where the great man's pupil Andrea is so disconsolate with his teacher's famous recantation that he says, 'unhappy is the land that breeds no hero'.

'No Andrea,' Galileo replies, 'unhappy is the land that *needs* a hero.' It is a beautiful truth when applied to the broad sweep of global political history and there's a lesson for the football fan too, especially when we pin longer-term aspirations on a new saviour. Nonetheless, sport will always produce those fleeting moments that do require a hero, even when it's not the one some expected it to be.

44

Rangers 5 Celtic 1

Scottish Premier League
Sunday 26 November 2000

'... In spite of Virtue and the Muse,
Nemesis will have her dues,
And all our struggles and our toils
Tighter wind the giant coils.'
(Ralph Waldo Emerson, 'Nemesis')

When taken out of context this match ticks so many of the relevant boxes that sets the greatest games apart from the rest. It's a thumping victory against old rivals, it was a genuine end-to-end contest for large parts, it had so many stand-out individual performances from established players, hope-inspiring cameos from old and new faces and, in the first and final examples, some high-quality team goals. However, football is always played within context and should always be remembered with that in mind. The key box remaining un-checked here is that one of impact and successful relevance. Other memorable games have missed the list because they existed in barren seasons. The two back-to-back league and Scottish Cup victories over Celtic at the end of the 1997/98 season didn't make the cut because, despite containing many memorable moments and imagery, they ultimately led to acute disappointment. Perhaps those cuts still run too deep and, amidst the farcical shambles of season 2000/01, the support is better able to compartmentalise and romanticise this particular November afternoon.

Where there has been hubris, nemesis will always follow. The distinguished historian Margaret MacMillan knew a thing or two about the rise and fall of powerful men. 'Hubris is interesting,' she once remarked, 'because you get people who are often very clever, very powerful, have achieved great things, and then something goes wrong – they just don't know when to stop. The more power you have, the more danger it is that you will only hear what you want to hear, that you will only be told things that flatter you, and you become convinced that you are right, and you persist in certain courses of action, even when the costs become very high, perhaps intolerable.' If there is a better precis of the story of Dick Advocaat's Rangers career by this point in time, I have yet to encounter it.

It is not difficult to see where the hubris came from in the first place. Five domestic trophies out of six, a winning margin of 21 points in 1999/00 and restoration of the club's European reputation. Add that to a personality that does not lack in self-belief and it should really be of no surprise that Advocaat's decision-making during the summer of 2000 very much resembled MacMillan's observations. The addition of Bert Konterman to an already established defence was misguided. The sheer lack of preparation to try and combat a very different, physical Celtic side under Martin O'Neill was professionally negligent. Any misconceptions that it would be business as usual despite some serious summer activity on the other side of the city were blown away in the fifth league game of the season. A 6-2 defeat perhaps didn't quite capture the evenness of the opening 45 minutes, but it did crystallise the sense of complacency and arrogance running through the club.

It was nothing new, of course. Rangers had lost heavily at Parkhead under Advocaat on his first visit there in November 1998; however, his lead was at the time sizeable and it was comfortably dismissed as an aberration. Walking out of the stadium that day we may have used the same words but few of us really believed it. Rangers were still in the hunt at the start of October, with a deficit of only three points, and had already chalked up two memorable Champions League victories, at home to SK Sturm Graz and away to Monaco, to start that new campaign in style. The rest of the month saw everything fall apart. Three league defeats in a row, the disastrous signing of goalkeeper Jesper Christiansen and two fatal, error-strewn closing fixtures in the Champions League left Advocaat under a pressure he had never previously faced.

He replaced his captain. His defence was that he felt the fans were getting on top of Lorenzo Amoruso and he wanted to remove that burden. Nearly 20 years on, the Italian doesn't buy it. Speaking to *Heart and Hand* in May 2019, Amoruso was still visibly livid with his former manager, whom he felt had made him a sacrificial scapegoat. 'I told him at the end of that conversation, "I don't like you, don't speak to me anymore as a human being. Speak to me as a manager and I will answer you as a human being. I will not answer you because if you don't like the way I play you drop a player to the bench but you can't take off the armband because you are blaming me, just me, for the way the team is playing on the field."' The new Rangers captain was his 22-year-old protégé Barry Ferguson.

Advocaat, in sync with his chairman's approach to problem-solving, also tried some retail therapy in order to alleviate the pressure and they spent big. The signing of Tore Andre Flo more than doubled the Scottish transfer record when he arrived from Chelsea for £12.5m and it was starting to resemble a very scattergun strategy. Rangers balked at spending half of that on John Hartson three months earlier, but that was then and this was now. Desperation was beginning to set in and gambling so much on a player who never had a consistent scoring record and was very much out of the picture at Stamford Bridge was the kind of example that kick-started a pattern of financial mismanagement that would have long-reaching consequences.

Flo started against Celtic as did Rangers captains past and present in a game that had to be won for there to be any remotely credible talk of a title chase. With a gap of

14 points and a game advantage, however, the word 'credible' was doing a lot of heavy lifting. This was a match in isolation. It was about pride, as Steven Harrigan recalls. 'This was one of those rare games where the crowd and the players were on exactly the same page. It was all about revenge and settling a score.' The pace was typically frenetic. Flo could have scored in the second minute after a great counter-attacking move involving Albertz and Reyna, a player who had been sorely missed in recent weeks. Rab Douglas did his job but it was perhaps the Norwegian's lack of match sharpness that cost him the chance. Rangers had a better one two minutes later. Amoruso launched a fairly standard ball into the Celtic box that managed to still cause havoc for Douglas and Johan Mjällby, but Ronald de Boer somehow managed to scoop the ball over the bar when there was an empty net in front of him.

Celtic had their chances too, most notably to Valgaeren and Sutton, however it was the new Rangers skipper who broke the deadlock just after the half hour mark. It was a beautifully timed run into the box and finish by Ferguson but this goal was as much about Claudio Reyna's drive, vision and perfectly weighted pass. Every moment of note for the rest of the first half seemed to involved Ferguson, from a handball shout in the box (his hands came into the body to protect himself) and luring Alan Thompson in for reckless challenge that brought him his first booking of the afternoon.

O'Neill made some changes at half-time that gave more presence to the Celtic midfield, most importantly Jackie McNamara for the anonymous Lubo Moravcik, and it reaped quick dividend. Konterman was posted missing as a Bobby Petta cross found Thompson in the penalty box, but Amoruso and Numan were alert to the danger and limited the damage to a corner kick. It was only a momentary reprieve, as Thompson's cross found Larsson with a free run in between Amoruso and Konterman, a partnership that was never destined to work, and Celtic were level.

For all of two minutes. The Rangers response was instant as they penned Celtic back and won a corner on the left-hand side. De Boer's ball was deep and it found Albertz, whose header rebounded off the crossbar into the vicinity of the new boy Flo. It was described by Davie Provan at the time as an easy chance, as admittedly those from less than two yards out usually are; however, the ball fell behind the Rangers forward and the instinct and skill he showed to effectively score with a cushioned back heel shouldn't be dismissed.

The pattern of the match was now set firmly in Rangers' favour, helped in no small part by Thompson's second yellow card from another wild tackle on Ferguson. Rangers pressed home their advantage in the middle of the park but the next two goals came once more from corner kicks. With 23 minutes remaining, Rangers scored from a mirror image of the previous corner as Albertz swung a deep back-post ball in from the right-hand side to be met by the head of Ronald de Boer, making his Old Firm debut. Ten minutes later, Albertz again delivered another devastating cross and this time it was converted by Amoruso, who thundered it home with relish, proving a point to fans and manager alike.

Incredibly, another debutant in this famous old fixture was Michael Mols. Injured the previous season before the first fixture came around, every Rangers fan inside Ibrox that day was eager to welcome him onto the pitch as a second-half substitute for a very young Kenny Miller. He scored the best goal of the match, which started with Amoruso carrying the ball out from the back, eventually making its way to Albertz, who caressed the ball with the inside of that famous left foot into the path of the onrushing de Boer, who swept it across the box for his countryman to complete the move and the day. His audience had waited a year to see that moment.

Revenge was sweet, and, although any hope of retaining the title may have been forlorn, there was genuine hope amongst the thousands streaming out of the stadium that this season was just a blip. Rangers were still in both domestic cups as well as the European consolation prize of the UEFA Cup. 'The league was gone,' said Steven Harrigan, 'but we had shown that next season it was our title to lose again.' This wasn't entirely ridiculous. The dressing room rifts seemed to have been mended, Amoruso still looked imperious despite the lack of an armband and the kid who was now wearing it led by example and could have potentially been at the club for life. We had a new striker who had scored on his debut and a returning one who looked like he had retained some of the ability to twist defenders inside out and could hopefully have the same impact on the season as Henrik Larsson was having for Celtic, after a similar injury layoff.

The resonance of this match might simply be explained by it being a farewell of sorts. It was the manager's final victory over Celtic and the last great performance by this Advocaat side, arguably the greatest technical Rangers team of all time. Klos was rock solid, Amoruso straddled the game like a god, Ferguson and Reyna's combination of movement and tempo was superb, Albertz looked like he could change the game at will and Mols looked close to how he did in that opening spell in Munich before his career was ruined.

It was also the end of another era, one of Old Firm dominance at Ibrox. This was the 12th game in succession that Rangers were undefeated at home to Celtic, a run stretching back to 1994. For historical comparisons, one has to go back to two of the greatest Rangers sides of all time. The legendary side of the early 60s managed the exact same record of 12 without loss and the great post-war team of Young, Waddell and Thornton were unbeaten in 16 games between 1945 and 1954. Modern Rangers fans would never see anything remotely close again.

The inclusion of this game, therefore, proves that some last hurrahs do echo into eternity and demonstrates the need that some fans have to cling onto the memories of hubris right at the moment that Nemesis takes her dues.

43

Celtic 0 Rangers 1

Scottish Premier Division
Sunday 16 March 1997

'I don't want to put you under a lot of pressure but this game is the most important game in the club's history so take it or leave it.'
(Archie Knox, pre-match)

Much has been written in recent years, by Michael Cox, Jonathan Wilson and others, about the tactical changes that have shaped British football since 1992, the year that introduced the Premier League in England, the Champions League in Europe and, perhaps more importantly, the back pass law everywhere. Although widely ridiculed today, getting the ball into 'the mixer' was once the prevalent school of footballing theory on these islands. As Cox described it in his book of the same name, it was the 'simplest tactic in football: launch the ball into the penalty box, take advantage of the ensuing chaos, perhaps following a goalmouth scramble, and hope to pinch a scruffy goal.' It is probably fair to assume that in Walter Smith's preparation for the defining final Old Firm game of the 1996/97 season, there wasn't much work done on the laptop. This was very much back to basics.

Although a perfectly fair observation, there are many reasons why this approach on *this* day should not be disparaged 20 years later. Firstly, the three other league games against Celtic, which Rangers won and were always going to be significant in the quest for this fabled ninth title in succession, were great adverts for the game, especially the second match which will feature later in this book. It was a familiar strategy of set pieces and lightning counters into the space that this Celtic side would always give up; however, the quality of its execution should be left in no doubt. Paul Gascoigne's bursting run and finish in the opener and the free kick from Albertz in January (Game 48) are evidence of that.

Secondly, needs must. As was becoming customary by that stage of the 1990s, the injury list was bigger than the number of fit players at the football club. Out of 58 first-team players, reserves and apprentices, 34 were injured. Erik Bo Anderson, hero of the previous league match, had suffered a depressed fracture of the skull against Celtic in the Scottish Cup the previous week, Gordon Durie had appendicitis and Paul Gascoigne and David Robertson had longer-term issues, although Gascoigne sought to treat his by spending time on the lash with showbiz pals. McCoist and Gough were not fully fit, but Gough was desperate to start whilst McCoist took his place on the bench. Perhaps most importantly was the loss of Andy Goram, the bane of Celtic's existence for the last five seasons. With Theo Snelders not trusted to withstand the heat of this particular battle, Smith dipped into the market for a free replacement. In a time before transfer windows, in came Andy Dibble from Manchester City, a goalkeeper who had spent the vast majority of his nine years at Maine Road on loan somewhere else. For a support growing more and more nervous, replacing their enemy's Kryptonite with a Welsh keeper who hadn't spent more than a full season at one club since the 80s didn't necessarily help matters. It was no different for his new team-mates who, after an early training session, said that they thought it was Officer Dibble that had signed.

Smith's other signing that week *did* provide fans and players alike with a tonic. On the Thursday morning, three days before the game, Mark Hateley had hung up on his agent more than once. 'I thought it was a wind-up,' he told *Heart And Hand* in 2018. 'But it took me a nanosecond to agree to come back.' Although 35 years old and described by Hugh Keevins in *The Scotsman* on the day after the game as 'more memorabilia than mobile', he still had a presence that terrified the rest of Scottish football. He also wouldn't be asked to drive the Celtic defence back as he used to do in his heyday. This was a clear sign of the game plan. Football boiled down to its fundamental elements. An afternoon that would offer up less in the way of nuanced quality than some iterations of the famous Kirwall Ba game, the annual Orcadian tradition where a scrum of men try and force a ball to the edge of either the town's north and south boundaries.

Smith had good reason not to be confident in trying anything too complex. March had not been kind and Rangers were deep in a slump by the time this game came into view. Two points were dropped on the first day of the month when an early two-goal lead at Pittodrie had been cancelled out and a shocking 2-0 defeat at home to Dundee United followed the first loss to Celtic since May 1995, this time in the Scottish Cup quarter-final at Parkhead. Returning there, just ten days later, with a lead of only five points in this season of all seasons and without an away win in over a month was only ever going to lead to one approach. There was simply too much at stake. A defeat would have brought the lead to within one more swing. Avoiding it would pretty much seal the championship. The performance of Celtic's pre-match huddle was nothing new, but their encore *after* that cup win was not well-received by this Rangers squad. Motivation was not something Smith had to manufacture.

The side that he managed to cobble together still retained the 3-5-2 shape, consistently in place since Gascoigne's arrival in the summer of 1995. In front of Dibble was a three-man central defence of Gough, Björklund and McLaren, with Alec Cleland and Jörg Albertz playing out at wing-back. Ian Durrant, Ian Ferguson and Craig Moore comprised the middle three, with Laudrup playing off Hateley's knock downs. From almost the first kick of the ball, there was artillery fire aimed at the Englishman where, not for the first time in the afternoon, he bullied Malky Mckay in the process of challenging for it. The opening exchanges were brutal. Craig Moore and Peter Grant were booked for cynical fouls. The Rangers' set-piece options were either a long ball for the Hateley battering ram or, as happened on three occasions, Albertz tried to re-create the magic of New Year but blasted straight at the Celtic wall instead. Their responses were limited to timid through balls for Cadete's runs, which Dibble was alert to, or a Laurel and Hardy free kick routine between Grant and Paulo Di Canio which led to another fine mess.

If one player wasn't going to be dragged into this swamp then it was always likely to be Laudrup. He retained composure whenever Rangers broke and fed Durrant and Hateley on a few occasions, but they couldn't reciprocate his coolness of thought. Although the word composure was far from the best way to describe Paulo Di Canio that afternoon, he did represent Celtic's best way of breaking through. With only six minutes left before half-time, he was taken out by Durrant on the edge of the box and rattled the crossbar from the resulting free kick. The place seemed to shake as much as the woodwork did. 'I don't know if it was just the angle of our seat but I thought that was in,' recalled Iain McColl, who was sat far back in the bottom tier behind Dibble's goal. 'They were getting close.'

With only a minute remaining of the first half, Rangers were seeing out the job as planned. Albertz had another free kick deep inside his own half and launched it yet again upfield for his target. If Hateley did flick it on, it was with whatever hair was left on his head, but it still caused too much of a problem for Alan Stubbs to deal with. His header was weak and Durrant took advantage of both that and Stewart Kerr ending up in no man's land, as he managed to lob the ball over the Celtic goalkeeper and towards goal. It was Laudrup who got the final touch in a goal-line scramble with Mackay to complete a goal that was almost beneath him. Cox could have been thinking about that exact move when he succinctly encapsulated that nature of route-one football. Not that anyone in the Rangers end that day cared a jot. 'It was sheer euphoria. It was the timing of the goal that made the difference,' said Iain. 'We drank a lot with Durrant and it felt so apt that he got the goal that could have sealed the nine. It wasn't until we got back in the pub that we found out that it was credited to Laudrup!'

The image of Richard Gough breaking from a wall to charge down yet another indirect free kick in a dangerous area was all that remained from the first half and was a perfect encapsulation of the team's attitude with their captain leading from the front. For all of Parkhead's noise in the opening exchanges, there was a sombre reflection at the break now that they were a goal behind. It wasn't just the recent scar tissue that had been built up, Celtic fans would have to go back to 1983 to find the last time Rangers went ahead at Parkhead and lost (a record that would stand until 2008). Something inside was strongly telling them that they were finished.

When Hateley left Enrico Annoni on his back inside the first minute of the restart, it was clear that it would be more of the same, just with more space and tired limbs. Di Canio was the only Celtic player showing up, although his control was eroding fast. Caught by the Rangers offside trap so often, he was booked when he blew up at the linesman for a correct decision, but no second yellow was forthcoming when he did the same following the ball running out of play. At the other end it was Laudrup again who was looking the most threatening for Rangers, and one of his counter attacks on 65 minutes resulted in the game's biggest flashpoint. After a sublime moment of control, Laudrup was free to run at the heart of the Celtic defence. After beating Mackay, he was brought down and then the Celtic defender appeared to stamp on him as he lay on the floor. Hateley, noticing the usually calm Laudrup's rage, confronted the Celtic players, which now included Stewart Kerr, who had run 20 yards off his line just to get involved. Hateley was pushed by McNamara and then faced off to Kerr with his head leading the way. That was all referee Hugh Dallas needed to see and duly sent him off.

Hateley's explanation years later that he was just keeping his chin tucked in to avoid being caught out isn't quite in harmony with the television pictures. This incident, coming just three minutes after Richard Gough had been forced to admit defeat with injury and had come off for Charlie Miller, with Moore slipping back into defence, meant that Rangers had lost their two key warriors in this major battle. 'The confidence at half-time had been lost, with Gough going off and now Hateley. You worried about momentum,' remembered Iain McColl.

Hearts were pounding in the stadium, but, in hindsight, we needn't have worried. Celtic were frozen by the fear that threatened to overwhelm them all season. When they did break the lines, such as the time Cadete lost McLaren in the box, Björklund's pace was there to snuff the danger out. When Mackay was finally sent off for a second booking after upending Laudrup, further wind was taken out of their sails. The best chance fell to Annoni after Dibble made his only mistake of the afternoon by not dealing with the cross ball, but his effort went tamely wide of the goal. When he committed arguably the worst foul of the match, on Laudrup late on, it sparked further scenes of pantomime aggression. When Di Canio, on a booking, confronted Ian Ferguson by gesturing that he would break his legs, Fergie suggested they wait until after the match. At the time of writing, he is still waiting.

The final whistle broke the tension and everyone knew that the league was over. There would be a match where that special title was confirmed but it would be all but ceremonial. This was the final step that needed to be taken and, regardless of the quality, it will never be forgotten. In retrospect, there were elements throughout this game that would foreshadow the season that was to follow. Celtic lacked quality in the middle of the park and a manager that was not blinded by the fog of obsession. They would get that midfield and a new boss, in Wim Jansen, who was more detached and analytical. Rangers needed a huge influx of new blood which is often costly and always a big risk. The spine of that new side, Amoruso, Thern and Negri, would not be fit enough for the entire season, hence the need to rely once more on this band of brothers, who were already showing large signs of breaking point in this fixture. It would prove to be a bridge too far.

But that was for another day. There was one final reason why Walter Smith's approach to this game should be venerated, even in these more enlightened times: it worked. Under extreme pressure, he sent his boys out for a battle and, as Brian Laudrup said when he recalled the story of Archie Knox's team talk, 'we went out there and lived up to the expectations.'

42

Rangers 2 Celtic 2

Scottish Premier Division
Saturday 17 October 1987

'Football is a physical game and we will continue to be a physical side.'
(Graeme Souness, May 1987)

There are plenty of examples in the annals of Old Firm history where the always-simmering and deep-rooted tensions have reached breaking point. There have been riots between fans from 1909 to 1980 and as recently as 2011, po-faced, opportunistic politicians brought to the attention of parliament the touchline war of words between Neil Lennon and Ally McCoist where some chin music was threatened, 'presumably in the keys of F and C'. Some moral arbiters may point to the 'Shame Game' of 1999 as a particular nadir where, as Scott Murray in *The Blizzard* so memorably put it, 'referee Hugh Dallas was quantitatively eased to the floor by the targeted injection of the pound sterling.' If the sole focus is on the behaviour of the players, however, then it is hard to look past the second clash of the 1987/88 season as the most infamous derby match of them all.

Sporting rivalries may have their historical roots in class, politics and religion; however, it's always when the sporting element gets interesting that one sees the temperature really rise. In the ten years before the arrival of Graeme Souness, Rangers players had seen red on three occasions against Celtic. That tally would be equalled in the first two encounters of this troubled season. After winning the title in such breathtaking fashion at the first attempt, Rangers were now there to be shot at in the summer of 1987, especially by a Celtic side in its centenary season. Souness would get the retaliation in early with an outrageous tackle on Billy Stark at Parkhead in August, which saw a straight red for the Rangers player–manager. It was nothing new, of course, as Souness had bookended that famous seasons with reds at Easter Road and Pittodrie, and by the end of this October clash Rangers would have chalked up ten red cards in all competitions in just over one season. It was an unashamed and deliberate attempt to create a side in both his own image and that of his all-conquering Liverpool side whom he always said were programmed to play but prepared to fight.

'Graeme always said that if your team is struggling, you have to try and get a reaction somewhere. A big tackle gets a reaction just as a goal does,' recalled Mark Hateley to

Heart and Hand in 2018. By October 1987 Rangers were indeed struggling. Just three points from the first five league games ensured a shambolic start to a title defence, and by the time Celtic came to Ibrox, Rangers were lying in fourth place, four points behind their old rivals and six behind the early pace-setters, Hearts. With just two points for a win, they had given themselves a mountain to climb but they had climbed a bigger one the previous season. Also, Souness had finally got the defender he had wanted for some time and whom he now considers his best-ever purchase – Richard Gough – who had signed for £1.5m from Tottenham earlier that month. There was still room for manoeuvre. On the same day that Gough arrived at Ibrox, Frank McAvennie turned up at Celtic for £750,000 and, along with a young Andy Walker from Motherwell, were tasked with filling the gap left by Brian McClair, Mo Johnston and Alan McInally that summer. Billy McNeil had also returned to the dugout. It was very much game on.

'Undoubtedly Britain's match of the day,' exclaimed Jock Brown from the commentary position, and he wasn't wrong. Ian Hogg was 12 years old, and for the first time was at an Old Firm game without his father, instead accompanying his brother in the notoriously vociferous East Enclosure. 'It might just be because I was in a different part of the ground, but when you listen back, you can hear that it's different. A lovely day to play football but it just felt a bit more electric. The atmosphere usually dies down after a while as everyone takes a breath, but it just didn't that day. It was as if the two sides were just going toe-to-toe all afternoon. It really had a kind of boxing feel about it.'

It wasn't long after the first bell sounded that those inside a sunlit Ibrox would get a portent of things to come. Tommy Burns, before being clattered by Ian Durrant, lofted a high, old-fashioned 'up-and-under' for Woods to deal with, with the sun in his line of vision. (Unlike any Old Firm game in recent memory, Celtic attacked the Broomloan Road end in the first half. This was where that low autumnal sun would be a problem in the first half but not for all of the second.) He did well to tip over the bar before being bundled into the net by McAvennie. The Celtic striker was high off the ground, arms and legs making contact with the Rangers keeper like something from the Nat Lofthouse era. There were many historical fuses lit, and heading towards this particular tinderbox, but this was the final one. It was as if McAvennie, now the new Celtic-minded poster boy, was too riled up as there was really no need to challenge for that ball in that fashion.

The top came off in 17 minutes. Celtic probed through the middle with McStay, who sent the ball out to Chris Morris down the right flank. His cross was tame and eased back into the hands of Chris Woods by Rangers left-back Jimmy Phillips. McAvennie, behind Phillips and at least five yards away when he blocked the cross, continued his run into the path of Woods. With the previous incident no doubt still in his mind, Woods shaped his body to defend himself against another McAvennie charge. McAvennie then took a left-handed swipe at the back of the goalkeeper's head and everything went up a gear. The two exchanged pleasantries before Woods grabbed the striker by the throat, before receiving a punch to the side of the face. The Rangers captain then intervened and shoved McAvennie, which knocked him off balance before another punch, probably by Graeme Roberts, although possibly by Woods, put him on the floor holding his face.

'... and here's trouble now. And this is what everyone was hoping would *not* arise,' lamented Jock Brown, belying the fact that the viewing figures for *Scotsport* on the Sunday evening would have been inflated exactly *because* people did want to see what all this fuss was about. Referee Jim Duncan from Gorebridge in Midlothian was handling his first Old Firm match and he was handed quite the baptism. Ultimately he had no choice, despite the protestations, to send off both McAvennie and Woods. Butcher was booked probably more for his dissent at the Woods red card than the push to McAvennie's chest. Before leaving the stage like a topless model, Woods handed Roberts, who had gone unpunished, the red jersey. In the days before substitute goalkeepers, Rangers would have a three-man defence, with John McGregor dropping out of midfield when needed.

It was a shambles. Celtic broke through the lines at will. Firstly, Peter Grant had an effort that the rookie goalkeeper did well to shut out, and then the first goal came. An agricultural clearance by Mick McCarthy was controlled well by Walker, who only had a desperately chasing Butcher for company. He made no mistake with the finish. Two minutes later Celtic doubled their lead, or rather Rangers did it for them. After some good work by Stark and Walker through a non-existent midfield, Butcher was left to deal with the through ball to Peter Grant. Under pressure, and rattled by recent events, he lobbed the ball over Roberts's head whilst Grant ran to the Broomloan Road stand in order to genuflect with his congregation.

'Everyone thought the roof was about to cave in,' explained Ian Hogg. 'Everyone feared an absolute doing. They were breaking at will.' No more damage was done before half-time, however, and Souness eventually plugged a gap he would have been better-served fixing as soon as the danger arose, when he replaced the forward Mark Falco with a defender in Avi Cohen. Any new-found stability was left it pieces on 63 minutes. John McGregor tested the Celtic goalkeeper Alan McKnight with a lofted ball into the box, but referee Duncan felt that the pressure exerted by Butcher was excessive. As both players tried to get back on their feet, Butcher ensured McKnight spent a little more time on the deck when he lashed out at him. Another easy decision for the debutante official and Rangers were now down to nine men. When discussing the incident on an episode of *The Time Capsule* Ian Hogg re-assessed his feelings about the incident: 'It's taken me a long time to come to this conclusion but I reckon that Butcher chucked it. I can't believe that a guy who has been to two World Cups already, very experienced in Europe etc, gets too caught up in the emotion of an incident that happened an hour ago.'

The fans weren't for chucking it, however. The songs, perhaps more of defiance than of hope, rang out as Rangers tried to find some way back. They were rewarded with 25 minutes remaining with a beautiful, albeit anarchic, goal amidst the violence. Some great close control and perseverance by Derek Ferguson eventually found the new right-back Richard Gough popping up in a number-ten role to lay it off to Ally McCoist, who finished brilliantly with a left-foot strike that went in off the post.

Celtic had most of the remaining possession but didn't put Rangers to the sword when they were surely still very vulnerable. Walker had a tame shot at Roberts and a speculative Stark header hit the bar but, with such a novice between the sticks, he should have been peppered. They were content to sit on the lead and weariness was also taking hold as demonstrated by a clash between Grant and Ferguson where both combatants seemed to just fall back against the ropes rather than square up for more of the same.

As the clock ticked into the 90th minute, Roberts had one final tired kick. It somehow reached Ferguson in the middle of the park, who controlled well and spun away to send Durrant an opportunity down the right hand side. He glided past the hapless Anton Rogan before fizzing a ball into the box that was cleared by McCarthy. The clearance went straight back to Durrant, who opted this time for a high, looping ball. It was missed by McCarthy, McCoist and, most importantly, McKnight and fell perfectly for Gough, the defender haunting the six-yard box, where he poked it home. The noise distorted the STV microphones and Ibrox lost itself in a frenzy. Terry Butcher, stuck in the dressing room with no television to keep him appraised, likened it to an aeroplane taking off. 'All I saw was the cross going in and then this noise and surge,' recalled Ian. 'For the first time at the football I feared for my life. It was just chaos and wild celebrations.'

'Someone was looking down on me that day,' smiled Gough when he sat down with *Heart and Hand*. 'My first home game, my first Old Firm. I've got a picture in the house and Peter Grant is behind me just watching it go in. It felt like we won the game.' There was still time for one final incident as substitute Owen Archdeacon again followed through into the Rangers goalkeeper. Roberts made a meal of it and took to conducting the Ibrox crowd as he wasted what little time was remaining.

If anyone thought that the 90 minutes were bedlam, the aftermath wasn't much quieter. Following 62 arrests and editorials calling Souness's side the 'common denominator', the calls for the Procurator Fiscal to get involved were immediate. The trial was heard in April 1988, where Woods and Butcher were fined £500 and £250 respectively, Roberts received a Not Proven verdict and McAvennie, who started the whole affair, was found Not Guilty. Of more concern was that Rangers would fail to hold onto their English stars; however, these were quelled a few days after the case had finished.

Violent drama on the football field may sell but it almost always overplayed. Far more serious bodily harm is done every week in contact sports than was unleashed in that skirmish in the Rangers penalty area. The willingness to get down and dirty did tarnish the reputation of that early Souness side ,which was able to play some excellent football in similarly hostile environments. However, it was clear that the balance between beauty and brawn was an issue and things changed soon after. Picking up one point in a season against Celtic simply wasn't an option going forward and neither was having key players missing for big games. In his first two seasons, Graeme Souness's Rangers picked up nine red cards in league matches. From 1988/89, the first of the nine-in-a-row dynasty, it would take until the sixth of those seasons before Rangers would reach that league total again. The immediate short term was impacted by the arrival of more creative players like Mark Walters, Ray Wilkins and Gary Stevens, which would naturally help change the overall approach.

It was only a draw in a season that was ultimately disappointing but it still means so much to those who were there because of a refusal to give in against all odds and another demonstration of outstanding character. Souness had made his point in those first couple of years. His team wouldn't be bullied. They'd be resilient to the end. Almost like an early tackle, he set the tone and then got on with playing winning football. As time went on, the capacity for fighting was still there if need be; however, the success that followed would have been impossible if they were not first and foremost programmed to play.

41

Rangers 4 Hearts 3

Coca-Cola League Cup Final
Sunday 24 November 1996

'The spark of genius again, just when it's required.'
(Jock Brown, Commentary)

Some games become etched in the memory not because of symbolic significance or the desperation for a particular trophy but simply because they were bloody good fun. This match was like a good night at the cinema: some star performances from the A-listers, some unexpected jeopardy but the troubled hero saved the day and everyone headed home happy, if a little cold. The match nearly didn't go ahead at all due to a blizzard in the morning, but a pitch inspection before lunchtime finally gave the go-ahead.

'I was sitting near the hospitality section which for some reason wasn't full,' recalled Andy McGowan. 'I actually jumped the wee mini barrier and sat there because they were cushioned seats and kept me a lot warmer! I remember it being quite a subdued atmosphere for a cup final. The new Parkhead structure wasn't complete and it wasn't raucous. Maybe because of the exhilaration of the game ten days before, I don't know.' It was the second trip to the east end of the city in short succession due to the redevelopment of the National Stadium, the other being a breathless classic league clash, packed with incident and ultimately a crucial win in the hunt for the championship. This final felt like relief from that intense pressure and against a team that we had good memories of facing. It was the second cup final against Hearts in 1996 and the Scottish Cup Final in May was an evisceration. An excellent overall team performance was overshadowed by one of the most graceful and superlative performances the old stadium had ever witnessed. Brian Laudrup was always going to get some close attention in this game; however, Hearts had to be careful to play within the limits of the law, after being reduced to seven men in the last meeting between the two sides, a 3-0 defeat at Ibrox.

Laudrup may well have been in a good place following that crucial winning goal earlier in the month; however, the club's other genius was already showing the sad signs of what was to limit his career and ruin the best years of his life. October had been a nightmare month for Paul Gascoigne as stories of domestic violence surfaced at the same time as on-field violence was being committed in a Champions League hammering in Amsterdam. Probably unthinkable in the modern climate, but the club publicly washed their hands of the private affairs of a married couple, and were criticised heavily for their silence, but carpeted Gascoigne internally. He showed flickers of his undoubted ability immediately in a 2-2 draw at home to Aberdeen but was quiet and missed a penalty in the Old Firm game earlier in the month. Fans were both worried and conflicted about their hero.

There were no concerns about this cup final, however, as they battled with the elements to take their seats. 'There were no thoughts of an upset. It just wouldn't have entered my mind at the time,' said Andy. Rangers were practically at full strength with just David Robertson missing the starting line-up and having to make do with a place on the bench with the ever-flexible Craig Moore deputising at left wing-back. Gordan Petric would partner Gough and Björklund in the three-man defence in front of Goram and Charlie Miller, Gascoigne and Albertz would constitute the midfield, supporting Laudrup and McCoist up front. Hearts, now managed by Jim Jeffries, allied the familiar experience of John Robertson and Gary McKay with exciting young players such as Paul Ritchie, Colin Cameron and Neil McCann. A famous goalkeeping howler in the May final by Giles Rousset hadn't been forgotten by anyone in the stadium.

One of those youngsters, Paul Ritchie, was given the unenviable task of man-marking Laudrup, the source of so much pain for the Edinburgh side six months earlier. Speaking to *The Scotsman* in 2016, Ritchie said, 'I was asked to do that a few times and, looking back now, looking at the quality player he was, it was a great privilege. There were certain parts of the game I was successful, certain games where I was successful; certain times when I wasn't. It was a very, very difficult job. Sometimes worked out better than others.' One of those 'others' was in the 11th minute of this final. Gascoigne did well to wriggle free of both Stephane Paille and Gary McKay and found Laudrup out on the right-hand side with his back to both the goal and Ritchie. In one turn he had flipped the situation on its head and his marker was lost. Pasquale Bruno then had to step out to try and get a bite of Laudrup, which left McCoist unmarked on the edge of the box. Laudrup found him with ease and McCoist didn't miss a beat before sweeping Rangers in front.

Ritchie's job could have been made even more difficult in the 20th minute when he should have followed Bruno into the book for a late challenge on his target. Gary McKay would enjoy the same leniency for an assault on Gascoigne. Rangers, however, were firmly in control of that early quarter of the match. McCoist had lost a volley in the floodlights and later tested Rousset from outside the area with a stinging drive that the Frenchman did well to tip over the bar. Ally was not to be denied from the resulting corner. The Albertz cross was a deep one, which Petric headed back across goal and Moore cushioned into the path of McCoist who, unmarked three yards from goal, completed the game of head tennis and gave Rangers a comfortable cushion. The marking was appalling but, even in the most congested of penalty areas, that man McCoist could always seem to find space.

'There was no danger here,' remembered Andy. 'We were on easy street. Let's just get the cup presented to us.' Hearts re-grouped, however, and started to make some inroads as Rangers sat back and became untidy. That lack of concentration was punished a minute before half-time when Stevie Fulton took advantage of a sleeping Rangers defence at a corner, controlled well first time to get away from Moore, and then buried one with power into Goram's left-hand corner. Petric was booked before the interval with a wild tackle on Paille and, most bizarrely, McCoist and Gascoigne feuded on the pitch when Gascoigne appeared to question McCoist's ability to get on his wavelength for a pass. This continued into the dressing room but it was nothing new in that Walter Smith era. Back in September 1992 Aberdeen headed down the Ibrox tunnel at the break with a well-deserved 1-0 lead. Rangers were appallingly lacklustre and Smith sat back with a cup of tea as the players 'discussed' their failings with gusto. The second-half performance was one of the best of that famous season and kick-started a glorious run.

The positive results of this particular argument, or of Gascoigne's supposed infusion of Dutch courage, were not obvious at the re-start as Hearts picked up where they left off. Smith had taken off Alec Cleland, who was getting a chasing by Neil McCann, and replaced him with David Robertson. Moore was asked to go out to the right and deal with that particular threat. Goram had to be alert as Robertson's rustiness was clear for all to see and Björklund had to do the same from a McCann cross as Moore proved to be as ineffective as his team-mate. With just over 30 minutes to go, McCann eased past the terrified Miller and Moore and delivered another wicked cross that found the Hearts equivalent of McCoist, John Robertson, just onside and only a few yards out.

The momentum of this cup final was now firmly in Hearts favour. 'It wasn't a shock they equalised because of the pressure,' said Andy McGowan. 'My arse collapsed a wee bit. All of a sudden there were zero guarantees, this could be a disaster here. But this side did have winners and you never ever lost faith completely.'

What happened next was a perfect example of why the rest of Scottish football at that time had to be at their best for the entire 90 minutes in order to upset Rangers. With their fans in full voice and everything pointing towards a Hearts winner, the game was turned on its head in three minutes by one man. The Hearts bench claimed a foul by Björklund on Robertson on the halfway line, but it was very much an even tussle, and eventually Gascoigne picked the ball up just under 40 yards from goal. One change of pace and body shape left McKay for dead and, perhaps with the first Rangers goal still haunting their mind, the four Hearts defenders lined up on the edge of the box and remained frozen to the spot. Before he got to the 'D', Gascoigne simply passed the ball with some bend into the corner of the goal. As the Rangers fans in the temporary stand behind the goal ran forward in celebration, the goalscorer's demeanour was more reserved. A jog, a big exaltation of breath, an acceptance of his brilliance, but no trademark grin as he was congratulated by his team-mates.

Not so the second time. Gascoigne picked the ball up from a short throw level with the 18-yard line on the left hand side of the park. He got a break of the ball as he skipped past the two Hearts players in close attendance but then he was off, driving at this defence with power and purpose, the trademark upper body strength coming to the fore. He saw the opportunity of the one-two with Charlie Miller, whose deftly weighted return ball through Bruno's legs should not be forgotten, before anyone else. He still had to bring the ball back with his left foot before clipping it beyond Rousett with his right. It was vintage Gascoigne. The kind of close control and free-as-a-bird endeavour that lit up the world at Italia 90 and had made him an instant hero at Ibrox the season before had won the cup when it seemed increasingly unlikely, and he was prepared to milk the attention this time. McCoist joined in with a welcome embrace. The tiff had been forgotten.

McCoist had two chances to get his hat-trick after good work by both Laudrup and Gascoigne, but he couldn't convert them. But McCann's effort never diminished and he was eventually rewarded with another assist, this time for Davie Weir, as the two future Rangers stars combined for the game's seventh goal. There wasn't enough time to make it too nervy for Rangers, but it was another special moment that was thoroughly deserved by the sponsor's man of the match, McCann.

'This game was a relief by the end of it. We knew that we were in a game and it was by virtue of our two geniuses that we won it,' remarked Andy. This was Walter Smith's 20th trophy and Ally McCoist's ninth League Cup winner's medal, where in doing so he set a record of 50 goals in the competition. It was a team that included arguably the greatest Rangers goalkeeper and the greatest Rangers captain. Yet the spell between 1994 and 1998 is characterised by two players more than any other. A duo who had the ability to demand the ball and change the course of history, almost at will.

40

Celtic 1 Rangers 2

Skol League Cup Final
Sunday 26 October 1986

'Well done is better than well said.'
(Benjamin Franklin)

At the time of writing we would have to go back to Scot Symon in 1954/55 in order to find the last successful Rangers manager who didn't win a trophy by the end of their first full season in charge. The pressures associated with managing modern-day Rangers are immense and few are afforded a sluggish start. By the time you are reading this, one hopes that Steven Gerrard has already bucked that trend by adding silverware following a barren, if still positive, first season. His arrival in the summer of 2018 attracted many comparisons, almost all of them unfair, with the spring of 1986 when Graeme Souness swept into Scottish football. Souness's natural swagger and ambition were consistent with a financial backing that was hitherto unheard of in this country, in addition to the British footballing market place being far more accessible than anything Gerrard could imagine whilst sitting in the same chair.

It was imperative then that the hype was backed up with tangible success and quickly. The new player–manager had brought an arrogance and assurance that the support both desperately needed and craved; however, it was an image that could look very much like insecure bravado if it wasn't backed up with the accumulation of shiny objects. Thankfully, the first opportunity to gather forward momentum arrived just as the clocks went back, in the shape of the Skol League Cup Final. Souness had already notched his first league win against Celtic, an Ian Durrant goal making the difference at Ibrox in the August, and it would be our most bitter rivals who lay in wait in this first opportunity for success. The start to the season had been less than smooth; however, Rangers approached this final still in the UEFA Cup and only three points off the top of the table. With such a massive transition from hopeless also-rans to a modern professional outfit, keeping the pace in the first quarter of the season was to be commended.

It was clear as he walked off the Ibrox pitch with a calf injury the previous Thursday night, a 2-1 UEFA Cup win over Boavista, that if Souness was to be successful at Hampden, it would be all manager and no player. Rangers kept the pretence of a possible starting berth going right up to the day itself (Souness said after that he saw 'no point in giving our opponents an advantage by saying so') but the players knew the he'd be missing and could prepare accordingly. When Souness envisaged being involved in his first trophy-winning match he must surely have assumed that he would be on the park and the frustration at missing out was clear as 3pm approached and he made his way to his main stand viewpoint. 'I can remember after saying "all the best" in the dressing room, coming up the stairs, it had just kicked off and I was late in getting up there. I actually paused for a moment to go through the doors. And I didn't want to go through those doors, I wanted to get back on the line because it's so hard watching the game. There was pressure on that one.'

He still exuded confidence, whether up in the stand or down on the bench in the latter stages of the game. His suit was so sharp it looked as if it was tailor-made for him in Italy before he departed Genoa. In contrast, his opposite number that day, Davie Hay, was sporting a green blazer over a mustard v-neck sweater, and, although the blazer and knitwear combination has been pulled off immaculately by Mourinho and Guardiola in recent years, Hay spent the entire afternoon looking like a coach driver who was worried that his party of pensioners were spending too much time at Southwaite services.

Celtic too had been in European action in advance of the final. A first leg 1-1 draw at home to Dynamo Kiev was generally considered to be the end of that tie; however, Hay remained defiant. 'You may think I'm a crank or a crackpot,' he said, 'but going there with a 1-1 draw might suit us better than had we been travelling having won the match 1-0.' Celtic would lose 3-1 but Hay needn't have worried about people's reaction to that particular quote. Despite being described by Archie McPherson before the game started as 'one of the most unflappable characters in the business', he'd outdo himself by the end of the weekend.

Cammy Fraser would start in the absence of Souness, although he too wasn't 100 per cent fit. Rangers packed the midfield with him, Ian Durrant and Derek Ferguson in the centre of the park and Davie Cooper and Ted McMinn operating further wide. McCoist would be up front on his own and, with Dave McPherson missing from the usual four-man defence, it would be Jimmy Nicholl, Ally Dawson, Terry Butcher and Stuart Munro lining up in front of Chris Woods. Celtic's only injury concern was Tommy Burns, who had been on the end of a terrible tackle against Kiev, and he was replaced by Tony Shepherd in midfield, but they still had a formidable front three of Alan McInally, Brian McClair and Maurice Johnston for Rangers to contend with.

The atmosphere was electric from the start, especially in the jam-packed Rangers end of the ground. In amongst it behind the goal was a young Scot Van Den Akker, on his first trip to Hampden to see Rangers. 'We sold the tickets out for that game in a day or two. Celtic had tickets on sale on the day of the game. They were league champions, they were top of the league, but they knew the possibilities of the Souness Revolution.' The two sides had met at this stage of the competition in March 1984 and there were large parts of the Celtic terraces empty on that day; however, this probably had less to do with a fear of a bumbling Rangers side and more to do with the fact that both team's seasons were fizzling out. This situation was different and it was indeed odd that there was such a struggle to fill their allocation.

The first half was characterised by half chances and full tackles. Celtic captain Roy Aitken was allowed two bad ones before a third, all of which inside the first ten minutes, finally warranted a booking. McInally was also booked before committing an even worse foul on Jimmy Nicholl at the corner flag, whilst Murdo McLeod was fortunate to escape a card following a common assault on Stuart Munro. The chances came from the scattering of inevitable free kicks, with McClair and Butcher going close from cross balls early on and Cammy Fraser hitting the post from a dead ball just outside the box. There was some fluency too. McMinn went inches wide, Durrant blazed over after some nice work with McCoist and Celtic had the best chance of the opening 45 minutes when Johnston hit the post after being sent through by Aitken, and Woods saved from the Mark McGhee rebound. It was evident early that, although Rangers had the bodies in midfield, they either weren't fully fit or tactically disciplined to maintain the shape as they had done in August. Derek Ferguson, who was succeeding in his attempts to model his play on his manager, was becoming increasingly isolated.

The same pattern continued into the second half, with Celtic always looking like they had options when in attack and Durrant and Cooper looking especially frustrated and tightly marked. Johnston and Nicholl went into the book and yet again Aitken was allowed to commit atrocities in the name of football without a second yellow card, this time on Cooper on the edge of the box.

With just over an hour gone, Cooper was fouled again, this time by Peter Grant near the corner on the Rangers right side. The free kick was swung in by Cammy Fraser, missing its intended target Butcher, but also Roy Aitken. Instead it came through to Ian Durrant, with Tony Shepherd in close attention. Controlling the ball instantly with his left thigh, Shepherd was taken out of the game, and Durrant drilled it low past Bonner into the net. For the second time in eight weeks the 19-year-old showed a level of composure amidst the madness that was well beyond his years. As was tradition, the bears in the Rangers end showed far less. 'He had the silky touch that others lacked,' recalled Scot. 'I'm so glad that it fell to him. The usual bedlam followed. You ended up 25 yards away, probably missing a shoe.'

Celtic responded strongly. Owen Archdeacon missed from a free header, McClair then hit the bar with a free kick before deservedly getting his side level with a superb goal that gave Woods absolutely no chance. Aitken was allowed to run freely through the middle of the park before giving to Johnston who laid it off to McClair on the edge of the box, where he unleashed a rocket into the top-right corner. With just 20 minutes left, the dreaded momentum swing was only going in one direction. 'Cammy Fraser wasn't fit. Derek Ferguson was our midfield. We simply weren't tracking runners. They were more connected. McCoist hadn't had a sniff and McMinn and Cooper were playing their own game,' said Scot. 'Strangely we all wanted the final whistle. Everyone was exhausted. Penalties would be a good result.'

Souness replaced the tired Fraser with Dave MacFarlane in an attempt to provide some much-needed solidity. The game was naturally becoming more and more stretched but the pattern remained the same: Rangers had good delivery from set pieces that caused concern and confusion in the Celtic box and Celtic were dangerous and numerous on the break, but the Rangers defence was becoming more adept at dealing with them. If Celtic had stopped conceding so many needless fouls in dangerous areas, they may well have won the cup.

With seven minutes to go Murdo McLeod's only answer to Cooper's skilful run was to take his legs away, and Rangers were handed yet another opportunity to cause chaos. The move started with some brilliant play by man-of-the-match Ferguson, and it was apt that he should then deliver the resulting free kick. Not for the first time that afternoon, it went to the back post, where Aitken and Butcher had been fighting for supremacy. In this instance Aitken lost his man and had to grab him back. Butcher offered little resistance to the pull and fell to the floor, whilst referee David Syme considered it briefly before giving the penalty. The Rangers captain may have been happy to fall, but it was unquestionably a foul, Jim McLean was in no doubt on co-commentary, and yet another from Aitken who had been on a booking since the tenth minute of the match.

The cracks in Celtic's discipline that had been visible all afternoon were now a gaping chasm as two further bookings (for Bonner and Archdeacon) were administered following a large delegation sent to contest the decision. Davie Cooper, meanwhile, was ice cool as he waited to take the penalty. 'Of course Cooper would score it,' said Scot. 'I believed he could colonise Mars.' He sent Bonner the wrong way, stood still as McCoist lifted him into the air and two iconic images were born. Firstly, the two of them, Rangers men who had waited a long time for the club to take off, locked in a celebratory embrace, and the second when Cooper was left to take his own ovation, the back of the number 11 waving at the raucous, wild crowd in front of him.

From the touchline, where Souness was now decamped, the instructions were to breathe deeply and see the remaining six minutes out. No one took any heed. McCoist was booked for a scything tackle on Whyte on the halfway line, which he made great efforts to make look like a 50–50 collision. During this period of stoppage time, matters got out of hand further down the pitch. Munro and Johnston had an altercation, involving a coming together of heads, that was spotted by the stand-side linesman and it resulted in a booking for both, meaning Johnston had to walk. He did so whilst making the sign of the cross, despite all players being warned beforehand about making religious gestures.

Confusion ruled Hampden at that moment, but Scot Van Den Akker wasn't in any doubt. 'I was miles away so couldn't see what happened. But I absolutely hated Mo

Johnston at this time so I was very sure that he had deserved it.' Syme got that decision correct, however he lost control soon after. A Celtic fan had hit him with a coin from the nearby stand and he mistakenly thought that it was Tony Shepherd so duly sent him off too. It wasn't until his linesman gave him the correct information that he rescinded the card and Shepherd remained on the field of play. The retraction didn't alter the fact that the match had ended in a shambolic farce that could have been avoided.

It was too much for Hay as he went on the pitch and seemed to suggest that he would take the ball and just go home. Later that day he would tell the press that, 'if it had anything to do with me I would apply for Celtic to join the English league tomorrow.' This feeling of robbery was backed by the club's official newspaper later in the week but it lacked any substance. Hay had an issue with the penalty, which came from a clear pull in the box, and felt that Munro should have been sent off as well as Johnston, ignoring the concept of multiple yellow cards. The truth of the matter was that Celtic's own indiscipline, made clear in those early stages of the game, cost them dear. Spooked perhaps by the changes at Ibrox and that early defeat, they had lost their head and Syme's, corrected, error gave them room in the press to deflect from those deficiencies. As Alan Davidson put it in *The Evening Times* the following day, 'To the victors the spoils. To the losers a sense of injustice that has hovered around them, like some maiden aunt, for the best part of a century.'

And how the victors enjoyed those spoils. Celtic had been the better side, although they could have been down to ten inside the first half, but Rangers had kept their cool when it counted. For the fans it was simply the confirmation of every assumption that they had made since 8 April 1986. Scot Van Den Akker feels that it cannot be understated. 'When someone comes in and says that they have a vision and then they deliver their first trophy, one out of one, you had better believe that it mattered to us. When Souness arrived and you had to queue around the block to get tickets, there was a feeling like you had been trapped in a very large box and someone had finally tipped open the box and you could now see the world beyond. That's what this game was to me. For all the fans there that day, for the first time since his arrival, there was a feeling that we could actually harness the huge support that we had. The stadium had been built for far better teams than we had been watching on the pitch. The trophy room was built for far better teams than we had seen recently. You could see what *could* happen. It was all possible. Everything was waiting for us. I would have bet on us winning the European Cup in the next five years right there. We hadn't even won the league yet. We weren't even top of the table! But we knew what was coming. It was exhilarating leaving that stadium that day.'

It wasn't that the League Cup itself was the springboard required for further success. Rangers had won it on three occasions in the last five years, but those were seen as brief intermissions from the grim atmosphere that had engulfed the club. It wasn't that this match was the immediate catalyst for a league-winning run of form either, as Rangers drew two and lost the other of their next three league games. The reason that this match is still loved to this day isn't just because it was an Old Firm cup final win where Celtic lost the plot entirely whilst our heroes looked supercool. It's because it was a confirmation that the support's trust was, finally, well-placed. It is because there is a childlike need deep within all football fans for a father figure at the head of their club that never disappears, no matter how old we get. Rangers was in good hands at last.

One of those hands was clenched in a fist of triumph as Souness looked up from the track to Chairman David Holmes in the main stand seconds after the final whistle blew. Not a thread out of place in the suit. A man in complete control amongst the bedlam. Everything was going to be alright.

39

Marseille 1 Rangers 1

UEFA Champions League Group Stage
Wednesday 7 April 1993

'Memory believes before knowing remembers. Believes longer than recollects, longer than knowing even wonders.'

(William Faulkner, 'Light In August')

If Rangers fans could turn any draw into a victory, I doubt that there would be any game further up that list than the club's 160th European tie. On a warm night in the south of France, a Rangers team walked onto the pitch just 90 minutes away from their fourth European final, but more importantly the first-ever Champions League Final. The inaugural tournament, in a two-group format at that time, had reached its penultimate round and AC Milan would lie in wait in Munich for the winners of Group A. Victory for either side would guarantee their place, a draw would mean everything would be decided in the final round of group fixtures, with Rangers at home to CSKA Moscow and Marseilles having to make the tricky trip to Bruges. It's hard to imagine a game with more excitement surrounding it.

Arguably there hasn't been a night like it for Rangers in the Champions League era. There have been plenty of thrilling games to enjoy since, domestic triumph to revel in and, of course, the road to Manchester. However, as exhilarating as a UEFA Cup final appearance was, it wasn't the big one and it wasn't the 'new' big one. Rangers stood at the forefront of European football in the spring of 1993. Or at least that is how we remember it.

It's how we felt at the time and this night was just another part of a whirlwind season. Rangers had secured a place in the Scottish Cup Final by defeating Hearts at Parkhead on the Saturday so, with such a commanding lead in the league title with just eight games remaining, the first domestic treble for a generation was very much on. In terms of sheer achievement, season 1992/93 produced a Rangers team that is unsurpassed in history with a clean sweep and 12-match unbeaten European campaign. Interestingly, however, only four games from that season appear on this list and they're all from that European run, involving only two clubs: Leeds United and Olympique de Marseille. The two qualification legs against Leeds would prove to be a relatively comfortable overpowering of a side overrated by both themselves and much of the media. The two group games against Marseille were a testament to the resilience of this squad in the face of a stupendously talented opponent, and none more so than here in the white-hot heat of the Stade Vélodrome.

Like Richard Nixon's involvement in Watergate, once the dust had settled on the Ligue 1 corruption scandal that season at Marseille, the shock wasn't so much the fact that it had happened, it was that the club's owner Bernard Tapie felt the need to intervene in the first place. Their starting XI that night boasted four players at the peak of their powers (Basile Boli, Franck Sauzée, Rudi Völler and Alen Bokšić) and three others who would go on to define the game in the 1990s (Didier Deschamps, Marcel Desailly and Fabien Barthez). However, control freaks will always seek to meddle rather than trust, regardless of the quality in the stable. That season alone, Tapie had reneged on bonus payments, refused the reserve goalkeeper Pascal Olmeta access on an official club flight, had a tempestuous relationship with his coach, 70 year-old Belgian Raymond Goethals and had literally placed the exciting playmaker Abedi Pele on the transfer market the day before this match.

Although Rangers lacked the combustible drama of their counterparts that season, the campaign itself was beginning to show its strain by early April. Rangers had played 53 competitive games by the time they arrived in France. By comparison, Marseille had completed just 40. However, it wasn't tired legs that was the major headache for Walter Smith, it was the absence of one of the season's key players and the one that the French champions feared the most. Mark Hateley, formerly of Monaco, had already received a call from a French agent suggesting that he would be richly rewarded should he miss this match, before Polish referee Ryszard Wojcik took matters into his own hands by sending off the Rangers striker in the home win against Club Brugge resulting in a two-match ban. It was a blow that meant that victory in France was always going to be highly unlikely.

As kick-off approached, both managers sounded as if they'd be happy to roll things onto the last game with a point apiece. Walter Smith, interviewed on the pitch by Gabriel Clarke of ITV and wearing what was now becoming a trademark navy blue cardigan, warned about the dangers of sitting back too much but he 'would be happy with a draw'. In the press the day before, Goethals felt that the match was 'dangerous because of the strength and attitude of the Scots,' but that 'a draw will be enough', seemingly very assured that his side would win on that final trip of the group to Belgium.

The Vélodrome was a cauldron of noise and colour as the sides appeared from under the pitch. Despite being promised 4,000 tickets by Marseille, Rangers instead got under 1,000 for the biggest match in 20 years. Club Secretary Campbell Ogilvie made a desperate plea for those without tickets not to make the trip. There were enough concerns about the safety within the ground for those who had official tickets. David Fleming had made the long coach journey from King's Park in the southside of Glasgow. 'Going into the stadium was like nothing I'd experienced before, being manhandled through every checkpoint by police, dogs almost at biting distance and hostility all around, although I did manage to swap a scarf with a Marseille fan through a fence which nearly got me walloping off the coppers. Unfortunately that part was only delayed. I was impressed with the size of the stadium and the noise was incredible, but the place was nothing like Ibrox and in reality it was getting well past its best. The netting was definitely a worry though as all sorts were getting through onto the bears below and it didn't look like it could keep the smaller stuff from getting through. There was reports of darts and coins being thrown but I never saw any and decided to stand in the front row for a better view.'

Despite being warned not to make the trip by Stuart McCall at a wedding on the Saturday before, Graeme Macdonald wasn't going to be put off despite the hostility upon arrival. 'I think we were being used as target practice for the locals as we seemed to get everything they could find chucked our way, bottles, fruit, all sorts.' John Cowden had a different perspective from other travelling fans, however. 'I was disappointed with the atmosphere. It was hyped to be a super-charged Old Firm game but it wasn't. They had an orchestrated banner display but maybe, as an open stadium, the noise went up and away.'

Regardless, on the pitch the early impact of the atmosphere on the Rangers side was clear to see when John Brown was caught under a long Barthez kick, but thankfully Völler couldn't manage a touch and the ball literally went from one goalkeeper to the other. Hateley may have been missing but Rangers played like they hadn't noticed, almost like a machine programmed to play one way to such a fulcrum of this legendary side, as they went long to McCoist. Somewhat isolated in a 4-5-1, Rangers struggled early to get the support to him from the likes of Huistra, Durrant and Steven. When the ball was played on the deck to McCoist, like one early example from John Brown, we looked a slightly different proposition.

Yet the nerves wouldn't go away. With 15 minutes gone the Rangers defence tried to retain some possession and control, and eventually the ball made its way out to avid Robertson. For some reason he let it go too long and before it rolled off the park ompletely, he tried to clear under pressure. In hindsight, a brief comedy moment uld have been a far better outcome. Robertson got the blame in my house that night he claimed responsibility quite candidly when he spoke to me for *Heart and Hand* 019. However, history has perhaps been harsh on him. The clearance is poor yes, auzée intercepted it with ease, but he did so a full 40 yards from goal. Völler have been closed down quicker by either of Robertson or McCall for the final d Ian Ferguson had 20 yards to track the Marseille captain's run. The shot from vas good; however, there is also an argument to suggest that Goram should better too. Ultimately it was a corporate failure by a team reeling at the start ne had feared.

r experienced noise like it when OM went forward, and when the inevitable e chanting was ridiculous,' said David. 'I couldn't hear myself think, but one thing that never waned was the Rangers support throughout the 90 minutes, they were incredible, singing for the full game and backing the team, sometimes with the hands over the eyes or the shirt over the head, but singing nonetheless.'

With the momentum and noise behind them, Marseille sought to capitalise, with Pele and Völler looking dangerous when they got in behind the Rangers defence. However, as time went on, confidence grew, and on the half-hour mark Rangers created a golden opportunity. Trevor Steven flighted in a free kick from out on the right-hand side. Gough won the header, Huistra controlled well and dinked a beautiful ball in behind Di Meco for Durrant. His intelligence was sharp, and instead of drilling the ball back towards goal, he cushioned it into the path of McCoist, who ballooned it over. It's impossible to shake the feeling that if an identical chance fell to him against Motherwell, the net would ripple and that familiar grin would be as wide as the Clyde. Especially in the context of his incredible domestic form over the previous two years McCoist, Rangers' record European goalscorer, was poor in this first-ever Champions League group stage.

Despite the infinitely better pitch and conditions, the game was scrappier than the first encounter with, of course, much more at stake. Rangers forced a number of corners, one of which led to a deflected Richard Gough effort just seconds after he was knocked over in the box by Boli, in today's money an almost certain penalty. Goram had to be alert to block a cross with Bokšić in space for a tap in, and Gough had to save Brown's blushes after he was caught in possession by Sauzée. The first half was an interesting mixture of nerves and determination. And that was just us at home, perched on the edge of sofas everywhere.

Those nerves were taken up a level early in the second half as a Franck Sauz
free kick rattled the Rangers crossbar, leaving Goram rooted to the spot. But
just seven minutes gone after the restart, everything changed. For once a Gorar
ball found Durrant in space between the lines and when the ball eventually f
Ferguson, his shot was charged down by Boli for a corner. Trevor Steven.
this game should have been made, swung in a pretty average corner that
away by Jocelyn Angloma but only as far as the onrushing, unmarke
inside the box. He met it perfectly. The French camera angle in line
box, which would become *de rigueur* at the World Cup five years la
finest light. The definition of power and precision, through a
with the outside of his right foot, it left Barthez without a pr
remembered Graeme. 'One of the best moments I've ever
ground and it only ramped up the hatred around us.' Dav
bitter-sweet. 'The Rangers support surged forward tow
the police finally got the chance to get their batons out
of Rangers fans indiscriminately and I took a few he
in particular right across the shin left me black an

bear from Belfast that got me back to my feet and pushed the cop off and gave him as good as he was giving out.'

For those of us watching at home, it was safer but still wild. 'It was an explosion of joy in my living room,' recalls David Edgar. 'Red Kola all over the sofa! The goal was so like something from "Roy of the Rovers" it might as well have had the white tracing from Durrant's boot to the net.'

There were now just under 40 minutes to win a place in the first-ever Champions League Final. Rangers would see a fair amount of possession, but once again the reliance on going long with no target man limited the opportunities at breaking through for that one final chance. In the rare moments when we did play sensibly, there was a lack of the required serenity to make it count. A perfect example of this occurred when Huistra brilliantly beat three Marseille players out on the left-hand side, and as he approached the box it was as if the realisation of just how far Rangers had come had suddenly dawned on him. Stuart McCall was available for a cut back on the edge of the box and McCoist was in space at the other end of it, but the cross would need pace and bend. He took too long to decide and by the time he played the safe option to McCall, it was too far behind the Rangers midfielder for him to capitalise. Similar would happen with the final half-chance to create immortality when Gary McSwegan, a late substitute as Smith tried to force the issue, found space on the right-hand side, but the ball across goal was timid and Barthez gathered easily.

At the other end Rangers had more than their fair share to deal with. As well as some more Sauzée dead-ball specials that whizzed and dipped over Goram's goal, Neil Murray, another young player thrown in at such a high level after David Robertson succumbed to a hamstring injury, was having a torrid time against Pele. After receiving one booking, he was lucky on two occasions not to pick up another, and one effort from his tormentor bulged the side of the net and hearts stopped all over Scotland. However, it came to nothing and a Rangers defence, marshalled so well by their captain, ensured that we all would have another two weeks to dream of Munich.

A match of such magnitude, undefeated away from home against such a majestic side, should always feature in this list; however, we must be careful when we assess it, lest nostalgia distort our memory (for over 20 years I was sure that McSwegan missed a good late chance with a header. It never happened but I wasn't the only one to have imagined it!) There is a danger that Rangers fans wistfully remember this whole Champions League experience in much the same way that England fans paint their experience of Euro 96. Two wins is ultimately difficult to write poetry about.

In a way the entire group stage was distilled in this 90 minutes. Although often producing a rearguard, Rangers weren't negative, not in the way Smith would be, successfully, in 2007/08. This side were tenacious and spirited but, handicapped but the three foreigners rule in place at the time, were simply up against players of superior technique. We compensated this with a level of bravery and effort that no other side in

Europe could match; however, as the coming years would show, it can only ever take you so far. There were moments of genuine quality, Durrant's goal here and at home against Club Brugge for example, but it was never sustained. Smith said immediately after the match that, 'I would hope that results like the one here this evening would confirm that we have established ourselves at this level.' By September, it would be a memory.

Nostalgia also lures us into believing that it was this night that decided it all or that Hateley would have made the difference. He may well have, but it was the game in Belgium that hurt us most. With Marseille failing to beat CSKA, Rangers roared back at Club Brugge with an outstanding second-half performance that just couldn't land a winning goal. Marseille would find one there and so the dream was over.

It's important to dream, however. For those of us at Ibrox that season, it wasn't ethereal. We really *were* one chance away from the biggest game of all. We really *did* have a side that we were immensely proud of and players, like Durrant, who could produce moments that left the continent in awe. Marseille would beat AC Milan and win the first Champions League. They would win that season's French championship before it was stripped away from them in disgrace.

They couldn't beat Rangers.

38

Rangers 1 Celtic 0

Scottish Premier Division
Sunday 31 August 1986

'... and if ever a team deserved a lead, it's Rangers.'
(Archie McPherson, commentary)

Essentially the story of that famous 1986/87 season was one of ignition. The big signings of Woods, Butcher, Souness and eventually Roberts were hugely significant; however, they alone were never going to be enough to win titles. It was their influence on others that did that. Igniting young careers like Ian Durrant and Derek Ferguson, re-igniting some more established ones, especially Davie Cooper, and in doing so firing up a sleeping giant. This match was a perfect example of that chemical reaction.

It was the first-ever televised league match between Rangers and Celtic and, because of that, it was moved to the Sunday. If anticipation wasn't high enough, the first Old Firm clash of the new Scottish champions and the new Rangers under their glamorous new manager, a troubled start to the season only intensified it. It wasn't just the position in the table (after four league games Rangers were seventh and three points behind Celtic at the top), it was the manner of the start that was causing some concern. The sheer extent of indiscipline, led by Souness, on the opening day away to Hibernian and then somehow contriving to lose 3-2 at home to Dundee Utd after going 2-0 up was exacerbated by the mess made of what should have been a routine Skol League Cup third-round tie on the Wednesday night. Rangers needed penalties to knock out First Division East Fife after the match ended 0-0 at Methil, with Ally McCoist missing one in regulation time amidst a flurry of other wasted opportunities. In hindsight it produces an interesting sliding-doors moment had Chris Woods not come to the rescue in the shoot-out; however, at the time nerves were frayed for those fans making their way to Ibrox on the final day of August.

One of those was a ten year-old Ian Hogg, travelling to the game with his father, two of his friends and their two sons. 'At this point my dad already thought Souness was a folly move and that the revolution felt like a gamble. As we all travelled together, all the children thought that we'd win and two of the adults, including my father, thought that we'd struggle. The third adult argued that we had strengthened significantly whilst they had remained largely unchanged. My dad countered by saying that we were asking too much of two 19 year olds and Cammy Fraser to dominate a midfield. We just listened.'

Any concerns about the midfield were valid. This was arguably Celtic's strongest area of the field, with Murdo McLeod, Paul McStay, Tommy Burns and the then highly rated Owen Archdeacon being able to control games and feed the very dangerous partnership of Johnston and McClair. Their defence was weak, however, with Peter Grant a makeshift right-back and Roy Aitken having to shepherd two young and inexperienced players in Derek Whyte and Paul McGugan. With Souness still serving the final game of his ban, there was indeed a huge responsibility placed on the three midfielders; however, Ted McMinn and Davie Cooper could come back to flood that area to make it a 4-5-1 if need be and there was increasing confidence about the backline that read Woods, Nicholl, Munro, McPherson and Butcher.

The infancy of a BBC Scotland live transmission from Ibrox was clear from the outset as Dundee United manager Jim McLean, on co-commentary duty, couldn't hear a word that Archie McPherson was saying in the introduction. The stadium was incredibly loud, too loud perhaps for the equipment, and it's difficult to think of many derby games with such a degree of expectation and anticipation. Both sets of fans were there to gloat, Celtic as newly crowned champions and Rangers as the biggest spenders in town. However, more than anything it was just a very noisy curiosity. How *was* this going to turn out now that the talking and spending had paused?

In comparison to the previous league meeting between the two, this was night and day. A ridiculous 4-4 draw at Ibrox in March 1986, an overrated cartoon of a football match in horrific conditions, didn't have too much in common with this clash other than the usual colour and fervour. And the difference was all in blue. Rangers were far more composed and tactically organised, smothering Celtic attacks quickly and efficiently. There weren't many Scottish talents that went unfulfilled quite as much as Derek Ferguson, but the teenager looked peerless that afternoon, whether that be constructing the play going forward or sniffing out danger before his opponent had even realised that there was an opportunity on. Butcher and McPherson would sweep up following his interventions and get it out to the full-backs as Rangers tried to widen the pitch going forward, mindful of the potential to exploit Celtic at full-back.

It is unclear whether or not it was written into the broadcasting regulations of the time, however there appeared to be some kind of obligation on commentators of the day to describe Ted McMinn as 'eccentric', 'gangly' and, especially, that 'sometimes even *he* doesn't know what he'll do next'. Regardless, he caused havoc down the right-hand side both with his crossing, which Pat Bonner never looked too comfortable coming to collect, and when he cut in and had a shot at goal. Cammy Fraser went over the bar with an acrobatic effort after Bonner and McGugan struggled to clear a corner before he cracked the post from a brilliant drive outside the box. Bonner did well to save the rebound but just how McCoist managed to miss is still a mystery decades later.

If Davie Hay tried to change things at half-time it wasn't entirely obvious as the pattern of the match continued into the second half with Rangers squeezing their opponent and looking the more dangerous, albeit too often from distance. Another Cammy Fraser effort from outside the area caused the first and only real controversy of the afternoon. Bonner stopped his low drive but spilled it back into play and Aitken clearly fouled Durrant when he picked up the rebound. It should have been a penalty, but Rangers continued to work away at finding a breakthrough. All in all it was a relatively easy day for the referee Kenny Hope. Both captains were deservedly booked, and, although Walter Smith would complain about it immediately afterwards, it was more than likely that he was just making a point about the other bookings that he had unfairly received and that perhaps the England World Cup captain was becoming something of a target in Scotland.

It is natural for fans to feel anxious if their team has been on top for so long without getting any reward and even more so when the opposition start to creep back into the game. A Murdo McLeod effort from range whistled past the Rangers left-hand post on the hour mark and a little bit of Celtic pressure was applied soon after, mainly from corners. Woods was more than a match, however, and looked imperious as he clawed the ball from the sky. All the Celtic fans could do in response was chant 'ARGENTINA! ARGENTINA!' a reference to England's famous quarter-final exit to Maradona and co only two months before.

With just under 15 minutes remaining, and those chants ringing in his ears, Woods launched another kick upfield, which was won in the air by McGugan over McCoist. The ball went only as far as Durrant, however, and he instantly moved it forward towards Cooper with urgency. The pass was slightly too long but Cooper managed to get his left foot to it before McGugan could retrieve it, and then, with another touch, he was in full flow. Aitken came towards him, expecting him to move further to the right to try and get past him, where the Celtic captain would be favourite to dispossess. Instead what happened was one of the most wonderful moments ever created by a Rangers player. Without looking up, and leaving Aitken on his hands and knees, Cooper played a reverse pass with the outside of his left foot, right into the path of Durrant, who had kept up with the pace. With one touch he was through on goal and, after pausing for that split second for Bonner to commit himself, he simply caressed the ball into the net as Ibrox erupted in both jubilation and relief. It is a moment that Ian Hogg still enjoys revisiting. 'In the hundreds of times I've watched the game back I now know and laugh at the celebration, Ian Durrant patching the architect supreme in Davie Cooper to run to the Enclosure. Then? I was being thrown around like a wet towel by adults and friends, desperate for success and glory. And I loved it. I loved being part of the feeling of winning amongst Rangers supporters. I hadn't had this feeling often, not in meaningful games anyway.'

Disclaimer: this is my favourite Rangers goal of all time. I've had the fortune to witness hundreds of them, and when I watch some again they always bring back the same reaction I had at the time the ball hit the net. Maurice Johnston's winner against

Celtic in November 1989, for example, never fails to produce an adrenalin surge every single time I come across it. However, none produce the kind of emotional response that this one does and I've never been entirely sure why I am so moved. Perhaps it is because it involves two Rangers idols whose lives were touched by tragedy; however, there are plenty of goals involving both of them that don't get me misty eyed. It could be the significance of the result and what we now know followed such a pivotal season. It may simply be the pure aesthetic of the goal itself. That amidst the usual cacophony of Old Firm heavy metal, Cooper and Durrant managed to produce a moment of pure ballet.

Durrant could have had a second but his effort was correctly ruled out for a handball by Butcher on the way past Bonner and into the net. Rangers were worthy of a more flattering scoreline; however, with only five minutes remaining it could have been worse. Brian McClair headed over the bar from four yards out following the only moment of poor marking from the Rangers defence all day. It would have been grand larceny had Celtic taken anything from this fixture and there wasn't even a complaint about the officials to make their pill sweeter.

In the end the older fans needn't have worried, the younger players had everything under control and in a way that was simply inconceivable five months earlier. The influence of a better attitude and professionalism was beginning to catch fire around Ibrox and, although there would still be some more setbacks in that first half of the season, by the time Celtic returned to Govan on New Year's Day 1987, Rangers were on a hot streak that wouldn't go out until the title had been captured in May.

There is one more reason why that goal resonates so strongly with me and perhaps the game itself with so many who voted. It was the first Rangers game I ever saw live on the television. I had a strip, of course. I knew who these players were and I knew where my dad went on a Saturday afternoon, but this was the first time, at five years old, when I had sat and watched Rangers play. And win. From that moment on I knew that I needed to go to Ibrox soon. A flame had been lit inside of me that has never gone out to this day.

37

Celtic 2 Rangers 3

Scottish Cup Final
Saturday 5 May 1973

'Football is the most important of the least important things in life.'
(Arrigo Sacchi)

It wouldn't be long before I made my first trip to Ibrox. Weeks of pleading meant that my father finally took me to my first game, aged five, a 2-0 defeat of Aberdeen at Ibrox on the Saturday of the September holiday weekend of 1986. For most of us, this addiction to following a football team is in the blood. If it's not something literally passed on through genetic material then it is a gateway opened by a relative, most commonly a father. From that flows the growth of a special bond as the two of you share in the searing highs and crushing lows, the beauty and the violence, witnessing together both instances of justice and injustice. Life in microcosm, projected by a simple game. After the first match there are other landmarks that have to be ticked off together. The first away game, the first cup final, the first European trip. The first Old Firm game. For both my dad and I, the first derby match we attended with our father was a Scottish Cup Final. His was certainly more enjoyable than mine.

They were only two bodies in a sea of over 122,000 crammed into Hampden Park on that cold, wet May afternoon. 12,000 more had tickets but would decide against attending due to the weather. This wasn't just any old cup final. It was the Scottish Football Association's centenary year; therefore, royalty was invited to present the trophy, in the form of Princess Alexandra, resplendent in blue and white. For generations, many fans were led to believe that 1973 would be 100 years since the formation of Rangers Football Club. It was a key milestone that needed to be marked with a trophy and this was the last chance. The May of 1972 had of course delivered the greatest achievement to date, the European Cup Winners' Cup in Barcelona; however, for most fans this felt like a very difficult time. Jock Stein's Celtic were dominant and domestic success was scant. The League Cup had been won in 1970 but the league championship hadn't resided at Ibrox since the great side of the early 60s won the treble in 1963/64. Celtic had secured their eighth title in succession on the final day of the season the previous weekend but, after a poor start, Rangers had finished the season strongly, undefeated in the last 25 games in both league and cup.

Not for the first time, or the last, the Scottish Cup was proving to be elusive, with seven years having passed since Kai Johansen's winner against Celtic in 1966. For the new manager Jock Wallace and his squad, the pressure was on to deliver something to the fans in this special season.

'There was a big debate and effort for me to be allowed to wear my scarf.' With my grandmother being a very nervous person by nature and my grandfather being incredibly protective, my dad did well to negotiate being able to wear his scarf to the ground at all, but only if it was zipped up under his coat. That garment in particular was needed, as they stood together in the old north terracing near the halfway line, wide open to the elements. 'We managed to get to a barrier to I had a semi-decent view of the pitch, with my dad standing behind me. I was excited beyond belief to be going to my first Old Firm game. It was like a coming of age. I had been to every home game on the road to Barcelona the season before but it was only now that I felt as though I'd made it as a fan.'

The Scottish authorities were also in a paternalistic mood, perhaps because they had visitors coming over. The Lord Provost of Glasgow, William Gray, made an appeal on the morning of the match. 'This is the first time that a member of the royal family has ever attended a Scottish Cup Final, and I know that the supporters of both our famous Glasgow clubs will give Princess Alexandra and her husband a warm, friendly Glasgow welcome. The eyes of the world are going to be focussed on Glasgow tomorrow, and I am relying on the vast crowd to be at Hampden Park on their best behaviour and to uphold the city's name. Let us make it a truly great royal and sporting occasion of which Glasgow can be proud.'

There were only a few changes in the Rangers starting line-up that afternoon from the legendary XI that walked onto the Nou Camp a year ago. Dave Smith would be on the bench for this one with Tam Forsyth, who had signed that season from Motherwell, starting the game that would make him famous. Colin Stein had been sold to Coventry City in a deal worth £140,000 (just over £1.6m in 2019 terms), which also included winger Quinton Young coming in the opposite direction. Taking Stein's place up front that day was a young man celebrating his 20th birthday, Derek Parlane. The third omission was perhaps the most notable. Willie Johnston, who it was said had a temper as quick as his feet and brilliant footballing brain, had received his second large SFA ban in the space of two years and it had made his Rangers career untenable. He had previously been handed a 42-day ban in 1970 and, when he threw a punch at a Partick Thistle defender in the second league game of the season, was out for 63 days. It was the final straw for Johnston and, despite Willie Waddell (now effectively the general manager) offering him a new six-year deal, he was sold to West Bromwich Albion for a then-record fee between Scottish and English clubs of £138,000.

Incredibly, given the size of the shadow that both clubs cast over the Scottish footballing landscape, this was only the eighth Scottish Cup Final meeting between the two in the hundred years of the contest (at the time of writing there have only been

13). The score was tied at 3-3, with the 1909 final being abandoned because of rioting and, at the request of both clubs, another replay not sought. Due to the relative rarity of such an event and because of the fascinating football context, a long-time champion perhaps showing signs of creaking versus a developing challenger and a European title-holder in incredible form, this game had a lot of hype around it before it kicked off.

It didn't disappoint. With the exception of the grim weather, it matched most of the criteria required for a model classic cup final. It was a fast, open, end-to-end affair. It had momentum swings and a fair share of skill and error. It also had an iconic goal quite unlike any other. Incidentally, the other model for a classic cup final, the David v Goliath type, was happening at Wembley at the same time as Jimmy Montgomery wrote himself and Sunderland into folklore with a sensational smash and grab against Don Revie's mighty Leeds United.

Rangers were the brighter side in the first quarter of the game and the impact was almost immediate as Parlane charged down a Billy McNeil clearance, beat two men before delivering a dangerous cross, for which there were no takers. The passing was accurate and fluid and corners were forced by Young and Conn, but the final efforts from Jardine and Greig were more suited to Murrayfield than Hampden. The Rangers fans were in full voice but it was clear early on that too many, perhaps because of the elements, had tried to get into the covered area at the Mouth Florida area of the ground and by three minutes there were fans spilling onto the track and helped away by ambulance men. The reporting of this in the newspapers, just over two years since the Ibrox disaster, suggests a wide acceptance that danger was still just a part of the football experience and that nothing was going to change nationally anytime soon, not when you could sell tickets to over 2.5 per cent of the population and hope to cram them into a ramshackle old stadium.

Rangers may have forced the issue in the opening stages of the game but Celtic were still dangerous on the break, with Jimmy Johnstone being afforded a free role operating in between the lines. Dalglish had gone close earlier when he forced an excellent save from Peter McCloy, but on 26 minutes he put Celtic into the lead. The threat became apparent when Johnstone beat Greig to a header in the middle of the park, but it was really made by an excellent and quick-thinking flick by Dixie Deans that gave Dalglish a golden chance and McCloy no hope at all. It was well-executed but perhaps too much space was afforded too early on in a cup final.

For around ten minutes it changed the dynamic of the match entirely. Celtic, now with the lead and the confidence of a side that was used to winning (this was an attempt to win three finals in a row), passed the ball with ease and security, whilst Rangers, with this centenary burden on their back, looked more desperate and anxious. Those fears were eased ten minutes before the interval, however, and it was the birthday boy Parlane who brought Rangers level. Willie Mathieson found Alex MacDonald out on the left-hand side. George Connelly came out to meet him, seemingly in slow motion, as MacDonald was able to create some space following a bobble and hooked the ball into the box, which Parlane met eight yards out after losing his markers with a clever run. It was intelligent play by the two Rangers men; however, if that goal was given the modern-day analysis, the state of Celtic's defending would be absolutely eviscerated. Connelly's attempts at closing down MacDonald, outside the box as it was, were comical, but Alistair Hunter's goalkeeping eclipsed even that. Nevertheless, Rangers were level and noise was deafening inside Hampden Park. 'I had read and heard all about it before,' my father recalled, 'but to actually be there and experience what it was like to score against them was magic.'

Rangers finished the first half the stronger, and less than a minute after the second half got underway Wallace's side blazed into the lead. Celtic kicked off and launched the ball deep into the Rangers half. Just as Archie McPherson said, 'anything could happen in this match,' Quinton Young played a long pass for Parlane, whose flick on to Alfie Conn was perfect. Conn then found himself in a direct footrace with McNeill but won it easily, turning his pace as comfortably as he would later turn his coat. Hunter rushed out to narrow the angle, but Conn got to the ball at the last moment and prodded Rangers in front. There was fighting in the Celtic end as the police had to make their way onto the terracing, but there was only partying at the other end of the ground. Rangers had their tails up and were playing at a pace that Celtic couldn't live with. According to Malcom Munro in *The Evening Times*, 'I have not seen Celtic so out-paced as they were here.' Rangers could have had a penalty when McLean was pulled down in the box, but the claims were to no avail.

Celtic had far stronger claims for one moments later, however. Jimmy Johnstone caused havoc with his more central role, turning his namesake Derek at the edge of the box before releasing Deans in plenty of space coming in from the right-hand side. McCloy was well-beaten but the Rangers captain sought to do his job for him by turning the ball around the post with his hands. It was a foul that didn't even merit a booking at that time, but Rangers would still be punished when Connelly comfortably equalised from the spot.

Yet again the cup-final momentum swung back and forth repeatedly for the next ten minutes. Celtic had the ball in the net two minutes after the penalty but the flag had gone up for an offside against Johnstone. No sooner had commentators and fans alike thought that Celtic were the most likely to get the fifth goal of the game, Alex MacDonald met Sandy Jardine's cross perfectly but unfortunately his header met the upright and Celtic were saved. It was only an overture, however. A Tommy McLean free kick on the left-hand side was swung in and it was Derek Johnstone's turn to hit the post with a header. Both of them, in fact, as the ball trundled across the line from one side of the frame to the other. From no more than a yard out, Forsyth managed to 'guide' the ball home with his studs and his famous stunned reaction was burned into Rangers history forever. Speaking years later, Forsyth said, 'To play in your first

Scottish Cup Final and score the winning goal was just a dream come true. As a boy, you dream about these things and it was unbelievable really. I just followed it in, but I honestly thought Derek's header was going in. They all say I nearly missed it but I tapped it in and they can't take it away from me.'

'I thought he had missed it!' my dad said. 'The place went absolutely mental and someone grabbed your papa's bunnet and chucked it in the air. He never saw that one again but he didn't care!'

There were no more dramatic twists and turns to be had. Rangers should have had more goals through Conn and Young but nothing further was required. Greig and Parlane wept on the pitch at the final whistle as a seven-year wait for the Scottish Cup was over. It was an important moment too for Jock Wallace, his first season in the hot seat, but he was keen to downplay his role in the day. 'Give praise to the players,' he said later. 'No one knows how hard they have worked. They were down, they picked themselves up. They're the men.' Words aren't required to get some insight into what it must have meant to a man who, as a boy, walked the 14 miles home to Wallyford after watching Rangers at Tynecastle, because he couldn't resist spending his bus money on a rosette.

Ian Archer, then of *The Glasgow Herald* and no friend of Rangers in his later years, summed up the afternoon by saying, 'The victors were Rangers in particular and football in general. People will still want to know about this sport in the aftermath of a fine afternoon and that is some legacy to bequeath to our children, among them the young son of Jock Wallace. "dad," he said yesterday, "can I have a ball to play with?" Moses McNeill would have approved and so Rangers entered their second 100 years.'

This match was one that certainly bequeathed a legacy in my family. Once my grandfather, a veteran of El Alamein, had plotted a way back home with military precision so as not to encounter any Celtic supporters, my dad was able to take it all in. 'It was a great day and it had wetted the appetite for more Old Firm games.' For most of us there is no way back after being at a match like this. We are hooked for life, always desperate for the next special fixture that gives us that kind of rush. The legacy of these memories is limitless. A ten-year-old boy from East Kilbride had made the journey to Hampden too that day. He would go on to become the club's greatest-ever goalscorer.

We are all introduced to our football team in different ways of course, all of them valid and special to each of us. However, there's arguably a deeper resonance when there is a blood bond, especially one between a father and son, who have usually inherited that male inability to communicate properly with one another. When relationships are strained, most notably in adolescence, they can always be salvaged by a 'what about the Rangers though?' Sacchi was right about football being the most important of all the least important things in life. However, there is nothing trivial about the relationships that grow out of a shared passion and the memories created that can transcend even death.

To Allan and Jimmy. Thank you.

36

Rangers 3 Celtic 2

Scottish Premier League
Sunday 24 March 2012

'Not today.'
(George R. R. Martin, *Game of Thrones*)

This match is arguably the most contentious choice of them all, but then the British have always had a soft spot for this type of story. The tale of one final glorious act of defiance, rendered redundant by the bigger ensuing calamity, has resonated to some degree as far back as Captain Robert Falcon Scott. Although his Norwegian rival Roald Amundsen reached the South Pole first, it was Scott's story that was romanticised throughout the century. As Clive James once pointed out, the British hero, battling not just against the elements but his own existentialism, may have been incompetent but he still remained the epitome of the stiff, indeed frozen, upper lip. By March 2012 it was becoming possible that Rangers may be gone from the top flight for some time, but not without one last hurrah.

The clues to the level of incompetence at all levels of management within the club were there early but were hidden by a blistering start to the league campaign. Although Ally McCoist's reign as manager had started badly in the cups (Rangers went out of the Champions League, Europa League and the League Cup at the first time of asking), few were asking too many questions because the league form was so good. McCoist's side were unbeaten after 15 league games, seven points clear of Celtic (having destroyed them 4-2 at Ibrox in September) and had amassed 39 points. One would have to go back to Alex McLeish's treble-winning side of 2002/03 for the same tally by that stage and even further back to Dick Advocaat's excellent second season of 1999/00 to find a Rangers side who had done better (they had managed 40 points). If we ignored the knock-outs, the transition from Smith to McCoist was going smoothly.

But we were ignoring a lot of things. Any initial concerns about the new Rangers owner, Craig Whyte, were relatively easy to dismiss. The 'billionaire' turning up at Ibrox for the 2011 title party in the back of a Vauxhall Vectra being one example. However, as the season wore on, reports of leveraging future season-ticket money and having absolutely no intention of paying the PAYE bill were far more difficult to keep at the back of one's mind. As the off-field apprehension became unshakable, so too did the impact on the field. A four-point lead on Christmas Eve was turned into a two-point deficit by New Year's Day. Nikica Jelavić was sold in the January window, and by Valentine's Day the club was in administration and the regulation ten-point penalty applied. The prospect of the league title being all but impossible was, incredibly, only a secondary thought for fans as they started to wrestle with the possibility of not having a club at all come the start of the new season. The prospect of Celtic coming to Ibrox at the end of March with the chance to win the championship on our turf was almost too much to take in.

The fear was swallowed, however, as Ibrox was ablaze with colour and hymns of defiance, the famous old stadium full sooner than usual on these occasions. The message to the beleaguered players, staring at an unprecedented fourth consecutive home defeat, was simple: Celtic may be crowned champions but not today and not here. For those old enough to recall 2 May 1999, a footballing joy almost without peer, it was essential to deny the Celtic support the same experience. At least, the fans cried, give us that.

The team responded. Sone Aluko, one of the few individual bright sparks in a dismal campaign, was already showing signs of being in the mood before he eventually put Rangers in front in the 11th minute. His early threats had come from playing off the knock-downs of Lee McCulloch, who was spearheading a 3-5-1-1; however, this was all his own doing. Picking up the ball from Steven Davis around 40 yards from goal, his first touch was enough to get away from Ki Sung-Yeung and then the slaloming run commenced. Thomas Rogne was nutmegged, Charlie Mulgrew was turned inside out and Fraser Forster attempted to close him down but could do little about the finish. 'A goal for Aluko. A goal for the fans. A goal for the cause,' said Ian Crocker in his usual punctuated commentary style. Ibrox was bouncing as if it was Rangers who had the chance to secure the title that day. A fine example of the football fan's ability to compartmentalise at will.

Celtic tried instantly to turn the tables, with Allan McGregor having to stand up to Georgios Samaras and Anthony Stokes in quick succession, whilst Aluko remained a threat as he created an opportunity for Lee Wallace who blasted over the bar. It was another one of those combinations that brought the first controversial moment of the match in the 28th minute. Aluko was at the heart of another Rangers break and he fed Wallace, who had beaten Cha Du-Ri, through on the overlap. Cha pushed him over just before he ran into the box and referee Callum Murray brought out the red card instantly. It was a goalscoring opportunity, even though the ball was possibly too far in front, and by the letter of the law it was a justified decision. In the Celtic dugout Neil Lennon was incensed and would wait until half-time to make his case before Murray in his usual calm and measured fashion. He did not return to the manager's chair for the second half, being sent off himself on account of the manner of his protestations. Even though the dynamic had flipped from 1999, it was still Celtic players and staff who were losing the plot in such a climax to the season.

Lennon's mood did not improve as he watched the second half unfold on television in the media room. Victor Wanyama gave Murray an even easier decision to make with a two-footed challenge on Steven Whittaker that may have won the ball but showed all of his studs in the process. With Celtic down to nine men, McCoist sought to capitalise and he brought on Kyle Lafferty for the excellent Rhys McCabe in the 60th minute. Lafferty made Forster work almost immediately and the Celtic keeper was called upon to deny both McCulloch and Whittaker soon after. Despite another short-range block from Lee Wallace, incredibly only four yards from goal, Andy Little, 30 seconds after replacing Aluko, made sure the advantage was commensurate with the performance. With just 13 minutes remaining, the future Rangers captain made it three with a move he started by robbing Adam Matthews of possession before receiving the ball back from Davis and cooly slotting it past Forster. Not only would Celtic be denied the pleasure of winning the flag in their rivals home, they were getting a hammering too.

This wasn't Walter Smith's Rangers, however, and calamity was always just around the corner. In what Ally McCoist described as a 'Michael Bentine five minutes' (there's a reference for the teenagers), the elation was almost extinguished. With just two minutes remaining, Carlos Bocanegra cynically fouled Samaras in the box as he was about to shoot and deservedly got a red card as Scott Brown converted the penalty. Unbelievably, it was pulled back to 3-2 in injury time as Rogne pulled away from Salim Kerkar in the Rangers box and powerfully headed home from close range. It wasn't enough though, and Rangers got the win that they deserved.

McCoist's picture of relief on the touchline was iconic. He said after that, 'it wasn't about stopping Celtic doing anything. We won it for us and for our fans.' Not only are the two not mutually exclusive, they are almost inextricably linked. The joy *did* come from stopping Celtic. It was literally the only thing on the line that day. There would be no bragging rights that could be derived from a standard end of season Old Firm win, not in the situation Rangers were in. The game *had* to matter in some kind of sporting context.

Did it really matter enough to warrant a place in the finest games in our history though? Iain MacLennan from Inverness is one of the many fans for whom this game still holds great significance. 'I had no reason to believe that we were going to win the game, my confidence in the team was shot and my heart was broken, with the off-field problems dictating front and back pages and also my every waking thought. The bus stopped at a warehouse somewhere outside Glasgow, I had been there once before, in the same season when we beat them 4-2 in the first derby of the season. The place was weird, I didn't know where it was. It felt like the back end of a distillery with a big lounge bar area in it. The bar, however, was *bouncing*. A party of epic proportions was in full swing and it was there, while sitting next to one of the elder statesmen of the bus, John Macbean said to me when I asked him how he felt the game would go, "they won't let us down today." Hearing it come from someone like him gave me a reason to believe, brought some confidence and belief and my mood started to lift. John is one of the founding members of the Inverness True Blues and has been following Rangers home, away and abroad since the 60s so he was no stranger to a big occasion.'

'Looking back seven years after the event, this match still means the world to me. During our darkest of days this one game is a ray of light. The only thing that mattered was football and we all know how close we came to losing it. The emotion of the day is best summed up by the pre-match atmosphere. Now, the celebration by Lee Wallace, running towards the Govan Stand arms outstretched, head back and roaring with emotion, just happens to be one of my favourite pictures. Every time I see it, I'm reminded of this one chink of light through the darkest of times for the club, a game that meant so much but also so little. Before the game, there were bucket collections for the Rangers Fans Fighting Fund, and because of this the stadium was a sea of Union flags. I love this game so much, because it reminds me of how lucky we are to still have a Rangers team to cheer.'

One wonders how this fixture would fare in a similar poll ten years from now. It meant a lot on the day without question. Denying our enemies that moment was an important crumb of comfort. But through a wider lens, of course, it was something of a hollow victory, merely delaying a more important success, that of securing a league title. It was a match that was far more about Celtic than about Rangers. It *was* about stopping them achieving rather than about us being triumphant. That Rangers fans consider a game of this nature to be worthy of the greatest 50 of all time is perhaps evidence that the emotions surrounding 2012 are still extremely raw. For those pouring out of Ibrox thinking that we had staved off the worst scenario imaginable, things were about to get infinitely worse.

35

Rangers 4 East Fife 0

League Cup First Round
Tuesday 7 August 2012

'Welcome back to Ibrox. Home of Rangers then, now and forever. After the most difficult period in the club's history, Rangers would like to thank their supporters for not walking away. We are the people.'

(Sandy Jardine, pre-match)

It might have been the sixth or the seventh title in a row, it's sometimes hard to remember. We stood up as the team came out to collect the League Championship trophy, each holding the A4 card lying on our seat with six, or seven, on it. The game itself was a dull affair, very much in keeping with the title 'race' that we had just won at a canter. It was then that I had the temerity to suggest to my old man that this was, perhaps, becoming a little boring. The look I got was enough. In my defence, besides being young and stupid and having literally never known a season where we hadn't won a trophy, these were the flat years of our nine-in-a-row era. 1993 to 1995, despite the introduction of Brian Laudrup, lacked the achievement and the quality team play of the first five. It wouldn't be until Celtic showed up with a Scottish Cup win in May 1995 that we would get into a higher gear with the introduction of Paul Gascoigne in July and the exhilarating race to the nine went into overdrive. It was simply because we *needed* to react. In those two years, Scottish football was very much supine under our dominance. My dad, however, had grown up through Celtic's own nine and their success in the old embryonic European Cup, and had also experienced the pre-Souness despair of the early 80s. The message was clear: never, *ever*, take winning for granted.

The trauma of summer 2012 would have been simply inconceivable to us then. Rangers stumbled from a protracted and somewhat bungled administration to the eventual entry into the liquidation of the holding company. The fans had to first wrestle with the uncertainty of where we would be playing in 2012/13 or if we would be playing at all, and then deal with the ignominy of starting from the bottom professional tier. There was the total ambiguity of who would be leading us there as Rangers-supporting buyers toiled but could never quite get their deal over the line and then, out of the shadows, came a consortium led by Charles Green who very quickly did.

There was the perceived treachery of former heroes, some of whom traded on their reputation as 'Rangers Men', who not only didn't stay and play in the lower leagues but refused to TUPE (Transfer of Undertaking (Protection of Employment)) over to the new company so as to generate some kind of transfer fee for the club. And then there was the blood lust. The rest of Scottish football sublimated rational economic considerations such as the need for the big-gate receipts that Rangers and Celtic bring, with a deep-seated tribal need to feast on the pain of those now firmly condemned as our national game's heel. Graham Spiers, arguably a spokesman for this constituency, captured that mood perfectly when he tweeted, 'All over Scotland I see people dancing on Rangers' grave. It is almost like a great cultural revenge for the varied sins of the club.'

The details of the 4-0 League Cup win over East Fife at Ibrox are entirely inconsequential to this book. This match does not have a place in the affections of Rangers supporters because of anything to do with the football that was played. It is purely the importance of the game taking place at all. The very first match back in season 2012/13 was at Brechin City, the hedge and all, and that game finished 51st in the poll. The resonance of that summer and the beginning of an unexpected and unwelcome journey should be of no surprise, but it was the return to Ibrox, a night of some kind of communal renewal at this sporting cathedral of ours, that made the final cut.

For Cameron Bell, the resonance of this fixture is well placed. 'Being consigned to the Third Division, the daily mockery and derisory comments from all quarters simply became the way of life for a good while, and through many dark hours when the unthinkable looked like a very real possibility, the very idea of starting another league season suddenly seemed like the promised land. Fear became acceptance, which became hope, which became defiance, and through one of the most difficult periods in the club's history, a team emerged against East Fife on that Tuesday evening who would be the physical symbol of a battered and broken club that was getting up off the canvas – taking a 15 count rather than ten as the game was delayed by a quarter of an hour to allow all of the disciples to get to their seats. I remember feeling acutely that it was the beginning of a new chapter as Sandy Jardine, the figurehead of fan togetherness and pushing back against the tide, spoke to the crowd to thank them for their patience and support, one of the few positive messages to come out of Ibrox in months. As we got back into some form of normality of simply wanting to see Rangers play football, I knew that it was something I'd taken for granted for nearly 30 years. It's easy, nearly a decade later, to show derision or disdain at the quality of the team that took to the field that night, given the summer exodus, but a small part of the club's history was written within that line-up. For the fans and staff alike, the previous months were the longest in memory as queues formed to take bites out the club and its name; however, the men from Methil proved to be the launchpad that allowed us all to – for a brief period – focus solely on the business on the pitch, with the off-field issues taking a lot longer to hear the final whistle. Defiant banners from the Broomloan Road Stand, the organic sense of freshness and relief and that feeling of togetherness within the stadium characterised the beginning of the long road ahead, with those small steps being always 90 minutes at a time.'

One of the 38,000 who returned to Ibrox on that beautifully warm and sun-kissed August evening was the journalist Iain Duff. Writing in '*Follow We Will*', he recounts that although he had fallen out of love a little bit with Rangers in recent years, and now living hundreds of miles away, it was more than the weather that made him feel warm that night as he walked up to the ground with both his father and his son, for the very first time. 'I'd seen the club I'd followed through thick and thin for 30 years come perilously close to disappearing and I wanted to be there when they returned to action. Not to send some sort of "get it up you" message to the rest of Scottish football, but because I had been reminded of what football was all about – the unity, the shared memories, the pride in your club and the people that represent it.'

Aside from being an excellent piece of contemporaneous evidence that captured the thinking of supporters in the middle of such turbulence, *Follow We Will*, published in 2013, is another example of this sense of renewal that was sweeping around the fan base at the time. All of a sudden, intelligent and passionate writing was flowing with more power and volume than it ever had before. This collection of pieces gives us a wide and varied appreciation of a support trying to get its collective head together and, especially with respect to its critique of the external circus engulfing the club, it still reads well. In other areas it absolutely doesn't. It is entirely understandable that there was a burning desire to get this new and motivated collection of voices out there into the wider domain and therefore publication couldn't wait. However, if even just 18 months had been allowed to pass in order to let the dust fully settle, the perspective would have aged a lot better.

There's a very thin line between a positive energy of renewal and a kind of born-again evangelism. The former comes from a rational reaction to a problem but can slip easily into a somewhat deluded, distorted world view. Bob Marley's 'Three Little Birds' became the soundtrack for this particular Rangers summer and the oft-repeated mantra was that 'every little thing gonna be alright'. Duff speaks of a feel-good factor being generated by the sense of 'adventure and excitement that had been missing for too long in the mundane, repetitive slog of the SPL'. The tour of the Scottish football's forgotten outposts was to be akin to some sort of sabbatical where we would re-discover our vigour and purpose. The twitter hashtag #ThisIsFun was ubiquitous. Except that it really, *really* wasn't fun. It was a self-preserving kidology, a mental crutch to ease the pain of this dark reality.

The ultimate manifestation of a born-again mentality is the need to place trust in a benevolent leader. When re-reading *Follow We Will*, the most jarring lines are the numerous examples in praise of Charles Green, his backers and some of the disastrous appointments that he made at an executive level. The overriding need for parental guidance at the top of our football club appears to be inherent within us all. It is therefore unfair to criticise too heavily when we all, especially during that period of time, desperately wanted the next guys to run the club well. However, there was enough information about his involvement with Sheffield United, the club he apparently supports, to have caused deep concern. His initial success, aided by the endorsement of high-profile figures such as the manager Ally McCoist, was partly explained by his willingness to grandstand to the footballing authorities and publicly slate the departing players who sold the club out. It was everything Rangers fans wanted to hear and it tapped into every grievance that had been opened up at an incredibly emotional time. It was, however, a stark, naked display of rhetorical populism, the kind that would later sadly define the decade. It worked though, and so did his subsequent Initial Public Offering, which raised over £20m for his investors.

The deluded evangelism would quickly dissipate but the spirit of renewal didn't. Although the tendency to seek rich men to pay for our enjoyment on a Saturday afternoon still remains, the ability of fans to mobilise behind change was a factor in the shift of power that finally occurred in 2015. On that front, the lessons of complacent trust can never be taught too often. The language used to describe 'The Journey' was bombastic and overwrought at times but rallying cries nearly always have to be. It is often mocked but the Rangers *are* coming. They *should* expect us. It is just taking longer than we desperately hoped that it would.

This calamitous experience has been one massive jolt to the senses. Not only should this generation never take for granted as fact that Rangers will always win or compete for the top Scottish honours, it also shouldn't assume that the lights will be on every week and that we will have somewhere to gather to unify behind our team. It has been a harsh reminder that institutions, no matter how old, beloved and great, can sometimes fall, and that it is *our* responsibility, and no one else's, to avoid the complacency and dependency that led Rangers to the very brink.

Years from now, when a Rangers captain lifts yet another trophy in that decade, parents everywhere should tell their children about East Fife.

34

PSV Eindhoven 2 Rangers 3

European Cup Round of 16, Second Leg
Wednesday 1 November 1978

'They shocked us. They played imaginative and stylish football, the likes of which I didn't expect from a British side. They are truly a fine team and they must have a splendid chance of winning the trophy which, frankly, I thought we were going to take this year.'
(Cees Rijvers, PSV Manager, post-match)

Even amidst such a celebrated selection, it is possible to discover a hidden gem. If truth be told, any Rangers win away from home in Europe has a high premium attached, especially against a side with a good reputation. This match ticks those boxes and it is the first of four of such wins on the list. Many of a certain generation would argue that it is too low and the context of the tie and the standard of the opposition alone would make a compelling case. The quality of the match itself makes it simply one of the greatest Rangers European performances of all time.

What makes this game so fascinating is the wider context surrounding it and what would follow immediately after this season. This sparkling run in the European Cup (the win over Juventus in the previous round will feature later in this book) shined so brightly because the domestic campaign at that stage was so dull. By the time John Greig's side travelled to the Netherlands, they sat fourth in the table after 11 games with only three wins to their credit. The six draws and two defeats were a huge frustration to the fans, given the side that Jock Wallace had bequeathed Greig, departing Ibrox soon after winning his second treble in three years. Fortunately, however, domestic draws were common place and Rangers were only three points behind leaders Dundee United in a very congested pack.

In stark contrast to the dull domesticity, the European Cup was throwing up some glamorous, if very challenging, ties. After the success against a star-studded Juventus side in the first round, Rangers were handed a challenge considered to be even tougher. PSV Eindhoven were UEFA Cup holders, had provided six players to the famous Dutch squad that reached the World Cup Final against Argentina that summer, were favourites for the competition after Liverpool's exit in the first round and, perhaps most importantly, had never lost a home European tie in their history. A 0-0 draw at Ibrox in the first leg, our 100th European match, was therefore a far from ideal situation when attempting to reach the quarter-finals.

For the renowned Rangers author Jeff Holmes, this was an impromptu opportunity that was too good to miss. 'I followed Rangers all over the country at the time. I'd have gone to England no problem but had never contemplated a trip abroad. I had two or three days off and was sitting in the pub in Maryhill with seven or eight friends at around 2pm on the Tuesday. We were all saying that we wished we were going to Holland the next day. Someone overheard and said that the bus from the Bristol Bar was leaving at 5pm. One of us used the pub phone to see if there were any spaces and, as luck would have it, they had a few. Seven or eight became just the two of us as we got a taxi over to the east end and bundled on the bus. No passport! To be honest we were herded in like sheep and no one checked. I was in Eindhoven by 2pm without a ticket, but eventually managed to get one just before kick-off but it was for the home end.'

Not for the last time that season, Rangers would have injury concerns on the eve of a big game. Colin Jackson and Davie Cooper were definitely out and Tam Forsyth, Tommy McLean and Peter McCloy were not 100 per cent but would start. Rangers lined up with McCloy in goal, Sandy Jardine, Tam and Alex Forsyth, Derek Johnstone and a midfield of McLean, Alex MacDonald, Bobby Russell and Kenny Watson, with Derek Parlane and Gordon Smith leading the attack. The PSV side would include their World Cup stars, the van de Kerkhof twins (René and Willy), Willy Jansen and Ardie van Kraay.

Officially, Rangers had 800 tickets for the 26,000-capacity Philips Stadion; however, the level of support was closer to 2,000. It would appear that many had the same kind of attitude as Jeff. 'There were plenty of Rangers fans milling around outside the stadium and locals were more than happy to sell tickets. Inside, the wire fences were up which did make us think that this could be dangerous, but the fans around me were absolutely fine. There wasn't a hint of trouble before the game, but of course I had no colours on as we only decided to go at the last minute.'

Whether that would change as the match developed would very soon be put to the test as Rangers got off to the worst possible start. With only seconds on the clock, a fine Willy Jansen cross was met perfectly by Harry Lubse, and McCloy was given no chance. Given the context of the tie and quality of the opposition, this was a nightmare scenario. 'I thought it was a wee bit early to go for the subway,' recalled Jeff. 'Yes it was deflating after the excitement of getting there, but I knew this side had characters and that it wouldn't be the end of the story there and then. Guys like Alex MacDonald wouldn't entertain it.' For manager John Greig, who in his autobiography prided himself on preparation, the plans were up in smoke almost immediately. 'I had just lit up a cigar when the ball hit the back of our net and I snapped it in two. Alex Miller, who was standing next to me in the dugout, turned and asked, "What are you going to do now?" "Light another one," I replied without any humour. Plan A had been binned inside 60 seconds and I wasn't sure exactly what Plan B comprised of.'

It would prove to be the only goal of the opening 45 minutes; however, there was still plenty of action. PSV were showing their class, especially Willy van de Kerkhof, who controlled a ball with snow in it before his cross was deflected for a corner. Gerrie Deijkers should have done better from seven yards after some panic in the Rangers defence, and an ill-advised back heel from Derek Johnstone on the edge of the penalty area right before the interval could have led to more trouble than it eventually did. However, this wasn't a nervy, backs-to-the-wall and hope-for-the-best performance, so typical of Rangers in Europe. Not long after the goal, Rangers showed great composure on the ball and no signs of being rattled so early. A classy move, which started inside the Rangers half by Johnstone and involving MacDonald, Watson and Smith, ended up with a good Parlane header at the back post that was well saved. Kenny Watson, a replacement for Davie Cooper, still possessed a fearsome left foot and van Engelen had to be equal to his shot from distance. In addition to another Johnstone chance from a corner, this was an even contest as the teams headed back down the tunnel.

If the midfield in the first half, MacDonald and Russell especially, was showing signs of control in the home of the Dutch champions, still in the era of Total Football, then the second half would produce even more Rangers class. A move soon after the break was just a sign of things to come as Smith and Russell combined to release MacDonald in the box but van Engelen had to time his intervention perfectly lest he concede a goal or a penalty. With just over half an hour remaining, Rangers got the equaliser they so richly deserved. Tommy McLean picked the ball up on the edge of the box. His cross was delicate but perfect and Alex MacDonald met it sweetly with the kind of late run and header that was by now a trademark. 'It didn't just give us hope, it gave us belief that we could go on and do this now,' remembers Jeff. 'This supposed European superpower had been breached. We went berserk and then sat down. We got some looks but no one said a word.'

If all the talk on the terraces was about keeping it tight for the remaining 30 minutes, it wouldn't last long as PSV were back in front only three minutes later. Tam Forsyth mistimed a header in the box, Gerrie Deikers did not mistime an overhead kick and the new-found belief must have been shattered. 'I couldn't believe it. It was right in front of me where I was sitting. However, we still had the players that could do it. That's what we kept telling ourselves.' The PSV pressure was intensified as they sought to kill off the tie and Lupse went inches wide from long range. Rangers, yet again, stood up and demanded the ball. Parlane missed a great chance when MacDonald sent him clear inside the box, and Johnstone tried hard to get purchase on another. All this within five minutes of going behind again. The match had really opened up.

At first glance, the second Rangers equaliser looks like a large stroke of luck. A moment to be placed into the European file marked 'Nisbet'. It is anything but. A free kick was laid into the path of Kenny Watson, who unloaded his left foot behind the ball. What happened next was actually quick thinking and skilful reaction by Derek Johnstone, and he was brave enough to just guide it into the net. For the second time in the match, against a club who had only ever conceded two goals in the European Cup before that night (both of those were consolations in heavy victories), Rangers hadn't folded in adversity and sought out opportunities from which to strike back.

The pattern of the game, however, just continued. PSV did have the ball in the net immediately afterwards, but van Kraay was offside and they should have scored a legitimate third soon after, but McCloy did well to shut down the chance and save from the next wave that followed. That was perhaps the break that Rangers needed, and with only three minutes remaining they took the lead for the very first time in nearly 180 minutes of football with one of the most sublime goals in the history of the club. Voted 24 in the 50 Greatest Rangers Goals poll in 2018, there haven't been many better Rangers goals in Europe than this. The finish from Russell, arguably the most gifted Rangers player of all time never to be capped by Scotland, is a beautiful cameo, but the pass from McLean, from deep, is the main attraction. It was inch perfect and a glorious example of the kind of telepathy on show from two intelligent footballers. Much of the football of yesteryear doesn't age well as the game develops in strength and intelligent preparation; however, that goal, a quick counter attack with precision passing and finishing, would have been at home throughout all of Sir Alex Ferguson's Manchester United sides.

'They had a chance late on that McCloy saved, but in reality there was no way back for them because of the away goals. We went berserk again at the final whistle and there was just a queue of PSV fans wanting to shake our hands and wish us well. There was no animosity at all and we simply headed back to the bus.' Rangers would make their way back from the Netherlands as second favourites to win the European Cup at 7:2 (Brian Clough's Nottingham Forest were 7:4). The champions of Europe were out and now so were Real Madrid, who incidentally had trounced Progrès Niederkorn 12-0 in the first round. Instead of drawing Wisla Krakow, Austria Vienna, Dynamo Dresden or Malmö, Rangers were handed the champions of Germany, FC Köln. After knocking out the best of Italy and Holland, this was one big hurdle too many, especially with more injuries by the time the competition resumed in March. Perhaps if the draw had been kinder, history could have been a lot different to John Greig and that Rangers side. Despite both domestic cups being retained, 1978/79 would end with the title being lost at Parkhead and the intriguing question, one for another book, of how a team who were only one game away from three trebles in four years and the quarter-finals of the European Cup could fall from grace so dramatically. Rangers were now at the edge of the wilderness.

None of what followed should take away from that night in Eindhoven. Described by Greig as 'a performance that was full of character and flair, and which has seldom been bettered by a Scottish team playing abroad,' it is one that is arguably underrated, especially by our own. Thirty-fourth place is surely too low a ranking for a performance of such class against the odds and the opposition. It suggests that we as a support and a club aren't good enough at showcasing our greatest nights for posterity, that we aren't good enough at educating the next generations about players such as Bobby Russell, who are far too easily dismissed.

It suggests, more than anything, that we need an interactive museum that properly brings our history to life. And we need it yesterday.

33

Celtic 0 Rangers 1

Scottish Cup Semi-Final
Tuesday 31 March 1992

'This has been a triumph rippling with character and courage.'
(Martin Tyler, commentary)

Everything that you need to know about this match can be derived from the on-field celebrations after the final whistle. It's not the normal reaction when beating Celtic, even in a cup semi-final. In terms of games that didn't directly produce a trophy, perhaps only Fiorentina in 2008 and the Scottish Cup semi-final from 2016 provided the same kind of wild scenes, and one of those led to a European final and the other followed a dramatic penalty shoot-out ending years of pent-up frustration. The footage of Walter Smith in his suit being held up by the hero of the hour Ally McCoist, punching and kicking the air with delight, tells a deeper story. Something was born that night that didn't just lead to success in the final two months later, it laid the foundations for the greatest season of all. This was a side coming of age.

Once again the Scottish Cup was a problem. No win since 1981, and, what's more, Rangers were on a terrible run against Celtic in the competition. For three straight seasons Celtic had ended our cup hopes. Firstly, there was the 1989 final defeat, stolen throws, terrible pass backs, disallowed goals and all. Then there were two exits in the earlier rounds, both at Parkhead: a 1-0 defeat in 1990 that saw Tommy Coyne kicked back into the net by John Brown after he had given Celtic the lead and then a horrendous match in March 1991 where Rangers had three men sent off (Hurlock, Hateley and Walters) in a 2-0 defeat. Rangers hadn't scored against Celtic in the Scottish Cup since the Centenary Final of 1973, let alone beat them.

In a period of dominance in the league, those results stand out as being somewhat anomalous. In that season, Rangers had beaten Celtic twice away from home very comfortably, with Hateley asserting himself all over the Parkhead pitch. At Ibrox, Rangers had sold a point with some careless play by Nigel Spackman and then, just ten days before the semi-final, had turned in their worst performance of the season in the final Old Firm league clash of the season. Celtic won 2-0 with goals in either half by Charlie Nicholas and Gerry Crainey. It was a fine showing, albeit amplified by the Rangers anaemia, and was one match in a 12-game winning streak. Much was made by the players in the press afterwards about how comfortable they found playing Rangers; however, they may have been better advised to keep that to themselves.

Celtic were at full strength for the semi-final and Rangers welcomed back Ian Durrant, Stuart McColl and Dale Gordon from injury but there was a key player missing once again. Mark Hateley, now in his second season and residing deep in the subconscious of every defender in the country, was not able to recover from the injury he got after leading Rangers to victory against St Johnstone in Perth on the Saturday afternoon. Smith's natural alternative was Paul Rideout, but he opted, not for the last time, for security in the midfield by using Pieter Huistra in a supporting role from midfield and Ally McCoist leading the line on his own. A 4-5-1 without the ball but the ability to be more of a very modern 4-2-3-1 Rangers lined up with Goram, Stevens, Gough, Brown, Robertson; Spackman and McCall; Gordon, Durrant and Huistra, with McCoist in front.

Hampden was engulfed by an incessant downpour that had not abated all day long. The match was a priority for Sky Sports, not yet into their English Premier League coverage, and they had bumped Milan v Juventus from the San Siro to the 10pm slot. David Livingstone, bringing the latest from trackside to Richard Keys, Ray Wilkins and Paul Elliot in a London studio, cut out now and again as he was rocked by the wind and rain. Conditions and context meant that it was never going to be a quality footballing contest but then that wasn't why people all over Britain were tuning in. They knew exactly the kind of battle that this game was always likely to produce.

They wouldn't have to wait long to witness the first flashpoint. On the BBC, Jock Brown had noted at kick-off that referee Andrew Waddell would have a 'key role' in proceedings. A well-worn commentary practice of stating the obvious to fill the time whilst literally nothing is happening it may have been; however, it only took six minutes for it to be proved correct. 'Joe Miller and I were mates at Aberdeen,' recalled David Robertson when I spoke to him for a *Heart and Hand* interview in 2019. 'We were very close and I didn't want a friend to get the better of me in a game. Walter and Archie were winding me up before the game saying "you need to sort him out early and do whatever you have to do to stop him". The ball was thrown out to Joe and I was going full steam ahead. He took a little touch past me and I thought "here's my chance" so I took him out. A little more than I planned to! In those days it was an unfortunate red card.'

Both Brown and Tyler assumed Waddell was going over to talk to Robertson and then show him the first of a few yellows that evening. They were stunned when the red card was brought out of Waddell's pocket, as was the director who didn't wait for the card to be shown and instead cut to another replay of the incident. Terry Butcher on co-commentary called it 'a disgrace'. Those who weren't commentating live and had a long time to digest the incident, Dougie Donnelly for the BBC and Keys, Wilkins and Elliot for Sky, were all convinced it was a straight red. As ever, the truth is probably somewhere in the middle. It's a clear obstruction and foul, Robertson is never getting to the ball once it was thrown out to Miller by Gordon Marshall. However, by his own admission, there was intent to cause some harm. Just how much, and to what extent a referee has to consider the conditions and match situation in the practical application of the rules, is another debate. The Rangers players and management were in no mood for a considered chat. Fourth official Joseph Timmons's attempt to restrict Smith from getting organisational instructions to his players was met with a ferocious riposte from an irate Rangers manager. Ultimately Smith's instinct to go with Huistra over the more direct forward worked a treat as the only alteration required was for Spackman to move back into the centre of defence and John Brown to replace Robertson at left-back.

Caught in the middle of a tempest, both literal and metaphorical, Smith's Rangers faced a challenge that would go on to define their era. The inevitable foul count mounted up, McStay pole-axed Durrant just seconds after play resumed but didn't see a card, and Tony Mowbray saw yellow for a tackle from behind on McCoist. Celtic's plan seemed to be to continue wide to Joe Miller. His delivery was average and a very tall Rangers defence dealt with the cross balls with relative ease. Rangers in the first half, on the other hand, were surprisingly technical although still tenacious. McCall and Gordon would press and Durrant and McCoist tried to link with each other nicely around the Celtic defence, but the state of the pitch and the absence of another runner made it increasingly difficult to penetrate. Stevens and Gordon both went wide from distance but, incredibly, as half-time approached, Rangers were the better side and fairly comfortable.

That position of comfort was about to get even better. With seconds of the first half remaining, Tom Boyd cut inside and played a ball to Brian O'Neill just inside the Celtic half. He was robbed, first by McCall and then McCoist, and the break was on. McCall took one touch out the right whilst McCoist made a run into space on the left. The cut back reached McCoist perfectly, and without breaking stride he buried the ball into the bottom corner from the edge of the penalty area. Gordon Marshall had a glove on it, but the surface made it nigh on impossible to keep out. There was only one tiny piece of the target for him to aim at successfully and, on pure instinct, he found it. 'Scenes of extravagant celebration,' shouted Martin Tyler. 'McCoist is almost in tears of joy and disbelief.' It really was a visceral reaction. A team felt their backs against the wall, under pressure, out of form and with a sense of injustice so early on. Archie Knox on the trackside resembled something from *Saturday Night Fever*, while McCoist was more like the poster from *Platoon* as he looked upwards to the heavens, open as they were.

'I had kicked the dressing room door in when I got there,' said Robertson. 'The guy came in and fixed it as I was waiting. I heard a noise from above and knew it was a goal. I thought "oh no, Celtic have scored". Wee Doddie (the Rangers kit man George Souter) came in and said, "Coisty's scored! Coisty's scored! We're going to be ok!"' 'I knew Celtic would throw everything at us in the second half,' recalled Archie Knox in his autobiography. 'I went out before the second half kicked off and grabbed one of the ball boys at Hampden. I asked if he was a Rangers fan and he said "yes". So I gave him a fiver and told him to get the message round his pals. If the ball went out for a Celtic throw-in, just leave it until the Celtic fans throw it back. If the ball goes out for a Rangers throw-in, just leave it full stop. I watched him go round all four sides of the Hampden pitch telling his pals not to go for the ball. We needed every advantage we could get and we managed to hang on for the win.'

Knox wasn't wrong and Rangers decided to sit in and defend what they had as Celtic, with the wind now behind them, sought to rescue their season in the remaining 45 minutes. They caused problems but rarely from direct range, with Joe Miller failing to properly connect with the only chance he had in behind Brown. O'Neill hit the post from distance with an effort that deflected off Spackman's hand. Mike Galloway, his replacement later in the half, stung Goram's hands from outside the area. Goram's goal frame was struck twice in quick succession, the first from a Paul McStay shot that left him rooted to the mud bath that constituted a six-yard area, and then he tipped onto the same crossbar from a Crainey header from the resulting corner. Almost like a game of rugby, Rangers were conceding both possession and territory as Celtic began to create chances inside the box and the game's second flashpoint was a case in point. With just less than ten minutes remaining, a tiring Rangers defence failed to clear a Celtic move and John Collins appeared to be fouled in the area by John Brown. In the replay, it is a fatigued and clumsy tackle, and Brown's left foot definitely makes contact with the right of Collins. However, the Celtic midfielder is already on the way down when the contact takes place, his body shape is that of the traditional simulation and perhaps that created enough doubt in Waddell's mind. If Collins had waited he would have been taken out and Celtic would surely have been presented with an opportunity to force a replay. As it happened, the Edinburgh referee spent the final ten minutes much in the same way he did the first, by ensuring that all of Glasgow had something to be incensed about.

Galloway had another pot shot from 30 yards, but Goram got behind it and Rangers saw the remaining time out. This failure, when it really mattered, was probably the beginning of the end for Liam Brady at Celtic, and it opened up a huge opportunity for Rangers to end their drought in the Scottish Cup as eventually Airdrieonians would face them at Hampden in the final. However, the repercussions of this result were not contained by the arbitrary nature of a season end. 'In the second half I was up in the stand,' said Robertson. 'I was kicking every ball but it shows the fighting spirit that squad had. Even in later years, if you were 2-0 down to Falkirk, you still knew that you were going to come back and win.' The greatest Rangers side of all time was arguably born that night. 1992/93 was characterised by comebacks and resilience, but that can only happen time and again, once you know how. Twice against Marseille in the

Champions League, famously at home to Leeds United and twice against Aberdeen in the league, this side had to fight back from adversity and the belief can be traced back here when all of the odds were stacked against them.

Speaking on Sky to David Livingstone after the game, McCoist said, 'We did not play well last week when Celtic beat us 2-0 at Ibrox. And then we picked up the newspapers on the Sunday and the Monday and some of the Celtic players were saying that it was the easiest game they've had all season. Maybe that was their second easiest. I hope it was.' The language may be slightly confused but the sentiment wasn't. When it really counted, Rangers had a team prepared to dig deeper into their own mental reserves more than anyone else, exactly the kind of characteristics that Rangers fans keep close to their hearts decades later. The hugs and roars on the pitch said it all. This wasn't just a team progressing to a cup final on a filthy, wet night.

This was now a band of brothers and one that would take some stopping.

32

Rangers 2 Juventus 0

European Cup First Round, Second Leg
Wednesday 27 September 1978

'After the flop of Argentina, after the defeat in Austria, Scottish football can hold its head high again – thanks to Rangers the magnificent and John Greig, planner supreme.'

(Hugh Taylor, *Evening Times*)

Scottish football was in a rather sheepish mood as the 1978/79 European club competitions commenced. In May, despite losing to England at Hampden in the Home International, Scotland manager Ally McLeod remarked that he was keen to get his hands back on that trophy next year but that 'it could be dwarfed by the World Cup'. McLeod, the self-proclaimed 'born winner', had whipped the country into a frenzy with the genuine belief that they would return from South America that summer with the big one. Thirty thousand fans turned up at the National Stadium to see them off, usually the kind of reception organised for returning heroes parading silverware. Why bother waiting for that? It was a formality. The inevitable disappointment quickly developed into abject humiliation. Peru, Iran, Willie Johnston's pills, rows over bonus, broken buses and, of course, typically, a fabulous win over Holland with one of the best goals ever scored. It was almost a caricature of Scotland at a World Cup.

Although they too returned home without the World Cup, Italy's stock was considerably higher. Denied a place in the final by an Arie Haan wonder strike, Italy had to settle for fourth spot, despite having beaten the eventual champions Argentina earlier in the competition. They were a side in the making, however, and, after another fourth-place finish at the 1980 European Championships, they would eventually triumph in 1982 when the World Cup was held in Spain. Many of the key components of that side were already established by 1978. Goalkeeper Dino Zoff, defender Claudio Gentile, sweeper Gaetano Scirea and midfielders Marco Tardelli and Franco Causio all won the World Cup in 1982 and played in that effective semi-final against the Netherlands four years previously. All of them, including Roberto Bettega (who missed out on that success in Madrid due to injury), were genuine legends of the game. All of them played for Juventus.

Eight Juventus players in total played in that World Cup match in Buenos Aires and all were an integral part of Giovanni Trapattoni's side. During his first spell at Juventus, from 1976 to 1986, 'Trap' won six *scudetti*, the Coppa Italia twice and one each of the European Cup, the European Cup Winners' Cup and the UEFA Cup. Both clubs may have been reigning champions but, with a new rookie manager at the Ibrox helm and Juventus having won the first of their European crowns just a year before (the UEFA Cup in 1977), this was an almighty test to overcome in the very first round of the European Cup.

Rangers lost 1-0 in Turin's Stadio Communale, however, perhaps as a sign of Scottish football's new found humility, it was treated as a triumph by both the home and continental press. That praise was for the performance which looked different from anything Scottish sides had displayed before. The Italian newspaper *La Stampa* called it 'the most grown up performance ever by a British team in a European tournament,' whilst Greig himself declared it 'the best Rangers display in Europe' that he'd seen. Perhaps the folly in Argentina accentuated it but it had been the staple approach for Scottish teams when faced with continental opposition: blood and thunder attacks and adventurous cavalier football. Not much in the way of planning, that was for Hungarians and the likes. McLeod had refused, unlike many of the other World Cup managers, to travel to Lima to watch Peru play Argentina a few months before the tournament commenced. It possibly led to him deploying Martin Buchan incorrectly because he believed that Juan Carlos Oblitas played on the right wing instead of the left, and he may not have had to sigh after the game and admit that his 'main fault' was not marking the brilliant Teófilo Cubillas, leading *The Guardian's* David Lacey to observe that it was 'much as a man might reflect, on falling out of an aircraft, that on second thoughts he should have worn a parachute.'

Greig's approach to this challenge was to be smarter than the average bears that had gone before, although he was quite open about it in advance. 'Our normal game is to attack and show non-stop aggression. Obviously we can't do that here. It would be football suicide against such a side as Juventus. There is no point in my beating about the bush, we are here for a draw and if it is a scoring one then so much the better, for no matter what happens in Turin, we'll still face a tremendous battle in the return at Ibrox.'

The start was sadly typical as Juventus scored in eight minutes when Rangers failed to clear their lines from Colin Jackson's clearance. Giuseppe Furino quickly turned the ball into Pietro Virdis (a £2m signing from Calgiari that summer), whose lighting-fast reactions were able to help him sweep the ball into the corner of McCloy's goal. Whereas Scotland had faltered in the shadow of the Andes, Rangers grew in stature at the foot of the Alps. It was a performance that had the old fashioned helping of courage allied with a disciplined organisation and the modern midfield energy of MacDonald, Russell and Alex Miller (brought in to replace the traditional width of McLean) squeezing the Italians out with Sandy Jardine looking as composed a sweeper as Scirea. Juventus were left frustrated and a little unlucky at the end when Cabirni's cross was deflected onto the post by Jardine, and McCloy made an outstanding save from the resulting Begetta header. It wasn't the comfortable evening that most had expected, however. 'Life will be very difficult at Ibrox,' said Trapattoni.

He wasn't wrong. Ibrox may have been missing the Copland Road end, under reconstruction, but it still produced a mighty noise as the tie, so finely balanced, got underway. Again Greig, unlike McLeod, got his team selection spot on. The defence was unchanged from Turin with McCloy in goal, Jardine sweeping up behind Colin Jackson and the Forsyths, Alex and Tam. MacDonald and Russell continued in the middle of the park, as did Derek Parlane and Gordon Smith further afield. Derek Johnstone returned from suspension and Kenny Watson made way for him. Tommy McLean was brought back in for Miller, which the Italians expected, but he was deployed on the left-hand side, which they did not. The resulting confusion gave Rangers an early foothold in the game and the advantage was pressed home within 20 minutes. Francesco Morini spent the night committing fouls for which he received no card but gave away numerous free kicks. It would be the decisive flaw in that very typical Italian game plan of the time. One of his fouls on Johnstone, just over 20 yards from goal, gave Rangers their first opportunity to restore overall parity. A pre-planned set piece involving McLean, Russell and Alex Forsyth led to a weak shot by the latter that ricocheted gently around the cluttered penalty area before falling at the feet of Smith. He controlled it with one touch before getting a shot away that Zoff could only deflect up into the air. Of course it was MacDonald, covering every square foot of the pitch at his usual pace, who was perfectly placed to nod Rangers in front on the night.

The rest of the story was one of patience and control, something MacDonald said Greig had instilled in them when preparing for this game. McLean was a revelation on the 'wrong' side, skilfully weaving patterns and dragging one of the world's best defences, enhanced by the returning Gentile, out of position and drawing foul after foul. It wasn't the hell-for-leather, blood-and-guts approach that had brought about two European trophies and three other finals for Scottish clubs but derived little else in 48 attempts other than mocking across the continent. This new found maturity reaped its reward with just under 20 minutes remaining and it was from a familiar pattern of play. Morini fouled Johnstone once more and this time it was left for Bobby Russell to swing in a cross from deep. The perfection of the delivery was equalled by the header at the other end. Gordon Smith somehow managed to find space between Gentile and Scirea and cushioned a header down beyond the despairing reach of Zoff.

One Juventus goal would still have killed the European dream but, as time wore on, not only were Rangers better organised than the Italians, they were fitter too, and opportunities were closed down by a mixture of both planning and stamina. 'Every Ranger was a hero on a great night,' wrote Jim Reynolds in *The Glasgow Herald*. 'But I must give special praise to MacDonald, who never gave the Italians any respite; Sandy Jardine, again used in the sweeper's role and making football connoisseurs forget all about Franz Beckenbauer; McLean, the magician who teased and tormented; and, of course, goal hero Smith. These men were out of this world. The rest? Only brilliant.'

Afterwards Greig was at pains to point out that, understandably given his keenness to position himself as a new modern coach, he would have preferred the goals to come from passing moves on the ground instead of the 'old fashioned sides of Scotland who relied on the high cross and the header'. That night would come in Eindhoven when the same controlled composure would create one of the greatest goals in the club's history as well as another famous scalp. For now, however, the nation needed this Rangers result, along with Aberdeen and Hibs who had also progressed that night. This was the same day that Ally McLeod finally left the Scotland job (incredibly he had stayed on to commence qualification for the European Championships but lost 3-2 to Austria in the opening match) and the press pack were desperate to hang their hat on any triumph but only dared to dream that one would come as big as this. Less was made, meanwhile, of Celtic's exit from the Anglo–Scottish cup as they lost 2-1 to Burnley.

Albion Rovers, Forfar Athletic and Juventus. Three football clubs that don't normally feature in the same sentence; however, by this, the 12th game of season 1978/79, these were the only three sides that Rangers had managed to beat. The early struggles to find league wins and even goals (four in six matches and only one at Ibrox) would ultimately provide us with a better sense of how John Greig's managerial career was likely to shape up rather than the two heroic European showings. Had his side been able to show the same nerve and discipline at Parkhead at the end of that season as they had shown against Juventus and PSV Eindhoven, then marching forward with a treble in the bag, a clutch of young talent and experienced winners might have been a whole lot easier for the new boss. This was evidence that a change in Scottish managerial approach was possible. Ultimately it wouldn't be Greig who developed it further, but instead two managers based in the north of the country: Jim McLean and Alex Ferguson.

The domestic context perhaps added to the delirium experienced by the thousands of Rangers fans who left Ibrox that night. But spare a thought for one young fan who had come all the way from Japan. Hitoshi Sato, a 20-year-old football coach, had come to Britain to watch his favourite sides, Rangers being one. Sadly, on the way back to his hotel on the number-15 bus, over £7,000 in cash and travellers cheques (adjusted for inflation) was stolen from his pocket. There was no robbery inside the stadium, however. Another match that suffers because of the legacy that didn't follow means that it is still under-rated despite making the greatest 50. Very few sides have turned up at Ibrox with such a depth of proven international class. To be beaten is one thing. To be outclassed is another. In addition, this Rangers side had to do something that night that no other had been able to do before them: overcome a first-leg deficit and directly qualify for the next round. To do that against this legendary side, first round or not, deserves more recognition than it gets. At the very least, it should be half as famous as the flop in Argentina is notorious.

31

Celtic 2 Rangers 4

Scottish Premier League
Sunday 31 August 2008

'The real glory is being knocked to your knees and then coming back. That's real glory. That's the essence of it.'
(Vince Lombardi)

I have a reputation for being something of a pessimist when it comes to assessing the chances of my football team. It's not uncommon at all, actually, this kind of self-preservation approach to the inevitable bumps and bruises associated with investing a great deal of emotional energy into a group of people that don't know or care about you. Nor is that reputation entirely justified in my case. Many a new season has arrived when I have felt league success was just upon us only to be let down in the spring. Only once in over 30 years of following Rangers have I felt at the outset that a league flag would be beyond the reach of that team and they have proved me wrong. Given the crushing disappointment of May 2008, which included the loss of a European final and a league title on the last night, the sale of Carlos Cuellar, who, despite being at the club for only one season, was genuinely loved by the support, and the return of Kenny Miller, who genuinely wasn't, I couldn't help but feel that 2008/09 wasn't going to bring the success that we were desperately hoping for.

The trip to Kaunas hadn't changed that feeling. After a frustrating goalless draw at Ibrox, Rangers looked set to progress in the return leg when Kevin Thomson scored just after half an hour but were pegged back soon after before succumbing to a long-range winner late on. European finalists in May, out in the first round by 5 August. The pressure really was on, as Thomson recalled when he joined me on *The Time Capsule* in 2019. 'We did struggle that night and got what we deserved. We lacked that wee bit of composure, class, know-how. Leadership maybe. I got the hairdryer from Walter that night and you're looking at the start of that season thinking that this is a huge year and we need to prove people wrong after thinking that you were top of the world a few months prior. This is part of being a Rangers player though. You have to deal with disappointment but I was lucky that I was part of a team and had a manager that could cope with that.'

The disappointment sparked life into the transfer activity. Steven Davis became a permanent fixture and Pedro Mendes also arrived with the American, Maurice

Edu. Fears about the loss of Cuellar started to subside when it became clear that Madjid Bougherra was an able replacement with an ability to form another successful partnership with Davie Weir, albeit in a very different style. All the focus, however, was on the return of Miller, who by this time had played for both Rangers and Celtic and had thumped the badge after scoring for Celtic in an Old Firm victory. It was a huge gamble by Smith to bring him back and one that didn't initially excite the dressing room. 'To be honest Kenny was an anti-climax for me when he was linked with us,' said Thomson. 'We were a bit surprised with that and weren't that excited about him coming in. In his first game at training I was over him like a rash, kicked him all over the pitch. He didn't like it but he changed my opinion in a couple of weeks. A great team-mate who would go that the extra mile for you, a huge character and he turned out to be a really good signing for us.'

The big test came at Parkhead at the end of August. Both sides had won two league games and drawn the other, but this had not been a happy hunting ground for Rangers in recent years, with only four wins in the previous ten visits. A key to any success was Thomson, a man with one of the best Old Firm records in history. In his seven matches, he won six and lost one, a dead rubber at the end of a season where Rangers had already been crowned champions. Perhaps most importantly in the ten games he missed during his spell at Ibrox, Rangers lost six, won only twice and drew the other two. 'The games were made for me. I liked the build-up, I thrived on the intensity. I liked to think that I was a big-game player and that my mates could rely on me to be a catalyst if the chips were down and we really had to win.'

With a mixture of Dutch courage and a buoyancy provided by the later signings, fans like Steven Campbell made their way to Parkhead full of confidence. 'Mendes was a huge signing. Very few have had debuts like that where you just knew right away how important they'd be in a season. Celtic hadn't really done any big business so, given that it was an 8am start and we were well lubricated by the time the double-deckers reached their neck of the woods, morale was high and the battle hymns were in full voice.'

Walter Smith's courage was of the more natural kind. His Parkhead Playbook was well-worn and a little frayed around the edges by now. He ripped it up by going with both Miller and Daniel Cousin, whom most had expected to leave Ibrox since the window opened following his red card in Florence, up front and with a ball-playing midfield of Charlie Adam, Pedro Mendes, Kevin Thomson and Steven Davis. Smith, in the past, when taking Rangers sides in far better form than this to the east end, would have focussed entirely on cramping Nakamura and McGeady. Although still a serious consideration, there was clearly more emphasis on what Rangers could do to Celtic. Fan reaction to the team news was mixed. One fan texted the BBC Scotland online coverage and said, 'Playing Daniel Cousin against Celtic is madness, and Kris Boyd isn't even in the squad; Rangers fans have the two most disliked strikers playing up front today in recent years. Wonder who'll get booed the loudest?'

It wouldn't take long for Cousin to get into the action, hitting the side netting with a header at the near post from a Davis cross, but it was Thomson who made the earliest mark with a scything tackle on Nakamura after eight minutes, for which he received the first booking of the game. 'Walter used to wind me up before the game by saying, "Right, who is getting it tomorrow?" And I just laughed and said, "I Dunno." He said, "I'll tell you something, if you're not booked within ten minutes you'll be sitting next to me." I looked at the clock and was getting a wee bit panicky, I hadn't been that involved and then Nakamura came into view. There were a few that wouldn't fight back. They weren't interested. They could be bullied. He was a good player but he certainly fell into that bracket. Getting a second yellow was a potential problem, but it was a role that Walter was happy for me to have. He had faith that I could boss an Old Firm game with the ball and without it and it was important for me, in order to do that, to leave a mark early.'

Much of the early exchanges took place in midfield, and when the ball did get into the forward areas, Miller lacked any touch whatsoever. The same couldn't be said for Cousin, however. The Gabon international had gone wide on 30 minutes with a volley where he should have done better, but he made up for that six minutes later. Picking the ball up on the right-hand side from a Mendes pass, he displayed an astonishing turn of power and pace like a middleweight champion to leave Mark Wilson for dead. Bearing down on goal, Artur Boruc must have expected a cut back to Miller in space but instead was caught flat-footed as the ball fizzed past his left-hand side and into the net. 'He was Walter's enigma,' according to Thomson. 'With the bit between his teeth he was unplayable, could swat you away like a fly. On other days he could be thrown around like a crisp packet. That day, however, he led the line and set the tone.'

The lead lasted for 100 seconds. Four minutes before Cousin's opener, Weir had found himself in trouble in the box and McGregor did well to save his blushes. It should have been a warning. Errors in midfield by Mendes and David were compounded in the penalty area as Weir and Papac combined comically to give Georgios Samaras a gift to bring Celtic level. For fans like Steven, there wasn't time to catch breath before getting that sense of Parkhead dread again. 'You're not even back to your seat yet. When you get that first goal I imagine players want five minutes to catch their breath, we certainly do, but we couldn't and there was the thought that "oh we've been here before".' The rest of the first half played out at blistering pace, but it was honours even at the break.

'Walter was great in the dressing room,' recounts Thomson. 'His man-management skills were meticulous, the timing of when to use the carrot or the stick. He gave you that belief that you'd win. Of course you lose games of football, the best teams in the world do, but they bounce back when others don't.' It wouldn't be long after the restart before the evidence of that was readily available. There was no panic or long hits in hope. Mendes, Davis and Adam knocked it around, kept the tempo high and probed for an opening. There was a decent shout for a penalty on Cousin before the ball fell to Thomson on the edge of the box where he chipped an inch perfect cross ball to where a Rangers player was waiting in space. It had to be Miller. Peeling off his marker he drilled the volley down into the turf and left Boruc with no hope. 'I didn't get enough praise for the pass! I knew what I meant to do, saw his run, and it was a terrific strike.'

Ten minutes later and it was three. 'At 2-1 up we were absolutely bossing it,' said Steven. 'Broadfoot had made a fool of McGeady down at our corner so morale was high, and when we got a corner at the other side we were singing the name of Pedro Mendes as Davis was about to take it.'

'Mendes is having a quiet game,' remarked David Begg on BBC Radio Scotland commentary one minute before. What happened next would guarantee his place in Rangers folklore. Davis rolled the corner out to the waiting Portuguese, who showcased the most incredible technique to keep it low and hard as it stayed on an unstoppable trajectory into the bottom corner of the goal. 'That wasn't off the training pitch,' said Thomson. 'That was off the cuff. Steve seeing Pedro, Pedro seeing Steve. He liked to stay back and had just unbelievable technique. Class is the only word I can use to describe him as a footballer and a gentleman.'

'Sometimes it takes half a second after the ball hits the net before you hear the boys next to you,' recalled Steven. 'And from then on we felt that we needed to give them a doing.'

Part of Cousin's success with both Gary Caldwell and Stephen McManus was the physical duel, especially in the air. Dougie McDonald had booked the forward for use of the elbow in between the second and third goal. It was a debatable booking. Just as Smith was in the dugout discussing making a change, probably with Cousin in mind, his second yellow card for use of the elbow was in no way ambiguous. With just under half an hour left to see the game out, Rangers were down to ten men. Confidence levels amongst players and fans was mixed. As far as Kevin Thomson was concerned, there was nothing to worry about. 'That look Walter gave Daniel I knew very well! Unless you did something stupid, though, he never gave you a hard time for being sent off. But I never worried at ten men. We had the players and experience to cope. We shuffled into position, no great tactical shift was required. We were comfortable.' Was Steven distressed? 'Aye! By this time the alcohol had worn off and you start to remember the recent record. Jan Vennegoor of Hesselink and Barry Robson had just come on for them and I felt they had been dangerous in the recent matches.'

The palpitations wouldn't have lasted long. One minute after Cousin's red and only five minutes after coming on as a substitute, Vennegoor of Hesselink aimed a swipe at Broadfoot and saw a straight red. It was a totally unnecessary moment of madness and Rangers took advantage of another one soon after. If the Miller and Mendes goals were examples of exquisite technique, Miller's second was not. A pretty harmless Broadfoot cross was spilled by Boruc and, when he was able to realise the gift horse that was staring him in the mouth, Miller steadied himself and knocked in the fourth. The travelling support were now in heaven. 'It was bedlam and so many of us hadn't been in this position at Parkhead. And it was a huge goal for Miller. Like so many I had gone into the game all "Billy Big Balls" and said that I wouldn't celebrate if he scored, but by God was I celebrating then. For boys like myself, winning at Ross County is all good fun, but being there and watching that stadium empty, knowing that it was only 3pm and you had a whole day ahead of you … it doesn't get much better than that.'

Some of the gloss was taken off a famous victory with a deflected free kick by Nakamura, which wrong-footed Allan McGregor with only two minutes left. For the fans, it didn't matter so much, but for the players, these things really do matter as was evident by McGregor, immediately following the final whistle in a heavy victory away to Celtic, moaning at Miller and Weir. 'That was just that team and it's why we had those high standards,' explained Thomson. 'It was a job. We would go and applaud the fans for five seconds and then I just wanted to get back in and get up the road. I thought we won with class and lost with class. I don't really have many pictures of me with cups and celebrating goals with fans, and it's kind of how that team was. It was business and we had to move onto the next game. I'm still raging at the only one that I lost. I saw them having a lap of honour after that win even though we had won the league. It hurt us all and it summed up that group.'

'It was the one time where we played Celtic there and absolutely battered them. Not just physically but on the ball. I've never played at Parkhead and created so many chances. Even with ten men we still kept the ball. As a Rangers player you don't get many opportunities to really put on a show in an Old Firm game, but we really let them off the hook that day when they scored their consolation. It could have been six or seven. It was the perfect blend of gritty determination and the flair in midfield. There was simply nobody beating us, nobody who would pass the ball better or rough us up.'

There were a number of players who could claim this game as being synonymous with them, especially all three goalscorers. However, more than anyone else, it was about Smith. To show the courage to deviate from his usual approach in this fixture after the debacle in Lithuania, to show the nerve and foresight to bring back Miller when he knew that the reaction would be so hostile and to be able to pick up a tired and devastated squad and led them back up the mountain again is exactly why his second spell is often revered more than his more decorated first. That's the real glory after all.

30

Rangers 2 Leeds United 1

European Cup Second Round, First Leg
Wednesday 21 October 1992

'I always look for the Rangers result every week. I supported them as a boy and that still stays with me. However, when it comes to a match between Leeds and Rangers, things will be different. I will have to forget any old loyalties.'
(Gary McAllister)

It is somewhat ironic that this match wasn't televised live to the vast majority of Scottish football fans. Due to the fact that Hearts were also in action at home to Standard Liege that night, European regulations meant that Border TV was the only region in Scotland to show it live, with the rest of viewers able to see the whole 90 minutes from 10:45pm. I say ironic because 1992/93 wasn't just a momentous year in the history of Rangers Football Club but in the history of the game as a whole. This was the season that the English Premier League and the Champions League came into being, and in doing so demonstrated how much television coverage could shape the game itself as well as ensuring that those leagues disappeared over the footballing horizon.

Yet it still had one characteristic that would become so typical of football coverage in the modern age: hype and plenty of it. Perhaps because of the demise of the Home International between Scotland and England three years before, an almost annual fixture dating back to the birth of the sport itself, the 'Battle of Britain' soon filled the column inches and gave tired old hacks the opportunity to re-hash the tired old clichés that had been denied to them since 1989.

The famous game was very close to not happening at all. Leeds had been paired with the German champions VfB Stuttgart in the first round. Despite a 3-0 defeat in the Neckarstadion with all goals coming in 17 crazy second-half minutes, Leeds rallied at Elland Road. A smart close-range volley from Gary Speed and a Lee Chapman penalty proved their intent in the first half, but sandwiched in between them was an equaliser from Andreas Buck, a dreadful goal to lose, with both centre-halves and goalkeeper at fault. A piece of Cantona genius and a close-range Chapman header with only 12 minutes to go set up the chance of the impossible. Leeds couldn't manufacture that decisive moment that would overcome the Germans' away-goal advantage; however,

Stuttgart helped them out with some admin. With seven minutes remaining, Christoph Daum brought on the Yugoslav defender Jovo Simanić to shore up his defence for a final onslaught. He was, however, their fourth foreigner, and in the days of a maximum of three foreign players, Leeds were brought back into the tie. UEFA's handing of the situation was shambolic. So long did they take to decide the outcome that Rangers fans received tickets for the match with 'Stuttgart or Leeds Utd' printed as the opposition. The Germans should have been removed from the competition for breaking the rules; however, as the footballing authorities often do, UEFA disappeared up its own procedures by ruling the second leg null and void, thus giving Leeds a 3-0 win, and tying the aggregate score. Instead of heading to Scunthorpe for a Coca-Cola Cup tie, Howard Wilkinson's side were now off to Barcelona to face Stuttgart in a play-off at the Camp Nou. The scoreline was tight, a 2-1 victory, but it was richly deserved. The tie everyone wanted was now all set to go ahead.

There had been 22 previous encounters in European competition between Scottish and English clubs and on only five occasions had the Scottish side progressed. Rangers had notched up one of those victories, the famous clash with Wolves in 1961, but had lost three other ties, including one against Leeds in the 1967/68 Fairs Cup. The old Anglo-Scottish Cup wasn't included in that statistic, but the shadow of Chesterfield in 1980 still strikes fear into fans of a certain age. This was a different Rangers vintage, however. By late October, Walter Smith's side were now very much into their stride, 14 games undefeated, and this first leg was the start of a busy run of big fixtures in the space of 18 days, including a League Cup final and a trip to Parkhead on top of this double header. Leeds were in relatively poorer form, lying eighth in the new Premier League and without a single away win, conceding 19 goals in their six league trips on the road. Most of these were from set pieces, but the introduction of the new back-pass rule, which meant that goalkeepers could no longer pick the ball up when a team-mate had kicked it back to them, had really caused problems with Wilkinson's penchant for direct build-up play. Something of a waste, given a midfield that included Gordon Strachan, Gary McAllister and Gary Speed.

It didn't need it, but there was another fuse lit under this blockbuster. It wasn't simply progression to the third round of the European Cup of old that was at stake. This prize was now access to the first-ever group stage of the Champions League, guaranteeing prestige, reward and an opportunity to still have a shot at the final come April. Walter Smith would enjoy a rare moment that season, and through much of his first spell, to have a fully fit squad from which to choose. Mark Hateley and Alexei Mikhailichenko were a doubt when they missed training but both were available by match day. Smith's only issue was selecting his third foreigner, with Hateley and Trevor Steven being pretty much locked in. In the end it was Pieter Huistra that got the nod over Mikhailichenko, but he had to make do with a place on the bench. It was the standard choice of Goram, McPherson, Gough, Brown, Robertson, Steven, McCall, Ferguson, Durrant, Hateley and McCoist that took to the field. Leeds had the energy of a young David Batty to add to their skilful midfield trio, with Cantona and Chapman providing the threat up front, especially in the air. However, it was the defence that looked to provide Smith with an obvious weakness to exploit, especially when they were away from home. John Newsome and Tony Dorgio provided stability at full-back, but Chris Fairclough and Chris Whyte were not at the level of the Rangers golden pair in attack.

Ibrox was loud but tense, the way big games should always be. It was also exclusively full of bears. Both clubs, with the hooligan issues that called a halt on the 'Auld Enemy' fixture still in their thoughts, took the decision to ban away fans from travelling. It rarely produces a satisfying atmosphere, however, as fans need to bounce off one another, metaphorically at least and not in the traditional fashion of the 1980s. The electricity provided by the stands ensured that the game kicked off at a pace resembling Pathé News reels from the 1930s. Within a minute, the power went out. Leeds had won a corner when John Brown beat Lee Chapman to a David Batty throw. Strachan's corner was average and easily cleared by David Robertson. Gary McAllister, a life-long Rangers fan, was in space at the edge of the box but everyone in the stadium would have expected at least a second for him to control whilst a blocker could rush out. There was no second's pause. The strike was immediate, arrowing straight into the corner, leaving Goram without a prayer. The silence, save for the screams of the Leeds players as they chased their captain, was eerie, but it didn't last too long before the support roared some belief back into their team.

'The first goal was out of nowhere,' recalls Ian Hogg, 'yet the crowd didn't know what to do. Total silence and bewilderment to the point that everyone is looking at each other trying to convince ourselves that the goal should not stand! A minute gone, written off by the English press and now 1-0 down. It took the crowd two or three minutes to start getting noisy again, but they did just that. Leeds had a fair amount of the ball, but they also seemed to be in a quandary. Do they stick or twist? They attempted the former and Rangers started to take back control of the game.'

Rangers responded in the only way that side knew how as they forced the issue for the next 25 minutes. McCoist should have won a penalty when he was brought down in the box by Whyte after evading the initial block from a clever Hateley knock-down from a Dave McPherson cross. The same three players, plus Ian Durrant, were involved in some nice work on the deck, but John Lukic was quick to get down to the ball before McCoist. It was good goalkeeping by the former Arsenal player, but it would soon be forgotten. Just after 20 minutes, Ian Durrant swung in a corner that held ever so slightly in the blustery air. Lukic was dominant in his attempt to punch it clear, beating everyone else in the close vicinity, but he lost it in the lights as it hung there for a split second and his punch was mis-timed, causing the ball to spin in the opposite direction. Dorigo couldn't make the ground up and it squeezed over the line. The relief at drawing level so soon was palpable.

Durrant was now becoming more and more involved in this game, as he would the entire European campaign. His beautiful scoop over the head of McCoist was touched back into his path by Hateley, but Strachan cut it out before he could take possession. At the other end Durrant was needed to block a Whyte header off the line before Strachan had a goal ruled out for offside following a great passing move. It was enough to spark Rangers into another siege of the Leeds United goalmouth. David Robertson forced a corner with a good drive that Lukic did well to keep out. Another corner followed soon after and finally Rangers got their noses in front. It was Trevor Steven this time who flighted it in from the opposite side to Durrant's, where it was met powerfully by the head of Dave McPherson. Lukic saved well but could only parry it back into the goalmouth where the poacher supreme was waiting. McCoist pounced, Ibrox rocked and the tie was back on. 'As Ally McCoist wheeled away, the West Enclosure went wild with delight,' said Ian. 'The first goal was relief, the second was ecstasy and it felt like we were now dominant and could go on and score a few.'

Durrant, McCall and McPherson all went close in the space of a few minutes before half-time and Rangers picked up where they left off when Robertson fizzed a brilliant ball across the box, but it just evaded Hateley. There was a strong feeling around the ground that we needed a bigger cushion and the fans urged the side on any time a third goal looked possible. The best chance of securing that fell to Hateley late on when he was sent clean through by Stuart McCall. It was an opportunity ideally suited to Hateley, as he would prove time and again, where he would power on and smash home the chance. Perhaps the Achilles injury was more of an issue than he let on, but he looked sluggish despite controlling well initially, and Newsome hunted him down easily to smother the weak right-foot shot. It felt like a real moment to everyone crammed inside the stadium that night. One that creates a nagging feeling that it might come back to haunt us.

Leeds counter-punched once or twice, Cantona being involved in both incidents, chipping in for a Chapman header that hit the side-netting and having an acrobatic effort of his own that sailed over the bar, but they seemed content with their lot. With an away goal and just the one-goal deficit, their manager, and the English media, was sure that this would be enough of a platform for the return leg in Yorkshire. Given their home record and the way they had approached the Stuttgart situation, it wasn't an opinion entirely without foundation. Rangers had certainly left themselves with work to do, however; as the next couple of weeks and months were about to demonstrate, this side very much relished that kind of challenge.

In many ways this is an obvious selection in this poll. A win at Ibrox over the English champions has only happened once in European competition and it was one of many special nights in this very special season. However, it still remains a curious choice amongst the 30 greatest of all time. The second leg is where the magic was. A genuinely big performance with iconic goals and a brave rearguard. A match that never gets old.

This game was a little untidy and nervy. Most fans left with an unshakable sense of unease that the job was far from over. Historical context doesn't do it many favours either as Leeds wouldn't win a single away match all season and the two scrappy goals Rangers scored that night were exactly the kind that they were shipping in at an alarming rate. Also 1992/93, for all its success, was something of a high water mark for the club. By the late 1980s Rangers were without question the biggest club in Britain. After this season, despite defeating England's best (twice), we would become engulfed by the sheer weight of the two new leagues that had now opened up.

We as fans weren't to know that at the time, though. Despite one of our own coming back to give us the fright of our lives, the team had shown the kind of character that would take them a long way. Rangers had beaten the champions of England at home and we knew, deep down, that we'd have to beat them away too. Just to make sure.

29

Rangers 4 PSV Eindhoven 1

Champions League First Group Stage
Wednesday 20 October 1999

'God made the world, but the Dutch made Holland.'
(Anon)

Of all the Rangers sides that took part in the Champions League era, none were better placed to make a big impact than Dick Advocaat's squad that started the 1999/00 season. Treble winners in his first year, even with such a high player turnover throughout the campaign, Advocaat's only major addition in the summer of 1999 was Michael Mols, a £4m signing from FC Utrecht. It was a talented, expressive and, for one more season at least, well-drilled football team, still very much wedded to the philosophy of attacking football. As would be demonstrated by the colour and style of that season's Scottish Cup Final evisceration of Aberdeen in 2000, the Dutch influence had well and truly taken a hold of Ibrox.

They started the new season in very much the same way that they left Hampden Park, having completed that domestic clean sweep. The first eight league games had been won and the first points were only dropped the weekend before the visit of PSV, as a one-goal lead was surrendered at Rugby Park when Rangers had to settle for a draw. It was perhaps a result that was in the post as Rangers faded out of the game late on, trying to see out the lead they had built up, such was the pattern of the last couple of away fixtures. It kick-started a more ruthless approach as the following two league clashes were a 5-1 victory at Pittodrie and a 4-2 home win over Celtic. October was merely the set up in the farce that was 'John Barnes: Celtic Manager'. The punchline was to come in February, but at this stage they were only four points behind Rangers with a game in hand. On paper anyway, everything was still up for grabs.

Europe was where the growing interest was, however. Handed arguably the toughest qualifying tie against the Serie A giants Parma, Rangers had delivered one of the greatest European performances in the club's history to book a place in that season's Champions League. If the luck of the draw had deserted Advocaat in qualifying, it was still nowhere to be seen when the first group stage was laid out in late August. Group B admittedly had the glamour as Barcelona and Gabriel Batistuta's Fiorentina joined Arsenal, playing their home fixtures in the competition at Wembley, although they did have a whipping boy in AIK Solna. There was no whipping boy in Group G, despite the Scottish media's best efforts to provide one. In an attempt to create false expectations, Héctor Cúper's Valencia were dubbed the 'Aberdeen of Spain' by Hugh Keevins of Radio Clyde before the opening group match, due to their slow start to that La Liga season. They would, however, reach that season's Champions League Final, despatching of both Lazio and Barcelona en route, before being humbled by Real Madrid in Paris.

Joining them were Bayern Munich, beaten finalists in dramatic fashion against Manchester United three months earlier. Bayern would reach the semi-finals of this edition before eventually winning the trophy in the 2000/01 final by beating, of course, Valencia in Milan. PSV Eindhoven completed the quartet and, although lacking the quality of Valencia and Bayern, they were still a very strong side. By the time they visited Ibrox on Matchday four, they had already drawn with Valencia, would beat Bayern in the next fixture and their Dutch title would be secured that season by 16 points, at a time when the national game was strong, sandwiched in between two semi-final appearances at the 1998 World Cup and 2000 European Championships. PSV had some emerging young defensive talent in André Ooijer and Mark van Bommel in addition to *the* hottest prospect in European football up front. Ruud van Nistlerooy had scored 15 league goals by this point, including two hat-tricks. To put it into context, his fellow Dutchman at Ibrox, Michael Mols, was considered a sensation in Scotland and he had scored eight. Even the great Romário hadn't started that well in Eindhoven. This was a team to be respected and there was surely no tougher group into which Rangers could have been placed.

It had started badly. Despite holding their own in the first half, including a great chance for Gabriel Amato, Rangers were blown away in the end by Valencia in the Mestalla Stadium. Keeping in line with those fine Rangers traditions abroad, there was a considerable degree of contributory negligence as Lionel Charbonnier gifted the Spaniards their opening goal; however, the trio of Gaizka Mendieta, Claudio López and Kily González pulled the Rangers defence out of position at will to create the second. There was a huge response at Ibrox two weeks later for the visit of Bayern, but a mixture of hideous luck and careless passing cancelled out a first-half Jörg Albertz goal and Rangers had to settle for a point. There would be no cancellation in Eindhoven, however, as Albertz struck late on to grab a famous win in Holland. Rangers were starting to look more comfortable on their travels under Advocaat. Following on from the win against Bayer Leverkusen in the previous season's UEFA Cup, it was no longer mandatory to watch away legs in Europe from behind the sofa.

The talk before kick-off was all about the Rangers team selection. Claudio Reyna and Arthur Numan were injured, but it was a tactical switch that had caused all of the shockwaves. A story would do the rounds in Glasgow later that week, almost certainly apocryphal, that supposedly originated from someone working in the hotel being used by the PSV squad. In the corner of their team meeting room, it was told, stood an A3 flip chart with just one word written on it, circled heavily in marker pen: Albertz.

He didn't start. Rangers only goalscorer in the Champions League so far, the man directly responsible for the four points we had gathered, would be sitting on the bench. His replacement was Derek McInnes, a bit-part player by that time who was reportedly going to be sold to Sheffield United for £450,000 before the game. Albertz had in fact not started the previous game in Holland but had famously come on and scored the winner. Surely Advocaat, despite the fractured nature of their relationship, would not risk going without the German again? There were more than murmurs rippling around the pre-match Ibrox crowd, but it was a selection that worked a treat. McInnes played at the base of a three-man midfield, allowing Barry Ferguson and Giovanni van Bronkhorst the freedom to pull the creative strings for a mobile front three of Neil McCann, Rod Wallace and Michael Mols. As usual, Numan's deputy was Tony Vidmar, who joined the familiar defensive unit of Moore, Amoruso and Porrini, playing in front of Stefan Klos, who returned that night from a near-ten-week injury lay-off.

It was an open game of football from the off, with Van Bronkhorst stamping his authority all over the pitch. He had gone wide from distance after setting up Vidmar, the hero against Parma, from a dangerous free kick. There was a scare too as Sergio Porrini failed to control a ball in his own box, which gave Johann Vogel an opportunity, but he was fortunately smothered out by Moore. It was Rangers who made the first clear-cut chance, however. A patient move involving van Bronkhorst, McInnes and Ferguson, so patient that you can clearly hear one punter shout, 'Move yer arse Gio!' (total football hadn't taken a hold of *everyone* then), and one which finally released Porrini down the right flank. The Italian cut a simple ball for McCann in the box, but he meekly hit it straight at the goalkeeper Kralj. The tension around the ground was palpable. Rangers had played well thus far in the campaign but hadn't been ruthless. These chances couldn't continue to be passed up.

No sooner had fans slumped to their seats in frustration, they were up on their feet in jubilation. The resulting corner was swung in by Van Bronkhorst and met powerfully by Amoruso from four yards out. It was a super delivery and a commanding header, but the Dutch defending was very lax. Soon after the opener it seemed as if PSV resembled the boy with his finger in the dike as Rangers swept forward again and again. Wallace had a good effort charged down by Stanga after an intelligent McInnes pass found Mols, whose ability to turn defenders to his will was now becoming something of a trademark, before cutting it back for the English forward. Mols missed a chance of his own, as did Porrini, before Wallace spurned perhaps the best one of them all when he dragged wide after a brilliant pass by Ferguson. Advocaat was struggling to keep whatever was remaining of his surgically enhanced coiffure.

With six minutes left before the interval, Mols saved his side a dressing-room tirade when he doubled the lead. He started the move himself when he won the ball just inside the PSV half before switching play out to McCann on the left-hand side. McCann paused intelligently before sending over a pinpoint cross for the Dutchman coming in at the back post. Mols had been a sensation domestically but had missed some big chances at home to Bayern Munich and in Eindhoven. This was a big moment, especially as he had been on the receiving end of a lot of Dutch abuse from the away end. 'I don't think we were quite at the Kris Boyd stage where you couldn't play him in Europe!' said David Edgar. 'The thing I remember about that goal going in was the delight on his face because there are some guys that you love to see score a goal because you can tell just how much it means to them.'

If the Rangers players felt that they had received their just reward with that bigger cushion, they were reminded right on the stroke of half-time that it takes a lot of work to maintain it. Porrini, under pressure out on the touchline, could and should have blasted it up to me in the rear of the Govan Stand. Instead he tried to retain possession with a ball back to Klos but it was woefully short. Suddenly van Nistelrooy, hitherto anonymous, skipped ahead of Moore before being bundled down in the box. A soft penalty according to Archie McPherson in the commentary box. The penaltiest of all penalties according to legendary official Pierluigi Collina, who wasted little time in pointing to the spot. Klos guessed correctly but van Nistelrooy left him with absolutely no chance as he rifled the ball high into the net. With a gut punch that somehow felt unjust, the collective enjoyment of 44 minutes of blistering technical football had been replaced at the interval by that familiar feeling of tense dread.

'Ibrox was so loud that night,' recalls David. 'It was just one of those nights, there's a secret to it but it can't be found in design, where you knew before kick-off that the fans were on it. Maybe it was because of a renewed confidence from the way we had been playing, but it was visceral. And it was like the oxygen had been sucked out at that moment. We should have legitimately been three of four goals up in a game that we had dominated and now they go off down the tunnel believing they're still in it.'

After the re-start it should have been Rangers on the spot, but incredibly the Italian referee waved away the appeals when McCann was assaulted by Kralj in the box. It merely delayed the restoration. A van Bronkhorst free kick on 56 minutes moved wickedly and could only be parried straight back out by the Yugoslav goalkeeper and into the path of Wallace. His reactions were fast but his toe-poke had no pace and, in what can only be described as a 'stramash', Wallace literally attempted to header the ball on the ground from one yard out. Neil McCann showed no such gentility as he nearly took his team-mate into the net with the ball. The juxtaposition was described perfectly by David Edgar on *The Time Capsule*. 'This was such a great goal because it showed the contrast you sometimes get in football. Here is a glamorous European competition, these two huge names, millions of pounds spent on the players on show and, in the case of van Nistelrooy, would be spent and there's a goal that comes from a Primary five lunchtime kickabout.'

There was no complacent let up this time as Rangers piled on the pressure. Vidmar, who had been letting off some steam in the press that week about being considered only as an understudy, should have done better when sent through brilliantly by Ferguson, but he instead hit the side-netting with the outside of his right foot where he could have drilled it low across goal or crossed for the waiting McCann.

The fourth goal finally came with just ten minutes left, although it didn't have the type of build-up befitting the performance in general. With tired legs all around him, Sergio Porrini just simply punted the ball long for Mols. After that, the play was far more refined. The familiar twists and turns were on display before he first settled himself and then settled the match. Due to be substituted with cramp for Jonatan Johansson before the goal, he had given himself the perfect setting in which to take his standing ovation. An instant hero of the Ibrox faithful, now showing a ruthlessness at the very top level as well as domestically, the fans and the manager had found the final piece in their puzzle. Rangers were now shooting for the stars! What could possibly go wrong? The problem, when your hopes and dreams are embodied by one man, almost always rests in the body of that one man. The careers of both Dutch goalscorers that night were shaped by exactly the same injury. Daryl King, writing in *The Evening Times* the following day, said that Rangers had saved themselves £11m by signing the better Dutch forward. Sporting injury, and more importantly the physical and mental recovery associated with it, is a capricious business indeed.

There were many Rangers players that night, other than Mols, who could lay claim to having put in an outstanding shift. Amoruso had kept the best striker in Europe very quiet and had firmly re-established himself with the support as the Rangers captain, van Bronkhorst, was sensational in pulling the strings, and Neil McCann, who had scored twice in a title-winning victory at Parkhead, described the performance as 'as sweet a moment as you can get in football,' as he relentlessly attacked the Dutch defence. The role of Derek McInnes can't be understated either. Sitting on the intelligent Belgian veteran Luc Nilis, he allowed Ferguson, van Bronkhorst et al the space in which to shine. For all the threats the PSV coaching staff may have seen in Jörg Albertz, he couldn't have done that crucial job.

Rangers finished that evening one point clear at the top of group G. One more win in the remaining two fixtures would have ensured progression to the next group stage and Champions League football into the spring. Barry Ferguson, subject of a £10m interest from Parma, committed himself to a new contract the following day. Plans were also in place for an academy to be built on a site at Auchenhowie. Everything felt on the up as the fans left Ibrox on that October night. PSV manager Eric Gerets said afterwards that, 'Rangers could have scored many more goals than they did. I thought they played marvellous football at times. We had a lesson in how the modern game should be played. This defeat will be in my mind and the mind of the players for a while.' As we have seen, such platitudes from PSV coaches are nothing new, but this wasn't 1978. Rangers had won a European trophy six years before that particular victory. With the exception of one season in the 1990s we, and the rest of Scottish football, were a laughing stock. We had pride back, with interest, and we could dream again.

Dreams rarely come true, of course. This team would ultimately fail to make it through. Another masterclass by Valencia, this time at Ibrox, and the heartbreak in Munich, left Rangers with the consolation of the UEFA Cup, an opportunity they treated like an uncool birthday present from an out-of-touch aunt. History has perhaps placed this disappointment into a fairer context. Rangers were drawn with two of the best three sides in European football at the time (Real Madrid being the other) and not only was it the toughest draw in that season's competition, it was the hardest Champions League draw Rangers have ever faced. Borussia Dortmund in 1994 and Lyon in 2007 were tough second-place sides but both exited the competition immediately once the knock-outs started and PSV Eindhoven were a far harder proposition than either Steaua Bucharest or Stuttgart.

Parma was the greatest knock-out achievement of the era, and, with a super performance to match, but for sheer dominance of a respected opponent, this may well be the peak of Advocaat's Rangers reign. The regression down towards the national mean may have picked up pace in the years that followed, but rarely has a Rangers side inhaled that kind of rarefied air at the summit of European football. An ironic metaphor, perhaps, for a side shaped by the continent's lowlands. That old Dutch phrase came from the fact that it was a nation literally dragged out of the sea and dried by drainage and building dikes. By October 1999 it felt very much like Rangers had been dragged out of European football's depths. Now glory awaited, unless, of course, arrogance got in the way.

Those bloody, but brilliant, Dutch eh?

28

Sporting CP 0 Rangers 2

UEFA Cup Quarter-Final, Second Leg
Thursday 10 April 2008

'As any athlete knows, momentum is the most unstoppable force in sports. The only way to stop it is if you get in your own way, start making stupid mistakes or stop believing in yourself.'
(Rocco Mediate, US Golfer)

One quirk of modern football is that some teams can reach European finals without the consistent upwards trajectory of the traditional cup run, that building sense of excitement and destiny that grows from such an inauspicious start. In the 20 seasons to date, where the UEFA Cup/Europa League has absorbed teams who were knocked out of the Champions League along the way, 19 teams have reached the final of one European tournament after having suffered the dejection of being eliminated from another. That figure includes eight winners. It's not how the traditionalists demand that it should be.

It is exactly how it was for Rangers, however, in 2007/08. Champions League qualification was ground out in the intensity of Belgrade and a difficult group was the reward. If anyone thought that the win at home to Stuttgart was a surprise, in a rather chaotic opening match, they would have needed smelling salts after the 3-0 victory over Lyon in France. A goalless draw at home to Messi, Ronaldinho et al left Rangers top of the group at the halfway stage. As this new-found momentum grew, so did the expectation, and Rangers found themselves frozen to the spot. No further points were picked up in the final three games and a place in the last 32 of the UEFA Cup was the consolation.

Perhaps if the results had been flipped and Rangers had managed to salvage the continuation of European football that season with an exhilarating surge and victory at home to Lyon, the mood over the winter would have been better. Many fans raged on internet forums and made it clear that they weren't interested in the UEFA Cup, only a place at the very top table would do. More than a few responded that they would happily take their UEFA Cup Final ticket in that case, as surely they wouldn't be interested in going to such a second-rate affair. Much laughter was shared, some gallows humour possibly, but there was many a true word spoken in jest. By April of 2008 the possibility of needing tickets for the final was becoming a reality.

There had been another swing in momentum, accelerated by an Allan McGregor save from Boubacar Sanogo late on in the siege of Bremen. It was Nacho Novo who had actually started it with his late equaliser in Greece, as Panathanaikos were eliminated following a drab home 0-0 draw in the first leg of the round of 32 and a pretty insipid display in the second, in keeping with the general glum feeling that had bled out from that Lyon defeat. Then came victory in a raucous home leg to Werder Bremen, lying second in the Bundesliga at the time, when Rangers won 2-0 by virtue of some courageous forward play and a disastrous goalkeeping display by Tim Weise. On a night of some literal thrills and spills, Daniel Cousin and Steven Davis were the beneficiaries as they speculatively and opportunistically created a cushion to take to Germany, where McGregor gave a masterclass in shot-stopping. The Brazilian Diego would breach his lines in the second half with a glorious 20-yard shot, but stops against Markus Rosenberg and Daniel Jensen paled in comparison to the late miracle that denied Sanogo inside the six-yard box. All of a sudden the magical, intangible force that is sporting momentum was gaining a rapid pace. There is a point in every unexpected cup run, sometimes a season as a whole, where the dynamic changes from an 'enjoy-it-while-it-lasts' whimsy to a 'holy-shit-we-are-going-to-actually-do-this' conviction. For Rangers in this season, that came in Lisbon.

For those who had travelled throughout the season, missing out on the next chapter was becoming impossible. The problem with this tie was that it took place in the middle of the Easter holidays and many had booked a spring break with the family long before it became apparent that Rangers might still be in Europe. I know of one fan who was long booked on a Mediterranean holiday where there was no household negotiation being entered into for a quick alteration. On that Thursday morning he quietly slipped away from his wife and kids at the hotel to get a newspaper, somehow ended up at the airport and booked a flight to Lisbon. Listen, who knows how these things happen? 'I'll be back tomorrow,' was the gist of the, presumably short, phone call. Something special was brewing and this game simply couldn't be missed.

One fan who had prior consent for the trip in place was Ian Hogg. 'I had left Ibrox after the first leg very frustrated. They hadn't been very good and we should have capitalised. There was a knot at the pit of my stomach that we'd maybe let an opportunity pass by. But as the week went on, the excitement built. It was akin to an Old Firm anticipation.' All the Rangers tickets had been paid for by the club as a thank you for an extended run of continental support. It would probably be the last hurrah after all.

It had started with some familiarity in the home leg of the quarter-final where the concession of no away goals seemed to please the manager more than scoring any goals of our own. Another dull stalemate set up a trip to Portugal as thoughts turned to the victory over Sporting at the same stage of the successful European Cup Winners' Cup campaign of 1971/72. These signs, completely irrelevant as they are,

are given meaning by this surging force of destiny. Coincidences became omens. It was a sense that was manifest on all four possible fronts as Rangers roared into the spring with dreams of a quadruple still fully intact. There were inconvenient and avoidable replays in the Scottish Cup, which would prove costly in the end, but the league form was exactly the kind that stirs belief. Thirteen straight wins, including a 1-0 defeat of Celtic at Ibrox, left Rangers six points ahead with a game in hand as they entered the first weekend of April, with Lisbon soon to follow. On the face of it, the results of that weekend were yet further evidence of this unstoppable cruise to glory as Rangers extended their lead at the top. The trick with momentum is that it is sometimes layered with hidden wobbles that won't be felt until further in the future. This *was* a wobble and a missed opportunity that would come back to bite. Celtic lost at home to Motherwell on the Saturday, whilst Rangers had to come back three times to draw 3-3 with Dundee United at Tannadice the following day. Seven points with a game extra should have still been enough; however, nine may have deflated the counter charge by Celtic that was to come.

Walter Smith was forced into making just one change from the XI that started the first leg with Davie Weir's suspension making room for Christian Daily to come into the heart of the defence with Carlos Cuellar. McGregor, Broadfoot and Papac making up up the rest of that unit, whilst Hemdani, Davis, Ferguson, Thomson and McCulloch comprised a tough midfield with Jean Claude Darchville, on a dreadful individual European streak, the lone man in attack.

The opening 15 minutes were an example of how different this Rangers side looked on the ball when away from home and with the pressure off. There was a composure about how they passed the ball and there were some good moves that just fell foul of the offside flag. It was Sporting who went closest, though, as McGregor was rooted to the spot when Liedson's header crashed back off the post following a wicked free-kick from Leandro. As the weather resembled Glasgow more than Lisbon, Darcheville's intelligent runs and Ferguson and McCulloch represented the only threats to goal, but Sporting were reasonably contained too, only the brilliant Joao Moutinho scraping the post from outside the box.

Sporting, under some pressure from their own support, started the second half with far more intent, in doing so pushing the Rangers line further and further back. Within ten minutes of the restart there were three scares. Firstly, Gladstone was inches away from converting a cross ball, Kevin Thomson (who picked up a costly booking that would rule him out of the first leg of the semi-final) precipitated a collective seizure amongst the support with a poor back-pass that put McGrgeor under serious pressure, and finally a Simon Vukcevic header that glanced the woodwork. 'I was at the opposite end,' recalls Ian. 'The third of those chances, the Vukcevic header, I was convinced was in from where I was. McGregor was nowhere near it, there was a big massive roar around the stadium and somehow it went wide. My chest was sore with the tension!'

Rangers were leading a charmed life but Sporting were playing further and further into a pattern that suited this team down to the ground.

On the hour mark the trap was sprung. With Sporting forcing the issue more and more, Broadfoot released the pressure with a hopeful punt up the field. The bounce of the ball beat the two closest Sporting players, Darcheville gave Steven Davis a cushioned header and the break was on. With two more touches of the ball, Rangers were incredibly ahead. Davis was able to cut the ball back into the box before Leandro could reach him and Darcheville, with the horror of that miss against Lyon still hanging over him, was in plenty of space to score one of the most crucial goals of the whole season with a classy left-foot finish past Rui Patricio. 'At the point when Darcheville released Davis I remember being behind the goal, grabbing the shoulder of my mate Duncan and saying "we are clear, we've got two on one!" I knew nothing of the iconic Darcheville salute at the time as I nearly lost my specs in the celebration. It was absolutely wild.'

With Sporting needing two goals, the tone was set for the remaining half an hour. With the exception of McGregor's goal frame being clipped once more, this time from a Yannic snap shot, it was mostly a case of impotent possession against numbers and close pressing around the Rangers box. Smith replaced one target man with another as Daniel Cousin took on that role whilst he took the seemingly defensive move of replacing Lee McCulloch with another defender in Steven Whittaker. The only disappointment as Rangers ran down the clock was the yellow card shown to Barry Ferguson, meaning that, if the job in the Estadio José Alvalade was completed, they would line up in a UEFA Cup semi-final without two key players in midfield.

With two minutes of normal time left, Cousin should have been the one that sealed a famous victory, but he let the ball roll too far away from him, after another brilliant driving run by Davis, and could only find the side netting. Given the away goal and the ever-decreasing time available, by the time Steven Whittaker dispossessed Abel inside the Rangers half none of the travelling support should have had any remaining concerns. This is Rangers, however, so when Cousin's run made space past Leandro it was no wonder the supporters, to a man and woman, were screaming 'PASS!' Miguel Veloso clearly thought that would be the most obvious move and so didn't commit to closing down the slaloming Whittaker, thus leaving him the space to complete the best moment of his career when he cooly steered it into the bottom corner. The esteem in which he is held by the Rangers support would plummet rapidly in later years, but at that moment he was a hero. Rangers were in a semi-final of a European competition with a classic counter-attacking performance and two of the greatest goals in the club's history.

'My immediate thought in the two or three minutes after the final whistle, as we were all calming down to just a mild frenzy, was that we could genuinely win it. This was the first time that I, a naturally cynical pessimist, had believed. As they kept us in the stadium it was just an overriding emotion of sheer pride. The players had to come back out from the dressing room and celebrate with us, such was the noise from the Rangers support.'

In purely footballing terms, this game doesn't quite exceed the achievement in Eindhoven in 1978 or even the draw with Marseille in 1993. Sporting won the Portuguese Cup that season but hadn't been league champions since 2002 (and are still waiting at the time of writing). It ranks so highly, however, because of the devastating nature of the two goals and because at this moment, frozen in time, it all looked on for Rangers. Fiorentina stood in the way of a UEFA Cup Final, a very difficult opponent but still beatable, especially as it was, for the fourth tie in a row, a case of having the home leg first. One domestic trophy was in the bag and, given Celtic's exit from the Scottish Cup the month before, the path was clear in the other. And surely, given such a big lead in the championship, a domestic treble was the least that we would manage.

'I don't believe in momentum,' said Bob Boone, the former Major League Baseball All-Star. 'Momentum changes with one hanging curveball.' There were a few of those for Rangers to deal with in the closing weeks of the season. Thomson's booking, which ruled him out the Old Firm double header at Parkhead, McGregor's injury in the first of those games, which probably would have prevented the 93rd minute Celtic winner and ended their chase there and then, and of course Celtic's 'Tour of Japan' rouse which meant that the season could not be extended and ensured that Rangers had to play 14 games in the final six weeks of the season. That momentum was now stuck in a sickly treacle.

Strictly speaking, both quotes by Mediate and Boone are contradictory nonsense. In two sentences, Boone states he doesn't believe in momentum before then, explaining how it changes, and Mediate declares something unstoppable and then subsequently tells us three different things that can stop it. They're not knowingly wrong, like a carefully constructed Groucho Marx or Peter Altenberg aphorism ('There are only two things that can destroy a healthy man: love trouble, ambition and financial catastrophe. And that's already three things, and there are a lot more'). However, they still make some kind of sense to us. Momentum is a purely psychological phenomenon. We *felt* unstoppable that night in the José Alvalde. It *was* going to be our big year. But, metaphorical hanging curveballs *do* happen in sport. Suspensions and injuries mount up and the thought of a fixture pile up can be mentally draining before the balls have even been kicked. It is the response to those curveballs that counts. It is in these situations where forced errors become unforced errors in tennis or two quick wickets leads to a batting collapse in cricket. A once unshakable belief can eventually turn into corrosive self-doubt.

As fans, however, we seem able to extricate the domestic season from the European one in 2007/08. There are countless Rangers games throughout history that were a snapshot of intense emotion and pride but are subsequently damaged by what immediately followed. Every element of that European run, however, in a time where Scottish football was at best a second-class citizen in continental society, still shines brightly. We are still very much in awe of those memories and the journey.

Thousands of bears slipped into the Lisbon night for an evening of celebration, dreaming of just one more bright European night. Three weeks later, they'd get their wish.

27

Rangers 4 Celtic 0

Scottish Cup Final
Saturday 14 April 1928

'I saw, in a flash, the whole picture of our striving to win the cup. I saw the dire flicks of fortune which had beaten us when we should have won. That ball should have been in the net. It was on the penalty spot instead. If I scored, we would win; if I failed we could be beaten. It was a moment of agony.'
(David Meiklejohn)

When I was 11 years old I received a Rangers annual as part of my Christmas. It was becoming something of a tradition, even at that young age. As always, this edition contained the usual trivia, interviews and photos, but it also depicted a game from yesteryear in a comic strip, *Roy of The Rovers* style. The names didn't mean much to me, save perhaps Morton and McPhail, and the old-fashioned style was little more than amusing. However, it was clear to me that it was something that I ought to know, something important. I was being handed down a piece of Rangers mythology. The Scottish Cup Final of 1928. The end of the hoodoo.

Despite the fact Bill Struth's side had won the Scottish League Championship six times in the previous eight seasons, they were literally a variety theatre joke. Before the 1928 final, George West, one of the most popular comics in the country, cracked wise in the city's Princess Theatre when he held aloft a cardboard cut-out of the famous old trophy (still the oldest national cup in existence) and claimed that it was a piece of genuine antiquity, the proof of which was the fact that the last name on it was Rangers. According to James Forrest, producer and host of many podcasts on the era, the cup was seen as 'the highest prize for a Scottish football club at the time', more so even that a league title. The *Official Biography of Rangers* called it the 'Blue Riband of the sport', much like the FA Cup was in England. The attendances for the final and the press fever around it was never matched at the time in the normal weekly contest.

For Rangers, as decorated and as big a club as they were, this was becoming a strain. It was puzzling many, not least the management, why a side used to going through league seasons with barely any defeats to their name (there was only one defeat in Struth's first season in charge (1920/21), in one season they kept it to three and on three occasions they only lost four league games) seemed to find a few rounds in the cup beyond them. Teams that were routinely taken care of in a league fixture seemed to grow in stature in this competition. As Ian Peebles points out in his 1973 'centenary' book *Growing with Glory*, the fans could always point to one reason or another. 'Sometimes the referee would be blamed, or the state of the pitch, or a fluke goal by an opponent, but always something happened to Rangers in the cup. They lost cup finals to Third Lanark, Partick Thistle, Morton, and, of course, Celtic. In their 25-year run of cup calamities the only thing Rangers fans could be sure about was getting through the first round.'

Recent signings such as the legendary Bob McPhail had won the cup with their previous club and, although it wasn't talked about in the dressing room, they'd have fun with the more senior Rangers players by attaching their winners' medal to their watch chain and flaunt it from the pocket of their waistcoat. David Meiklejohn, according to McPhail, 'would often growl and let rip with some choice language, though not if the manager was within earshot.' Nobody swore in front of Struth. It may have been unspoken, but the bonus for this final told the story. McPhail would take home £20 (just over £1,100 adjusted for inflation) which was incredible for such a payment in 1928.

Meiklejohn was only the skipper that day because Tommy Muirhead was injured and had to be replaced by the 37-year-old Andy Cunningham. Fans who treated this blow as a bad omen would have doubled down when Rangers lost the toss and had to face a gale in the first half, in the days when Hampden was a swirling wind bowl. Upon reflection six years later, Meiklejohn felt that it was the best call for Rangers in the end: 'I knew our supporters were glum when we were forced to face the wind, but it suited us for we were a very fit and strong team and we liked to start against the wind so that we could end with it at our back and go and launch massive attacks.'

The Rangers side that day was Thomas Hamilton, Dougie Gray, Robert J. Hamilton, John Buchanan, David Meiklejohn, Tully Craig, Sandy Archibald, Andy Cunningham, Jimmy Fleming, Bob McPhail and Alan Morton. For the latter this would cap off an incredible month as, only a fortnight before, Morton had written his name into Scottish footballing folklore with a devastating performance at Wembley when Scotland beat England 5-1 and the 'Wembley Wizards' were first crowned. The Wee Blue Devil's pace, dribbling and accurate crossing would be needed at Hampden too.

The first half was very much as expected by the 118,000 fans crammed into the home of Scottish football. Celtic, with the wind behind them, hammered at the Rangers goal and the league champions were rocking in the cup once again. The familiar pattern looked set in place when Celtic's Paddy Connelly met the ball flush from outside the box with a volley that convinced many it was surely goal bound. Hamilton, in the Rangers goal, stretched every sinew to keep the ball out of the top corner, but it still rebounded back into play for yet more anguish on the terraces. Adam McLean, perhaps assuming Celtic had taken the lead the second the ball left Connelly's boot, paused too long and stumbled before the ball was safely retrieved.

Celtic had to make the most of the first half conditions, and going in at half-time goalless was akin to passing up a much needed away goal in a modern European tie. The pressure was reverted in the second half and it was only 11 minutes old when Rangers thought that they had taken the lead. Jimmy Flemming's goal-bound shot had beaten John Thomson, the Celtic goalkeeper, but was punched clear by their captain Willie McStay, even though McPhail and Meiklejohn were convinced that it was already over the line. Referee Willie Bell instead pointed to the spot and the chance was presented for a Rangers legend to be born. Everyone involved or watching seemed to understand that this was it. Score and Rangers would be comfortable, especially in these conditions; miss and the hoodoo was still clearly in force.

Bob McPhail, in the book he co-wrote with Allan Herron, chief sportswriter for the *Sunday Mail* for 26 years, *Rangers Legends* said, 'I still remember there was a silence when Meiklejohn put the ball on the spot, but if I was nervous just watching, he looked his usual calm, cool and collected self. I got ready to move incase there was a rebound, but Meek just stepped up and drove the penalty kick low to Thomson's right. I knew at the time that, had our skipper missed, then Celtic would have gone on and beaten us, and every other Rangers player out there on the field at Hampden that day believed the same, and Meek himself told me that he wanted to take the kick quickly for he didn't want to have time to think about what would happen if he missed.'

'For ten minutes afterwards I was in a trance.' recalled Meiklejohn. 'I have only a hazy idea of that period, and now I feel that if Celtic had realised my condition and had played on to me, I would have been clay in their hands,' Perhaps he offered some degree of modesty but more likely this was further evidence of what tense situations in sport, where the mind is manufacturing all kinds of supernatural nonsense, can do to the best and, in that era, 'Meek' was. Rangers legend George Brown described him as 'the best of them all. In attack he could spread around the most delicate passes, yet if he had to fall back to defence he was as hard as nails. More than that, he could read a game brilliantly.'

Rangers were liberated by that moment and they didn't look back. Despite his moment of trance, the Rangers captain still felt able to keep Jimmy McGrory contained in his pocket as McPhail and winger Sandy Archibald unleashed years of pent-up frustration. Three minutes after the penalty, McPhail stole one off the toe of Jimmy Flemming (he should really have had two cup-final goals), from an Archibald corner and Archibald himself lashed in two late, long-range, low drives. The hoodoo was over and Rangers had won their first-ever league and cup double. After taking so long to break the duck, Rangers would go on to win five of the next eight Scottish Cups, and this perhaps propelled the league juggernaut to further success. Of the 11 titles available before the outbreak of the Second World War, Bill Struth's Rangers would win eight, making it 14 in the first 19 seasons of his stewardship.

It is not difficult to appreciate why this game meant so much to Rangers fans of the time. Of more interest is why this legend lives on as strong to this day, and why others instead have faded. Being the only match from the Struth era on the list and only one of three games before the 1970s that made the cut, it is an obvious stand out. Considering the demographic of the listenership, the increased quality of footage over time and the natural bias towards recent memory, why does a Scottish Cup Final from 90 years ago resonate more than great European triumphs at home and abroad or Old Firm cup finals still available to us in technicolour?

Conscious or otherwise, there is perhaps a need to salute the greatest figures in the club's history. As time fades in the memory, one single game will have to do. Not a token gesture as such but as a way of distilling years of service and achievement down to the format we love most: a tale of 90 minutes that can be passed down from generation to generation. Struth has one, as does Symon. Waddell, Wallace and Greig have two each. Perhaps a poll in 20 years will find them limited to a solitary match too. McLeish, Advocaat and Souness have 17 between them, with Smith bestriding the whole poll with 21 entries featuring him at the helm, none of which is surprising given that this relatively recent success is still so visceral. Again it raises questions of how well we 'do' history, but one game is better than nothing. Rangers simply wouldn't be the club it is without Bill Struth, and the levels of success he produced demand some recognition.

Why not the famous Moscow Dynamo friendly of 1945, however? Or a key game from the first-ever treble-winning side of 1948/49? There are four Scottish Cup finals on this list, and all of them are synonymous with an individual player. The 'Meiklejohn Final' would be joined by the 'Forsyth Final', the 'Laudrup Final and the 'Lovenkranks Final'. None of the Scottish Cup victories that comprised a treble season are anywhere to be seen. In fact, of all the 340 games that were played to give Rangers seven domestic trebles, only two of those games features in this greatest 50. That fabled domestic clean sweep is perhaps given more kudos than we actually mean.

From a managerial career that touched four different decades, there is arguably one major reason why Rangers fans continue to select this as the one Struth-era game that gets kept alive throughout the generations: we are incredibly superstitious. All football fans, all sports fans, no matter how rational they consider themselves to be, cannot go through their lives untouched by the little manifestations of this ridiculous mindset. Hoodoos and curses take on a greater narrative power because the intricate details of fortune, psychology and the basic ability of your team to win matches is too prosaic. In baseball, the 'Curse of the Bambino' was said to have caused the Boston Red Sox an 84-year wait for a World Series win after they sold Babe Ruth to the New York Yankees, whereas the football equivalent can be found at Benfica. In 1962, after steering the Portuguese champions to back-to-back European Cups, Bela Guttman left after being refused a pay rise. He said that Benfica wouldn't be a European champion again in a hundred years – 57 years and eight European finals later and its 'power' is still going strong. A great game of football alone sometimes isn't enough to be remembered. There needs to be a story, preferably with an inexplicable side to it, that can jump off the page and spark wonder and interest in a time long before we were born.

There was nothing faded about that Rangers team's memory, however. A quick stop was made at the Princess Theatre, where they would present the Scottish Cup to the audience and force George West to cut a joke from his act.

26

Celtic 0 Rangers 1

Scottish Premier Division
Thursday 14 November 1996

'You carry on Martin, I'm absolutely speechless. This game is unbelievable. Unbelievable.'
(Andy Gray, commentary)

It is often the case, in tight league title races between Rangers and Celtic, that the derby matches provide so much of the colour but aren't overly decisive. Often they can cancel each other out and, such as in 1997/98 and 2010/11, there are occasions when the champions actually end up in negative equity when it comes to the head-to-head record. Scottish titles are often won away from home. The trips to Edinburgh, Dundee and Aberdeen. A real champion is the one who can most often leave Scotland's other towns and cities with maximum points. 1996/97 was always going to be a different kind of season. The season of destiny for the Rangers nine-in-a-row dream would be tense beyond imagination. As a direct result, runs of form were difficult for both sides to create. It really would come down to the four iterations of that famous old fixture.

Rangers won them all. For a title that was won by only five points and a campaign that included six defeats (there were only two of the seasons in that sequence where Rangers suffered more losses, the flat seasons of 1993/94 and 1994/95) it is fair to say that these 12 points were significant. Naturally the four games are still remembered fondly. The final two have already been featured on this list. As important as they were, both were arguably examples of the darker side to the fixture. The media circus of paranoia that enveloped the New Year game and the brutality, both in conduct and style, of the final episode of this saga, which is unsurprising as the tension grew.

The first two, however, were different. The opener in September doesn't feature here, although it has much to recommend it, not least the period of seconds it took for Celtic to hit the Rangers crossbar in search of an equaliser before Paul Gascoigne's lung-bursting run and header finished the game off. It was the second game, however, a Thursday night match at Parkhead, that is, rightly, considered to be the greatest of the lot. There was no shortage of pressure, certainly not for Rangers, for whom this was the most precarious position of the season, but it lacked the sensationalism or claustrophobic attrition of the later games and filled the entire 90 minutes with action.

This was as good an exhibition of the two sides in a mid-90s footballing microcosm. Celtic typically throwing abandon with Rangers seeking to break dangerously at will.

For only the first time since 1989, Celtic went into the second Old Firm game of the season ahead of Rangers in the league, albeit only by goal difference in this case. Winning the first seven league games and qualifying for the Champions League in some style with a 10-3 aggregate win over the Russian champions Alania Vladikavkaz, Rangers ended September five points clear and in good form. There was a stumble at Easter Road, where Brian Laudrup twice missed a penalty, and it precipitated a fall as points were dropped at home to Aberdeen, despite being 2-0 up, and away to Raith Rovers. Paul Gascoigne's private life was starting to become a bigger story than his performances on the field, which included a sublime free kick at home to Aberdeen following a stupid red card away to Ajax, all in the same four days as revelations about domestic abuse started to surface. It meant that Rangers made the short journey to Parkhead under some strain and jeopardy. A defeat would leave them three points behind and, because of the upcoming appearance in the League Cup Final against Hearts the following weekend, Rangers could have gone into the next league match six points adrift.

Despite having failed to defat Rangers in the last seven attempts, sheer form meant that Celtic went into the game as heavy favourites. There was also the football fan logic that *'it has to happen sometime'*. If the big Rangers injury doubt hadn't made it, it almost certainly would have. Andy Goram had missed the last six weeks with a hip injury and Rangers downturn may not have been entirely unrelated. Crucially, he returned behind a back three of Gough, Björklund and Petric, with Cleland and Robertson at wing back as normal. The midfield was ostensibly a quartet of Derek McInnes, Craig Moore, Jörg Albertz and Paul Gascoigne, with Brian Laudrup playing the role of a 'false nine' long before it was fashionable. A 5-4-1 without the ball and the intention to get Albertz and Gascoigne breaking in behind Laudrup when it was won back. Celtic, meanwhile, had an Old Firm debutant in goal as Stewart Kerr had displaced Gordon Marshall earlier in the season, but the rest of the team was as expected, with Boyd, O'Neill, Stubbs and McNamara in defence, Peter Grant and Morten Weighorst doing the donkey work in midfield, with Di Canio, Thom, Donnelly and contract rebel Pierre van Hooijdonk in attack.

I had been to Parkhead a few times for these games and, having grown up watching football in a modern stadium, it always felt like a time machine, back to the days my grandfather would speak of, a mixture of danger, grime and excitement. The Rangers end was literally a toilet, with a wall running the length of the back end being used for that very purpose. It was dangerous, it was overcrowded, but it did feel incredibly special when we won. The wild scenes of celebration in there have never really quite been recaptured in later years. We were away from home but, given the sheer numbers crammed in there, it didn't feel like it. This night was different in two ways. Firstly, it was the first time inside the stadium since it had been re-developed. It was incredibly high and, because of the material used at the back of the stands, unbelievably noisy. It really did feel like a lion's den. Secondly, it was the first time I had gone to one without my dad. Unable to attend, I was briefly the most popular kid in the class as I had a spare ticket, for anyone who could part with £19. My friend John Kennedy was willing and able and it was a first for him as well. 'I had never been to Parkhead before. It was always considered too dangerous. I had been abroad for Champions League games but not to the other end of the city. Now it was re-developed, and, at 16 years old, it was considered safe enough.'

Live on Sky, it was easily the biggest game in Britain that week, and Martin Tyler and Andy Gray were still being sent to cover it, as they would for one more season before the Premier League took their full attention. As expected, Celtic started the brighter, with Goram being called into action early and Gough doing well to see off van Hooijdonk from Boyd's cross. With an early foothold in the game there was no need for Celtic to take risks, to be overly expressive in dangerous areas or to take a revolver to said foot. As ruthless as Rangers often were during this era, Celtic have always acquiesced by providing a fall guy in defence. A clownish figure. Someone whom you felt did well to take to the field safely in the first place without first stepping in a bucket and somehow setting themselves on fire. Brian O'Neill had perhaps earmarked himself for that role by the tender age of 16 when he missed the crucial penalty in the final of the FIFA Under-16 World Cup, held in Scotland in 1989. In fairness to O'Neill and the rest of the Scottish fledglings, the Saudi Arabian goalkeeper looked as old as Peter Shilton, and the rest of his team-mates just marginally younger.

It was O'Neill, vaunted as a new example of a ball-playing centre-half, who would provide Rangers with an early sight on goal when he slipped, trying to control a flicked header from a Goram clearance. His chest control was fine, it was the mere matter of kicking the ball that seemed to cause him problems and he ended up flat on his back. Of all the players on that field to offer the ball up to on a plate, he'd surely have chosen anyone but Brian Laudrup. Still with much to do, nearly 40 yards from goal and two other defenders in behind O'Neill, he pounced on the opportunity nonetheless. 'We got a great view of this from up where we were,' recalls John. 'From the minute O'Neill slipped we were shouting, "Go on! Go on!" I thought he actually shot too soon, that he could have taken Stubbs on, but he was just world class and that's what can happen if you gave him a sniff.' There's a good chance that both Stubbs and Kerr expected the same. They didn't give Laudrup much in the way of a target, but he hit the bullseye regardless. Not for the first time in this game, the sublime and the ridiculous would collide in the same breathless collection of seconds. After only eight minutes Walter Smith had exactly what he wanted.

To their credit, the Celtic players got straight back to approaching the task at hand exactly as they had been instructed. Gaps were being created in the Rangers defence and when Björklund wasn't able to run back to plug them, Celtic were wasteful, most notably Weighorst, who blasted high over the bar after being played onside in plenty of space by David Robertson. Peter Grant would go higher but from much further out. It was the standard pattern of play that we all expected. 'It changes with age,' remembers John, 'but, perhaps it was the naivety of youth, I was never in fear in those days. We had a genuine threat, we just won big games all the time and the support was in great voice. You felt part of that bigger thing.'

Watching Rangers dig in to set the Parkhead trap wasn't always easy, but at least with this side, as we had already seen, Rangers had the ultimate counter attacking threat leading the line. There's a lot to be said for the target man approach – the bullying centre-forward who can hold the ball up and create a bit of havoc whilst willing runners occupy the space. There's a lot more to be said for what we had. No one in Scottish football has ever combined explosive pace with graceful skill like Brian Laudrup, and just after the 20-minute mark he was demonstrating that again. Skipping past a lunging Celtic defender on the halfway line, yet another break was on. At one point the television frame contained only Laudrup and five Celtic players, all of whom were running towards goal. He had the presence of mind and the ability to hold the ball up and Boyd off, as he waited for the cavalry to arrive. The ball into the box was decent, but Albertz, never being the most powerful header of a football, couldn't trouble Kerr with it.

The pace of the game was frankly ridiculous, more akin to a basketball game. Because of the searing tempo, fouls and bookings mounted up, especially against Laudrup. Albertz tried his luck from 25 yards but it struck the wall, immediately springing a Celtic counter attack, which Derek McInnes cynically stopped and picked up a yellow of his own. Van Hooijdonk stung Goram's palms with his own set piece and Simon Donnelly's short-range cross was cut out by the Ranger keeper. Perhaps the single most incredible moment of the first half occurred when Laudrup robbed the Celtic high line once again and was clean through on Kerr, a far closer range than his previous effort. Kerr did well, his footwork excellent, but Laudrup would have been disappointed not to have given his side an even bigger cushion at the break. There was a half chance for Albertz, which came to nothing, and Sky couldn't show a replay of the Laudrup chance for a full two minutes, such was the frenzy of activity on display.

If there were tactical instructions laid out in either of the two dressing rooms at the break, they were ignored. Within the space of 15 minutes, Laudrup and Donnelly went close at either end, O'Neill headed over from a good opportunity, Albertz had a dreadfully anaemic header from close range straight at the goalkeeper, Goram intercepted a good Thom cross, David Robertson tested Kerr from distance, Weighorst had a goal-bound, penalty-box shot stopped by a diving Richard Gough tackle and a fox ran a full lap of the Parkhead pitch. The latter provided a much welcome lull in play and a chance for both sets of supporters to check their heart rate.

There is a long-held misconception that reactive football is necessarily dour and cynical. Apart from ignoring the beauty of a well-paced and devastating counter attack, it misses the point entirely. When you know that your opponent will offer space and have defenders who aren't good enough with the ball at their feet, this is simply the best opportunity to create clear and open chances, which Rangers did in a 17-minute second-half spell. Four of them, in fact. The first was one created purely by Gascoigne's vision and Laudrup's intelligence, as he slipped the ball through the Celtic defence for him to run onto, and wait for Kerr's intervention and the inevitable foul. Laudrup perhaps still had Easter Road in his mind (although he did take one at home to Aberdeen), Albertz wasn't yet the penalty king and so Gascoigne, maybe seeking to atone for recent troubles, stood up to take it. If the goalkeeper is sent the wrong way it is called a super-cool penalty. When he guesses correctly, as Kerr did, it is a terrible one. Still, Celtic left space and the next two opportunities fell to Albertz, but sadly neither his legs or brain were quick enough and he was closed down on both occasions. When he found himself 30 yards from goal with seven minutes remaining and only himself and team-mate Peter van Vossen (a substitute for Derek McInnes who was seriously close to a second yellow card) standing before Stewart Kerr, he chose to square it for his team-mate to tap in and seal the three points. You can hear Martin Tyler's voice break as he exclaims, 'oh my goodness!' John and I used other words but the sentiment was the same.

'It came just a few weeks after he scored from an impossible angle at Rugby Park. An absolutely excellent goal. This was just incredible and it doesn't get any better with repeat viewing years later. There's not even a bobble, it almost defies the laws of physics how he misses.' In retrospect, although not quite as jarring as watching that chance again, it is strange to watch the performance of Jörg Albertz. He'd have to wait a couple of months before properly announcing himself on this stage, and from that point on he wouldn't look back. Roll those three breakaways on another year and Albertz wouldn't just have scored, he'd have taken the net away too. In the moment, however, the Rangers support were being put through the wringer. Chance after chance had been passed up. The growing doubt in the mind that we'd have to pay a price was unavoidable.

It was too much for Tommy Burns as well. A month after being fined £3,000 by the SFA for threatening a referee at Kilmarnock at the tail end of the previous season, he was sent off again for complaining about the officiating, but it was not clear to see why. Every call Dallas made that night was spot on, and he was about to get his final big decision correct as well, one that I imagine Burns approved of up in the main stand. With just over five minutes remaining, Celtic launched a ball in the box which was met by Cadete back to Donnelly just inside the box. Gough saw another opportunity for a trademark courageous block, but his mind worked faster than Donnelly's as the ball made contact before the Celtic striker was able to gather full control of it. A certain penalty and utter despair in the Rangers end. A victory that was necessary and should have been certain was now hanging by a thread.

Seconds later we were celebrating more than we had for the goal. Van Hooijdonk struck it low and hard, but not wide enough, and Goram, never renowned for stopping spot kicks, was placed perfectly and erupted in a triumphant anger. 'It was better than the Gascoigne penalty, but it wasn't exactly low into a corner or high into the roof of the net. Take nothing away from the save though. This is yet another huge performance in a huge game. As far as we were concerned, I believe the modern day phrase is "limbs."'

And, despite Andy Gray giving up trying to capture this match adequately enough, Albertz was yet again caught by Tom Boyd through on goal, this time with a 20-yard head start. If 30 seconds could sum up 90 minutes, it was a penalty save at one end finishing with a counter attack being snuffed out at the other. Celtic would throw more at Goram's goal, but to no avail. With seconds remaining, he had the ball in his arms, gum in his mouth, waiting for the moment to launch it upfield to signal the end of an exhausting game of football.

In over 30 years of following Rangers, I can't think of many nights when I've personally witnessed as breathless an encounter at this. And yet, so much of the Rangers play in the final third was poor. Although Smith was quick to credit Stewart Kerr's performance, there was no excusing much of our finishing. However, one moment of brilliance was enough and it encapsulated so much of the era. Celtic would present those opportunities and we would capitalise. It simply didn't change. 'Great things are built from perseverance,' said Burns immediately after the match, 'and we will not change our style of play. It will one day get us to where we want to be.' Except that it wouldn't. Celtic needed a cooler, analytical head at the controls. This was the eighth straight game against Rangers without success and there would be two more to come in the league as chances slipped away to stop us equalling their record. A more considered approach was almost anathema to Burns, as if pragmatism was a dirty word strictly for protestants.

Pragmatism runs through Walter Smith's DNA, however; and on this incredible night, he used it to unleash a genius.

25

Rangers 3 Aberdeen 3

(After extra time, Rangers won 5-3 on penalties.)

Skol League Cup Final
Sunday 25 October 1987

'He was a unique player, not comparable to any other. No, Davie Cooper was one of a kind.'
(Ruud Gullit)

Sandy Jardine would often complain, tongue slightly in cheek, if not firmly, that one of the best goals he ever scored hardly gets a mention because of the goal that followed. Jardine ran the length of the field against Celtic at Hampden in the Drybough Cup Final of 1979 before hammering the ball past Peter Latchford to put Rangers 2-0 up. It was the Rangers third, however, with only 12 minutes remaining, that was all anyone would talk about. A goal from the footballing heavens, the kind of close control and presence of mind that aren't bestowed on mere mortals. Davie Cooper had stolen the show. To score a goal that dominates a local pre-season tournament is one thing. To score one so iconic that it overshadows one of the greatest national cup finals in modern history is something else. Eight years later, on the same famous old ground, he would arguably do just that.

The build-up to this Skol League Cup Final was as far from the kind of mesmerising Cooper grace and serenity as you could imagine. It had only been two weeks since Ian Durrant had handed in a transfer request following a bust-up with Souness relating to an altercation Durrant had ended up in after a night out. Thankfully for all parties, it had been smoothed over and the 20-year-old midfielder had kept his place in the heart of the Rangers team. The weekend before the final saw the carnage of the Old Firm league encounter at Ibrox, which resulted in goalkeeper Chris Woods and captain Terry Butcher being sent off, and they were later joined by Graham Roberts in the dock (Game 42). While all hell was breaking loose at Ibrox, the reserve fixture was taking place at Parkhead, as was the custom at the time. Nicky Walker, who hadn't played for the first team in over a year and managed only two appearances the season before following Woods's arrival, had taken a knock on his knee. Peter McCloy had to run on to tell him to get going. 'Woodsy's just been sent off.' He'd be needed in the cup final against a side which he had never experienced the satisfaction of victory in his entire professional career.

Aberdeen sat four points ahead of Rangers in the league and had only lost one game all season thus far in all competitions. They warmed up for the weekend with a 2-1 home win over Feyenoord in the UEFA Cup, and although they had lost the influence of Alex Ferguson in the dugout, replaced by Ian Porterfield in the autumn of 1986, they were still a strong outfit containing many of the side that had won the European Cup Winners' Cup in 1983. Rangers were also in European action in midweek with a 3-1 home win over Gornik Zabre of Poland. A 12-year-old Ian Hogg had a ticket in the North Enclosure for the cup final but had been at all three games that week. 'The Gough equaliser against Celtic felt like a winner. It gave us so much momentum that we were 3-0 up by half-time against Gornik. I only really realised on the Thursday or Friday that "shit, we are without our goalie and captain on Sunday". The games were just coming thick and fast.' Rangers were also without their player–manager Graeme Souness for this final for the second year in a row, after exceeding the cumulative penalty points. There was no touchline ban, but he would let Walter Smith take care of things on the bench as he sat up in the Main Stand.

Rangers may have been 6:5 favourites (Aberdeen were 9:5 and the 3-3 draw was 80:1) but this was a huge test. A goalkeeper who had been shielded from this pressure for over a year, a makeshift central defensive pairing of Graham Roberts and Richard Gough and a midfield missing their leader. However, there was no doubt that Souness trusted the youth and energy of Durrant and Derek Ferguson in the heart of his team. They had performed for him at Hampden the year before after all, plus he would have his lieutenant in there in the form of John McGrgeor, a recent transfer from Liverpool, on the right-hand side and the guile of Cooper on the other. Also, McCoist was hot. With 20 goals in 20 games, he was the form striker in the country, and, with Robert Fleck in support, Rangers had enough threat of their own.

There was a defiance about the 50,000 or so Rangers fans that made up the 71,941 that were packed into that stadium. A very loud defiance. 'Anytime I went to Hampden, including Scotland games, it felt as if all you could hear was the Rangers end,' said Ian. 'Acoustically it suited us. The noise at the Celtic end just doesn't travel. It disappears up into the sky.' It was noticed by former Liverpool legend Ian St John, on co-commentary duty for STV, when he said that, 'the Aberdeen fans are being out sung today but that's just because the Rangers fans know more songs.' Perhaps it worked better when Jimmy Greaves was there to laugh on cue. The team wasn't quite as steadfast on the pitch. Despite an early effort from McCoist that flew over Jim Leighton's bar, it was Aberdeen who looked most likely to score. Stuart Munro almost deflected a John Hewitt cross into his own net in the fourth minute, whereas Roberts looked all at sea when tussling with Willie Falconer, whom he would foul outside the box. Jim Bett's free kick was deflected and Walker did well to save from Neil Simpson.

With only six minutes gone, Rangers were heavily under the cosh, and two minutes later Walker would concede a penalty. Alex McLeish's ball over the top was intelligent and it caught the Rangers defence completely square, leaving Falconer with the space where he waited to be fouled by the stand-in keeper. Without Woods and Butcher, such a foundation stone of the recent success, the Rangers defence in those early minutes was a total mess. Always reliable from the penalty spot, Jim Bett did enough to give Aberdeen the lead as Jock Brown reminded television viewers that in the last eight finals only once has the team that conceded first gone on to win the cup. It should have been two for Aberdeen after 15 minutes as McLeish got away from Gough in the box, but his effort from six yards out was cleared off the line by Derek Ferguson.

Right from the first minute, Willie Miller had been committing the kind of fouls, without a booking, that would dominate discussion for weeks in the modern-day football media. His prime target was McCoist and he floored him with another bad one just inside the 'D' of the Aberdeen box. It was both brave and clever work by McCoist as he turned Miller instinctively, knowing that his calves would pay the price. 'I'd be upset if I was Miller,' said St John. 'His foot makes clear contact with the ball.' Neither Jock Brown beside him or referee Bob Valentine on the field agreed and Rangers had an opportunity 20 yards from goal.

'Watch it back with the sound up and listen for the ball hitting the net,' urges Ian Hogg. 'It's like an old carpet beater.' Davie Cooper had hardly touched the ball in the opening 21 minutes. That was about to change. If his Drybrough Cup goal was all finesse and guile, this goal, at the same end of Hampden, was sheer power and precision. With relatively little back-lift, a cannon was unleashed on the Aberdeen goal and neither the wall, who had moved further out to meet the ball, or Leighton, had the faintest hope of diverting it from its chosen trajectory. Cooper would famously later joke that Leighton had told him that he nearly got a hand to it. 'Aye,' replied Cooper, 'on the way back out.' Voted the second-greatest-ever Rangers goal by the listeners of *Heart and Hand*, it was a simply stunning strike to roar Rangers back into a cup final where they had been shaking. 'I had the wind behind me and just blasted it,' he said after the game, as if it was so simple that all you or I needed was a bit of a breeze too. 'A Brazilian trapped in a Scotsman's body,' is how the late Ray Wilkins described him, no stranger himself to playing football in a fashion not entirely in sync with his national heritage. It was certainly a goal of which Rivelino or Roberto Carlos would have been proud as Cooper raced away to embrace the wild celebrations in the North Enclosure, in which he would have been standing had he not been a genius.

The equaliser had settled Rangers down and they played the next 20 minutes with far more assurance and cohesion at the back, although Falconer did have the ball in the net but it was correctly ruled out for a foul on Walker. With five minutes remaining before the interval, Rangers went ahead with a goal that would have been fêted for generations had it been scored in any other cup final. Admittedly it started from an Aberdeen error, a Bobby Connor throw deep inside his own half where he looked in about five minds before trying to go long up the line, and it was intercepted easily by

Jimmy Nicholl, whose header was laid back out by Fleck for Ian Durrant. Durrant managed to get a header of his own towards McCoist, who provided a beautiful return pass which put Durrant clean through with just Leighton to beat. He did so with the outside of his right boot in the most impudent fashion, finishing off a move of lightning pace, intelligent movement and incisive passing. Once again it was Cooper and Durrant, at either ends of a career, fully relishing the opportunities opened to them by Graeme Souness.

To the modern eye, where cup finals seem more cagey and conservative, this shimmers like something from another time. Which, of course, it is. Those grainy news reels of the 1958 World Cup, the introduction of Pelé that I watched as a child are closer to this final than the time I write now. The Scottish League Cup Final has lost over 0.5 goals on average in the first 20 finals of the 21st century compared to the final 20 of the previous. The spirit of carefree abandon was still in evidence as the second half got underway, with both sides having their opportunities. With Cooper becoming more involved in the central areas, tackling hard and spraying it around like his manager, he released Durrant, who went inches wide after good link-up play with Fleck. Falconer had another great chance where he was sent through by Hewitt. The Rangers defence was sleeping but Walker was alert and was able to salvage the situation in contrast to the early events of the first half. On the stroke of the hour Aberdeen made a change that would alter the game as Neil Simpson was replaced by the mercurial Peter Weir. He would take up his post on the left, meaning that Joe Miller would come over to the right flank and Hewitt would support the target man Falconer in a more central role.

With 18 minutes remaining, Aberdeen got the equaliser their pressure merited. Joe Miller escaped Cooper down the Rangers left and flighted over a decent cross which Walker initially came for and then changed his mind, hoping that Roberts would win the aerial duel with Falconer. He did, but it wasn't a powerful header out and Hewitt had plenty of time and little attention around him, as he drilled a shot low through the bodies and into the net. 'I'd gone from a position of "This is easy, the cup is ours" to "Oh my God the world is going to end". I'd aged from a 12-year-old Hoggy to my adult state of mind inside a few minutes.'

Rangers should have been ahead once again soon after, however, as Durrant was clearly clipped inside the box by the untouchable Willie Miller. A tired but obvious mistimed tackle, not dangerous, just clumsy. Valentine waved it away, however, and Aberdeen then sought to capitalise. The danger was now all down the Rangers left-hand side. Souness had been down south the day before looking at the England and Nottingham Forest left-back Stuart Pearce and this is perhaps why he thought that there was a need to strengthen in that area. Miller was involved again before the ball came back to Bett just outside the box, where he sent over a delightful ball for Falconer to attack if he could just beat Roberts. He did, Walker was stationary and, with only eight minutes to go, Aberdeen were ahead in this cup final.

It is the fashion now for football fans of every team to see bias everywhere they look. From commentators to columnists, if they don't confirm our very own biases and re-affirm our hopes, we take deafening umbrage. There is no modern equivalent, in a domestic game at least, for Ian St John's off-mic exclamation of 'YES!', as Falconer's header hit the back of the Rangers net. A quite remarkable moment in the coverage of what was now becoming a classic match. 'I thought we were done,' remembers Ian Hogg. 'I always used to giggle when I heard adults swear but not that day because it's exactly how you felt in your gut. You knew fine well that Aberdeen were a very good side and you knew Rangers were just being picked off. I didn't see any way back for us.'

There was no panic or despondency in the Rangers side, however. Perhaps it would have been if this had been in the Scottish Cup, a troublesome competition where players can easily convince themselves that it's not theirs to win. However, this was very much 'our' trophy. The team continued to probe, almost expecting that there would be one more chance to come. McCoist tested Leighton before Ferguson went over the bar, his last action before being replaced by Trevor Francis. Gough was sent up, with the events of the weekend before in mind, as Cooper twisted away trying to find that one perfect angle. In the end that vital chance came from something a little more agricultural as Jimmy Nicholl sent a ball in the air, like a rugby up-and-under. Graham Roberts may have had his moments of insecurity in this game, but this wasn't one of them as he met the ball flush whilst cementing Willie Miller in the process. Durrant was first to it with the presence of mind to lay it cutely into the path of Fleck, who swept it away, not boasting the aesthetics of the first two goals but the same sharpness of thought and instinct. With only three minutes left, the match was tied again. There were no cheers from St John. There were plenty from Walter Smith on the Rangers bench.

Extra time gave us more of the same but with tired limbs and minds. Both McCoist and Falconer had clear cut chances to win the cup. Falconer headed straight at Walker from close range (which induced another shout in the commentary box) and McCoist lashed over the bar following an excellent flowing Rangers move, at the centre of which, once more, was Durrant. Fleck brought a save from Leighton whilst, in a moment that would have repercussions, Joe Miller cramped up late on in the second period as the breakaway was possible. His namesake and captain was finally booked when he ended John McGregor's afternoon and he was replaced by Avi Cohen whilst leaving the field in a stretcher. By the end there were a lot of socks rolled to the ankles, typical of an elongated game in that era and, whilst the action raged from one end to the other, Trevor Francis strolled the Hampden turf as if it was his front room. He'd have one of the final chances of the extra period, which whistled past the post, but he'd have his say eventually.

And so one of the greatest Hampden cup finals would fittingly become the first Scottish final to be decided by penalty kicks, previously the exclusive preserve of competitions like the European Cup and World Cup. The first two takers, McCoist and Bett, were the kind you would put your mortgage on, and they didn't disappoint, with McCoist going low and Bett going high into either corner. The third taker was the kind that you'd bet your neighbours mortgage on too. From the same spot where he won the previous season's trophy, Davie Cooper blasted home his penalty with the utmost confidence. It should have been Joe Miller next, but he was cramped up. Four Aberdeen players had put up their hand, one had to be coerced.

The Welsh international Peter Nicholas had missed two penalties for Luton Town the season before, and he would add another to his collection at Hampden as his effort clipped the top of the bar. 'I wasn't quite sure what had happened from the North Enclosure. I just saw Walker jumping up even though he had been sent the wrong way. Much like at the goals the place was going berserk.' Robert Fleck compounded the advantage when he wrong-footed Leighton, but Weir did the same to Walker to keep Aberdeen in the frame. The fourth Rangers penalty, even in this game that had everything, was something special. With Jim Leighton trying his best to channel Bruce Grobbelaar on the goal line, Trevor Francis was forced to re-spot the ball, after which he took two steps back and one step forward before perfectly placing the ball in the bottom left-hand corner. Leighton, who guessed correctly, was absolutely incensed at being beaten by such insouciance. 'I'd honestly never seen a penalty like that before. Usually mere mortals collapse after being asked to re-spot the ball. He was just so super cool.'

John Hewitt, another star turn on an afternoon full of them, was the eighth player to convert an excellent penalty before the stage was set for Ian Durrant, the man of the match, to win the cup for Rangers. As Joe Miller prayed on the halfway line, Leighton wasn't given a chance in hell as Durrant found the corner before running to the Rangers end where he turned around, arms aloft at only 20 years old, to take the adulation of his teammates. 'You have to feel for Willie Miller and his team,' was St John's immediate response and, in fairness, most would. In a week that hardly showcased the best of Scottish football, here was a game that was a genuine exhibition in attacking and entertaining football. Two good sides, at the time evenly matched, going at each other with pace, skill and power for 120 exhausting minutes. Graham Roberts looked a touch sheepish, climbing the stairs as he stood in for his skipper to collect both trophies. Rangers were to keep the Skol Cup, basically a silver tankard, as it was the fifth time that it had been secured, whereas the League Cup had now been retained for a record 15th time. It would also be a final for individual records as Davie Cooper overtook Billy McNeil when he picked up his seventh League Cup-winners' medal.

This match is rightly considered to be the greatest of all the League Cup games in which Rangers played as there are no more to come on this list. A competition that has given Rangers so much and, when played in the autumn, it could provide a platform for a season, but nevertheless it is always seen as the weaker part of the domestic triumvirate of honours. The magic of those finals from the 80s and 90s has been retained, however. Rangers would contest eight out of the nine finals from 1986, winning seven, set within a perfect window of time where fans could enjoy them live in colour on a Sunday afternoon but before a time where the footballing landscape on television would be blown wide open and, as such, the fixture would grow more and more parochial. In that era it felt like the most important game in the world to younger bears watching at home, sheltered to the wider world of football but still spellbound by a contest that was consistently exciting and entertaining. None more so than in 1987.

It is the third time on this list that Durrant and Cooper would combine to produce a memorable Rangers performance. It will be the last match featured here where both shine as brightly together and it would be the final time that both names ended up on a Rangers scoresheet. We'd never know exactly what insight and instruction Cooper could have brought to future generations as his life was cruelly cut short in 1995. We'd never know if Durrant could have done what Cooper decided not to do and take the continent by storm, as those crucial years of his career were robbed from him. Both with a mischievous sense of humour and a burning love for the club, they had a dark lull in the middle of their Rangers careers that was contrasted by the startling brightness at either end. Both players would surely win a great many votes in any fans poll to select an all-time Rangers XI.

When Ruud Gullit was asked to select an all-time greatest XI of those he had played with or against, he chose Davie Cooper, who had mesmerised him whilst playing against his Feyenoord side in 1984. Zinedine Zidane and Ronaldinho were left on the bench.

24

Rangers 0 Callander 0

Friendly Challenge Match
May 1872

'All great deeds and all great thoughts have a ridiculous beginning. Great works are often born on a street corner or in a restaurant's revolving door.'
(Albert Camus, *The Myth of Sisyphus*)

If this poll had been conducted in 2006, it is doubtful whether this match would have made the list at all, never mind take its place in the top half. It would have garnered some votes for sure – everyone understands the importance of those first steps – however, for so long it had remained very much a statistic in dusty books. By chance, a football writer, Gary Ralston, and two keen fans, Iain McColl and Gordon Bell, had begun delving into the Rangers origins story, one they all felt had been too keenly brushed over, and crossed paths with their research in 2007. Ralston's book *The Gallant Pioneers* and *The Founders Trail*, an interactive walking and bus tour created by McColl and Bell, suddenly brought this tale to life. What was once distant history had now been made vivid in the minds of thousands of Rangers supporters.

But what about the 'centenary' year of 1973? For decades, fans believed 1873 to be the year of origin. Indeed the club itself had recorded it officially for as long as anyone could remember. The reason for the error dates back to the early 1920s when John Allan, a journalist friend of Bill Struth, was commissioned to write a book about the first 50 years of Rangers Football Club, to be published in 1922. He underestimated the volume of work required to complete the job at hand and, like history students the world over would have loved to have done in the decades that followed, he simply changed the facts to suit his needs. Rangers were now founded in 1873 so that Allan could meet his deadline. The year of formation had been in the Wee Blue Book, the official Rangers handbook, as 1872 for years. In the 1923 and 1924 editions, that particular detail is missing. By 1925, it was 'corrected' as being 1873. It is frustrating, as McColl often points out, that Rangers lifted the European Cup Winner's Cup in Barcelona a full century to the month that those boys first played under the name of Rangers, and it couldn't be recognised accordingly.

Little is known about the inaugural match itself. What we do know, from former Rangers player and later journalist William Dunlop, is that it was hardly a classic. In his article 'The Rangers F.C', written for the SFA Annual of 1881/82, he describes it as a 'terrible game' and where 'both sides were quite pleased when time was called, without any definite result. If they could lay no claim to be players, at least both sides has exhibited true British pluck.' In other words, they kicked the living daylights out of one another. If there was a Man Of The Match award in those days, according to Dunlop, it would have been given to the 16-year-old William McBeath. Such was the multitude of his scars, he was in bed for a week.

None of this is why the story resonates, of course. Even by the time Dunlop was writing the early history of the club, his message was one of perseverance against the odds. 'Eager, earnest persistent endeavour is ultimately crowned with success,' he wrote, in a sermon so typical of Victorian Britain. Only five years since their first outing on Glasgow Green, a team of boys carrying an 'aged bit of leather' and needing the help of guests from Queen's Park, Rangers were in a Scottish Cup Final where the famous Vale of Leven needed three matches to eventually triumph. (Dunlop himself scored two goals in the first replay, although one, crucially, wasn't given). Within 20 years of their formation Rangers were the inaugural Scottish League champions, sharing the honour with Dumbarton in 1891. At a time when thousands were intoxicated by this new craze of Association Football, new fledgling clubs vanished as quickly as they appeared, including the very first opponents Callander. The fact that a football club, born out of a quiet conversation in what is now Kelvingrove Park, between four country boys from the Gareloch frustrated at not having a team of their own, enjoyed such rapid prominence was already noteworthy in 1881. For 21st-century fans, the fact that the world's most successful football club and a Scottish institution originated from such humble origins casts an even more romantic spell.

There was nothing romantic about the explanation for such early success. The four boys, Moses and Peter McNeil, Peter Campbell and William McBeath, set standards for dedication right from the start. According to Dunlop, the three nights set aside for practice were usually doubled, such was the enthusiasm of the members. If it wasn't for the mandatory observance of the Sabbath, the Rangers would have been on Glasgow Green training every night of the week. Unlike rowing, which was enjoyed in tandem with the football before dissipating into the background, this was no mere hobby. It was a passion that ensured Rangers didn't go the way of so many of their early opponents and it set a standard expected of a Ranger for the next century and beyond. In unearthing tales such as this, McColl and Bell have helped fans reconnect with their roots, especially post 2012. 'Around that time people would often come up to us at the end of the tour and say thanks for giving them something to cling onto. These boys persevered against the odds at the very beginning and so too, will we now,' said McColl.

The Trail's biggest emotional impact comes from literally being able to go on the journey from Glasgow Green via the various stops touched by the nomadic existence of the club's early decades and finally arriving at Ibrox Stadium. From a 'ridiculous beginning' to our cathedral of sport, shaped as it was by the iconic eye of Archibald Leitch who gave us the main facade which is still the envy of the footballing world. Where once Peter McNeill had to cross the city to plant poles in the ground at the most desirable part of the green, a following soon developed. Dunlop noted that, 'the sacred spot became the Mecca of the green, the God football being there worshipped by thousands of devotees, whose piety would not bear either a journey to Hampden Park, or the necessary subscription … Football was their Allah, and the Rangers, if not at the time *the* prophet, were at least *their* prophet.' Very little would change over the next 150 years.

****

If it wasn't for his tuberculosis, Albert Camus may well have been an obscure Algerian goalkeeper instead of one of the greatest post-modern philosophers of the 20th century. Despite having to give up the game at 16, Camus still held a great deal of love for football, which he felt was a 'real university'. 'All I know most surely about morality and obligations I owe to football,' may have been a famous misquote but he did grasp the notion that the game would teach you more about yourself than a book ever could. That it was able to 'possess wisdom about life in an immediate way, not from a great distance.'

Those lessons were equally prescient for the followers of the game. Camus was an absurdist. He wrestled mainly with the problem that the human need for reason and contentment is in total contradiction with the silence that comes back from the world around us. Where religion and mythology used to present comfort, there was now a deeply uncomfortable void. He famously used the Greek legend of Sisyphus, whose punishment from Zeus for trying to put Death in chains was to push a heavy boulder up to the top of a mountain, where it would roll back down and the pattern would be repeated for eternity. The only option Camus felt appropriate was to deal with the reality of our predicament and to put our shoulder behind own particular boulder. 'The struggle towards the heights,' he wrote, 'is enough to fill a man's heart.'

There are few interests in life more absurd than following a football team, especially as passionately as millions of us do. When you stop to consider it, delusion is a pretty fundamental part of being a football fan. Just as it is necessary for a full appreciation of the arts, the 'willing suspension of disbelief' is a pre-requisite for immersing yourself in the entire experience. Not that the game itself is a contrived fiction, more that the importance we place on the fortunes of professional athletes is something that, as grown adults, we tend to resist analysing too closely. These are 'our' teams. This is 'our' game. In fact sponsors, who have more to gain from spinning this mirage than most, will tell us that fans 'are football'. We talk of 'our' victories and defeats despite the impact of our combined efforts requiring subatomic equipment to detect. We declare a passionate interest in total strangers and act like jilted lovers when they make the perfectly normal human decision to change employers when the opportunity suits. As Jerry Seinfeld once said, 'You're actually rooting for the clothes. You are standing and cheering and yelling for your clothes to beat the clothes of another city.'

Our weekly ritual, started by those who crowded around Flesher's Haugh and then handed down from one generation to the next, is perfectly encapsulated by the struggle of Sisyphus. MM Owen, in an article on the subject for *The Blizzard,* wrote that 'supporting a team is an investment with no hope of any permanent happy ending. If we lose, we'll have to roll the boulder back up the hill. And even if we win, even if we keep winning, we'll eventually lose, and then we'll have to roll the boulder back up the hill. There is no moment forthcoming when any football team, no matter how good, will solve football's last theorem, allowing us all to pack up and go home. Such an aspiration is nonsensical precisely because it belongs in the realm of the rational. The point, as with theatre, is to keep taking to the stage even though eventually the lights will always come up and you'll remember it was all a make-believe. It's about imagining celebration, when the world is quietly promising you further dismay. Perhaps the only sort of faith left for a people who have traded gods and saints for playmakers and number nines.'

There truly is some solace in the absurdity of following football. The vicarious hobby that allows us to share in the supreme talent of others who are able to do the kind of things we have dreamt of doing ourselves ever since we could remember dreaming at all. The joy derived from attaching profound meaning to an inflated sphere crossing an arbitrary painted line. The sense of belonging that comes with projecting an imagined community onto a team of professional footballers or convincing oneself of the belief that their sporting contest be a further manifestation of historical ones.

Never has the Myth of Sisyphus resonated more with the Rangers support than in the years immediately following 2012. The continual empty promises and false dawns that saw the boulder tumble back down the mountain as the club were forced back to square one, without even the joy of getting it to the top. No wonder then that there was an acute need to re-connect with those very early struggles that four boys faced in order to establish the greatest football club in the country. No wonder, either, that their remarkable story and those first steps in particular should continue to echo through the centuries.

One day soon, perhaps, the struggle to the heights will indeed be enough to fill our hearts. I would like to think that Camus would have rejoiced in the glorious irrationality of it all. I know, for certain, that I will.

23
Zenit St Petersburg 2 Rangers 0
UEFA Cup Final
Wednesday 14 May 2008

'Most things are never meant.'
(Philip Larkin, 'Going, Going')

As the sun set on 27 May 2000, never before, or since, had Rangers looked down upon Scottish football from such a distance. The league season had concluded with the gap between first and second an unprecedented 21 points and then at Hampden Rangers secured the double, to add to the previous season's treble, by defeating Aberdeen 4-0 in a final where the champions barely moved out of second gear. With Jim Leighton stretchered off inside the opening minutes and Aberdeen not having a nominated substitute goalkeeper, Rangers toyed with their opposition like orcas sometimes do with baby seals. Dick Advocaat had fulfilled most of his remit since taking over from Walter Smith in the summer of 1998. Domestic dominance had been restored, the quality of football was outstanding and the reputation in Europe had been somewhat salvaged. With a bit of fortune in the draw and some improved focus, perhaps there would be scope for continental forays beyond Christmas. Fans would have laughed anyone out of town that evening, at supporters' clubs or family barbecues, if they had said that it would be two years before we would enjoy such celebrations again. However, if one was to suggest that, at some point in this first decade of the new millennium, Rangers would be in a UEFA Cup Final and Dick Advocaat would be left holding the trophy, most fans would have taken it seriously. This was, after all, the plan.

The Manchester 2008 story is really one of unintended consequences. The mass migration that the authorities refused to plan for and the avoidable impact on the league title race have been discussed ad nauseam over the decade since. The intriguing footballing story is of the two men in the opposing dugouts. A tale that really wasn't supposed to turn out this way at all. Smith had been replaced by Advocaat ten years before primarily because the prospect of Rangers turning out in such a showpiece event seemed as distant as St Petersburg itself. Smith's side, this ageing band of brothers, was perfectly calibrated to winning Old Firm clashes and thus creating the upper hand domestically. It was, however, a machine that consistently malfunctioned when faced with continental tests. Most were in agreement with David Murray when he felt that it was time for a new approach.

As the 21st century dawned, the new broom had swept almost all before it. The comprehensive nature of the gap between Rangers and the rest at home cannot be overstated and the gap in Europe was closing. Exits to Parma in the 1998/99 UEFA Cup and to Valencia and Bayern Munich in the 1999/00 Champions League were frustrating but still respectable given the opposition. The collapse of a two-goal lead in Dortmund during that season's UEFA Cup was more galling. There was work still to be done but Advocaat had built a great platform upon which to build the next stage of the development.

Or so it seemed. As discussed in Game 44, the platform disintegrated at a rapid pace and Advocaat would depart the manager's office in the December of 2001, soon after guiding Rangers past Paris St Germain and into the last 16 of the UEFA Cup. What should have been a legacy of modern European football and an infrastructure set up to cultivate technique was instead one of bloated and frivolous spending. This would be a legacy that would shape the rest of the decade at Ibrox and beyond, as Advocaat's successors would have their hands tied as a result of the lack of fiscal responsibility he and his chairman had shown once the tide started to turn.

Walter Smith had been working with his hands behind his back ever since he left Govan. His retirement lasted one month as he was tempted to Goodison Park to replace Howard Kendall at Everton. For a club already struggling, this would be a period characterised by the consistent sale of their best players, including Duncan Ferguson to Newcastle United without Smith's prior knowledge. A far cry indeed from land of milk and honey that was Ibrox in the 1990s. After a 3-0 defeat to Middlesbrough in the FA Cup and the club just one point outside the relegation zone, Smith too found himself departing the manager's chair, just three months after his successor had done at Ibrox.

Both men soon sought solace in the international game. Advocaat, who had taken the Netherlands to the quarter-finals of the World Cup in 1994, where they were eliminated in a classic by eventual champions Brazil, returned to his old job following their failure to reach the finals in Japan and South Korea. His Euro 2004 performance was labelled a failure despite their tournament only coming to an end against the hosts Portugal in the semi-finals. Tactical mistakes in the group defeat to the Czech Republic and his general tone and manner resulted in media pressure that he and the KNVB couldn't resist and Advocaat resigned shortly after the tournament. His showing at the next World Cup in 2006 with South Korea could more accurately be labelled a failure as they didn't manage to qualify from a realistic position in a group including Switzerland and Togo. Advocaat's next port of call was Russia. Where steel had helped fund his Rangers success, natural gas would provide an irresistible draw to the Baltic Sea where he smashed internal transfer records to take Zenit to the 2007 Russian title. After a sluggish start to the 2007/08 UEFA Cup campaign, where they only qualified out of their group in third place, the momentum began to build in the knockout rounds where Villareal and Marseille were dispatched on away goals and then, with the Russians in their stride at the start of their domestic season, Bayer Leverkusen and Bayern Munich were obliterated on the road to the final. Zenit would have been European football's big surprise package that season, if it wasn't for their opponents in that final.

After turning up at Old Trafford, completely out of the blue, to be Sir Alex Ferguson's assistant for the final few months of the 2003/04 season (where Manchester United won an FA Cup), Walter Smith was back in the limelight when he answered the call from the SFA to replace Berti Vogts in December 2004. Vogts, whose appointment was designed to have the same kind of foreign impact as Sven-Göran Eriksson was then currently having on England, only had one full qualifying campaign (for Euro 2004) which ended in a play-off against Holland. In typically Scottish fashion, Scotland won the first leg 1-0 at Hampden before being thrashed 6-0 by Advocaat's side in Amsterdam. Smith regained some credit at the end of the next campaign before getting the Euro 2008 qualifying off to a solid start with a memorable victory over France. They may well have managed that necessary win in Georgia later on the campaign, but Smith had since returned to his first love.

The culmination of the post-Advocaat downsizing was the hiring of a much sought-after continental coach to rebuild a squad that had just finished third in Scotland and supporting him with whatever loose change could be found floating around the house. Following Alex McLeish's fluctuating spell of glory and misery, the appointment of Paul Le Guen was destined for disappointment right from the outset. In early January 2007, with the team both in disarray and in outright mutiny, the call was sent for the return of the steadiest hand on the tiller that the club had known for generations. When Churchill returned to the Admiralty in 1939, a signal was reported to have been sent out to the naval fleet that simply stated 'Winston Is Back!' A similar message was sent out to the thousands of Rangers fans angry and confused as to what direction the club was supposed to be going. Walter would bring us back on an even keel – in Scotland, at least, as it would be wise to assume that our European dreams were being shelved.

Just how this second iteration of Smith as Rangers manager managed to transform his approach to the continental challenge will be discussed in more depth in another chapter; however, by the spring of his first full season back in charge, Rangers were incredibly still on course for all four competitions. What that kind of run generates in heart-pumping excitement, however, it saps from the legs. Where the league championship looked certain at the start of April, it was now precariously poised a month later after four dropped points on the road to Dundee United and Hibs sandwiched two back-to-back defeats to Celtic at Parkhead. It was still within the control of Rangers by the time the UEFA Cup Final arrived but there was now no room for error and also no space being afforded by the national body to prepare properly for a European final. Every game mattered, even when you had to play three in the five days.

'Most of our group around the dinner table in an Italian restaurant on the eve of the game, astonishingly, wanted this Scottish team beaten by the Russians. A text message to the editor from a producer back at home left nobody in any doubt that she hoped the Zenit manager Dick Advocaat would triumph. Most of the football chat was about what effect the result would have on the league title race with Celtic, not the European final itself, thus proving that there is no escape from parochial, tribal thinking,' so wrote *Scotsport*'s Archie MacPherson in his autobiography, recounting his team's own preparation for the final. It would be fair to say that the thousands of us who made the short journey south did not do so with the best wishes of the Scottish footballing public.

Not that any of us cared particularly much. Any Rangers supporter born in the 20th century who is able to tell you about that day will do so in great detail if allowed. My day started at 4am as my flatmate Alex and I left our street behind a neighbour's people carrier with flags and scarves already flying out the window. What could have been a blissful, not to mention profitable, festival if proper arrangements had been made at one of Manchester's public parks instead grew steadily in its claustrophobia as the day wore on and the sun beat down. Alex had to make do with Albert Square as my dad and I decided to just get to the City of Manchester Stadium as soon as possible. His ticket was sourced earlier in the week from a contact at the SPL which meant he was in the middle tier of the main stand. Bedecked in Rangers polo, jeans and scarf, he was looked up and down with disdain on the main concourse by the UEFA President Michel Platini. My ticket arrived in my hand at 2pm in the Millennium Hotel via Arthur Numan, the Little General's Lieutenant back in 1998. It had come from the club so I was sat in with the players' partners which is, as it turns out, a very effective deterrent for the outward expression of vociferous individual criticism.

'THIS IS YOUR CHANCE. THIS IS YOUR TIME. BECOME LEGENDS' roared the banner behind the goal to my left. Part of the build-up felt like a standard big game but so much of it was just surreal. The seat to my left was empty for the entire night, the boy behind me was practically comatose for the duration and the gentleman next to him spent most of the match on the phone to either his wife or someone whom his wife may have been interested in speaking to as well. Behind them was Frank Lampard and Robbie Earle and about 70 yards to my right was the UEFA Cup. I felt like a prize-winner at a fixture so alien to my match-going experience, which of course it was. This was unchartered territory for two generations of Rangers fans. The grass seemed shorter, the ball shinier. I could feel the fire as the pyrotechnics exploded for the teams appearing from the stand and, despite 'Best Of You' by Foo Fighters blaring around the ground, I couldn't help but be overwhelmed by the emotion of what had been achieved by my club at a time when it was not expected to do anything of the sort, especially after the disappointment of the 90s, when we hoped to be a regular visitor to such occasions.

In all honesty it never felt like the team fully believed that they deserved to be on that stage either. Immediately after the quarter-final win against Sporting, Smith said that 'it will be one of my proudest moments if we get to the final.' Ever the pragmatist, it is interesting that there was a realistic limit to his public ambition, even after such an exhilarating win in the last eight. It is a common occurrence with unlikely cup runs. Plenty of FA Cup giant killers not only meet a better opponent but also the limitations of their own belief. World Cup shocks often end in the quarter-finals or semis because the team eventually looks down from their new-found perch and feel uneasy. 'Never!' said midfielder Kevin Thomson when I asked if that perhaps affected this Rangers side that night. 'That changing room wanted nothing less than winning every day. Getting beaten and taking part was never an option. It was a great run, brilliant for everyone involved, unbelievable playing in a European final, but it was no consolation for me because I had no interest in a runner's-up medal.'

Thomson took his place in the starting line-up despite worries that he'd miss out due to injury. 'I had a real issue with my feet. It felt like I had nails in my soles. I'd have played through anything though. I could hardly walk but it was just a case of pain killers and strapping them up!' Thomson's predicament said much about the real obstacle in the way of glory. This night in Manchester was the 64th match that season, with four more crucial games to follow in the next ten days. It was a squad at the end of their collective resources against a sharp and dynamic side just getting into the swing of their own season.

Rangers lined up with Neil Alexander in goal and Broadfoot, Cuellar, Weir and Papac in front of him. Brahim Hemdani and Thomson were there to provide an extra shield with Ferguson, Whittaker and Davis providing support for Jean Claude Darcheville in the lone striker role. Zenit's danger man had made it. Andrei Arshavin had been considered a doubt but took his place in the Zenit side that included its Ukrainian captain Anatoliy Tymoschuk but not former Rangers player Fernando Ricksen, who had to make do with a place on the bench and no place at all, due to suspension, for the slayer of Bayern in the semi-final, Pavel Pogrebnyak.

The tone was set from the start. A nervy Rangers were mostly on the back foot as Zenit played with an extremely high tempo of both movement and passing. Arshavin hit the side netting early on with a drive to Alexander's right and Anyukov stung the hands of the Rangers goalkeeper with a wicked first-time drive from outside the box. Rangers had their moments but it was very much a willingness to sit deep and wait for the moment that would inevitably come later in the game combined with an inability to use the ball properly, the perennial cause of those 90s failures. Smith's side did pass eight hours without conceding a UEFA Cup goal and, given the pattern of success on the road to the final, being in the mix when it mattered was infinitely preferable to hunting too soon and being out of it by half-time.

As chaos reigned near the big screens in the city centre, the second half lost its controlled predictability almost immediately. After good work from Broadfoot, Davis released Darcheville who tried to drill it across Malofeev's goal from the left. His save produced a melee in the Zenit box, with Barry Ferguson claiming a handball against the onrushing Igor Denisov before his own effort scuffed the post and then went wide. A penalty perhaps at the 2018 World Cup, but sadly not in the 2008 UEFA Cup. The game was becoming more and more stretched as Arshavin had an effort cleared off the line by Papac after a series of Zenit corners hemmed in the Rangers defence. With 20 minutes left, it was perhaps the time to be proactive, to use fresher defensive players and the wild card of Nacho Novo, the hero of Florence, in place of the hard-working Darcheville. Whilst Rangers remained passive, Zenit pounced. A long ball for the Turkish striker Fatih Tekke was won by Weir but the second ball wasn't picked up as Denisov beat Thomson to it and played it to Arshavin, with space to die for, before he threaded the ball back through the Rangers defence perfectly for Denisov to collect and wrong foot Alexander and beat him low to his left.

It was heartbreak as the game plan that had served Rangers so well on this journey lay in ruins. Zenit should have been two in front when Zyryanov blasted wide from close range but there was one more opportunity for glory. One more moment for us all to relive in the years to come, albeit that we would always change the outcome. Smith had thrown on Novo, Kris Boyd and Lee McCulloch within ten minutes in a desperate search for that equaliser. A long throw from Ferguson on the right-hand side, 15 yards from the byeline, caused havoc in the tiring Russian defence as it bounced out of the reach of almost everyone. All three Rangers subs were within four yards of each other and the ball as it finally landed in the vicinity of blue shirts. Novo, ten yards from goal but with McCulloch trying to change his natural run to his immediate right and Boyd blocking the best sight of goal, blasted the ball high over the bar.

It was the one chance that managers, players and fans alike always believe that they will get as long as the game remains tight and we all knew that was that. Two minutes later, deep into injury time, with Zenit basically playing keep-ball in the Rangers half, the fate was underlined with a second from Zyryanov, although the strings were being pulled by the wonderful Arshavin, who wouldn't receive the full respect due to him until the following month for Russia at Euro 2008.

It was a crushing disappointment to those fans inside the stadium, the city, at home or all around the world, but it was a final that was never supposed to happen this way at all. Smith had returned to provide resolute, domestic stability. No one dared dream we would witness a Rangers team under these kind of lights. In his role as Rangers Supporters Trust Spokesman, David Edgar once asked the Rangers chairman why we didn't make more money from this run, the final especially. 'Bonuses,' Murray replied. 'Why were the bonuses so high?' pressed Edgar. 'Because we didn't fucking think they'd actually get there!'

This game is another that resonates because it took place at all rather than because of the outcome or moments therein. There was another reason why it probably felt so important, other than those very special personal memories of being part of the day.

By this stage in the modern evolution of elite European football, Scottish clubs were not supposed to be making finals such as this. And that is also an unintended consequence of our own making, as Rangers pressed ahead in the early 90s to ultimately create a continental landscape that more and more resembled a closed shop. We knew that would happen, it was just that we fully expected to be inside it by then. Philip Larkin was talking about the state of England in the early 1970s when he wrote 'Going, Going' but the final stanza could apply to many a dark romantic's view of the direction of 21st-century football.

'Most things are never meant.
This won't be, most likely; but greeds
And garbage are too thick-strewn
To be swept up now, or invent
Excuses that make them all needs.
I just think it will happen, soon.'

As the 20th century closed, many of us genuinely believed that Rangers would be a 21st-century European finalist. Few of us imagined that we would need to go back to the future in order to get there.

22

Rangers 1 Celtic 0

Scottish Premiership
Saturday 29 December 2018

'I can testify that there is nothing to compare with them in terms of their intensity and ferocity, not to mention the sheer noise. I found it quite disturbing.'
(Gary Lineker on Old Firm games)

It should be no surprise that over a third of the games selected in this list involve Celtic. It is perhaps more curious to note that, as the air gets more and more rarefied in the pantheon of Rangers' greatest moments, the Old Firm clash becomes rarer. This match is already the 14th to have featured in the first 30 matches. By contrast there are only four more to come in the top 20. Important to us yes, but possibly not as much as we sometimes appear to think. The resonance of this particular fixture, coming just five months before voting opened, can easily be explained by the recency, and fans still being firmly inside the fresh Gerrard bubble. However, it also provides a welcome moment in proceedings to examine why other derby matches fail to stick so firmly in the memory. What then *does* separate the great Old Firm games from the rest?

It would appear that the high-scoring draws don't find enough favour with the *Heart and Hand* community. Jock Wallace's final dose of the Battle Fever, a 4-4 draw in the incessant Ibrox rain where Rangers were 3-1 down, 4-3 ahead and then eventually pulled back, only made it to 55 on the list. A game that is either considered to be a classic or chaos, depending on your footballing outlook, seems to be losing its aura. Seven places further down, and two goals fewer, is the 3-3 tie from 1995 that had more quality, just as much drama and an added bonus of outstanding controversy when David Robertson was judged to be offside despite running past his marker to get the ball. No, entertaining these matches may well be, but unless there are three red cards, court appearances and a last-minute equaliser, truly great Old Firm games require a Rangers triumph.

Perhaps it is because the League Cup has thrown up so many great finals that we only have the mental space to hold a handful of them close. Four of those triumphs found their way onto this list and only one of them saw a defeat of Celtic; however, there are at least four others that could have laid a claim. Three of those arguably made the name of some of our greatest strikers. Derek Johnstone was only 16 when he rose between Billy McNeil and Jim Craig to meet Willie Johnston's cross and head home the only goal of the 1970 final, thus starting a legendary career in the best possible way. Ally McCoist's Rangers career was still in the balance in those early three seasons, but performances such as his Roy Race hat-trick at Hampden in the 3-2 win over Celtic in 1984 helped keep enough credit in the bank until 1986 and his stratospheric lift-off, but the match itself didn't even make the top 100. He may have had nowhere near the Rangers career that Johnstone and McCoist had, but there have been few, if any, more graceful forwards leading the Rangers line in the second decade of the 21st century than Nikica Jelavić. His short spell at the club shouldn't simply be defined by that science-defying spinner that won the cup in 2011, but it's where most fans' minds go when his name comes up. The 2003 final was very much a fine team effort, a dismantling of Celtic in the first hour that was nearly thrown away, save for a wonderful John Hartson penalty miss at the death.

For all the romance around the fixture, the New Year game only appears once in the 50. Not enough love was shown to the 1987 evisceration at Ibrox where Souness finally made his debut in the fixture and not since Jim Baxter had a Rangers midfielder conducted such a match. Nor the 1994 iteration at Parkhead where Rangers were 3-0 up inside half an hour and chocolate bars were being thrown at the Celtic directors' box. The match finished 4-2 but it could only finish as high as 56 on this list. We have two famous 5-1 home victories but no room for the same scoreline at Parkhead in 1960 or the 4-0 win a few years later. Not even Mo Johnston's late winner at Ibrox in November 1989 was enough to resonate stronger than Mo Edu's in 2010. There's only so much analysis one can attempt in order to explain how that fact comes to pass.

Another curious omission is either of the league and cup double headers in April 1998. Two victories, one at Parkhead and then one at Ibrox that were steeped in drama, context, iconic goals, debuts, as well as goodbyes. It was about a team of heroes going into this special battle for the last time and coming out on top. Those battles may have been won, of course, but the war wasn't. What should have set up a glorious league and cup double that secured the Scottish Footballing Holy Grail of ten league championships in a row, ended in bitter disappointment. Moments of genuine greatness cannot be extricated enough from the ultimate context. The 2-0 league win at Ibrox, with Thern and Albertz at the fore, was left far in the distance, although the 2-1 cup victory, McCoist and Gough's tears and all, wasn't that far behind in 61st place. By the same rules, then, this fixture in 22nd place should have also fallen by the wayside. It produced hope at the time but was ultimately fruitless. How, then, did it break the mould?

The chaos of December 2018 should have been the real guide as to how the second half of Steven Gerrard's first season at Ibrox was going to pan out, rather than simply the final 90 minutes of the month that we all clung on to. Commitment and control at Tynecastle followed immediately by a limp and pathetic display at home to Aberdeen.

The frustrating draws against Hibs sandwiching the late drama up in Perth against St Johnstone. A pattern of inconsistency that was to be expected of a new manager and a new squad. It left Rangers with no room for manoeuvre as the final game before the winter break approached. Beat Celtic at home and re-ignite the title race. Fail to win and, with a game more in the bank, and it would have been all over at Christmas yet again. A simple formula, but with an inexperienced team carrying injuries and the early exertions of European competition starting to show, it would be no easy task, especially since they would have to do what no Rangers team had done in six years: beat Celtic in 90 minutes.

'Nobody enjoys going to Old Firm games,' David Edgar once said in Richard Wilson's book *Inside the Divide: One City, Two Teams*, where he makes an excellent attempt to make sense of this fixture. 'It's a really strange, queasy sensation. You can't sleep, you try to force some food down, the heart's beating, your hands are shaking, you're twitchy, you're nervous, you're talking through your arse.' From the ten minutes it took us to walk from the John Grieg statue to take our seats at the rear of the Sandy Jardine stand, David had gone from 'well who knows what we are going to get today?' to 'I definitely don't think we'll lose' before reaching the 'we're going to fucking win this!' stage. It's a path well-travelled by Old Firm veterans of all shades. As the teams came out onto the pitch on that crisp, sunny winter's day I wanted to say that I agreed with him. We *were* going to do it today. But I couldn't dare open my mouth and verbalise it. I was literally paralysed with the fear of even saying it out loud!

From the earliest moments it was obvious that there was no fear in this Rangers side, in the way that there unquestionably had been in the first clash of that season at Parkhead. After only two minutes Andy Halliday charged 20 yards before crunching into a fair and perfectly timed tackle on Olivier Ntcham. These tackles are celebrated with almost as much fervour as goals are in these fixtures, and with that the tone was set. It wasn't enough on its own to throw Celtic off their game, with both Forrest and Christie passing up chances to put the visitors in front. It was only a short respite, however, as Rangers pressed high and dictated the tempo of the first half. Mistakes were becoming more pronounced, Dedryck Boyata the guiltiest culprit, as Rangers forced a succession of set pieces that kept Celtic penned in for long spells. Scott Brown nearly headed in an own goal from a Halliday corner but the glance hit the crossbar instead. Connor Goldson drew a brilliant save from Craig Gordon whilst Daniel Candeias and Alfredo Morelos should have done better from various efforts in that opening 30 minutes.

It was the Rangers play without the ball that was initially more impressive. Ross McCrorie, Ryan Jack and Scott Arfield hunted down green and white shirts in packs with an unrelenting vigour, and on the half-hour mark one of them got their reward. Ryan Kent wasn't yet the fêted hero that he went on to be by the end of that season. The loanee from Liverpool had a fairly inconsistent end product in his first few months at Ibrox, understandable for a wide attacking player with so little regular game time under his belt. He almost always showed for the ball, however, and this day was no different as he picked it up on the Rangers left, around 30 yards from goal. There was no obvious opportunity available to him as he ran directly at the covering Mikael Lustig and Ntcham. The Swedish full-back was left to shepherd out to the byeline to safety, with a possible corner being the highest cost to pay. With two touches in two seconds, Kent changed the game. The first was inspired as he sold Lustig with the hopeful attempted cross before dragging back at the last moment and leaving his opponent on his backside and off the field of play. Now that danger had been created, his second touch had to be just as well-executed. The ball into the path of Ryan Jack, thought to be of no threat as the move was seemingly breaking down, was perfect and his low, controlled right-foot shot deflected off the foot of Scott Brown and into the Celtic net.

There won't have been a noise celebrating a Rangers Old Firm goal at Ibrox like that for some time. Earlier that year, the club had decided to significantly curtail the Celtic allocation to the 'normal' number for away fans and provide the opportunity for more Rangers season-ticket holders to take their place in the Broomloan Road stand that day. In doing so, it created a cauldron that fuelled the Rangers players rather than inhibit them. Every one, to a man, was putting in their biggest shift of that season so far. Jack's goal, his first for the club, won the Rangers Goal Of The Season award and it's no secret why. There were other goals in that campaign around which you could have built more of an aesthetic case, but none more emotionally significant.

Celtic were rattled on and off the pitch that afternoon. When they did show signs of threat in the first half, both Joe Worrall (a loanee from Nottingham Forest who, if he had displayed in all games the same excellent concentration and attitude that he did in this big one, things may have been very different) and James Tavernier were inch-perfect in their tackles. Rangers were in the zone with seemingly everything in control, whereas Celtic players were dropping like flies. Filip Benković was subbed before the interval and the hapless Lustig wouldn't return from the tunnel as he was replaced by the 20-year-old Anthony Ralston.

The consistent evidence of the impact on Celtic was how bad their distribution was and, inside only two minutes of the restart, it nearly created a second Rangers goal. Craig Gordon's dreadful pass to Boyata left him in a whole world of trouble as blue shirts swarmed him. Rangers played their own part in a comedy of errors as Kent and Morelos all passed up the responsibility before Arfield's effort was cleared off the line by Boyata. The pattern didn't really change for much of the second half. Rangers made the play, had good efforts by Jack and Morelos stopped and were seemingly winning every ball. However, a second goal was not forthcoming and as the minutes go by the fear of a sucker punch increases. That devastating blow that Rangers often used to land in the past. The kind of thing that winning teams know how to deliver and that hopeful challengers don't seem sure of preventing.

Celtic did have the ball in the net on 66 minutes but Callum McGregor was just offside. It was a good move but the only moment of sloppy play in the Rangers backline all day. A reminder, however, of how little possession and intensity mean when they are not converted properly. Rangers kept punching in the final 20 minutes but with a more cautious eye on the back door and with those energy levels approaching the warning sign. With only six minutes remaining there would be one final heart-stopping moment to contend with as Odsonne Edouard, Celtic's final substitution, ran at the retreating Joe Worrall and created space for Ntcham to have a clear sight of goal. Andy Halliday's block epitomised the entire Rangers performance. With a squad suffering from injury, illness, fatigue and pressure, this was one final, desperate push before Scottish football closed down for a while and they could all enjoy a recharge in the sunshine. Everything could be left out on the park that day. There was no tricky away tie to consider just three days later.

Rangers did indeed leave it all on that Ibrox turf and it was enough to secure the first Old Firm victory since 2012. Morelos's cheek and attitude, Arfield's drop-ball challenge against Scott Brown and the endless pressing and working. It felt like it was for us, the long suffering support, and the communal celebration after the final whistle reflected exactly that. 'I just looked round and I thought "this is the most united Rangers support in my lifetime,"' David Edgar reflected some months later. 'That was why I got so emotional at the final whistle and that it why this game represents so much more to me than just an Old Firm win. I've been very fortunate, I've seen loads of vital ones, but that day, just a league game in the middle of the season, you were very well aware that you didn't feel like an individual in the ground, you felt like a member of the Rangers support and that is what made it so special to me.'

Even younger fans like Stuart McColl didn't escape the emotion of it all. 'When I heard that Arfield and Kent were starting for us [they were doubts] and Edouard and Tierney weren't for them, I started to believe. When the game actually kicked off and you could feel this fuller atmosphere than normal, we were definitely winning that day. Rangers, as they do, put us through a tough second half with some missed chances, but when Morelos had the ball in the corner and we got a throw-in deep into injury time, I had a tear as I hugged my old man. It wasn't just a win. It was because it had been way too long.'

It was three points that got Rangers right back into the title race at the halfway stage. That there was no success as the season developed, however, doesn't take the shine off this win. The games in 1998 *were* different. They *were* dependent on leading to something tangible for us to celebrate them long into the future. This was always more than a potentially pivotal win in a title race. Ibrox that day, with its louder voice than usual, was a communal outpouring of relief that we had tasted that kind victory once more, a necessary stage on the journey back to the top.

21

Rangers 5 Hearts 1

Scottish Cup Final
Saturday 18 May 1996

'The manager used to tell the players before games, "Give Brian the ball, he'll do something good with it." They could find me anywhere on the pitch – left, right or centre.'

(Brian Laudrup)

Stan Mortensen was a post-war professional footballer of high regard. Over 300 appearances for his beloved Blackpool and 23 goals in 25 caps for England, including the first-ever World Cup goal by an Englishman at their ill-fated tournament in Brazil. The highlight of his career was arguably the FA Cup final of 1953, when he became the first and, thus far, only player to score a hat-trick in that famous match, including a thunderous free kick as Blackpool came back from 3-1 down to win 4-3. It remains one of the famous finals in the competition's long history and it was quickly named in honour of one man.

That man wasn't Mortensen. Sir Stanley Matthews was arguably the most famous player in the world at the time and this realistically was his last chance to win an elusive cup-winner's medal. Such was the romantic desperation to see him succeed, his two assists (the final one bringing about the winning goal) ensured that it was his name that was forever associated with the 90 minutes. When Mortensen died in 1991 it was said that his final moment would no doubt be known as the 'Matthews Funeral'. If he carried any bitterness with him about such a performance being overshadowed into eternity then surely Gordon Durie would know how he felt. He had made a bet with Paul Gascoigne at the start of the English superstar's first season at Ibrox that he would outscore him, and going into the final game of the season, the Scottish Cup final at Hampden against Hearts, Durie was one ahead of his rival. His three goals that afternoon would win him the bet but not the Man Of The Match award as once again a genius stole the limelight.

I got his signature before Walter Smith and David Murray. As I was preparing to fly out of Glasgow Airport on a family holiday, Brian Laudrup had just flown in to seal the deal, after being lured by the promise of a free role and an easier life compared to the shackles of Italy and Serie A. It was an exciting signing, quite literally in the form of my boarding pass, but there were genuine questions over his love for the game following such an unhappy spell in both Florence and Milan. Rangers' other high-profile signing that summer of 1994, the former Marseille defender Basile Boli, created more of a buzz. It wouldn't be long into the 1994/95 season before it was clear that in actual fact a Rangers legend had arrived. He was simply playing football at a different level than any other player I had seen pull on a blue jersey.

'It wasn't that at the start,' recalled David Robertson when he spoke to me on *The Time Capsule*. 'I remember the first pre-season game against Clyde at Broadwood. I remember coming in at half-time thinking, "This guy is not as good as people make out!" But it turned out that we weren't as good as he was and we had to catch up to him. He was making passes that I simply wasn't reading. But as time went on I knew that if the ball got to Laudrup, I could make a run and nine times out of ten he would find the pass to me. He made our lives so much easier.' By October Laudrup couldn't go to take a corner without the fans visibly showing that they weren't worthy of him. He was an instant sensation that, along with the redoubtable Mark Hateley, brightened those two seasons between 1993 and 1995 when Rangers in general were relatively flat. It was therefore no surprise at all that if a Scottish Cup Final was going to be named after a player, it would be him. What was a little surprising, however, was the season in which it happened.

1995/96 – Laudrup's second season at Ibrox was more subdued than his first. His 13 goals from 38 appearances from his free role in his debut year was impressive, not to mention the umpteen assists for Mark Hateley. By this cup final he had only managed four goals in 32 games, although the last of them was the decisive moment in the semi-final against Celtic, a brave but brilliant lob that sent Rangers back to Hampden. However, this was the season that Rangers had another genius creating magic. If Laudrup's complete freedom the season before showcased his individual talent, it arguably caused problems in the overall Rangers shape, resulting in a disappointing campaign where 'only' the league was won. Smith changed formation to get the best out of Paul Gascoigne, using wing-backs, deploying three at the back and ensuring some real workforce around the England midfielder in order that not just he but the entire unit flourished. It worked. Gascoigne scored 19 goals and Rangers averaged over 2.5 points a game in the league, the only time in the nine-in-a-row era when this was achieved (where all seasons are adjusted to three points for a win). Even if Laudrup was playing a more reserved role, this was a Rangers side in top gear.

Hearts, however, had proved to be a problem that season, winning the previous two fixtures and scoring five goals without reply, including an Allan Johnston hat-trick in a 3-0 win at Ibrox in January. Unlike the last Scottish Cup Final that Rangers appeared in (two years before when they had slumped to a calamitous 1-0 defeat to Dundee Utd, who had also notched up a 3-0 win at Ibrox that season), it felt like a team on an upswing instead of one in a slump. All the talk that week was about the possible arrival in the summer of Gianluca Vialli from the soon-to-be Champions' League winners Juventus. He instead chose Chelsea, citing the draw of the capital and the need for press attention. On the eve of the final, Richard Gough remarked that he should have a word with Gascoigne about how intense life can be as a Rangers player.

No Vialli that summer and no McCoist for the final. He cut a pensive and withdrawn figure as the team paraded the league championship around Ibrox three weeks previously and speculation had mounted about his future. A new two-year deal was signed during the week, however, but sadly a long-running calf injury flared up in training and he would have to make do with watching from the stands as Rangers took the field with no out-and-out centre-forward. Goram took his place in the Rangers goal that afternoon for the 47th time that season, a fact that might explain the cohesion of that Rangers season as much as the creative firepower Smith had available. Only Alan McLaren played more often in 1995/96 and he made up a three-man defence with Richard Gough and John Brown, with Alec Cleland and David Robertson providing the width as normal. Gascoigne was partnered with the familiarity of Ian Ferguson and Stuart McCall, with Laudrup and Gordon Durie the nominal Rangers forwards. In typical mid-90s fashion, Hearts matched the Rangers shape with Giles Rousset, the popular French goalkeeper, behind Allan McManus, Paul Ritchie and Pasquale Bruno in defence, former Ranger Dave McPherson in the right wing-back role and Englishman Neil Pointon on the other side. Gary Locke, the 20-year-old Hearts skipper, was in midfield with Gary Mackay and Steve Fulton, with John Colquhoun and the dangerous Allan Johnston leading the line.

The game took a significant turn after only three minutes when Locke, the source of so much energy in the Hearts midfield engine, caught his studs in the turf trying to tackle Stuart McCall and was stretchered off. In a time of three substitutes, one of whom was a goalkeeper, Jim Jeffries had to make a fundamental change to his shape before anyone had broken a sweat. Alan Lawrence, a forward, took his place, meaning that Johnston, his main threat, had to come back into midfield to shadow Gascoigne. The movement of Laudrup and Durie was evident early on and Ferguson and Robertson made Rousset work, but in that first 30 minutes Rangers were scrappy, with Ferguson and Cleland booked for persistent fouling and a wild swipe on Johnston respectively. Even though they were imbalanced, Hearts had a good long-range effort from Lawrence, and Colquhoun missed a free header. Rangers, sporting the next season's new kit on cup-final day for the third time in four years, were struggling to find their rhythm. Billy McNeil on co-commentary duty had started to criticise the lack of a penalty box threat without a number nine.

As is so often the case with the most dangerous of threats, for Rangers that day it was one hidden deeper. Durie and Laudrup were not being picked up by a defence set up for the tip of the Rangers team being much further forward. After 37 minutes there was a seemingly harmless exchange just inside the Hearts half, with Laudrup lobbing to Durie, then an exchange of headers before Durie sprung the trap with a more adventurous lob over the top of Bruno that spun perfectly for Laudrup to take on the volley, low beyond the despairing reach of Rousset. It was a fantastic piece of play that took seven seconds, four touches, covered 40 yards and changed the dynamic of the cup final. From that moment on, Rangers stepped it up. Gascoigne nearly scored a carbon copy of his season-defining goal the month before against Aberdeen but got swamped by maroon shirts, Gough tested Rousset with a brilliant header and Durie should have done better as he rounded the Frenchman before running the ball out of play. Hearts should have been further punished when Paul Ritchie, later of the parish, took Gascoigne out of the game with a cynical and dangerous foul right on the edge of the box. He was the last obstacle in the way of a Gascoigne goal and should have seen red. Hugh Dallas perhaps prioritised the spectacle of the showpiece event over the strict laws of the game.

There was no let up after the restart as Alec Cleland was in behind the Hearts backline within 30 seconds. Four minutes later the match was ended as a contest in the most bizarre and cruel way. Giles Rousset wasn't just a cult hero at Tynecastle, he was as responsible as anyone for turning around Hearts' fortunes that season. Laudrup had created an opportunity over in the right corner after turning McManus inside out, but his delivery was well below his usual high standards. No one was entirely sure if this insipid ball was a cross or a shot and there was an initial groan that it was a good chance squandered followed by an almighty roar as the ball was inexplicably rolling over the line and into the net. A surreal moment that a genius should win the cup by way of some kind of slow-motion accident.

'It was probably Laudrup's worst pass of the season,' recalled Ian Hogg, who was sat high up in the South Stand in its final Hampden match before redevelopment. 'He did the hard work and then just scuffed this left-footed pass that was weak and straight at the keeper. Then it's as if Rousset thinks, "I'm not going to follow the goalkeeping manual which says get my knees and body behind the ball. I'm going to go to try and get it with my hands only and keep my legs open." At the time everyone found it funny, but when you watch it back I have real sympathy for Rousset. It was a howler and his reaction was iconic in that cup final.'

There was sympathy for him in the commentary box too but more a sense of disappointment that the contest had concluded early. There was little sympathy for him in the West Stand as 'There's Only One Rousset' bellowed out behind his goal as Rangers pressed on for more. Jeffries replaced Bruno with veteran striker John Robertson and elected for a back four in order to get Johnston into the game, but it was still Rangers who remained on top, with Gascoigne driving at will, Ferguson hitting the bar and Durie popping up everywhere. Jock Brown feared a rout but that would require some better finishing. Durie had five efforts and they were all off target. Perhaps he needed a chance without the time and space to overthink it.

With 66 minutes played, another Rangers counter attack completely exposed a young and rapidly tiring Hearts defence. When McCall started the move by slipping a ball through to Durie, Rangers were once again 40 yards from goal. Durie sprayed the ball first time with the outside of his right boot for Laudrup to chase in plenty of space. He returned it across the box at pace for Durie to run on and take instantly in his instep, ten yards from goal. In another beautiful example of blistering and devastating football, Durie's endless endeavour had finally been rewarded.

It was now exhibition stuff, especially from the two chief architects, shirts untucked, as they indulged in ball juggling and back heels in the brightening sunshine. One move ended with John Brown just taking too heavy a touch in the box, where the Brown of yesteryear would have taken it first time and perhaps finished one of the greatest team goals in the history of the club. The showboating was also maybe indicative of a creeping complacency and it was punished when Colquhoun pounced on a loose ball at the edge of the Rangers box before Alan McLaren could, and rifled a low consolation past Goram. It failed to change much as Rangers continued to attack in droves. Stuart McCall went very close whilst Laudrup drifted past defenders as if they were ghosts, before forcing two more good saves from Rousset. McManus looked as if he was playing on sand trying to catch Laudrup, after being fooled by a cute David Robertson flicked pass, but the Dane broke away and gifted Durie his second of the afternoon, although he nearly fell over the ball, before finally dispatching it past the now-tormented Rousset.

Durie got his Mortensen moment with five minutes remaining, rightly taking his acclaim as part of a star-studded cast. Yet again it came from a triangle with Laudrup, this time originating from a long ball that Durie managed to flick on to the Rangers number 11. Such were the weights draining the Hearts legs, Laudrup had time to ponder life's greatest questions before sending the ball right back onto the head of his partner. An extra-special roar greeted a brilliant cup final hat-trick that sealed a relentless display. 'We really felt it in the first half hour because we didn't have a number nine,' said Ian Hogg. 'But once we got the first goal and Hearts had to come out, it was entirely different. All of a sudden you had Durie running into space, Laudrup doing whatever the hell he liked and Gascoigne doing the same at the front of the midfield instead of his earlier quarterback role. The final hour of this match was up there with any attacking performance that a Rangers side would provide.'

It was a hugely enjoyable day at Hampden, somehow free of the tension and pressure of the other Scottish Cup finals of that decade. There is shot of Walter Smith, however, as he watched his boys go up to collect their medals, barely cracking a smile. Soon after, in his on-field post-match interview with the BBC's Hazel Irvine, once the standard platitudes and clichés were over, he was asked about the pressure now to deliver nine-in-a-row and what new faces would be arriving at Ibrox. Barely ten minutes had passed since he had delivered his third 'double' in four years, the 13th in the club's history, and the focus was already on the forthcoming season of destiny. Few moments summed up the pressure on Walter Smith's shoulders at that time more than this exchange with Irvine, but she was only tapping into the reality. He had delivered 11 trophies in five years as Rangers manager but, such was this growing obsession with matching this sequence, it would have been rendered meaningless if he didn't bring home one more. For Smith, there was no real mental space in which to properly enjoy such a fantastic performance.

His two maestros had plenty of space, however. The last enduring image of the post-match celebrations is of Gascoigne and Laudrup sharing a genuinely emotional embrace on the Hampden turf. Perhaps he had cup-final ghosts to exorcise from 1991 but Gascoigne, who had been in the wars all afternoon, effectively refused to come off for Ian Durrant as an 88th-minute substitute. He was soaking it all up on that stage even if he was playing a more supportive role on this occasion. Two more different personalities you would struggle to find, but the blend was alchemic. Because of the impeding suffocating circus with Celtic or the never-ending promise of even more glamorous new signings to come, those of us there that day may have taken for granted what we had just witnessed. From 1994 to 1998 we had watched two of the greatest, if not *the* greatest, Rangers of all time carve open Scottish football with ease. Plenty of Rangers greats have shone in big games but only the best have *owned* them. Within the final three weeks of a tense season, these two delivered the double seemingly of their own free will.

As time has passed and our ability to compete in the transfer market has diminished, these performances have grown in our love and esteem. We really weren't worthy.

20

Rangers 2 Marseille 2

UEFA Champions League Group Stage Wednesday 25 November 1992

'We can reach the final again. Our only problem is the Glasgow team.'
(Bernard Tapie, pre-match)

'The European Cup has become a historical anachronism … it is not modern thinking,' remarked Silvio Berlusconi when Diego Maradona's Napoli were pitted against six-time European champions Real Madrid in the very first round of the competition in 1987/88. 'It is economic nonsense,' he said, 'that a club such as Milan might be eliminated in the first round.' The AC Milan president's primary motivations were no doubt for his club and, by proxy, his media company Mediaset which owned Italy's first private TV station Canale 5; however, there was a wider point too about how European football was structured. It wasn't that he wanted to eliminate the chances of a David v Goliath story as is often said, it's that he wanted to prevent a Goliath v Goliath happening before the competition had time to even gather pace.

A league format amongst Europe's champions was nothing new; in fact, it was the initial plan of the original creator of the tournament, Gabriel Hanot, in 1955 but the quality of travel and communication at the time was the biggest logistical obstacle. Liverpool raised it again soon after being knocked out at the first go by Nottingham Forest in 1978 but these ideas had never caught fire. The time for change was now more pressing and Berlusconi approached the leading name in advertising, Saatchi and Saatchi, to draw up a proposal. As it happened they had an executive by the name of Alex Fynn who had, just that year, given a speech at the launch of the *Rothman's Football Yearbook*, advocating a European Super League that made better commercial sense for the champions of the continent. 'The key,' according to Fynn was, 'more event games between the big clubs in the big television markets.' He proposed an 18-team league comprising of two or three clubs from Europe's four big leagues and representation from Scotland, France, Portugal, Holland and Belgium.

It was a step too far for UEFA and they didn't entertain it. The pressure for a better structure couldn't be ignored forever though, and a suitable compromise came from inside Ibrox Stadium. Rangers were at the time the most influential club in British football and changing the landscape had been on the club secretary Campbell

Ogilvie's mind for some time. 'Domestically, there was a ceiling,' Ogilvie said to *The Daily Telegraph* in 2018. 'In Europe, you could be out after one round. I remember we played Osasuna in 1985/86 and went out. That spurred on discussion for all clubs of our size – how do we take this forward? Can we get European football into some sort of structure where we could at least be guaranteed six games, three of them at home? That was where it started from.' At the third attempt, Ogilvie's plan was accepted and a group stage replacing the quarter-finals was introduced first in the 1991/92 competition and then at an earlier stage in 1992/93 where it would be re-branded in its own right. Berlusconi's charge, it was thought, had been headed off a pass; however, the media magnate was happy. The original plan was a stalking horse, never imagined to be accepted so soon. This gave him, and the other owners of Europe's biggest clubs, something that they could work with.

'It felt like the European Cup with a group stage, a shiny new badge and a theme tune. Instead of being knocked out in November or February, we knew that we would now still be there by April at least,' said Ian Hogg. We weren't to understand just how big this would be as we turned up to Ibrox on that soaking wet night, but it did feel important that we had this amount of European football guaranteed, with no away goals causing instant elimination. Rangers would make nearly £5m from these six fixtures, which was a significant windfall at the time. The eight stars logo, symbolising the eight teams to make it to the two groups, were everywhere around the stadium, including the match ball itself, and music inspired by Handel's *Zadok The Priest* thundered out for the first time to those in the ground and watching at home on television. This was an instant marketing drive that hasn't stopped at the time of writing. The whole structure of European football was changing and Rangers were at the heart of it.

The unseeded group draw in Geneva could have been a lot worse. Berlusconi's AC Milan, the best side in Europe, were on the other half along with PSV Eindhoven, who still had the dynamite of Romário up front, and also FC Porto. It was clear, that Marseille were the favourites to qualify for the final in Munich from Group A. This was their second trip to Ibrox in four months after visiting for a pre-season friendly in July where they were exceptional in a comfortable 2-1 win. By November, however, all was not quite plain sailing in the south of France.

The week before this game, Marseille had sacked their coach Jean Fernandez due to indifferent form and replaced him with their technical director Raymond Goethals, a wily 70-year-old Belgian in a Columbo trench coat who was tactically gifted but no stranger to the darker arts, as evidenced by his conviction for match-fixing whilst manager of Standard Liege in 1982. One would assume that is the kind of business that would normally end a managerial career, but these were not normal times. It was the era when club owners started to become as famous as the managers and star players, whose mouths they stuffed with gold. Bernard Tapie had much in common with Berlusconi in that he had charisma, wealth and a burning desire for footballing and political glory that wouldn't be curbed by the mere triviality of ethics. He had also given his club the same charismatic injection in 1986 that Rangers had received from Souness, and the two clubs' fortunes were eerily similar in that both had won four domestic titles in a row and were well in contention for the fifth by the time they met here. Red Star Belgrade had defeated both clubs on their way to winning the big prize in 1991; however, their win over Marseille in the final was infamous for its boredom. Tapie was now obsessed with this over everything else, but realised that because of their physical and mental strength Rangers were a serious obstacle.

It was also a Rangers side in good form. A run of 18 wins in all competitions had come to an end at Tynecastle on the Saturday but a 1-1 draw still kept Rangers in a comfortable position at the top of the pile in Scotland. Walter Smith had his headaches, however, as fitness and the requirement to play a maximum of three non-Scottish players left him threadbare. The biggest blow was the loss of Ally McCoist, who had already scored 32 goals by this stage in November, whereas captain Richard Gough declared himself fit despite being nothing of the sort. 'It was the kind of situation that littered that first Champions League campaign,' remembers Ian Hogg. 'We played a strict 4-4-2 with not a great deal of flexibility so it needed both Hateley and McCoist. It was a devastating blow to lose either (they'd play together in fewer than half of the matches) and it changed how we would have to play significantly.'

Smith appreciated the significance of the fixture but seemed to suggest that this season was viewed as a stepping stone towards future success. 'My ambitions for Rangers must lead there. The experiences gained this time will help next time around.' Like the majority of us he was excited, but aware that we probably weren't yet ready. His defensive unit was a familiar one to anyone following Rangers that season, with Goram behind a back four of McPherson, Gough, Brown and Robertson. The midfield would comprise some experience in the form of Trevor Steven, Alexei Mikhailichenko and Stuart McCall but also saw 19-year-old Neil Murray making his first appearance since an outing against Stranraer in the League Cup back in August. Ian Durrant was pushed further up the field to support Hateley. The Rangers bench for the inaugural Champions League fixture included three youngsters – Steven Pressley, Gary McSwegan and David Hagen – goalkeeper Ally Maxwell and the 34-year-old reserve-team coach Davie Dodds, who had to come out of retirement to be registered. Marseille could afford to leave the likes of Dragan Stojković at home and fielded a standard 3-5-2 with a young Fabien Barthez in goal, Basile Boli and Marcel Desailly being marshalled by the sweeper Bernard Casoni with Éric Di Meco and Jocelyn Angloma on either side. The midfield that night was a three of Franck Sauzée, Didier Deschamps and the highly rated Ghanian Abedi Pele, leaving just Alen Bokšić and Rudi Völler up front.

The common telling of this story is that Rangers were pulverised for 75 minutes before coming off the ropes to snatch point and the continent's hearts. It's generally accurate, although the first half an hour was fairly balanced. Marseille had more of the ball, dominated midfield with that extra man in there, but it was Rangers who had the best early chances. Durrant and McCall were involved in a clever bit of work around the box and Mark Hateley was a nuisance to both Barthez and Basile Boli, who had boasted during the week that he would keep him out of the game. The 21-year-old goalkeeper, whom Ray Wilkins had described in the *Scotsport* studio before the game as 'a bit iffy at crosses', flapped when under pressure from the Rangers target man and a fantastic opportunity to put Rangers in the lead was spurned by 'Miko' as he dragged his shot wide when most of the goal was gaping open.

If Rangers were happy to pass up gifts, Marseille were not, and on 31 minutes they were in front. Richard Gough came to clear an aerial ball but went too soon and found himself quickly underneath it. Völler, waiting behind him, controlled the ball immediately and took it into the corner, where he was followed by both Brown and the recovering Gough, keen to make up for his error. This left Bokšić unmarked in the box if his partner could find him, which he duly did. The Croatian could have controlled and steadied himself, such was the space afforded him, but instead he drilled it low past Goram first time. Ibrox, as it had been for much of the Leeds United game, was relatively flat, a mixture of nerves and awe at what the fans were watching. This goal didn't help and nor did the French pressure before the break, when both Deschamps and Pele could have added more goals.

The Rangers captain was nowhere near fit enough to continue, and the 19-year-old Steven Pressley would replace him at half-time, moving out to right-back with Dave McPherson tucking back into central-defence. The difference in the teams, as the second half got underway, was the ability to keep possession, even on a filthy night and a dreadful pitch. Rangers never tried to build from the back, using Goram's artillery fire for Hateley as often as possible. Ten minutes after the restart John Brown lost the ball in the Rangers half to audible groans, attesting to the tension and frustration from the stands. Marseille kept the ball for a bit before Sauzée attempted a cute but speculative lob over the backline. Pressley took the bait and stretched out a leg to knock the ball past the outrushing Goram when, perhaps on a non-monsoon night, it may have rolled out for a corner. On this night it stuck in the mud and Völler wouldn't score a simpler goal in his long and illustrious career.

The initial thoughts of many in the packed Ibrox was that it might have been better to be knocked out before Christmas after all if we had to watch six drubbings, which is what we all feared. 'You were genuinely thinking that this might be a cricket score,' said Ian Hogg. 'We have both experienced players and kids all making mistakes against a side littered with world class talent.' Rangers tried to respond, this team always did, but Casoni has the offside trap set perfectly so playing through wasn't working; however, there was still some hope when we could get in some wide deliveries. Free kicks led to a penalty shout when Desailly stopped the ball with his arm and a John Brown effort that was blocked off the line by the same player. The French champions had plenty of opportunities for a third themselves as Goram saved once from Bokšić and twice from Angloma, whilst Völler had two more chances which he wasted.

With 15 minutes to go, Rangers didn't have a pulse. Smith made a change by replacing the very ineffectual Trevor Steven (playing in a fixture that was always going to either inspire or inhibit following his one disappointing season at Marseille) for another young player, the striker Gary McSwegan. This allowed Durrant to fall into a deeper position and it changed the game. Picking the ball up just inside the Rangers half on a counter attack, his vision and speed of thought released Mikhailichenko on the left-hand side in some space. His first-time cross didn't go into the mixer, as so many had done, but to the back of the defensive line where McSwegan was waiting. With no time to realise the stage he was on, his header was instinctive and brilliant, looping over Barthez and into the top corner. Ibrox Stadium was no longer flat. Nerves had disappeared, hope was replenished. As a young 11-year-old, just starting to get a taste of these nights, I had never heard a noise like it as people went mad around me in the stand. 'If you were at the back of the enclosures in those days, in moments like that, you'd be ok, but if you were in the middle, you'd end up at the front pretty quickly,' said Ian, who was in the West Enclosure that evening. 'I was beside my mate and there was a massive surge in front of us, leaving this empty space for us to dance about in. Ibrox was rocking and there was a real sense around the ground that we should be losing about 3 or 4 nil but it's now 2-1. We had a chance.'

For the next three minutes it was all Rangers, and the goal that we seemed to feel was inevitable was scored. Such was the rush of adrenaline from McSwegan's goal, the move started from Mikhailichenko tracking back and robbing Pele of the ball on the left-hand side. Durrant then pushed from midfield, linking up brilliantly with McSwegan on the edge of the box as he evaded Di Meco's lunge before returning the ball with the outside of his foot. Durrant's cross was low and it deflected off Casoni into the six-yard box, where Hateley was waiting and Barthez was not. The noise was sensational. Rangers had been out of this, dead and buried, and now there was parity.

The natural reaction for Marseille would have been to dig in and survive the continual aerial onslaught; however, that would have just invited trouble and a side this good went back to what it did best: attack. They created a flurry of late chances with free kicks being blocked and corners punched away. There was a particular moment that could have led to cardiac arrest when the ball stuck in the penalty-box mud the wrong side of Pele before he had a free shot on goal. Both sides simply ran out of time, however, and the very first Champions League match at Ibrox ended all square.

For those Rangers fans pouring out of the ground, the season expectations had just dramatically increased. 'The second goal changed everything,' recalls Ian. 'Before then we were playing for second place. Now there was a feeling that this was going to become a shoot-out. It was now about who could deal best with Club Brugge and

CSKA Moscow. Domestic football already felt under control so now Europe had a real focus. It felt on.' The game typified that team and that season. The example was set, perhaps foolhardily by their captain, when the odds were stacked against them they simply had to keep fighting until there was nothing left. Rangers may have felt like a modern European football club, at the heart of reforming the game to realise its market potential, however we were still fighting continental prestige with an old-fashioned gritty desire.

No one inside the ground that night had any idea of the monster that had just been unleashed as European football would change beyond all recognition by the end of the decade. Rangers and Marseille felt that this progress would be beneficial for upwardly mobile and ambitious champions like themselves but didn't see that it was where the television markets were that would dictate the shape of things to come. 'Mine was a football model,' argued Ogilvie. 'I was of the view it was a champions' competition. I never for one moment thought four teams from the same country would be playing in it. Things evolve and it became obvious that to get the higher TV revenues it was going to need more teams from the big countries that command the TV rights. But we have created super-clubs. There are a limited number of teams that are going to win the Champions League.'

The day after Rangers scrapped their way to a result that fans still feel so proud of to this day, Manchester United bought Eric Cantona for just over £1m. The money wasn't newsworthy, Rangers had matched that more than once before, but it was a move that would turn the Premier League into a marketable narrative that would soon dwarf our game and has yet to slow down at the time of writing.

That night, however, Rangers were the dominant force in Scottish and British football and that horizon seemed endless. We were now playing on a whole new stage. As the new UEFA anthem proclaimed, 'Ce sont les meilleures équipes, Es sind die allerbesten Mannschaften, The main event'. For the next five months it felt that we could genuinely be kings of this new European game. Die meister. Die besten. Les grandes èquipes.

The champions.

19

Rangers 2 Dynamo Kiev 0

European Cup First Round, Second Leg
Wednesday 30 September 1987

'The noise was absolutely phenomenal. It was like winning it out there that night.'
(Ally McCoist)

At the impressionable age of 11, the experience of the Marseille game was overwhelming. It was pretty much all I talked about the whole way home as I had never known Ibrox to be like that. The noise, the passion, the wild celebrations and the communal growth in belief during those last 15 minutes alone. Surely, I asked my dad, that was the best atmosphere that there had ever been in that famous old stadium. He agreed that it had been a special night but ultimately dismissed my suggestion with one word: Kiev.

For Rangers fans of many generations, this still appears to be the benchmark for what we consider to be the greatest of all nights at home. This is the level that needs to be matched, a charge of energy that is impossible to quantify but we know when we've been close to reaching it again. Ibrox has often been loud of course. The loudest nights have sometimes been those which have ended in disappointment but where there was a clear need to try and generate a response from first-leg adversity, against all odds – Steaua Bucharest in 1988 or AEK Athens in 1994, for example. Noise and atmosphere are different, however. Much of the tiresome discussion about modern football is around the plethora of new stadia and their homogenous uniformity. Acoustic design is a big consideration for new projects so that teams end up with something like the new Tottenham Hotspur Stadium and not the new London Stadium that has been bequeathed to West Ham United. Specific group sections, safe standing and other contrivances are toyed with to improve atmosphere. All of those things can raise the noise levels. That is something that can be measured. Sound is a slightly different, more ethereal concept, which struggles to be. It is the latter that makes your hairs stand on end. It is the latter that we still search for.

The latter will always need sporting context. One can bang a drum for the entire 90 minutes but if there is no jeopardy around the result or if the competition itself doesn't turn the heart rate up a few clicks then it's just noise. Atmosphere is dependent on the result not being a foregone conclusion either way and the prize being worth the world to you, especially one that you've not been involved in for some time. That is where this game comes into its own, like a kind of goldilocks zone for football fans.

Rangers hadn't been in the European Cup for eight years. The Souness Revolution had delivered the league title back and a League Cup for good measure but, with the money spent and the European ban still in force in England, there was always an assumption that this was the competition that the manager saw as being the real test of our mettle. If the excitement about being back in the big time had been building since the Pittodrie hangovers had worn off in May, it would have been checked back by the first-round draw. The same unseeded process that locked together the champions of Spain and Italy paired Rangers with Dynamo Kiev, at the time one of the most feared sides in Europe. Semi-finalists the year before after disposing of Celtic on the way, this Kiev team contained eight of the players that the USSR would use in the European Championships at the end of the season, where they would reach the final. The side boasted two Ballon d'Or winners in Igor Belanov and Oleg Blokhin, the former picking up his award only the previous year. Their manager, the legendary Valeri Lobanovsky, had a duel role in charge of both Dynamo and the Soviet national side. This was a well-drilled but very flamboyant footballing machine.

'We're out,' recalled Ross Hendry, when he first heard news of the draw. 'That was the instant reaction: one of deflation. But the performance in the first leg gave us a bit of buoyancy going into the home leg. There were some things that happened, Kuznetsov's treatment of McCoist, for example, that just gave us a bit of fire in the belly.' The away game, a match played in front of 100,000 people in Kiev and beamed back on a screen to thousands at Ibrox on a Wednesday afternoon, was better than many first feared. A 1-0 deficit lacked an away-goal threat but was still something that could be overcome and the performance itself was one of maturity and resolve. All the perfect ingredients for setting up a magical night for the return.

'I didn't appreciate how long we'd been away from the big cup,' said Ross. 'That's what accounted for that special buzz that had been in the air. The pace walking to the ground was quicker than usual and I remember getting into the ground a lot earlier than we normally would. Ibrox was just buzzing from the moment that we stepped foot in there. It makes the hairs on the back of my neck stand up whenever I see that game now. We knew that we were in a fight. It wasn't a lost cause. It's the magic sweet spot in football when you go into a fixture knowing that you can get a result but also knowing that you won't get steamrolled.'

Ibrox instantly felt a little different. A packed stadium for a European Cup tie for the first time in a generation. It also looked a little different too. 'It was one of those things that we didn't all notice at the same time. It was a gradual realisation as to why Ibrox didn't look right. Why the Copland seemed further away from the East Enclosure, which was the beating heart of the support at the time. There was no forewarning, no rumours that he might do it. He had pulled it from nowhere. No one had heard the likes of it before.' Graeme Souness, wary of the Dynamo threat from wide areas, had narrowed the Ibrox playing surface, already the largest in the country, by eight yards and did so at the last minute so that it was a different pitch than the one Kiev had trained on the night before. 'There are no gentlemen at Glasgow Rangers,' complained the club secretary Mikhail Oshenkov after the game, whilst Lobanovsky refused to comply with the mandatory post-match press duties. It was perfectly legal, however, and, given the travel difficulties Rangers had suffered behind the Iron Curtain in the first leg, it would be a stretch to argue that Dynamo had any kind of moral high ground.

Graham Roberts was a late call-off with a groin injury, whilst Davie Cooper's absence was known well in advance. The Rangers team that night read Chris Woods in goal, Jimmy Nicholl, Terry Butcher, John McGregor and Jimmy Phillips in defence, a midfield four of Avi Cohen, Souness, Durrant and Trevor Francis and a strike pairing of Ally McCoist and Mark Falco, a summer signing from Watford, who had both notched up a hat-trick each in the 7-0 demolition of Morton the previous Saturday. Throughout his time as Rangers manager, Souness was very adept at bringing in experienced players for short-term roles, but there does seem to be an imbalance there throughout this particular starting XI. One or two old heads have a great value but when they comprise half the team, it limited the dynamism that so characterised the championship-winning side from the season before. Souness would rectify that the following Friday when he signed Richard Gough from Tottenham Hotspur and later in the season, when Mark Walters, John Brown and Ian Ferguson arrived, all of whom were integral parts of future Rangers success. Notable names in the Kiev line-up included the goalkeeper Viktor Chanov, who would have a memorable evening, captain Sergei Baltacha, later of St Johnstone, Oleg Kuznetsov and Alexei Mikhailichenko, later of Rangers, star of the 1986 World Cup Vasili Rats and the world-class strike force of Belanov and Blokhin.

The frenzy in the stands perhaps led to the false start when Kiev kicked off before the referee's whistle, but when the action did get properly underway it was Rangers who were fuelled by the energy coming at them from all four sides. The pattern of consistent but controlled home pressure and dangerous counter attacks by the visitors was set early as Falco, McCoist, Nicholl and Francis all had efforts in the first 20 minutes, McCoist in particular was lacking the composure in front of goal that he had shown so often that season already. Kuznetsov clearly fancied his chances from range, as he would go on to demonstrate on his Rangers debut three years later, and Belanov was unlucky not to get a free kick on the edge of the box when he was clearly fouled by Butcher. Rangers concluded that first quarter with a great move between McCoist and Falco which left the former with the chance to drill it straight across goal but, under pressure, he instead shot straight at Chanov.

The altered dimensions become more and more obvious to the viewer as Kiev, so used to a wide-open pitch at their own Central Stadium, struggled to break out of the claustrophobia and perhaps the lack of such a wide out-ball played some small part in the curious opening goal on 24 minutes. It came from an inauspicious Jimmy Philips high cross that Chanov collected with ease. He looked around at his options but where his intended target was we shall never know as the ball comically spilled out of his hand like some aborted overarm delivery, and hit Baltacha's rear end as he walked away completely unaware. McCoist was very much aware and he poked into the path of Falco, who rolled it into the empty net to level the tie. 'The noise I still maintain is like nothing that I've ever heard before,' recalls Ross. 'I don't know if it's just me being misty eyed but I'll maintain to my dying day that this is as loud as I've ever heard Ibrox. The place was literally bouncing. The structure was moving. The best thing that happened after we scored was that we just kept piling it on.'

Durrant and McCoist had chances to put Rangers in the clear before half-time but both showed a very uncharacteristic loss of poise. That's the trade-off with having such an atmosphere. There is often an incompatibility between passion and aplomb and both Rangers stars appeared to be over the level when presented with their opportunities. McCoist's, however, should arguably have led to a Rangers penalty. As Chanov saved from the close-range effort, the ball spun into the air and appeared to be punched over the bar by the chasing Besanov. Archie Macpherson was incandescent with rage but referee Ulf Eriksson from Sweden remained unmoved. If some fans thought that they could finally enjoy a breather for 15 minutes, they were mistaken, according to Ross. 'Half-time got swallowed up in this visceral memory of Ibrox just heaving. This thing of steel and bricks, an inanimate object, became alive. It started to have a heart and the East Enclosure just wouldn't let anyone have a rest.'

Kiev responded to the noise and pitch conditions early in the second half through the sheer class of Rats, driving and probing from midfield and eventually creating a half-chance for Blokhin, but Woods got down well to smother the danger. However, any immediate resurgence was short-lived as on 50 minutes Rangers were two ahead. Some patient midfield passing eventually led to the ball going out to Trevor Francis on the right. His control was instantly nonchalant, as if a local child had rolled the ball towards him as he was casually talking to a neighbour about hedge trimmers. His cross was deep to the back of the box where Falco, an experienced target man and a UEFA Cup winner with Spurs, headed the ball back across the Kiev line where McCoist had expertly worked his way in behind. His header was less than expert – it was a mistake – but it bamboozled the hapless Chanov and Rangers were now in control. McCoist's joy at the goal was visceral. He would, of course, later explain that he meant exactly that and was 'just testing the goalie out with my eyes' as the ball came off the opposite side of the head to where he directed it!

The threat from the Ukrainian side was not extinguished by the McCoist header, deliberate or not. One more goal and they would be back in control, and Blokhin was soon on a one-man mission to get it. With perhaps the only slack bit of Rangers play all night, this time by Butcher as he collected a pass on the edge of his own box and dawdled on the ball, Blokhin was in direct range. The last line of defence, however, was in top form and Woods simply ushered him out wide to relative safety and the chance was eventually blasted high and wide. He could do nothing but watch Blokhin's second effort as he breezed past McGregor before unleashing a shot that left Woods well beaten but thankfully flashed wide. Rangers didn't sit back and invite trouble as Durrant and Souness probed away for openings, and when they weren't on Durrant was prepared to try from distance. Robert Fleck, a substitute for the tiring Francis, was also unlucky as he badgered the Kiev defence, who were having a very different evening compared to having just McCoist to deal with in the first leg.

As the clock ticked on, Ibrox was cheering the most mundane of passes back to Woods and they'd get a collectors' item at the very end. With another late Rangers attack looking on, Souness collected the ball 35 yards from Chanov's goal but, with the game in its final minute, he chose to launch it all the way back and into the safe hands of his own goalkeeper. Not for the first time that evening, a cynical but legal option for the man who knew a thing or two about success in this competition, having won it on three occasions as a player. FIFA's patience with the back pass would last three more years when their technical report for Italia 90 showed that the Republic of Ireland goalkeeper Pat Bonner, in their dire 0-0 draw with Egypt, had the ball in his hands for a total of six minutes throughout the game. It was abolished two years later but celebrated like a pass of great beauty and intelligence here, which of course it was.

The final whistle was treated like a goal itself, with McCoist on the floor drained of all emotion and fans literally jumping for joy behind him. 'Souness! Souness!' boomed down onto the pitch from all corners of a stadium that had come alive throughout the evening. It was most appropriate as there was no way that this night would have happened without him. His decision-making throughout the rest of that season can, however, be questioned. The squad was infused with new blood over the next five months, but there was nothing up front to cover McCoist. This was especially an issue when Fleck and Falco were sold soon after this tie. Falco said in 2016, 'I might have been there a short time but it was still enjoyable and I will always be part of the history of a wonderful club. Sometimes things just don't work out in football and I suppose you could say that about my spell at Rangers.' When Ally McCoist suffered a knee injury before the quarter-final tie against Steaua Bucharest in March, he was forced to play in the first leg in Romania despite having undergone keyhole surgery just seven days before. From the final 13 games of the season McCoist scored six goals, three of which were from the penalty spot. No other Rangers striker got on the scoresheet in 1988 until Kevin Drinkell scored against Clyde in a Skol League Cup game that August.

It was arguably a very costly gamble. Many, correctly, lament the opportunity to win the trophy in 1992/93 but Rangers faced genuinely world-class sides. PSV Eindhoven, under a young Guus Hiddink, would win the European Cup in 1988, having only won three matches, none of which were from the last eight onwards. If Rangers had been better equipped to face Steaua then a semi-final against Benfica and a final against PSV was a far better prospect than Marseille and Milan five years later.

None of that removes the shine from this night over 30 years later, however. It rightly takes its place in the top 20 due to the context, the opposition and that ethereal connection that so many fans still have when reminded of the game itself. Not until Parma 12 years later would Rangers defeat a more cultured and gifted opposition. For those crammed into Ibrox that evening, screaming their hearts out, this match, perhaps even more than Aberdeen earlier that year, was a symbol that the Rangers really were back where we belonged.

18

Hibernian 1 Rangers 1

Scottish League Division One
Saturday 29 March 1975

'If you can achieve winning a league championship, that, to me, is the full test of the team and management because it is over the full season and you have a lot of problems you have to overcome.'
(Walter Smith)

It is arguably around this point where the answer to the original questions about resonance and what really makes a Rangers game great start to crystallise. There have been some incredible moments, memories and symbolic meaning brought out in the previous 32 chapters but only a quarter of those matches resulted in a trophy and only one of those was a league decider. Eleven of the next eighteen chapters will deal directly with Rangers winning something and there are three semi-finals to add to that. Half of the remainder of this book will centre around Rangers winning the league title, something that has for decades been at the very heart of the club's identity. In order for a Rangers game to be truly considered great, if it doesn't include silverware then it better have a remarkable story attached to it. Winning trophies, championships especially, is what Rangers is all about.

That came from Struth. Although not exactly a minnow of Scottish football when he took over as manager in 1920, Rangers trailed behind Celtic in terms of titles by 15 to ten. By the time he retired in 1954, Rangers were eight in front and, due in no small part to the standards he set for the future, the gap was still five when Stein's run of titles reached nine in 1974. However, that bigger picture was scant consolation to the Rangers fans who were living through a league championship drought that was unheard of in the club's long history. When would this end?

John Cowden was eight years old when the 1974/75 season kicked off and, coming from a strong Rangers family on both sides, the bug had him bitten so early on he was already going every week, home and away. How did his family cope with this never-ending barren spell? 'The reaction was split generationally. My father and uncles were scarred completely. We had gone close early in their league streak (1966/67 and 1967/68) and then close again in 1972/73 with that strong finish. There was a mystique around Stein's Celtic that they just knew how to get the job done, how to score late. It didn't matter if we had a great side, they had a great side plus one. My grandfathers' generation started going in 1925 so for the first 40 years of watching they had seen Rangers win the title 20 times and Celtic only four. So for them it was very much a case of "Who are these upstarts?" Celtic were on a par with Partick Thistle or Clyde. They weren't our rivals. Hibs would have been, but Celtic were really nothing before Stein.'

By the standards of 2019, the word 'barren' being used for a spell that included two European finals, one of which was successful, and a few domestic cups jars somewhat. Surely Barcelona helped get people through without a title? 'No,' was John's very straightforward answer on *The Time Capsule*. 'Barcelona was a sideshow, a huge and very enjoyable sideshow of course. The League Cup Final was the only win against them in 15 games for Waddell. It was pretty poor. Conn and Parlane burst their bubble and gave us a belief in January '73 and then of course the cup final, but in terms of dominance it's only the league that counts.'

As usual the season started slowly, so slowly in fact that Rangers were out of the League Cup by the pre-league season group stage and drew the first league game at Ayr United. What was unusual, however, was that the rot didn't set in as Jock Wallace's side won 11 of the next 12 league games, drawing only once away at Hearts and, perhaps crucially, beating Celtic at Parkhead for the first time since 1968. There would be stumbles, such as a 1-0 defeat at home to Hibs (who had already beaten us twice in that League Cup group) and a 4-3 loss at Airdrieonians before Christmas, but the 3-0 defeat of Celtic at New Year ensured enough momentum to leave Rangers a point clear as February started.

That month would see Rangers go out of the Scottish Cup to Aberdeen after extra time was required in the replay at Ibrox, but it also provided evidence of something necessary if a challenger was to take the crown of a long-term incumbent. Celtic were showing signs of creaking when they managed to draw twice from winning positions to the two bottom sides in the league, Arbroath and Dumbarton, the latter a 2-2 draw at home when they were 2-0 up at half-time. Experience is vital to win over the course of a long season, and when a team doesn't have much of that, it invariably requires a lot of encouragement from the side on its way down. In Scotland that appears to happen as winter turns to spring. At the start of February 1998, Rangers were three points clear at the top of the table in their quest to outdo Stein's achievement and make it ten titles on the spin. The legs were wobbling though, and by the middle of March Rangers sat five points behind in third place. Hopes were raised in April, however, as Celtic, completely unaccustomed to seeing out a title race, were pegged back. The Rangers legs and minds sadly weren't there and, despite Celtic drawing at Dunfermline when a win would have sealed the championship, there simply wasn't enough left in the tank to push them further.

In 1975 Rangers suffered from similar altitude sickness as they failed to initially capitalise on Celtic's stumbles with a 3-3 draw in the game in hand at home to

Kilmarnock, never once being ahead in the match. By this time John was concerned about managing to see out the month in one piece. 'You'd read the papers and they'd say "Rangers don't have the bottle. They can go so far, match Celtic stride for stride, but when they have to burst through that tape and say 'It's Ours!', they freeze." And it wasn't just the press saying that. The evidence seemed tangible that when we had the opportunity to build a lead, we would falter. The fear was that Celtic would pick back up and we had some tough away games coming up. There was no social media thankfully or the thing would have imploded.'

But Celtic wouldn't pick back up. Defeats for them at Hibs and Aberdeen in late February and early March sandwiched a run of three gritty wins for Rangers by the odd goal over Clyde, Hearts and St Johnstone. Next up was a trip to Dens Park where nerves would be tested to their very limit. Dundee went ahead in two minutes and Colin Stein (who had just returned to Ibrox for his second spell) was sent off for dissent in 37, which resulted in a pitch invasion. John Grieg hit the bar before half-time before then going off injured minutes after the re-start. Some fans said it and many more thought it. This is exactly the kind of situation, up against the scoreline, the extra man and the Dens Park slope, where the mental frailties would come to the fore. They didn't, however. A clever Tommy McLean goal and a late Derek Parlane winner snatched the full points.

'I was buzzing as I got out. We had heard rumours that Celtic were behind at half-time but that's all they ever were. There must have been 50 or 70 buses behind the Rangers end and you simply got on yours and you waited for the scores to come through on the radio. There are 46 games in the English league to wait through and then it came up … Celtic 0 Dundee United 1. Eight points clear and only six games to go. In my mind as a nine-year-old, it was going to happen. I don't think *everyone* believed it, but I did. It was a matter now of when and not if. It was a weird and scruffy game but that's what broke the dam.'

Rangers continued with a 3-0 victory over Motherwell at Ibrox and even better news came through the radios that day as Celtic had lost 1-0 in Airdrie. 'Now it was all set for the following week at Easter Road,' recalls John. 'For that week it was mental. It was the stuff of dreams. It was all I could talk about. My dad effectively had to tell me to shut up about it during dinner. Will we clinch it on Saturday? Maybe or maybe not. But it *was* going to happen that season. Some older fans were waiting for something ridiculous to happen, however – that we'd be deducted 20 points or something! It's the fatalistic streak in us Rangers fans in general and for those who had lived through their dominance. "It cannot be this easy surely?" Eleven years since we had won a title. We now only needed a point from Hibs. It's not like Aberdeen '87 where you could have gone into the final game with just a one-point lead if you lost.'

The day that a generation of Rangers fans had been desperate to see had finally arrived. 'If you wanted to be there you'd be there,' said John. 'You'd get in. Easter

Road was a big ground, the biggest outside Glasgow, with this massive double-banked terracing. You could feel immediately that this was a big game. The sheer number of people for an away game for one thing, easily 100 buses went. I'd been in big crowds, the '73 cup final being the biggest. However, there was something in the air because there was something really big on the line. It's an edge. It's an anticipation. It's not just the usual teenage/early-20s energy either. It went across all demographics. We *should* do this but are we gonna cock it up?'

As was the norm for British football in the 70s, violence was never far away and it was already heated on the terraces, on which Rangers fans dominated, before a ball had been kicked. 'It was something that, if you wanted as part of your match-day ritual, you could find it, but it's not something that ever affected me. I was taken to the enclosure that day as I normally would at Ibrox. In the 70s the enclosure was the quieter and safer part. I was on the opposite side from the trouble on the double bank. You'd watch it, you'd see it all. Cans, bottles, even snooker balls. But there was an acceptance that this was just what happened.'

Eventually the teams came out and the real action started. With John Greig still not fully fit, he had to make do with a place on the bench as Rangers lined up with Stewart Kennedy, Sandy Jardine, Alec Miller, Bobby McKean, Colin Jackson, Tam Forsyth, Tommy McLean, Colin Stein, Derek Parlane, Alex MacDonald and Derek Johnstone. Both sides had early periods of pressure, mainly through free kicks from distance; however, both Tommy McLean and Joe Harper had better sights at goal without success. But Hibs took the lead on 20 minutes when Ally McLeod headed down and in from a good Erich Schaedler cross from deep on the left-hand side. Stewart Kennedy had enjoyed an excellent season for Rangers but should have kept that out. His reputation would be defined two months later at Wembley, as Scotland farcically lost 5-1 to England.

It should have been two only a couple of minutes later, but Arthur Duncan snapped at the effort and fans would have been forgiven for thinking that it was going to be another one of those days. 'I always believed that it was going to be our day, but that Hibs would probably score first,' remembers John. 'By now we had a confidence that this team had a backbone. They had the full support of the crowd.' MacDonald had the ball in the net but there was to be no equaliser as Stein had been adjudged to have fouled in the build-up. Tensions on the terraces were being replicated on the pitch as a flare up in the box ensued when the Rangers defence were less than impressed at Iain Munro's challenge on Kennedy from a Hibs corner. Forsyth may have landed a punch but both were booked for good measure.

Rangers started the second half with much more intensity and pace than the first 45 minutes, with Stein thundering a shot towards goal that was tipped around the post for a corner in the first minute. Just before the hour mark it looked as if the perfect situation had been created by the sporting gods when Bobby McKean was tripped in the box by the Hibs goalkeeper Jim McArthur following a dreadful pass back by Shaedler. The stage was set for the Rangers captain on the day, Sandy Jardine, to score the goal that ended the wait. 'It was a very strange penalty,' said John. 'Even the corner he went for. All season he had gone for the same corner. On this day he changed his mind, second guessed himself perhaps. He came to the club in 1967 and had carried a lot of scars by this point. It was a real shame, but it didn't get us down.'

Five minutes later it happened. Jardine was involved in the build-up but it was all about the patience and cross from McKean and the powerful header at the near post from the returning hero Colin Stein. 'If you listen to how that generation describes Stein as a player, it is no different to how the current one describes Alfredo Morelos. He was a one-man wrecking crew. He will make chances, things will happen, he's rambunctious, he's temperamental and we love that kind of player, flaws and all. He was one of those heroes that a west of Scotland male loves.'

'It is one of those rare things,' recalls John, 'where I see it on the television and I hear Arthur Montford's commentary but if I close my eyes I see it from the other side where I was. Stein seems to come from nowhere, it's like a flash of blue. He seems to be outside the front post and bullets this header and that huge double bank … it's pretty difficult for people nowadays to imagine a) the size of it and b) what it's like on a standing terrace when a big goal goes in and there might be 15 or 20,000 there and it just goes up. It's a wondrous sight. The whole place just lifted up. Eleven years of hurt just disappeared with one header.'

There was little else of note on the field of play, save for a very late sentimental substitution when John Greig took to the fray for the final two minutes. It had been pre-arranged between Wallace and Jardine that, if the situation allowed, Jardine would come off so that not only was Greig on the pitch when the famous moment arrived, he would be captain. Greig, alongside Colin Jackson and Willie Mathieson, were the only ones left from the last Rangers championship side, the great treble-winning team of 1963/64 but only Greig, of that three, was an established part. He had been the Rangers captain through grim times on and off the pitch. He had led Rangers to cup glories that illuminated the darkness for a while but only now had he led them to domestic dominance. The be-all and end-all, of course, for any Rangers captain.

For John Cowden, it was just beginning. 'When it happens you try to take everything in but you never do. Nothing is wrong in the world for that instant and indeed for the half hour after it. Despite the sea of blue that flooded Easter Road on the way out, it was actually very calm. Like a second breath, post-coital even. There was a buzz but it was a mellow one. There was a guy hanging out of a window with a union flag, probably the most animated of everyone.'

For all the nervous energy that was burned by Rangers fans over the course of 1974/75, especially in that early spring period, it is no surprise that there was an element of blissful contentment immediately after the initial surge. It was, in the end, a coronation, rather than a dramatic climax. Only the mental damage of years gone by created any tension. 'The signs were there before Dens Park but we just wouldn't believe it. We couldn't look at it like a bookie would or like non-Old Firm fans were telling us. Looking back it looks so obvious but it's the scars that create the doubt.'

The following season would see the introduction of the brand new Scottish Premier Division, which meant that Rangers would be the first and last team to win the old Division One league title, which they did 35 times. The total at the time of writing is 54, and is still a world record that Rangers fans hold dear because it so clearly defines the club to the footballing world. Managers from Struth to Smith, via Symon and Souness, have understood and cultivated that. Those younger Rangers fans, for whom 55 will be their first, will no doubt see plenty of anxious older faces surrounding them, even if that coronation day comes before Easter Sunday, like it did in 1975.

17

Lyon 0 Rangers 3

UEFA Champions League Group Stage
Tuesday 2 October 2007

'Players lose you games, not tactics.'
(Brian Clough, post-Euro 2000)

Very few, if any, saw this one coming and any who say they did are lying. In the burning embers of New Year 2007, most expected the Walter Smith and Ally McCoist galvanisation to bring Rangers back to domestic parity – they knew the Scottish game better than anyone after all – but to imagine that night in Lyon? It might as well have been in Narnia. The Paul Le Guen debacle, an inherited mess from the end of the McLeish era that was tackled with very little financial support or managerial zeal, had been put out of its misery soon after the bells. Two Old Firm victories in March and May had provided hope that there would at least be a challenge in the new season and the early signs were promising. The European campaign had also started in line with expectations: a bit of a struggle. Smith had left Ibrox in the summer of 1998 with 13 trophies in only seven years but the shine of that memorable Champions League run in 1992/93 had been well and truly dulled by a stream of embarrassing disappointments to both the continent's elite as well as their also-rans. We spent as well as a challenging club from a second tier nation could do, and although it was dwarfed by Serie A and La Liga outlays, it was in line with the English Premier League at the time and way above the budgets of Grasshoppers Zurich, IFK Gothenburg, Steaua Bucharest, AEK Athens and Auxerre. Money wasn't the problem in the 1990s. Smith was tactically out of his depth.

He wasn't alone at the time on these isles. Initially it appeared that the post-exile English were going to pick back up in the early 90s where they had left off in the mid-80s, as Manchester United beat Barcelona to win the European Cup Winners' Cup in 1991 (the first season after the European ban was lifted), with no little élan sprinkled in with the traditional directness and width. It was a bit of a false dawn for United and for most of the other representatives from dear Albion. Ferguson's side never failed to provide excitement and entertainment, but there was the absolute chasing by Romarió et al in the Nou Camp before a series of disappointments, notably against Borussia Dortmund and Monaco, where the personnel was of equivalence but the organisation was not. Even the famous Champions League triumph in 1999 had more than a bit of fortune about it and was arguably more the result of a side on a mission, overflowing with self-belief, rather than detailed planning bearing fruit. The English national side had something of a rekindling in their home tournament in 1996, after the embarrassments of Euro '92 and the failure to even reach the World Cup in 1994, but even that was limited to some famous moments and, ultimately, glorious failure. Glenn Hoddle's arrogance against Romania in the group stage of the French World Cup ultimately cost them a more manageable knock-out path and their showing at the European Championships in 2000 was a tactical mess. There was quality available to Kevin Keegan, underlined by the blistering start in the opening match against Portugal when they were 2-0 up in no time, but the fact that they contrived to lose that match and the final group game against Romania was more to do with approach than anything else.

It was presumably Philip Neville's careless foul in the dying moments of the Romania game that cost his side a fatal penalty, that Brian Clough was referring to when asked to explain another early exit. Although Clough was good for a soundbite when his methods were working in the late 70s, his quips were, if still catchy, a touch more anachronistic when he hadn't won anything in 20 years (see also his thoughts on foreign players and women's football). Clough's focus on Neville's error ignored the story of why England had found themselves in a place in the game where human error could so easily torpedo their entire hopes. At the same championships in Portugal four years later, Jonathan Wilson relays a story in *Inverting The Pyramid* where he and his colleagues were discussing the need for Sven-Göran Erikkson to change the England shape, when one English writer said, 'They're the same players. The formation isn't important. It's not worth writing about.' It was an Argentinian contemporary who had to interject and make the point, slightly exaggerated for effect, that 'the formation is the only thing that's important. It's not worth writing about anything else,' however the anti-intellectualism and failure to grapple with the abstract was too deep within our footballing culture to make much impact. The lack of understanding around why a game takes the form that it does probably explains why British coverage spends so much time being outraged by moments of controversy and chance. There is only the capacity to deal with soundbites and not theses.

One British manager who didn't look out of place in the mid-90s was the Arsenal boss George Graham. For him, shape really was the only thing worth talking about and his Arsenal side managed to triumph over Parma in the 1994 Cup Winners' Cup Final and, although Graham had departed by then, his team would lose out at the same stage the following year against Real Zaragoza, only because of a freak goal by Nayim from almost the halfway line. There's only so much planning one can do after all. By that stage there wasn't much evidence of any planning when Rangers took to the field under the bright European lights. On the occasions we did make the Champions League proper, the twin individual threat of Laudrup and Gascoigne, so potent at home, was comfortably isolated by better sides than Motherwell, Falkirk and Celtic. As confidence on that stage eroded, year upon year, Rangers looked more and more a shadow of the side that came so close in 1993. 'Holidaymakers' was the impression made in the 3-0 defeat in Zurich in Match Day 1 of the group stage in 1996. The Swiss were being kind.

Initially 2007/08 didn't look much different. Qualification was secured but it was via a couple of scrappy showings against FK Zeta and a Red Star Belgrade that had seen better days. Those performances were more like Anorthosis Famagusta than Alania Vladikavkaz. The first proper match was at home to Stuttgart and it was going very much to type when Mario Gomez turned the ball in to secure a well-deserved German lead. The whole season arguably changed with the swing of Charlie Adam's left boot bringing Rangers level and creating a sense of havoc amongst the visitors that was compounded when Allan Hutton was downed in the box and Darcheville rattled in the winner from the penalty spot. A good start but with French champions Lyon on course for seven titles in a row and a Barcelona side just approaching true greatness, this was a vital three points in a search for third place and the chance to keep the European season alive in the UEFA cup.

Most of the damage of Smith's first spell was inflicted away from home, with a solitary point in a dead rubber in Dortmund all we had to show for our group efforts post 1993. Rangers visited the Stade de Gerland then, without much in the way of positive experience to fall back on. Although nowhere near the level of Marseille 15 years earlier, they still had that blend of players in their prime such as the Brazilian free kick maestro Juninho, along with Milan Baroš and Fabio Grosso, and youngsters who would be stars of the future like Karim Benzema. Rangers were level at the top of the table with just the one draw and one defeat in eight matches, but that draw had come at the weekend's tussle at Motherwell, with Jean-Claude Darcheville not recovering from a hamstring injury in time to take his place on home soil on the Tuesday night. Rangers lined up with Allan McGregor in goal and a back four of Sasa Papac, Davie Weir, Carlos Cuellar and the red-hot Alan Hutton at right-back. The now typical midfield five of Hemdami, Ferguson, Ferguson, McCulloch and DaMarcus Beasley supported Daniel Cousin in the lone role in attack.

The game started as most expected, with Lyon bright and dangerous from distance. Juninho caused havoc as early as the third minute when Hemdani had to block his shot and Weir had to snuff out the threat of a mazy Baroš run soon after. Then, on the 23rd minute, after some good work by Hutton down the right-hand side, against the run of play, Rangers won a corner. Beasley hung the cross perfectly just outside the six-yard box and Lee McCulloch's desire and strength pushed him higher than anyone else in that cluster to thunder the ball home with his head past the stationary Vercoutre in the Lyon goal. 'It came out of nowhere,' said Graeme Harvey, on his third European trip of the season. 'The stadium looked both modern and traditional but it helped create a good atmosphere in that lower tier in the corner, behind that goal. We knew that we'd be up against it so we had to grab the chances when they arrived.'

Lyon had plenty of purpose and intent but, with that midfield protecting an already solid defensive unit, they couldn't get close to McGregor's goal, instead being limited to shots from distance, the latest of which was a Kim Källström effort that fizzed wide of the Rangers goal. With Juninho around, Lyon were always keen to get a free kick somewhere inside his monstrous range, fairly or otherwise. The Brazilian's outrageous dive got Davie Weir a yellow card and an opportunity right before half-time. McGregor hardly moved as the ball smashed off his crossbar and Rangers cleared in order to keep the lead intact at the interval, although the breather didn't change much as Lyon's number eight was at it again from long range minutes after the restart. It was all intense pressure without ever getting too close. How long could we see that out with only a one-goal lead?

That question became redundant a minute after Juninho's latest attempt flashed wide. A Rangers break was once more instigated by Hutton as the full-back's cross found Cousin in the box. His control was instant but with two defenders in front of him, nothing immediately looked on. In a flash, Rangers were two in front. Cousin rarely procrastinated in the penalty area and only one more touch created the space he needed. Neither Lyon defender seemed threatened enough to show more urgency, and before they could the ball had been lashed into the back of the net. It was a magnificent example of modern centre-forward play – touch, strength, power – and one example of the frustration he caused within the support. If he played like that all the time ...

Four minutes later, celebrations of fist-pumping adrenaline at the thought of surely getting an away win turned to stunned laughter at what we were witnessing. Cousin's strength again made the difference, but this time in his own half as he beat Réveillère to launch another counter attack. The ball was a high, hanging 25-yard effort over the top of Cleber Anderson, which Archie Macpherson described it as a 'lovely little ball' as if he had dinked it forward whilst looking in the other direction. Beasley was first to it, with his initial touch making him favourite but still inviting Rémy Vercoutre to come out and claim it. Vercoutre stayed still and Beasley ended the contest with a simple finish.

Smith now had the match exactly where he wanted it and his unit stayed strong despite Juninho hitting the post, of course, and Anderson hitting the bar from a corner, the result of a brilliant McGregor tip over the crossbar. At times it felt too close for comfort, but those moments were sparse and from turns of genuine quality, which is to be expected in the Champions League. However, Lyon weren't able to create incessant pressure on the Rangers goal, the type of which leads to the inevitable collapse. For much of this incredible night, the Rangers defensive shape was solid.

'I properly started travelling away in Europe during the 2005/06 season,' said Graeme, who only missed one single match throughout that marathon season. 'So although we had some good results over the previous two seasons and had done well in Europe, this was entirely different level to any other result I had experienced. Even the old guard that I travelled with had the result up there with one of the best they had seen. Some of these guys have been travelling with Rangers away in Europe since the late 70s so I was very lucky to see a result like that so early in my days of following Rangers around Europe. I remember a lot of chat about the performance and you'd expect everyone to be discussing the three goals but it was all about the Cuellar–Weir partnership and how Hemdani had the game of his life pulling the strings.'

It was a result that not only shocked Europe but us too and yet, if we had looked back ten years, we shouldn't really have be so surprised. If we replace the performance in Lyon with an Old Firm away game, especially during the Tommy Burns era, it wouldn't look out of place at all. Regardless of league position or form, Rangers were never as well-organised and as disciplined as when we went there. Every year, at least once, Smith's side would show the same characteristics as this display in France. It was as if a match at Parkhead took on a nature of its own. For reasons which are unclear, Rangers were almost always cast by the media as the underdogs for those fixtures and, through the nine-in-a-row period, Smith never lost a crucial game there. At Ibrox, when we were expected to take the game to them, we seemed less sure of tactics and shape. When asked to take the initiative, we seemed uncomfortable and encouraged disaster. In the period 1991–1997, Smith took 26 points out of 36 away from home (adjusted to three points for a win) and only 15 from Ibrox. Eight wins away, at least one a season, compared with only three at home. In fact, up until the 1996/97 clean sweep of league matches, we had only had Trevor Steven's header in the New Year fixture of 1993 to celebrate.

Compare the organisation, discipline and attacking execution in Lyon to the shambles of Zurich, Athens *et al* and the difference is stark. So was the money spent, the talent available and the strength of our position at either time. The Rangers fans did, rightly, expect a great deal more in the 90s than we did on this night and therein perhaps lies the answer. Smith and his teams revelled in being the dark horse in the pressure games. He appeared to be more comfortable providing a rear-guard action than taking the initiative. This expectancy created a paralysis in the Champions League as well as being easy to tactically negate. There was no Gascoigne or Laudrup by the time Smith took back the reins, nor were Rangers spending the kind of money on a par with Europe's elite. The perfect conditions, therefore, only in retrospect, for a remarkable performance that set the tone for a remarkable season.

16

Rangers 2 Bayern Munich 0

European Cup Winners' Cup Semi-Final, Second leg
Wednesday 19 April 1972

'I think Rangers will be too strong before their big crowd.'

(Franz Beckenbauer, pre-match)

It was the kind of compounded pain that no other club support in Europe has endured. Borussia Dortmund avoided it in 1997 when they stunned Juventus in the Champions League Final in Munich only a week after their bitter Ruhr rivals, Shalke 04, had put the pressure on by defeating Internazionale over two legs in the final of the UEFA Cup. The extra-time loss to Bayern Munich in Bavaria's second city, Nuremberg, was bad enough for Rangers. It was the second failure in six years at the final stage to win the European Cup Winners' Cup, an understandable sporting frustration at not getting over a particular line. What made it doubly unbearable were the events in Lisbon six days previously. It wasn't only a trump card in the bragging rights for that summer, it was seen as further evidence that Celtic seemed to be adapting better to a changing sport, whilst Rangers had been caught on the hoof. Although director George Brown would later admit that they should have been ahead of the game in the post-war era, no one in the Ibrox boardroom had seen the need for modernisation at the time, trusting fully in the gentlemanly methods that had been so successful under Struth and Symon.

Berwick Rangers had caused shockwaves and panic at the start of that year that were still reverberating in Germany by May as Roger Hynd, out of position, famously toiled up front in that 1-0 final defeat. That Scottish Cup exit, widely regarded as the worst result in the history of the club, led to scapegoating instead of sober and calm analysis. Jim Forrest and George McLean, the two forwards on that day, were forced to carry the can, with the former being the most controversial. Forrest was only 22 years old and had scored 146 goals for Rangers in three and a half seasons. He'd never start for the club again following the trip to Berwick, which meant that Rangers went into that final against Bayern with a centre-half leading the line. Football, however, often has a funny way of providing opportunities to turn the tables.

Five years later, Glasgow once again stood on the precipice of having two clubs in European finals in the same week. 18 per cent of the city's population attended the football on that spring evening as the two '67 finals were replayed at home, with 80,000 people at Ibrox to watch Rangers v Bayern and 75,000 at Parkhead to see Celtic face Inter. (One poor soul had taken a portable television to Parkhead so he could watch the first 15 minutes of the Rangers game and keep in touch during lulls in play!) Much of the intervening years since Nuremberg had seen the Rangers high command at a loss trying to comprehend the changing dynamics of football. Without anyone quite as supremely gifted as Jim Baxter, the individual flair of yesteryear was no answer to an extremely well managed and organised Celtic. The experiment with the youthful Davie White as a replacement for the statesmanlike Symon was heavily criticised, not least by the man who would eventually take his job. Willie Waddell had won a league title as manager of Kilmarnock in 1964/65, the season that split the two great Old Firm dynasties, but was by then a sportswriter for the *Daily Express*. He answered the call to return to management, with Rangers top of the league, as, not for the first or last time, the club looked to past glories as the answer to future ones. Domestically, Waddell never really laid a glove on Stein, with the famous exception of the 1970 League Cup Final where a 16-year-old Derek Johnstone scored the only goal at Hampden, but that was the only win in 12 Old Firm matches, with eight defeats into the bargain including a clean sweep in 1971/72.

Europe, however, was different. This Rangers side wasn't lacking in ability, both with players at the peak of their careers and some very exciting younger talent coming through. However, the success of the Cup Winners' Cup run in 1971/72 was down to Waddell's utilisation of that talent as much as anything else. His meticulous preparation was a departure from the past, as Willie Mathieson explained in *To Barcelona And Beyond*. 'We could adapt depending on which team we were playing against and were tremendously prepared. Willie Waddell would give us a photograph of the player we would be up against and on the back he noted all of that player's strengths and weaknesses.' A little different then to a jolly appeal to work hard and, when in doubt, give the ball to Baxter.

Also important was Waddell's tendency to change the traditional role of his players, especially the front two, for the away ties, where Rangers never failed to score that vital away goal. This season was also one of the toughest series of draws in the club's European history, with a major nation represented in every round: Stade Rennais, third in Ligue 1 at the time, the first-round encounter, Sporting Lisbon, who were second in Portugal by the time of the crazy tie that had everything, the quarter-finalists Torino, fighting it out at the top of Serie A with city rivals Juventus, and then Bayern, Bundesliga leaders and eventual champions, were the toughest opponent of all. Conquerors of Liverpool in the second round, this was an exceptional side. Six of the team that lined up against Rangers would play at Wembley ten days later, as West Germany defeated England in the quarter-final of the European Championships, which they eventually went onto win, beating the USSR in the final. It was a West German side that would be world champions two years later, the same year that Bayern won the first of their three successive European Cups. Five of those six were crucial to both club and country. The goalkeeper Sepp Maier, sweeper and captain Franz Beckenbauer, attacking left-back Paul Breitner, midfield general Uli Hoeneß and the legendary marksman Gerd Müller. They were also well-known to Rangers, having knocked us out of the old Inter-Cities Fair Cup (which had started in its new guise of the UEFA Cup that season) in the first round the year before.

'The biggest hiding I've ever had in my life,' said Sandy Jardine about the opening salvos in the first leg in Munich, the match held at the Grünwalder Stadion, the home of 1860 Munich, with Bayern not getting into their iconic Olympic Stadium for a few more weeks. Every single outfield Bayern player had a shot on goal within the first 20 minutes and the onslaught ended with a beautiful Paul Breitner goal, being fed through by Müller. Rangers stood up strong, however, with Derek Johnstone, still only 18, stepping in front of the robust line of four in defence to mark the 'spielmacher' Hoeneß. Waddell's side weren't simply booked into their own half for bed and breakfast, there was an intent to get forward when possible and the risk was rewarded three minutes after the break when Colin Stein's low cross was deflected high into the roof of his own net by Rainer Zobel. Strangely then, according to Jardine, Bayern 'just shot their bolt' as Rangers held out to take a priceless 1-1 draw back to Ibrox. It was, by all accounts, a performance of great maturity against such pedigree. Hoeneß and Müller were marked out the game by Derek Johnstone and Colin Jackson, whilst Dave Smith at sweeper more than matched his opposite number, *Der Kaiser.*

Udo Lattek, the balding Bayern coach, was not in a bullish mood as he reached the Normandy Hotel in Renfrew before the game: 'We have little chance of winning tonight,' he told the press, presumably not his choice of words in a stirring address to his players before the match. 'Our chances are not good. To come to Scotland I wanted at least a two-goal lead. This is necessary in European football against a good team such as Rangers. We only drew and now it does not look so good.' The Rangers squad, meanwhile, were down on the Ayrshire coast where captain John Greig was instructed by assistant manager Jock Wallace to paddle in the freezing cold water in an attempt to try and heal a stress fracture in his right ankle. Incredibly, this was not a breakthrough in modern science and Greig missed the game, to be replaced by another Ibrox youngster, the 18-year-old Derek Parlane. The announcement of his inclusion over the public address system drew gasps from the huge crowd and he would be assigned the man-marking job on midfielder Franz Roth, scorer of the only goal in the final five years ago. Parlane would have the game of his life.

Rangers lined up, in all blue, with the same team that had defeated Torino, except that one notable change. Peter McCloy was in goal, Jardine and Mathieson at full-back, Derek Johnstone and Colin Jackson being marshalled by the sweeper and captain for the evening Dave Smith, Parlane joining Alex MacDonald, Tommy McLean and Willie Johnston in midfield, with Colin Stein leading the line. If the capacity Ibrox crowd was noisy with excitement and anticipation at kick-off then all records were going to be broken within a minute. Bayern had quickly lost possession from their own start and that nervousness was exploited soon after as Rangers probed with Johnston down the left before moving the ball over to Jardine on the other side. As Breitner stood off him, he let fly with a speculative left-foot shot that seemed to completely deceive Maier in the air and ended up in the top corner. 'A sensation!' roared Arthur Montford, barely above the din of the crowd.

It was the perfect start but Rangers didn't sit back on it. Bayern were not allowed to recover and didn't register a shot on goal until the 33rd minute, such was the role reversal from the start of the first leg. By that time, the tie was all but done. Colin Stein had hit the bar with a header and then on 23 minutes Parlane doubled the advantage. Koppenhöfer had put the ball out for a corner, under pressure from little else but his own mind, when a controlled back pass safely to Maier would have been the better option. Willie Johnston's cross wasn't dealt with properly by Maier, under close attention from Stein, but Parlane, although unmarked 12 yards from goal, was still no favourite to score. It was the instinct that would make him a hero of Ibrox Park over the decade as he latched onto the half chance with such power and accuracy. Five Bayern players, including two on the line, had no chance whatsoever as the ball rattled the underside of the bar and into the back of the net. It was Parlane's only contribution to that European run but it was crucial in finishing the most difficult of ties. There was a bravery about his performance, balancing the man-making job with the willingness to get into those dangerous areas himself. It could be explained by the naivety of youth but it was something that Waddell had no fear of, perhaps dating back to his own introduction as a teenager for Rangers against the mighty Arsenal at Highbury where he scored the winning goal. Parlane, of course, would be better known as a forward and it was this positional flexibility, like Derek Johnstone too, that gave Rangers a very different look in continental battle than ever before.

'After Derek's goal, they fell to pieces,' said Jardine years later, the perfect manifestation of which was an on-field set-to between Maier and Beckenbauer that filled everyone's hearts with joy. Hoeneß escaped the shackles of Johnstone only once, in the first minute of the second half, but McCloy superbly tipped his powerful effort over the bar. It was really all the Germans had to show as they became further and further squeezed out of the contest, the most notable evidence of which was Gerd Müller, the most prolific penalty-box poacher in world football, having to come back to collect the ball from Beckenbauer in order to get into the game, such was the job Jackson did on him. Outshining even the teenagers that night was perhaps the stand-in skipper, Smith. Another example of tactical flexibility, Smith's performance at sweeper, when he was normally a midfielder, received most of the plaudits, especially when you consider who his opposite number was. 'I've got a photo of the Kaiser and myself exchanging pennants which he's signed "to my friend Dave Smith",' he said to *The*

Guardian in 2014. 'He was a better player than me, no question, but that time I maybe had the edge.'

It is a fact that most of us run a mile from accepting, but the very nature of sporting rivalry, especially the tribal city rivalries of football, means that it is a relationship that is locked together by each other's successes and failures. The most glamorous of victories can be tarnished, even just slightly, by the other side matching it. The nightmare scenario is the one that occurred in Nuremberg where the disappointment was amplified. The sweet spot, however, is the kind of situation that happened on 19 April 1972 as a Dixie Deans strike crossed the bar and kept flying, as Celtic were knocked out on penalties by Inter. A sweet, sweet bonus ball for the Rangers support to enjoy, by now back in the house or in the pub, watching on the box. An incredible night for Scottish football, and Scottish policing(!), had ended with some kind of redress and revenge for a fanbase searching everywhere for some light.

The standard of the game has moved on in step with time. Rangers faced some mighty opposition in the 1970s but none would be able to live with the fitness, strength, pace and technique of the Serie A opposition in the 1990s, for example. We can only assess these things relative to the context of the day, however, and in that case, given the strength that this Bayern Munich side had and would demonstrate on the domestic, European and international stage almost immediately, there is a very strong argument to suggest that this is the greatest opponent that any Rangers team defeated.

There wasn't much time to revel in it, however. Every bear was searching for travel agents. Every bear was booking for Barcelona.

15

Kilmarnock 1 Rangers 5

Scottish Premier League
Sunday 15 May 2011

'This club is different. This is Rangers Football Club.'
(Walter Smith)

No single figure dominates this poll like Walter Smith does. 21 of the 50 games chosen involve him as manager and in a further eight he was assistant to Graeme Souness. Not since Bill Struth has such an indelible mark been made on the club than by the man with 21 trophies to his name, only seven behind the great man himself. He is the modern godfather of Rangers, universally beloved. It wasn't always that way, of course. The fickle nature of football fandom in general, in addition to the high standards of this club's support, meant that the glory years of 1991–1998 were not always serene. Smith was the man who delivered nine but whose ill-disciplined and jaded side dropped ten. He was the man responsible for giving us such European pride in 1992/93 but such embarrassment on the continent for the next five years. The man who regularly skewered Celtic and Aberdeen but had budgets that sometimes dwarfed both combined. It would be wrong to paint this period as a constant love-in and that tension was often felt both ways.

The passage of time, and its natural distortion, is one reason why that tension is no longer detectable; however, the main reason is the quality of Smith's second spell. Far less of a blockbuster, under far more trying circumstances and constantly in the role of underdog rather than incumbent king, this term of four and a half seasons where he gathered up eight trophies gained the manager far more love and respect than his first period when he scooped 13. It is a view shared by no less than Sir Alex Ferguson. 'What he has achieved this time, in his second spell, is better than the nine-in-a-row success. And to do it this year, taking everything he has had to deal with, away from football, into account … well, I can't speak highly enough about him.' What Smith had to deal with – indeed what Scottish football had to deal with – in his final season of 2010/11 could fill an entire book in itself.

That season was not one for the football purists with the action on the field forever punctuated by bitter acrimony off it. Referee strikes, death threats to officials and managers and a Holyrood summit, led by First Minister Alex Salmond, who said, without a hint of irony, that 'people in positions of responsibility must – absolutely must – behave responsibly.' All of this was painted on a backdrop of ever darkening clouds over Ibrox as the interminable and ultimately toxic takeover by Craig Whyte rumbled on. It was no surprise at all that Walter Smith decided that, for him personally, enough was enough.

Seven Old Firm games in three competitions didn't exactly help dampen the simmering resentment between the two clubs. Rangers only won twice, the opening league game of the season and the CIS Insurance League Cup Final. Celtic won three times, two comfortable league encounters and the Scottish Cup replay at Parkhead where the lid blew off completely. When Rangers won 3-1 at Parkhead in October, the 13th straight league win in a row at the start of that season, the narrative was about refereeing. Only the week before, Neil Lennon, in his first full season in charge, had gone public with visceral criticism over Dougie McDonald's decision to overturn a penalty in Celtic's 2-1 win away to Dundee United and piled the pressure on Willie Collum ahead of the arrival of Rangers. Lennon's rage was no lighter following the defeat and he fell into the trap that almost every manager in every league around world succumbs to when they call out officialdom: selective memory. Collum could have shown Lee McCulloch a second yellow card for pulling back Georgios Samaras and the penalty he awarded Rangers was on the softer side. However, the righteous indignation schtick only holds weight if you recognise the decisions that you benefitted from, including the decision not to send off Anthony Stokes for an horrific challenge on Sasa Papac in the very first minute.

It was an early insight into one major reason why Rangers would win that title: the difference in the two dugouts. Smith carried years of experience with him and, although mellowed somewhat, his sharp tongue was still active but used with judicious prudence. He was a statesman. Lennon was very much the opposite, the midfield terrier, whom opposition fans always loved to hate, hadn't really accepted that he was no longer there to kick every ball and that there was now a need to be more detached. A perfect example of this was the Scottish Cup fifth-round replay at the start of March. Celtic deservedly won the match 1-0, and after losing the goal Rangers lost their head and some numbers as Steven Whittaker, Madjid Bougherra and El Hadji Diouf were all red-carded. At this moment Lennon held the cards. Celtic had knocked Rangers out of one competition, were five points ahead in the title race and had an aggregate score of 8-2 over the four fixtures held in the space of two months. Instead, however, he sought to get involved with Diouf on the trackside, which led Ally McCoist, then delegated the 'cup manager' role in preparation for his upcoming promotion, to tell Lennon something in the region of 'Don't you ever fucking speak to my players like that again!' and all hell broke loose, thus prompting the Scottish Government to get involved so that they could secure an easy Public Relations win. He could and should have walked away, laughing even, at the fact that Rangers were imploding under the heat. He wasn't, however, in full control.

The League Cup Final later that month would highlight the second reason that Rangers eventually triumphed at Rugby Park. Much of Smith's travails in that sticky period between January and March came from the sale of Kenny Miller, who had been in red-hot form that season, and the injury to summer signing Nikica Jelavić. As winter turned to spring, however, the Croatian was back in the groove and his winner at Hampden, with the ball spinning from post to post, made him an instant hero and really helped kickstart a push to the end of the season, igniting form from the likes of Kyle Lafferty and Steven Naismith too. The game also saw another refereeing *volte-face* as Craig Thomson gave Rangers a penalty for a foul by Thomas Rogne on Jelavić only to be surrounded by Celtic players and subsequently change his mind and book the Croat for diving. Smith was angry but was perfectly placed to make the comment that 'if you are good enough, you will win, despite a refereeing decision.'

Defeat for Rangers at home to Dundee United meant that Celtic were still ostensibly in control as the league split for the final five games of the season. A win at Ibrox at the end of April would have practically sealed it for Celtic and they were presented with a gift late on when Steven Davis was adjudged to have brought Stokes down in the box and it was Thomson again who pointed to the spot, this time without changing his mind. Allan McGregor's fantastic save from Samaras kept Rangers top by a point but, with one game more in the bank, destiny was still in Lennon's hands. What happened at Inverness ten days later was a fine illustration that it is one thing for Rangers or Celtic to cope with the intensity of the Old Firm battle, but it is quite another to go to difficult grounds and consistently grind out points. There were no officials to blame in this instance as Caley Thistle deservedly won 3-2 and Lennon was left kicking water bottles in the air and suggesting the remainder of Rangers' opponents wouldn't try hard enough.

It was straight out of the Ferguson playbook from 1996, but Walter Smith was no Kevin Keegan. Perhaps he wouldn't even have taken the bait in 1991 when he was just starting out in the hot seat, but by this time, lacking the need to prove anything to anyone, least of all a jack-in-the-box rookie, there was no bite. He responded about the lack of respect shown to Scottish football, of course, but cooly reiterated that it was the long duration of a season that decided a title and that Rangers wouldn't lose focus in its final stretch. They didn't, swatting Hearts and Dundee United aside at Ibrox, the latter providing the final home farewell for Smith before business was to be concluded at Rugby Park, Kilmarnock, on the Sunday. His final battle. Just the win required to earn the tenth league title of an incredible career.

Rangers fans jammed the M77 and took over Rugby Park like an invading army. The two stands behind the goal were the official away sections, with the longer trackside stands supposed to be mainly the provision of the home support. David Edgar was one of thousands of bears who had a main stand ticket and the test of his discretion would be earlier than anyone imagined. Smith sent out a pretty, attacking line up for his final-ever game, stating his intent from the off. The usual defensive unit of McGregor, Papac, Weir, Bougherra and Whittaker had Maurice Edu and Steven Davis in front of it and then a fairly fluid and interchanging four of Jelavić, Lafferty, Naismith and the youngster Gregg Wylde. 'On you go Rangers,' said Ian Crocker on commentary. 'But if there's any hint of a problem today,' he continued, 'Celtic, it's over to you.'

There wasn't. There were already two attempts at long balls up to Lafferty within the first 20 seconds before some head tennis in the middle of the park. From a lovely flick by Jelavić, Davis instinctively saw a third opportunity to get him clear behind Manuel Pascali and bearing down on Cammy Bell in the Killie goal. Two bounces, one touch and the ball arched perfectly over the goalkeeper's reach and in under the bar. 46 seconds on the clock. 'I had said to young Stuart McColl beforehand, "If we score, don't lose your shit. A wee smile and a wink. There's no point in getting chucked out,"' recalls David. '40 seconds gone and we instinctively reacted and immediately caught ourselves but then saw 80 per cent of the stand rise. It was the Kilmarnock fans that then just got up and sat somewhere else. They left us to it, together. It was then the scarves came out the jacket and you can see on the tv that it now looks like a home game.' Lafferty started his celebration with a facade of calm arrogance before it all erupted from within him and the rest of his team-mates who piled on behind. A season of incredible tension and aggravation was coming to an end and it was exclusively on our terms.

Despite Lennon's insinuations, Kilmarnock came back at Rangers immediately with a little bit of pressure, possession and set plays, but when Davis released Naismith from the edge of his own box, the champions were about to pounce. Wylde was next to be involved out on the left and he showed patience under close attention from Clancy before squaring it back to the former Kilmarnock striker Naismith. As Jelavić peeled off, so did the Killie defence, expecting another pass. They got one, but it was perfectly into the left-hand corner of Bell's goal. Within five minutes, Rangers had a two-goal lead. For a side that hadn't conceded an away goal in six games, all the nerves and worries about a last-day disaster disappeared in jig time. It was the stuff of dreams, not a start anyone had realistically imagined and two minutes later it was about to get even better.

Again it was Davis who started the move, involved in all three opening goals, and he once more set Naismith on the move. His ball to Jelavić was decisive and spread the Kilmarnock defence with the waiting Lafferty on the other side. Rangers were too quick for them, thinking and moving at a rate they simply couldn't cope with. The Croatian and the Ulsterman shared two touches of the ball and Rangers were 3-0 up. The noise in the crowd was different. If the other two induced sounds of hope and anticipation, this one brought about a full stop. Walter Smith cheered fanatically up in the stand, like he once did in the 1950s when he was introduced to a life-long love. 'Everything was all in the zone,' said David. 'Individually and collectively. A side that knew that this was their day and this was their destiny.' The game had received the usual 'Helicopter Sunday' hype all week. It was over in seven minutes.

The early Rangers blitz had settled the title race but had created a sporting vacuum, if not for the next 83 minutes, then certainly the remainder of the first half, save for a few Rangers corners, a Davis shot that hit the post and some fine McGregor saves from long range. Ally McCoist talked on television at half-time about the need to lift the levels again as they understandably dropped after the seventh minute. As so often in that final stage of the season, Smith's troops carried out his instructions to the letter. Fittingly, for his own contribution that season as well as his influence on the other attackers, it was Jelavić who got the fourth from a free kick just outside of the box. It was turning into the kind of day where there was a general sense of inevitability for all of those watching in the ground or at home. It looked so straightforward as he somehow powerfully caressed the ball high into the corner and was able to take his well-deserved bow. The fifth came four minutes later from Naismith pressing deep inside the Rangers half and then breaking at pace once he won the ball. In Smith's final three championship-winning seasons you could time Kyle Lafferty's form by the daffodils and tulips. For the third spring in succession he turned up with vital goals to get Rangers over the line and, with a bit of instinct and fortune, he found himself on the end of the Naismith through ball to poke it beyond the onrushing Bell for his hat-trick.

James Dayton's freekick that defected off the posterior of Maurice Edu and into the net is forgotten by many today and most fans pretty much instantly, save the raging Allan McGregor who berated his wall as if the goal had meant all the difference in the world. Naismith rattled the woodwork with one more blast but all anyone in Rugby Park wanted for the best part of half an hour was the final whistle and for the celebrations to begin.

For a generation of Rangers fans this was the 17th league championship they had seen won but few have felt as sweet. That, and the fact that, at the time of the poll, it was the most recent, make it an understandable selection so high on the list. 'Everything that happened during that season and the fact that it was Walter's last would have made this sweet anyway,' reflected David, 'but there was this unavoidable sense of foreboding about the future of the club. I therefore had an acute appreciation of the moment. This was amazing and I was going to savour it because who knew exactly what the future had in store.'

Once the dust had settled, Smith took the opportunity to say his piece on the issue that had permeated the whole campaign. 'I hope Celtic realise that if their team is good enough, they will win. If they are not good enough, they'll not win – and they can't look at anybody else, whether it's referees or any other influence. I don't say that in any smug way. I just felt it set the tone for what has been a poor season for our country, in terms of publicity.'

It wasn't a poor season for Rangers or Walter Smith, however, no matter the concern about when the next time we'd feel that way again would come. F. Scott Fitzgerald once thought that there were no second acts in American life. Walter Smith had no fairytale ending to his first act as Rangers' manager, being told to go and then watching on as his players ran out of life at the final hurdles. Given the opportunity again nearly a decade later, he ensured that he went out in his own way: by choice and holding aloft the biggest prize in Scottish sport.

Smith often said how fortunate he was to get another chance to manage Rangers. Not as fortunate as we were.

14

Rangers 2 Celtic 2

(After extra time, Rangers won 5-4 on penalties.)

Scottish Cup Semi-Final
Sunday 17 April 2016

'Illusion is the first of all pleasures.'
(Voltaire, 'La Pucelle d'Orleans')

The Scottish Cup Final of 1995 was not a classic. Alex MacDonald's Airdrieonians were in their second cup final in three years but were edged out 1-0 by a nervy Celtic side, winning their first trophy in six seasons. 'Celtic winning the Tennents Scottish Cup is only the beginning. We're back on form,' roared the club newspaper advert the next day, urging fans to buy season tickets for the newly refurbished Parkhead.

It wasn't. The relative Rangers slumber of 1993–1995 (only the three domestic trophies from six), to cope with the exhaustions from the exhilarating spell of 1991–93, had come to an end and it was arguably this afternoon that did it. Celtic had come close earlier that season but had lost the Coca-Cola League Cup final in comical fashion to Raith Rovers on penalties at Ibrox, but now a watchful Rangers had to take heed and put the foot down. Nearly £10m was spent that summer, £4.3m of which on Paul Gascoigne from Lazio, and the results were instant as Celtic failed to win a thing over the next two crucial seasons and only tasted Old Firm victory once in the next eleven games. Be careful what you wish for.

Or rather, be careful how loud you trumpet that initial, transitory success. Over two decades later it was another post-Hampden act of hubris that didn't quite have the desired effect but this time the roles had been somewhat reversed. For the first time since the horror of 2012, Rangers fans had genuine reason to believe that there was light at the end of the tunnel. The first two years in the lower leagues had brought the expected promotions but little else, especially in the cups where there were more than a few embarrassments that can only be talked about now in hushed tones in a darkened room. The journey back to the top flight stalled in 2014/15 as Rangers failed to climb out of the Championship via any route and used three managers (Ally McCoist, Kenny McDowall and Stuart McColl) in the process. The shame of losing the Challenge Cup semi-final (a competition purely the preserve of lower league clubs) away to Alloa Athletic when Rangers were 2-0 up with 18 minutes to go and contrived to lose 3-2 in normal time, was threatened when a beleaguered side were finally drawn against Celtic in the League Cup semi-final two months later. The fact that so many in the Rangers support were happy enough with just a 2-0 defeat perhaps sums up the situation at the time perfectly. On and off the park, this truly was the darkest point before the dawn.

The brightness of that on-field dawn was provided by Mark Warburton, who arrived at Ibrox in the summer of 2015 with a decent reputation in youth football and some excellent work with English Championship side Brentford. The assessment of managers at a club is usually coloured by the end of their spell, as the distinction between Walter Smith in 1998 compared to 2011 would testify. It is easy, therefore, to paint Warburton's time as Rangers manager as a disappointment; however, as much as the end of it certainly was, it would be unfair to dismiss the fact that the majority of that first season gave fans not only hope, but genuine enjoyment watching their team on the park. Although the lack of a second or third plan would become a problem soon enough, the fact that we seemed to have any plan at all was a breath of fresh air as Rangers started the season on fire, hammering our rivals that season Hibs 6-2 at Easter Road in the first game of the Challenge Cup and then winning the first 11 league games. The return to Leith brought about the first defeat, as well as early signs of fragility at set plays, and also precipitated a wobble in form. An eight point lead had been whittled down to just three by the time Hibs came back to Ibrox, but Rangers responded to the pressure, and an early concession, to win a brilliant game 4-2. Hibs didn't just wobble, they crashed and burned, as Rangers stormed ahead into the spring with a 17 point lead over Hibs in third place as they made their way to Falkirk in the middle of March.

Alarm bells should have sounded that night as Rangers, 2-0 up and cruising with 18 minutes left, managed to lose 3-2. The echoes of Alloa may have been there but they were faint. Even the failure to wrap up the league title and promotion back to the top division at Kirkaldy a fortnight later, when Rangers contrived to concede a 94th minute Harry Panayiotou equaliser seconds after Wes Foderingham had saved a penalty, was dismissed by some as just one of those things in football. The league was a certainty anyway, it would be won at Ibrox against Dumbarton three days later. Instead the whole club's focus was on the Scottish Cup semi-final, and had been since a brilliant 4-0 win over Premier League Dundee on 5 March had booked the place against Celtic. Rangers wouldn't be favourites, literally in a different league and a team that had been re-built with just over a million pounds, but in the space of 13 months the support had gone from fearing a double-figures defeat to thinking that there was a puncher's chance of success. A success that the fans had been craving for four years: the sign of all signs that we were on the correct path back to where we belonged.

'We were so nervous,' recalls Caroline Morrison. 'We left from Partick on a bus from The Rosevale. I don't think we even had a drink before we left. I was still of the mindset that I just wanted to escape a doing! I didn't think truthfully that we could get the result that we ended up getting.' Her friend Marina Bannatyne, however, was more positive:

'I thought we could win, and because I wanted it so badly that's where my nerves came from. I'm confident that we will win every game, until the thing kicks off!' The mood on the bus, however, was jovial, as Marina explained: 'It wasn't long before this game that Celtic had written to their fans to remind them about hygiene standards so we all had surgical masks on for the trip. I shared a picture on my Facebook of the two of us with the masks on and someone complained that they were sectarian! Sectarian surgical masks! This fixture does weird things to people.' The previous season's game was hardly even billed as a contest, the attraction to the neutral was perhaps only how many Celtic would score. Now the biggest fixture in British football seemed to be back, with Crystal Palace players watching the game on mobile phones as they took their first steps on the Emirates pitch before the warm-up began.

The performances during the six fixtures in between this semi-final and the quarter-final always felt like Rangers were a team deliberately stuck in second gear just trying to do enough to win and then get to Hampden unscathed. It wasn't a ridiculous notion at all as Warburton was ultimately only able to choose five substitutes when seven spaces were available to him, due to injury and eligibility. One of those missing through injury was Harry Forrester, who had started the rout against Dundee in only 13 seconds, and he was a big miss. In fine form that spring, Forrester was injured at Hampden only the previous weekend as Rangers finally won the Petrofac Challenge Cup with a comfortable 4-0 victory over Peterhead. Rangers were stripped to the bare bones but had been keeping energy in reserve. Everyone felt confident that they wouldn't disgrace themselves, that they'd throw absolutely everything at this Celtic side, soon to be champions for a fifth season in succession, although in lieu of any challenge whatsoever and not having been able to complete a domestic treble in four seasons with a clear run. Ultimately, it was a free hit.

Hampden, never known for cultivating great atmospheres since its refurbishment in the mid-90s, was a frenzy before kick-off. The famous old bowl was filled with noise and colour, bangs and smoke, anticipation of what was before us all. Finally this fixture was back with a purpose. Warburton's side was as expected, with Forrester being ruled out during the week and Martyn Waghorn, the club's top scorer that season, a longer-term problem. Foderingham took his place in goal as he did for every single competitive game that season, behind a back four of James Tavernier, Rob Kiernan, Danny Wilson and Lee Wallace. Andy Halliday and Dominic Ball were tasked with providing midfield cover, with Jason Holt delivering energy and support to a front three of Dean Shiels, Barrie McKay and Kenny Miller. Celtic combatted the 4-3-3 with a 4-2-3-1, which saw Gordon in goal behind Lustig, Boyata, Mulgrew and Tierney in defence, the double-pivot of Brown and Bitton and Roberts, Johansen and Mackay-Steven feeding Griffiths in attack.

The previous encounter had been won in the tunnel or in the obligatory handshake procession, where the Rangers team looked cowed and like they'd rather be literally anywhere else. The tone to these games can often be set here and it couldn't have been more different on this April afternoon as Warburton's side had their chests out and had the look of a team who couldn't wait to get started, none more so that lifelong fan Halliday, whose look to the Celtic captain told the television viewers all that they needed to know. The game itself played out in a slightly different fashion, with Celtic clattering into early tackles. Gary Mackay-Steven was especially lucky not to be booked inside three minutes for a tackle that might have brought him a yellow card in any other fixture, and Rangers were content to keep the ball and probe for openings. One such fell to Kenny Miller in the sixth minute from a brilliant through ball by McKay but Gordon stayed strong enough to block his goal-bound effort. Celtic broke with purpose, with Brown going inches past the post when he should have scored. Celtic were fortunate again not to pick up a yellow card soon after, this time the already struggling Boyata who clattered Jason Holt to the floor. The resulting free kick, however, led to a moment that so many had been waiting for.

If anyone ever needed an example of the perfect Kenny Miller goal, it was this one. First to react to a break of the ball in the box, no time to think, an instant execution of technique with no other considerations to get in the way. The original free kick by Tavernier was a poor one and the second delivery from Halliday, once the ball was worked over to the other side, wasn't much better. However, Scott Brown's intervention was perfect and laid the chance on a plate for Miller, who had escaped the stationary Boyata, and filled his boots. For Caroline the ecstasy turned to anxiety, as it so often the way on these occasions. 'It was crazy where we were in the South Stand but then my initial thought was "oh this is a very early goal! How do we hold on for the rest of the 90 minutes?"' All of this in only 16 minutes. There is no fixture in world football where the pace of the game feels absolutely frantic but the clock, if I may quote *Blackadder,* appears to be going at the pace of 'an asthmatic ant with some heavy shopping'. An Old Firm game has its very own theory of relativity.

The remainder of the first half saw a familiar pattern being weaved. Rangers happy to be on the front foot, looking for options down either flank with the over-lapping full-backs and Celtic happy to wait and counter at pace. From one counter in the 33rd minute, the chance of the season fell to loanee Patrick Roberts. Intelligent hold-up play by Mackay-Steven allowed Griffiths space to get a shot in. It beat Foderingham but not the post as it rebounded back into the Rangers penalty area where the wide-man was waiting. As a fan, the brain automatically adjusts in these moments and accepts that there's going to be an equaliser. When it becomes clear that the only netting the ball hit was the side, it felt like a bonus rush. The Rangers keeper did well to get back quickly but there was still a gaping goal for Roberts to pass the ball into. It was a quite incredible moment. 'It was almost as good as a goal,' Marina recalled. 'How different the game could have been if they had scored at that point.' Rangers continued to see most of the ball, 78 per cent of it in fact for the last ten minutes of the half, prompting

Sky's studio guest Maurice Johnston to question, with gleeful delight, whether he was watching Barcelona or Rangers.

Celtic responded well after the interval. Having not forced a single corner in the first half, they managed four in the first four minutes of the second and from the last of those came the equaliser. Sviatchenko, a first-half substitute for the disastrous Boyata, rose above Wilson and powered a header into the net, somehow managing to beat the towering presence of Jason Holt guarding the goal line. The momentum was now with them, but despite the pressure they couldn't make it count. For most of the second half the two sides looked a little punch drunk from the exertions of the first hour, with some careless play in the final third and a general lull in proceedings. Rangers were expected to tire, the options from the bench were thin, and there was a concern in the stands that we had spent our chance as the final minutes were dominated by Celtic, with Bitton perhaps having the best chance with a close-range header with only a minute of normal time remaining. The ball flashed wide and we would all get 30 extra minutes of this tension to savour.

With Kenny Miller substituted for Nicky Clark, Rangers had no out ball in extra time and no real experience of success in this fixture, especially in the creative areas of the field. Many felt that penalties, an unknown quantity in competitive Old Firm football, would be our only chance, unless of course someone was able to produce something really special. It came from an innocuous complaint over a throw just inside the Celtic half. Craig Thomson gave the throw-in to Rangers, having missed the slightest of contact from James Tavernier, and the game continued to flow. Tavernier worked the ball inside to Barrie McKay who, surrounded by Celtic jerseys, turned around to assess options ahead. With no pass available and four men bearing down on him, there was only one to choose. McKay will never score a better goal in his career, both in terms of technique and importance. 'What a goal!' said Marina. 'The kind to win a cup tie. We are going to do this now. It *is* going to happen here.' In much the same way as the Miller goal and Roberts miss, this appeared to knock Celtic for six as they played out the remainder of the first period in a rather anaemic fashion.

Yet again, however, they re-started with a kind of focus that a rapidly tiring Rangers side lacked. Less than a minute had elapsed in the second period of extra time and Celtic were on level terms again. Tierney strolled past the ghost of Nicky Law on the left-hand side and his cut-back found substitute Tom Rogic in enough space to just pass it into the Rangers net. 'I'd like to say that it was unbelievable but it was exactly what I feared might happen,' recalled Caroline, 'especially with the way both teams started the second half of normal time. From then on we were fresh out of energy and ideas and there was little else we could do but try and absorb this pressure and take it to penalties.'

Penalties it would be, despite an extremely close call from a Griffiths free kick which hit the bar and then the back of Foderingham and rolled past the post instead of over the line. Lee Wallace won the toss and chose to go first, despite that meaning they would be taken at the Celtic end of the ground. It was statistically the correct decision as the majority of shoot-outs are won by the team who step up immediately. There was very little doubt about Halliday, reliable from dead ball situations, as he sent Gordon the wrong way as the ball nestled safely in the corner of the net. Charlie Mulgrew had a similar reputation and his penalty was equally clinical.

There was a time earlier in the season where a James Tavernier free kick felt like a penalty, such was his prowess from a set piece. That calmness deserted him as he skied his penalty over the bar, handing Celtic the advantage. 'I could hardly watch, could hardly speak. I had enough focus just breathing!' said Marina on *The Time Capsule*. That was it for me. I sat down, legs unable to prop me up. Listening for the reaction was now preferable to watching the potential agony. Parity was instant. I heard and watched the celebrations around me as Callum McGregor's effort smashed the bar and pinged directly back out.

Barrie McKay's effort lacked the sweet spot of his earlier strike but it managed to squeeze past Gordon, creating a kind of audio tennis as the Celtic support thought it had been initially saved, only for the cheers from the other end to welcome the final outcome. Nir Bitton, who at one stage in the game seemed unable to continue due to a hamstring issue, was very able from the spot as Celtic drew back level. Miller's replacement Nicky Clark never looked confident. His penalty wasn't the worst but Gordon guessed correctly and it was the perfect height to stop it going in. His father Sandy reacted in the stands like we all did. Thankfully, Scott Brown's effort was even worse. A huge run up that seemed to suggest a good old-fashioned blast but a change of heart led to a feeble shot which Foderingham saved with relative ease.

'The Celtic captain misses, what will the Rangers captain do?' asked Iain Crocker on commentary. The answer was never in doubt as another reliable ball striker put Rangers back in front. This meant that Leigh Griffiths, who had missed four penalties that season and had said in the run-up that he was off them, had to score to keep Celtic alive. He did, and onto sudden death we went. Much of Rangers' transfer activity in the summer of 2015 was based around young loanees and one of those was tasked next with handling the most extreme of pressures. Perhaps it helps when you don't have a lifetime of emotional baggage locked up in the outcome, but Gideon Zelalem looked like he was taking one in training and let the Celtic fans know how easy he found it. Foderingham got close to Lustig's penalty but not close enough, and so the agony continued.

My friend Stevie, an adult, kept me, a child, updated from my position of looking directly at the floor at each penalty. 'Who's up next?' I asked. 'I'll tell you later,' was the response on this occasion. Nicky Law was never the most popular Rangers player of all time with a support who value courage as much as skill. Once again, despite the doubts of those watching on, the penalty was exquisite. A man felt to be invisible too often in games had turned up on stage when the lights were brightest.

It had started with the previous Celtic penalty but it was louder now. Replacing the traditional boos and whistles during an opposition player's run up, the Rangers support instead turned to the defiant hymn of 'Derry's Walls' as Tom Rogic picked up the ball at the end of the loneliest walk in the football. It was over, in more ways than one. 'Derby Day in Glasgow belongs to Rangers. They've beaten Celtic and quite simply there is no better feeling than that and after the last four years Rangers are loving this.' It is Crocker's style to ham it up, to make the most mundane seem life-changing. Barry Davies he isn't; however, on this occasion he summed it up perfectly. The journey back would still have struggles to overcome, but on that day Glasgow did belong to Rangers and that's all we needed to experience again.

There have been few matches in history when Rangers' players have celebrated like that at the end of a game. Penalties add to that closing drama of course, but even Fiorentina was more sedate than this afternoon. Loan players and new signings who had no experience whatsoever of playing against Celtic were wild with delight and adrenalin. A huge obstacle had been overcome and naturally we couldn't resist extrapolating. 'It didn't feel like we were that far away in terms of standards, as we were continually told we were, so yeah we bought into the idea that we could challenge next season,' said Caroline and that would chime with just about every fan who floated out of Hampden with no voice left and few dry eyes either.

This was, however, Warburton's final. His summit. Rangers never won a game for the rest of that season and, with no competitive game for the next six weeks, couldn't lift themselves to beat Hibs in the final, a side who had just failed in the play-offs but were match sharp and more desperate for success. His team never recovered and went sleep-walking into the new season failing to heed any of the warning signs that the close of the previous one had laid out for him in massive neon lights.

Like Rangers in 1995, Celtic responded strongly. Ronnie Daila was sacked at the end of the season (according to Roddy Forsyth of the *BBC* and the *Daily Telegraph*, Celtic fans gathered at the Hampden's main entrance after the game to demand that he be hanged!) and spent big on their new manager and players. It is impossible to fully extricate this game from its full context, but it is not surprising to see it so high on the list. It was an incredible afternoon of football, the likes of which have literally never been seen before in the history of the Old Firm.

We read too much into it but that is what football fans do. The memories of that afternoon, however, are still burned on the hippocampus of many Rangers supporters, especially the younger generation who have fewer blockbuster with which to compare. The years in the lower leagues were always going to be a source of general embarrassment, but in one way we were protected from greater emotional pain. Only the vagaries of the cup draw could bring us head to head with our rivals, the clubs who would find glory in our problems the most, and that turned out to be fairly kind. Once back up in the SPL, Rangers, still re-building, were now in a competition where they'd be pegged to Celtic every single week and the pressure would become too much for that manager and that group.

Those disappointments would follow but they were for another day. On that afternoon we wanted to indulge the illusion that we were back where we desperately wanted to be. We weren't. On that afternoon we wanted to revel in the fact that our city once more belonged to us. It did.

13

Aberdeen 1 Rangers 1

Scottish Premier Division
Saturday 2 May 1987

Jim White (STV): 'Now, how much did you pay for that ticket?'
Rangers Fan: '50 quid.'
White: 'And what is the face value of it?'
Fan: 'Two fifty.'
White: 'You were obviously prepared to pay that kind of money to see Rangers…'
Fan: 'Aye. Ah'd have went mare. Nae problem.'
(The Rangers Revival, STV)

It wasn't the greatest fixture involving these two sides. It wasn't even the greatest example of a match against Aberdeen where Rangers secured a league title. It lacked the sheer individual brilliance that Paul Gascoigne displayed to wrestle control of the league championship in April 1996. It didn't have the nerve-shredding jeopardy that engulfed the winner-takes-all showdown at Ibrox in May 1991. In the end, Rangers could have lost this game and the scenes of wild celebration at its conclusion would have been no different. It doesn't make the list because of what these 90 minutes showcased, rather because of what they symbolised. It was more a moment than a match. Nine years of being also-rans overturned in one whirlwind season. From being a running Scottish joke to being the biggest force in British football. At around 4:50pm on that grey May afternoon, from Pittodrie to Kilwinning to Blackpool and beyond, nearly a decade of pain and shame simply dissolved. The message to the rest of the footballing world was loud, clear and triumphalist: the Rangers were back.

Rangers travelled north on the penultimate day of the league season firmly in the driving seat. Souness's side had assumed that position by setting a pace in the second half of the season that Celtic simply couldn't match. Their home draw to Dundee United the previous fortnight had given Rangers a lead of three points with only four left to amass. Given the goal difference advantage of ten, Rangers would realistically need to lose both remaining fixtures, this trip and the visit of Scottish Cup finalists St Mirren to Ibrox, whilst Celtic took maximum points at home to Falkirk and away to Hearts. Despite the comfort, two doubts would surely have been in the back of the minds of the thousands of fans travelling or glued to their radios. Firstly, the psychological pain of perennial league failure had not yet been eradicated. Secondly, this was Pittodrie, a ground where Rangers had registered just two wins in 13 years at the cost of conceding 40 goals.

Doubts there may have been, but they were drowned out by an increasing conviction of manifest destiny. 5,000 tickets was the standard allocation; however, the Rangers support crammed inside Pittodrie that day was nearer 12,000 and many more without tickets were up on the hill behind the South Stand trying to catch a glimpse of history. Whether Jim White's incredulity at fans securing tickets for 20 times the face value was genuine or an example of the confected, yellow-tied schmaltz we'd come to know in later decades, there was never any question that the fan he interviewed before the game would have paid much, much more. For the thousands who had been caught up in the excitement of the Rangers revival, missing this match was simply not an option.

One of the lucky 5,000 who didn't have to scramble and call in favours was a ten-year-old Andy McGowan. Although he had attended games with his dad for a few years, *Star Wars* would have captured Andy's interest more than the light blues until he had his epiphany the season before. 'All of a sudden I couldn't get enough of Rangers. It just exploded, it was my life. And then I was blessed to have the arrival of Souness right on that mark. It was just the greatest time to be a kid and a Rangers supporter.'

The Pittodrie tunnel being as tight as it was, Rangers came out first to a deafening roar. Stuart Munro's aggression was visibly overflowing before a ball had been kicked and the players seemed to share the same burgeoning fervency as the 'away' support. This was not going to be a cool, tactical battle for the football purists. It was to be a day of destiny and at any cost. Rangers lined up with Chris Woods in goal, a back four of Jimmy Nicholl, Graeme Roberts, Terry Butcher and Stuart Munro. The midfield was centred around Souness and Ian Durrant, with Davie Cooper taking responsibility for creativity on one flank whilst Davie McPherson was tasked with stopping Aberdeen down the other. Robert Fleck would partner Ally McCoist up front. Although Alex Ferguson, not yet a knight of the realm, had left the Granite City for Manchester earlier in the season, Aberdeen were still a strong side and were chasing points to guarantee European football the following year. Captain Willie Miller had returned from suspension and Neil Simpson was enjoying a new lease of life after returning from injury. Their line-up was familiar, if starting to become stale, and read Leighton, McKimmie, Willie Miller, McLeish, Robertson, Irvine, Gray, Bett, Joe Miller, Simpson and Hewitt.

The early exchanges met with the low footballing expectations. Not helped by that famous Grampian light breeze, the ball was the victim throughout. Durrant had a weak effort from outside the box that never troubled Leighton, and Brian Irvine had a good header from a corner saved well by Chris Woods, one of the two signings Souness felt were necessary in order to propel this band of underachievers to the championship. Even Woods wasn't immune to the nerves associated with such a day, however, as he and Roberts tangled outside the box due to a lack of communication.

The tension was affecting everyone, especially the most experienced and decorated player on the pitch. Graeme Souness had already received an early warning for a high-footed challenge and then a booking for a wild tackle on Brian Irvine on the half-way line. Neither the informal or formal cautions were effective and when, after 31 minutes, Souness committed an even worse foul on Irvine, two feet both off the ground and halfway up Irvine's left leg, referee Jim Duncan didn't hesitate to give the Rangers player–manager his marching orders. It would be easy to blame the context and emotion of this day alone in pushing Souness beyond the point of control. It would also be too simplistic. This, of course, was not Souness's first red card that season. He opened his account at Easter Road on the first day of the revolution and, as discussed in Game 42, he and his players would add to that copiously over the next 18 months. For a player who never saw red in his entire career in England, this seems a deliberate ploy to re-assert the club's authority. They wouldn't be anyone's punch bag again.

In this case, however, it could have been damaging and the fans, most of whom worshipped their new player–manager, had absolutely no sympathy for him at that moment in time. 'I distinctly remember thinking "He's fucked it for us,"' recalls Andy McGowan. 'This guy is our hero, this guy is our saviour and he has gone and done that. We are so close, we can taste it. After all this time, he's put it in jeopardy.' Even once the dust had settled on the game, Souness's reaction was in some contrast to the wild expressions of joy surrounding him. The man who created it couldn't allow himself to enjoy his reward completely. 'I have rather mixed feelings at the moment,' he said afterwards, 'for, on a personal note, I have clouded the occasion by being sent off. I feel I've let myself, the club and my family down.' Crucially, however, he went onto say, 'I'm not at all proud of that, but it won't affect our style of play. Football is a physical game and we will continue to be a physical side.' The vociferous nature of his players' appeal to Duncan, for such a clear straight red card, is indicative of the attitude that he instilled in a team of hitherto losers.

The Rangers fans wouldn't have to wait long for another example of their team's new-found resilience under pressure, and fittingly it came from the captain. Davie Cooper was blocked unfairly by Stewart McKimmie on the edge of the box and he took responsibility for the free kick himself. A beautifully flighted ball from Cooper's left foot was met with the thunderous power of Butcher's head. It's hard to think of a player who enjoyed more of a renaissance that season than Davie Cooper. It's hard to imagine it being possible without the arrival of Terry Butcher. A fusion of craft and power, it was the perfect way for this team to make their mark on this day of destiny.

'Christ almighty! How did I survive that?' A young Andy McGowan had experienced some big atmospheres that season but hadn't yet been involved in a celebration like the one that followed Butcher's goal. 'It just added to the feeling that this side was an unstoppable juggernaut.' That feeling may not have lasted through half-time. With almost the last kick of the ball before the interval, Aberdeen were level. With the whistles around the ground urging the referee to follow suit, it was McKimmie's turn to win a free kick and then deliver the perfect ball to the back post, which took Woods out of the equation. Joe Miller did well to steal a yard and head the ball back across the box, where Brian Irvine, legs incredibly still intact, managed to hook the ball home. For all the heightened need for concentration, it was a poor goal to lose right before the break. Any disappointment might have been assuaged in the dressing room with the news from Glasgow. Celtic were a goal down.

Rangers decided to stiffen up the midfield by replacing Robert Fleck with Jimmy Phillips and it set the tone for the second half, which was dominated by the former powerhouse. Joe Miller rattled the post with a deflected shot from outside the box after a period of unchallenged possession and then McLeish tried his luck from distance, which Woods did well to get behind. The two combined to give Aberdeen their best chance of the match. A McLeish header at the edge of the box from a corner found Miller unmarked three yards out, but he couldn't divert his header towards goal.

Rangers were hanging on but the clock was ticking towards glory. A Celtic equaliser from the penalty spot ensured only the status quo. Then, with just four minutes remaining, transistor radios around Pittodrie Stadium buzzed with excitement. Falkirk's Jimmy Gilmour, the nephew of Jimmy Johnstone, had scored a long distance effort that comically bounced over the despairing Pat Bonner. What had felt within touching distance for a whole week was now firmly in our grasp. The final whistle at Parkhead sounded before the one at Pittodrie, thus creating the surreal situation where a battle rages on but the result doesn't matter a jot.

'That result came through to us and it was pandemonium. I was totally and utterly bewildered about what I was seeing around about me. There were growing men crying. There were folk itching to get on that park when that final whistle blew.' Although Mr McGowan Senior would not allow young Andy onto the field of play, he had the perfect viewpoint of a quite literal outpouring of joy as the pitch was flooded with fans who could finally revel in being champions again. This communal elation was replicated in towns up and down the country. 170 miles away in Kilwinning, an eight-year-old David Edgar was celebrating with friends and family. 'People were just moving from garden to garden, dancing and singing. There was no music, it was just Rangers songs all night. It was a grey, overcast day but no one cared.'

This match isn't revered because it signalled the end of something; a long championship-winning season. It is so loved because it signified the start of something; a long period of sustained dominance the likes of which a generation of Rangers fans had only ever known being on the wrong side of. This isn't the hindsight of a nine-in-a-row-era fan writing over 30 years later, this was highlighted by Alan Davidson in the *Evening Times* the following Monday. 'Right now, any bookmaker prepared to offer any kind of odds against them retaining their championship is entitled to qualify as a philanthropist. Rangers are firmly back in the driving seat of the game and it might be no exaggeration to say that Scottish football could be in for a spell of one-club domination similar to that enjoyed by Celtic under the late Jock Stein.' Rangers wouldn't in fact retain their title in 1987/88, but it was a mere blip in the decade of supremacy that was to follow.

As a six-year-old, my memory of this day is limited but clear. We were in Blackpool on a bank holiday weekend trip. My dad, none too pleased to be at the Pleasure Beach instead of the Beach End, used a pay phone to check the state of play. 'Celtic got beat?' he exclaimed before turning to me smiling and raising his fist in triumph. It was an exact mimicry of Souness when he gestured up to the Main Stand at Hampden after the final whistle blew on the Skol League Cup Final earlier in the season.

He had a new hero and, now, so did I.

12

Rangers 3 Aberdeen 1

Scottish Premier Division
Sunday 28 April 1996

'Those who become famous are up there for our use. The most they can hope for is to be used well, but used they always are. They are our dreams come true, not theirs.'
(Clive James, 'Fame In The 20th Century')

'I've had 14 operations and I deserve it more than anyone. I've knocked back the critics. I knew how good I was,' so bellowed Paul Gascoigne in the post-match interview down the Ibrox tunnel, a reflective breather between a brilliant demonstration of individual brilliance five minutes before and picking up the Scottish Player of the Year award a few hours later. A career that seemed to be forever intertwined with genius and tragedy appeared to finally have some stability and consistency. The joyful revelation that was his international introduction juxtaposed with those tears in Turin. Tottenham's FA Cup campaign of 1991 was propelled in the semi-final by his free kick against Arsenal, that started in a different postcode of Wembley, but was then shaken by his reckless wild challenge on Gary Charles in the final against Nottingham Forest, an incident that delayed his transfer to Lazio. His header in the Rome derby that endeared him to the *Irriducibili* proved to be a false dawn in a spell littered with serious injury and clownish idiocy. Finally now, under the reliable hand of Walter Smith, there appeared to be genuine happiness in the world of Gazza as those gifts were harnessed to drive Rangers towards a double. Never was that more in evidence than on that bright April afternoon at Ibrox when his talent sometimes simply transcended a hitherto team sport. The problem with such unbridled natural ability, however, is the adulation that comes with it and, especially when embodied in such a vulnerable soul, it can be almost impossible to control.

The league title race of season 1995/96 was a lot closer than is often remembered. Only the famous final-day decider in 1991 were Rangers under greater pressure during the nine-in-a-row era. Tommy Burns's Celtic would famously lose only one league game, to Rangers and Paul Gascoigne in the opening Old Firm clash back in the September. It was the 11 draws that were fatal to their challenge and two of those, home and away to Kilmarnock, came on the same weekends when Rangers lost to Hearts. Any slip by the champions could never be fully exploited and, despite the tiresome poetry written about that side's 'cavalier football', they scored 11 goals fewer than a more balanced and clinical Rangers. With a single point advantage by the penultimate game of the season, Walter Smith knew that a win at home to Aberdeen would seal the title and anything less would roll it onto the final day of the season, at Rugby Park, and a situation that he had managed to avoid for five years.

It was the following night that saw the famous Kevin Keegan outburst live on Sky, the week after Alex Ferguson had suggested that Leeds United had raised their game against his side and perhaps wouldn't when Newcastle United visited. With that in mind, Richard Gough attempted to play the same kind of mind games with Aberdeen by saying that they were the 'Leeds United of Scotland'. This prompted a degree of rage from captain Stewart McKimmie and manager Roy Aitken, who claimed that 'there's been nothing much between us this season.' If we ignore the 30-point gap then Aitken had a point. Rangers had won 1-0 on their two visits to the North East but had lost 2-1 on a very disappointing night at Hampden in the Coca-Cola League cup semi-final. The other remaining encounter was a torrid 1-1 draw at Ibrox when Paul Gascoigne should have been sent off by John Rowbotham when he head-butted John Inglis, and Billy Dodds and John Brown were involved in another altercation. Eoin Jess and Oleg Salenko threatened to bring the game into repute with a couple of fine goals, but it was a long-standing bitterness that endured.

For such a decisive fixture, Smith decided on a very attacking line-up. A familiar rearguard of Goram, Brown, McLaren and Gough was in place, with the reliable David Robertson, who had told Craig Brown not to bother with him at Euro '96 if he wasn't first choice ahead of Tosh McKinley, at left wing-back and the ageing Trevor Steven on the other side. It was only Stuart McCall who provided any defensive cover in midfield, with Gascoigne, Laudrup, Durie and Erik Bo Andersen providing the attacking threat. The latter, with six goals in four games, was picked ahead of Ally McCoist, who had to make do with a place on the bench amidst intense speculation that this would be his final season at Ibrox. (He would sign a new two-year deal within the fortnight.) Aberdeen matched the 3-5-2 shape, with Michael Watt taking his place in goal, Gary Smith, John Inglis and Brian Irvine in defence, Stewart McKimmie and the highly rated Stephen Glass on the flanks, David Rowson, Paul Bernard and Dean Windass in midfield with Billy Dodds and Scott Booth in attack.

The visitors were comfortable in their defensive shape, cutting out the threat of David Robertson on the few early occasions that he was able to break free. They had a threat themselves from Billy Dodds, booed by the home support, who had a good effort from distance in the first ten minutes. Just before the 20-minute mark, Aberdeen were ahead. A Stephen Glass corner was missed by Richard Gough, bandaged already after a head clash with Brian Irvine, and it was his opponent who was well-placed to opportunistically bundle the ball past Goram and Trevor Steven on the line. If an Ibrox party atmosphere had ever pierced through the tension then it was dampened quickly with a quite dreadful goal to concede. 'The prevailing mood around the stadium was, "Ok we're going to make it hard for ourselves,"' remembers David Edgar. 'We are going to do this in the proper Rangers way by putting everyone through the mill.'

The lull didn't have time to take root and create a permanent state of anxiety. Rangers forced a corner two minutes later and Laudrup played the ball to Gascoigne on the front edge of the box. The rest was purely on him. He glided past Dodds and then Windass before managing to get it onto his right foot to rifle it past Watt and up into the roof of the net. 'They're aware of what he is going to do. They're set for him. They know what's coming,' said David. 'But to do it, to adjust his body, to generate the power with no back lift and get it past Watt who, for his other faults, was a good shot-stopper, was incredible. He could do it in big games. A game where we needed our special players to do something special.'

The narrative of the rest of the first half was one of Rangers trying everything to get through a solid defensive set-up with just the odd moment of concern at the other end. Laudrup and Gascoigne buzzed around the Aberdeen half, taking up different positions to try and carve out another opening, Alan McLaren's looping header onto the post the closest Rangers got. It was Aberdeen, however, who created the best chance of the half. On 34 minutes a Billy Dodds knock-on released Scott Booth one-on-one with Andy Goram. The Rangers legend simply stood up, whereas the striker fell to pieces and could only manage a tame effort. A sense of building frustration then, was very much the half-time mood. 'We didn't want to be going into the last day looking for a point at Rugby Park. We wanted it done. We were at home. We were all there. We all had plans for afterwards. Carry-outs had been bought. Days off had been arranged for the next day.'

The match of the 3-5-2s resulted in the game getting bogged down at times, but when there was freedom Rangers were very wasteful, especially Bo Andersen who squandered four chances before being replaced by McCoist just after the hour mark. McCoist was one of a few players who went closer with headers, Durie and Gough being the others and even Laudrup lost his composure when he made the wrong decision with just over 20 minutes to go. When Aberdeen attacked, it was down the Rangers right with Trevor Steven being badly exposed by Glass, but Goram as always provided a reliable last line of defence, the best example coming from a Windass header that he tipped over the bar. Steven was replaced soon after by Gordan Petric, who had only made the squad after recovering from the most Petric of all injuries: a poisoned arm.

It was after 70 minutes that Gascoigne started to warm up for the big finale. Two of his corners found McLaren, who went close both times and he also created some openings for McCoist and Durie, but simply nothing was breaking down the stubborn resistance. With only ten minutes remaining and nerves frayed, it happened. Billy Dodds received the ball from a throw-in in the Rangers half but was dispossessed by McLaren, who gave a vocal instruction to Gascoigne as he won the ball from Windass:

go and do something with it. From his own half, on he went. Easing past Bernard, he would be tracked all the way to the Aberdeen penalty area, but his strength and conviction held off all challengers. Laudrup's intelligent run dragged Inglis away with him and for the first time the other two defenders seemed strangely frozen in the beating sun. It was the first bit of freedom he had seen in an hour of football and it was all he needed to seal the title. Voted the greatest Rangers goal of all time by the listeners of *Heart and Hand,* it was as if, for three or four seconds, none of the other 21 players mattered. It wasn't their game. For a brief moment it was suspended in Gascoigne's spell. 'There is something absolutely intoxicating, still, about watching a player with the complete conviction that the ball is their property,' said the writer and Rangers fan Alasdair McKillop in a piece about Gascoigne for *Nutmeg.* 'As he surged through the melting Aberdeen defence in the hot sunshine, his arms threshing, Gascoigne had that conviction: he powered towards the goal with a sort of gallus brutality.'

'There was relief of course but also that feeling that I had witnessed something very special,' recalled David. 'Sometimes great goals are amplified by the occasion. If he scored that goal in a 5-1 win over Falkirk, we'd remember it fondly, but it wouldn't become the legendary goal that every Rangers fan can play in their mind without the need to search it out online. Then we all said one of the stupidest phrases known to man but one that makes perfect sense in that kind of moment. "Did you see that?!" As if you're seeking confirmation from others around you that the extraordinary event that you think you've witnessed actually took place. But of course there were over 40,000 roars confirming that it did. It was a world-class goal and it will live forever.'

It was very much a Gazza goal. Anyone who saw him in Italia 90 wouldn't be surprised by that. There's bustle. There's strength, like a street fighter. Laudrup scored goals that looked like he had a shield around him, such was his effortless grace. This was a kind of beautiful chaos, running straight into danger but with a heart of a lion. The coolest man in the eye of the storm. Everyone else seemed paralysed by his wizardry. Only he was in control of proceedings. The debate would rage amongst Rangers fans of the time about which of the two superstars was better. A question of taste, of course, but there is some similarity between them and the likes of Messi and Suarez at Barcelona ten years later. Laudrup and Messi looked as if they were stars of the Royal Ballet. Gazza and Suarez looked as if they had never left the streets. There was an undoubted appeal there, an everyman genius that Laudrup's regality could never have, with which supporters felt a different bond.

There was time yet for another Alan McLaren assault on goal, but it flashed wide before the stage was set for the encore. From a Goram punch at an Aberdeen corner, the break was on and Durie was eventually felled by Bernard in the box. After pleading with McCoist, Gascoigne had the chance to crown his season and he duly did with ease to make it 3-1. Walter Smith had matched Bill Struth's record of winning five successive championships as manager for the duration of a season, but there was only one man being carried shoulder high around Ibrox stadium. A man who needed to be loved and adored would struggle to find more of that during his time at Ibrox.

Not so throughout the rest of Scotland, however. For those who questioned the signing as an injury liability, a player whose best days were long behind him, any praise of his match-deciding abilities was through gritted teeth and packed full of caveats. Any criticism of his dark and daft sides was more fulsome. The 'man-child' schtick was a regular trope of the Sunday columns and Gerry McNee, who was able to describe the action at Ibrox for STV that day so well, could barely use Gascoigne's name when writing for the *News Of The World*, instead opting for the 'Number Eight' moniker. In doing so McNee was effectively dehumanising a man, not without obvious mental health issues. A superhuman footballer but a very real fragile human, for whom reading the Sunday papers was often a very difficult experience.

'Most soccer fans have a need to get hooked on the fortunes of a single player, to build a team around him so to speak,' wrote the poet and critic Ian Hamilton in his biography of Gascoigne, *Gazza Agonistes*. A Tottenham fan with Rangers blood in his ancestry, Hamilton didn't take too long to fall for him, and neither did I. For me, no player provided more quality in a Rangers shirt, a catalyst of intelligence and individual character who sparked Rangers out of a relative slump and powered them on to fabled glories. I bought into it from the very start, waiting for hours outside the main door in the boiling July heat to see him finally paraded in a Rangers jersey and to shake his hand. I was too young to fully appreciate the signing of Souness. I was perfectly placed to understand this.

And yet my adulation, and that of thousands of others, was ultimately counter-productive as we projected onto him an ultimately unrealistic concept of perfection. Hamilton's attraction to the genius of Gascoigne was that of the poet and how out of this chaos and unlikely frame came such beauty. There was also the acute understanding that a failure to bottle the brilliance can easily lead to self-destruction. 'What's at issue is the idea of a life given over to creativity; and the belief that because a person believes himself to be possessed of some profound and special gift, he has certain rights to live his life in a certain way.' McKillop extended this further by correctly identifying that, 'it was others who invested most in the idea that Gascoigne possessed something special so he was offered a certain leeway that wouldn't have been offered to less talented players.' Our need for heroes, our need to distil team sports down to the individual often creates a mania that would be hard enough for the more well-adjusted to cope with.

Any hope Paul Gascoigne had of a well-adjusted life was up against it from the start. His troubles can probably be traced back to the childhood trauma of seeing the younger brother of a friend killed in a car accident at the age of seven. Gascoigne had persuaded his mother to let him come with the boys to the sweet shop and that he would look after him. It was whilst he was 'mucking around' in the shop that the accident happened. 'It was the first dead body I'd ever seen – and I felt Steven's death was my fault,' wrote Gascoigne in his autobiography. 'I had said I would look after him and I didn't. I couldn't understand why he had died when he was so young and hadn't harmed anybody. It didn't make sense.' Even before that, when he too was only seven, he had demonstrated considerable anxiety when he started to ponder his own existence and death. 'Suddenly I was scared, and I ran all the way home, screaming and crying. I got into bed with me mam and dad, squeezed in beside them, cuddled close. I didn't tell them why I'd been screaming, I just sort of hid it in my head.'

There was no proper treatment of these demons during his professional career and their outward manifestations were indulged, not managed. Hamilton summed it up well when he said, 'some feared … that he so little understood the nature of his own genius that he would be unable to protect it from the excesses to which his personality was irreversibly inclined.' Some of those excesses, the loveable larrikin sort, were ignored despite the fact that he was supposed to be a professional athlete. Because he was doing enough on the pitch, however, the excuses were excusable.

There were, of course, much darker excesses, such as that awful week in the October of 1996 when his lack of discipline in the Champions League clash with Ajax in Amsterdam, where he saw red in a desperate 4-1 defeat, was put into context when it soon emerged that his lack of control on the football field extended into his home life. Domestic abuse can't be excused by footballing prowess, but yet that is exactly what happened. Vice-Chairman Donald Finlay QC said, 'None of us here are going to get involved in somebody's private life. If Paul Gascoigne, or anybody else connected with the club, asks for help or advice we will give it. We are not going to interfere. It is entirely a private matter. We will stand by anybody who works for the club who gives us 100 per cent loyalty. They will get the same back.' Walter Smith fined him and hinted that there was a limit to the club's patience but that it hadn't been reached yet. The club officially washed their hands of it and so did the fans. Generally speaking, the Rangers support went into deep compartmentalisation and did all of the mental gymnastics possible so as to avert the cognitive dissonance that wasn't far from the surface. There were the odd brave voices of condemnation, none more so than the editor of the *Follow Follow* fanzine, Mark Dingwall, but they went very much against the grain. Myself included. Albeit I was only 15 years of age, but any deep unease was quashed by what he could potentially win for us that season: the nine. It really was a kind of mania. It was Aberdeen again who visited Ibrox for the first game following those revelations. Gascoigne sent a free kick into the top corner from 30 yards. All seemed instantly well again.

It wasn't, of course, and although future success would come, it would eventually unravel for Gascoigne at Ibrox and then, with his dramatic exclusion from Glenn Hoddle's squad for France '98, sadly for the rest of his career and his life. His story was never black and white. The horrendous behaviour was seized upon by those who seemed to revel in tragedy because it provided the opportunity to attack Gascoigne, and by association the club, with no interest in discussing any deeper psychological explanation. In much the same way as his best moments on the field were sometimes distorted by his worshippers as evidence of the norm, despite it being a career that never got close to meeting its potential. 'There was something in his personality that ran counter to the fantasies his soccer gifts induced,' observed Hamilton. 'Wasn't the whole drift of Gazza's story a drift towards some calamitous comeuppance, some terrible bringing-down-to-earth?'

Ultimately this was really the familiar tale of fame. Otherwise rational observers getting close to believing in supernatural power. Devotees willing to ignore the worst human behaviour, lest it reduce the aura of the gods. John Lennon committed the same offences and yet few of us enjoy The Beatles with any such caveats. More importantly it is the human being who gets lost when the fame takes over. Gascoigne was the loveable, footballing hero for his fans and the thuggish, overrated oaf for his detractors, but he was the troubled human being for far too few of us.

At the very end of his excellent documentary series, *Fame in the 20th Century*, Clive James summed it up perfectly: 'If fame comes from achievement, it's worth having and worthy of admiration. But achievement without fame can be a good life and fame without achievement is no life at all. Finally, what separates human beings is less important than what joins them and the famous people we like most seem to tell us that by their way of staying human. As if there was a frail, fallible human being behind the glory. Which there always is.'

11

Rangers 5 Celtic 1

Scottish Premier Division
Saturday 27 August 1988

'Is this how it's going to be? We win one, they win one, we win one, they win one? Because I'm not fucking interested in that.'
(Graeme Souness to his players, 30 April 1988)

How worried were you in the summer of 1988?

In the pub, once we have exhausted the issues of the day, this is a question I often enjoy asking older fans. Graeme Souness had swept into Scottish football like a force of nature, spending money like no Scottish manager ever had before and winning the title back at the first time of asking. The following season, however, despite seeing the League Cup being retained and a run to the quarter-finals of the European Cup, finished under a cloud of doubt regarding the future of the revolution. Rangers finished a distant third in the league, suffered yet another early exit from the Scottish Cup and had only taken one point from four games against Celtic, who had gone on to complete the double. Had 1986/87 been a flash in the pan? Most supporters, secure in the benefit of hindsight, assure me that they were never concerned. Poor recruitment up front and terrible luck with injuries, most notably the captain Terry Butcher who broke his leg in November 1987, were squarely to blame. Others were more honest. In 2016 I had the opportunity of asking the man himself, who seemed to dismiss the entire concept of worry altogether. Souness re-trod the same old Butcher narrative regarding 1987/88, but it was the talk with his team after the final home game of the season that left him confident that we would respond with strength. He had thrown down a challenge to them. *Was* this how it was going to be?

There was an early reply. Glasgow was still revelling in the inexplicable success of the 1988 Garden Festival by the time the first Old Firm game of the season came around. Over four million people had visited the site on the Clyde, which was a Michael Heseltine innovation to encourage regeneration within Britain's urban decay. The state of the Rangers regeneration was the primary thought on the minds of the majority packed into Ibrox that afternoon, however. Jock Brown, commentating for STV, would remark that, despite having witnessed countless matches between the two clubs, the atmosphere on that day was 'something special'. David Edgar was only ten years old and was going to only his second Old Firm game, but his father concurred with Brown. 'My dad had said that he felt it was bubbling up a bit more than usual. It might have been due to the news at the time (six British soldiers were killed by the IRA the week before) but also this was the season after the 2-2 draw in which four players ended up in front of a judge.' It was also simply the case that the Rangers players had the bit between their teeth. They wanted their title back.

Both sides had stumbled in their opening two league games, Rangers sharing a goalless draw with Hibernian at Ibrox whereas Celtic had lost to Dundee Utd at Tannadice on the same day. However, they had filled their shooting boots in the midweek League Cup fixtures, with Celtic beating Hamilton 7-2 and Rangers knocking six past Clydebank with no reply. Graeme Souness played a game of cat and mouse with the media about whether or not he would start, but his main focus was on the fixture's importance. In the official end-of-season video the previous summer, Souness had famously said that he wouldn't care if he lost four times to Celtic as long as he won the league title. The experience of 87/88 would be a painful reminder that the two were almost mutually exclusive. 'The longer I'm with Rangers the more I realise just how important the games against Celtic are. In particular to the supporters, but they also figure prominently in the minds and hearts of the players.' The emotional and psychological impact aside, the league arithmetic was simple: giving up eight points wasn't an option.

His opposite number Billy McNeil had issues at both ends of the park. Due to the sale of Alan McKnight and Pat Bonner's injury, Celtic had a goalkeeping crisis. Alan Rough was rushed back but had never played in this derby before and their new backup, Ian Andrews, signed from Leicester City in the summer, was also completely untested. 'Whichever of our goalkeepers plays,' said McNeil on the Friday, 'it will be a new experience.' It certainly would prove to be an unforgettable one for Andrews who eventually got the nod. McNeil also had to deal with speculation about Frank McAvennie returning to London permanently following a pay dispute between the club and their cup final hero. He was defiant, however, as he stated, 'There's as much chance of McAvennie moving as there is of Rangers beating us 5-1 tomorrow.' It was a bold claim but, to McNeil's credit, it proved to be wholly accurate.

Rangers started with a selection that was very nearly what Souness would regard as first choice by then. Stuart Munro was the only injury to contend with as we lined up with Woods in goal, Gary Stevens making his Old Firm debut at right-back, the central defensive pairing of Gough and Butcher, with John Brown filling in at left-back. The midfield four consisted of Mark Walters, Ray Wilkins, Ian Ferguson and Ian Durrant, with Ally McCoist partnered in attack by Kevin Drinkell, who was also making his first appearance in this famous old fixture. Celtic matched the 4-4-2 with a back four of Morris, McCarthy, Aitken and Rogan in front of Andrews. Burns, Grant, McStay and Stark were in the middle, with the genuinely dangerous partnership of Andy Walker and McAvennie up front. What stands out from these line ups is the lack of genuine width. Only Mark Walters could claim to be a natural in that role and he would get, and exploit, that space as the game went on.

The Govan weather was atrocious as the game clattered into life at its typical tempo. Rangers could have had a penalty in the opening two minutes when Durrant was tripped in a clumsy coming together with Anton Rogan, but nothing was given. After five minutes, Celtic were a goal in front. Any younger fan who believes that the high press is a new footballing innovation would only have to watch this goal to be disavowed of that notion. The Rangers backline were hounded down the right-hand corner and all of Stevens, Gough and Butcher made poor attempts to clear, allowing Grant to eventually get a shot at goal. His effort hit the post but removed Woods from the action and McAvennie instinctively poked the ball home from the rebound. Any Celtic goal at Ibrox is unsettling for a Rangers fan, but when it is scored at the Copland Road end there is a split second of eery silence between you knowing they've scored and that news reaching the other end of the ground. A wave of sound then proceeds to hit you in the stomach. Bears around the ground must have been thinking 'not again …'

Crucially, Rangers hit back quickly. It was an equaliser that was similar to the opener in that the Celtic defence produced comedic attempts at clearing the danger and a cool finisher, this time McCoist, did what the best penalty box strikers do. This fixture can frazzle the mind of very experienced players. One only has to look at the combined number of caps shared by both defences as they resembled amateur footballers on a hungover Sunday morning. For McCoist it seemed to happen in slow motion as he exerted total control in sweeping the ball into the net. His face as he returned the ball to the centre tells the story of the pre-match context. Not Ally the joker, the famous image of the smiling assassin. It is contorted, full of anger. 'There wasn't the joyful explosion that normally accompanies such a goal,' remarked David Edgar. 'He was saying, "Fuck that! We are *not* losing this game".'

As the sun came out, the game developed into an open and enjoyable contest. McCoist left Aitken for dead but waited too long to pull the trigger and later he went very close with a great effort that shaved the post. At the other end Billy Stark should have done better with a header after Woods was caught out by a big looping high cross that held up in the wind. He would tell his team-mates at half-time that the conditions were causing problems. As was tradition, the tackles were flying about thick and fast. McCarthy left a dreadful one on Durrant after a free kick had already been given, John Brown was booked for a cynical, professional foul on Morris and arguably the worst was a bodycheck by Ray Wilkins on Paul McStay. Midfield niggle wasn't what Wilkins was remembered for and it wouldn't be why people associate him so closely with this match either.

With ten minutes to go until half-time, he put Rangers in front. The long throw by Gary Stevens and the flicked header by Butcher weren't cleared well by the Celtic defence and Wilkins met it perfectly. This goal, 'a goal made in England' as Jock Brown memorably described it in commentary, would illicit only joy in its celebration. Voted sixth in the recent *Heart and Hand* '50 Greatest Rangers Goals' poll, it was a goal so good that it transcended the tense and febrile match situation and all the Rangers players were either smiling with glee or disbelief. Overall, Graeme Souness was successful in the transfer market whilst at Ibrox, although not a trait that would necessarily follow him for the rest of his career. The big signings mostly had their intended impact, but he was especially good at short-term moves. Senior pros who were here for a while fulfilled a job and moved on. Some were forgotten as soon as they left, but Wilkins left a mark that was still felt after his sad passing in 2018 and will continue for many years. He got us and we got him. That moment would crystallise this mutual affection for generations.

Celtic were forced into a change at half-time due to an injury to Tommy Burns. Instead of replacing him with the direct attacking wide option in Joe Miller, McNeill opted for Derek Whyte, normally a centre-half, thus pushing Anton Rogan into the left of midfield. It should be remembered that, although Rangers deserved the lead, the match was still very much in the balance. It wasn't yet at the point where Celtic were camping in and playing for pride. If it was McNeil's plan to shore up his side, it was left in tatters less than a minute after the re-start. The ball switched from Stevens out on the right to Durrant on the left-hand side of the Celtic box. With three opposition players coming out to meet him and the rest gathered in the six-yard box, he clipped a short, flighted pass over to McCoist, who was left in plenty of space between two clusters. In what must have been a deliberate ploy following the advice from Woods at the interval, he managed to hang the ball up in the swirling air with a cute backwards header. Chaos and confusion ensued for the debutant goalkeeper as, under little pressure from Kevin Drinkell, he allowed the ball to sail into the net. Aitken pursued referee Kenny Hope faster than Ben Johnson after a trip to his doctors but his complaints, correctly, fell on deaf ears.

The floodgates were now open. Rangers should have had a penalty when Whyte checked Walters in the box after displaying some sublime control. Kevin Drinkell had an earlier chance to score before he did finish off arguably the most aesthetically pleasing goal of the afternoon. The skill shown by Mark Walters down in the corner against McCarthy wasn't for show. It bought him the extra space he needed to find the cross, which Drinkell met in a fashion that can only legally be described as a 'bullet header'. The Copland Front seemed to rise together in a beautiful unity and the noise was now different. There is a subtle distinction between celebrating your team going 3-1 ahead in a big derby and them extending it to four. With the former you know you're going to see your team win an important match. With the latter you know you're watching history.

The fifth goal came on 62 minutes after a disastrous attempt by Aitken to deal with a long ball from Brown. McCoist nicked it away and was fouled for what would have been a certain penalty if it wasn't for Walters being there to stroke it home. Speaking to me as a special guest on *The Time Capsule,* Walters fondly remembered the afternoon 30 years later. 'It was just a fantastic occasion really. Once we got level there was never any doubt who was going to win the game. Ray Wilkins was running the show amongst other individual performances that day but as a team we really sorted them out.'

With just under half an hour still remaining, Ibrox was baying for more goals. Three more to be precise. Folk memory of the 1957 Old Firm League Cup Final, when Celtic won by seven goals to one, still resonated with many. There was a record there to be broken but Graeme Souness wasn't interested. For him, there was more than one way to mentally scar an opponent than by running up a cricket score. In echoes of Scotland's famous win at Wembley in 1967, where Denis Law was keen to keep pushing on so as to try and avenge the 9-3 thumping from England six years before and Jim Baxter reportedly told him that he would just prefer to take the piss, here was Souness bringing himself on as a substitute, lording it up in much the same way.

This was much to the consternation of the support and players such as Durrant, Brown, Ferguson and McCoist, who wanted blood. How perfectly typical of a classic Rangers victory that it still produced something for us to complain about. Not for a young David Edgar, however. 'For me it was all about the elation. There were a few around me who were frustrated that it should have been eight. But I hadn't seen anything like this in my lifetime. 1957 didn't happen to me, it had no relevance. This did. And for any Celtic supporters around my age, it happened to them too.'

For those who weren't at Ibrox, like me who had only been released from hospital on the Friday following a hernia operation, the 24-hour wait to see the highlights was interminable but was never going to disappoint. Such was the magnitude of the result, *Scotsport* had a feature with Tommy Burns, filmed from his living room, effectively offering a public apology to the Celtic support. 'In all my years with Celtic I have never been involved in anything quite as humiliating,' he said. 'The whole thing was unbelievable. However, it won't happen again.' (It would.) It was also an answer to the consistent jibes that the English invasion at Ibrox was purely mercenary and, when they chips were down, they wouldn't want it as much as the Celtic players. For the first time in the fixture's history, three Englishmen scored and put that slur to bed.

The ten games that follow this one, the highest tier of this particular pantheon, are full of classics, but it is both surprising that there is no room for this almost perfect afternoon and the fact that Souness doesn't feature there at all. This game, the eighth on the list under his control, was considered the greatest of his reign, but still not good enough to reach the truly greatest of heights. It feels unfair that the chief architect of modern Rangers history is declining in his significance to Rangers fans, when his profile in the game, on television, is still high. The Skol League Cup Final win in 1986 is also extremely low, down in 40th position, another indicator, perhaps, that the natural freshness of recent success is tough to overpower. Again, this is where our ability to showcase history comes back to the fore. Nine of the games that make up the rest of this line-up post-date this match and that entire spread of success seems impossible without victories such as these.

Most iterations of this fixture in recent years before 1988 had been won by the odd goal. Only three times in ten years had it been 3-0 and there had been plenty of draws in there too. This was a landmark result. If it were ever possible to psychologically win a league title after three games then this was it. Rangers finished August five points ahead of Celtic and would never end any month that season with a cushion smaller than that.

Celtic wouldn't compete seriously for a league title again until 1996. It would be too convenient to draw a line from this bodyblow, however significant it was. They would beat Rangers 3-1 in the next meeting in November and would spoil our treble ambitions in the Scottish Cup Final in May. However, they were teetering on the brink of an implosion. Every exertion possible was made to paper over the cracks in their double-winning centenary year and now they had little left with which to fight. The 5-1 would be followed up with a 4-1 rout at New Year and in April Rangers would win at Parkhead for the first time since 1980.

Clearly the balance of power was shifting; however, it would be a signing that Souness made in the July of 1989 that ultimately answered his own question and would help put Celtic to sleep for years.

10

Hibernian 0 Rangers 1

Scottish Premier League
Sunday 22 May 2005

'If, for some reason Celtic drop points, and you don't do your jobs and win the game, you will regret it for the rest of your lives. You will wake up in the middle of the night with cold sweats.'
(Alex McLeish, half-time)

This was the kind of sporting drama that only league football can conjure up. Whenever lists are compiled of the greatest comebacks, collapses or swings in momentum, they're almost always made up of head-to-head clashes. Ali v Foreman in the 'Rumble in the Jungle', Faldo v Norman at the Masters, Hendry v White at the Crucible. This kind of magic moment wouldn't be seen in US sports, such is their demand for playoffs and finals. Even the English Premier League's most dramatic denouement is only such because of the nature of the injury-time goals that Manchester City scored, not because it was actually them, heavy favourites on the morning of that game, who lifted the trophy. Game ten stands unique on this list because the most significant action happened in another game 38 miles away, that didn't involve Rangers at all. On five occasions in the new century, the title race between Rangers and Celtic went down to the final day of the league season, and in four of those seasons the side in the driving seat, no matter how slender their grip on the wheel, did what was required and took home the prize. Such is the rarity of this gift from the sporting heavens that the rush that fans experience endures years on into the future.

In many respects it was a day that perfectly encapsulated the schizophrenic nature of the Alex McLeish era, a four-and-a-half-year spell that saw Rangers bounce from glory to calamity and back. His first 18 months saw him win the first five realistic honours available to him, with his side playing some exceptional football into the bargain. The second full season was entirely barren, this year saw a league and League Cup double, whereas the final campaign ended with Rangers finishing third in a two-horse race. The summer of 2004 had been better for McLeish than the previous one, where the spine of his treble-winning side was ripped apart. Lorenzo Amoruso and Barry Ferguson were sold and Ronald de Boer was later out injured for half the season. This summer transfer window was both smart and ambitious. In came dado Pršo from

Monaco, second top goalscorer in the previous season's Champions League, in addition to the experience of Alex Rae and Marvin Andrews and the potential, after impressing at Dundee, of Nacho Novo. The free transfer of Jean-Alain Boumsong from Auxerre was a pure business decision as Rangers cashed in on the French defender in the winter market and in return brought home Barry Ferguson and the highly rated Belgian Thomas Buffel from Feyenoord.

The need for the upturn in transfer activity and intent was due in no small part to the fact that Celtic had won five out of five Old Firm fixtures the season before, the first time such a clean sweep in all competitions had been done since 1971/72. That run continued into 2004/05, albeit with a degree of misfortune at Parkhead in the August and looked set to continue at Ibrox when John Hartson thundered home a header from close range in the League Cup quarter-final in November. Rangers had done enough that evening to win two or three cup ties and finally their endeavour was rewarded when Pršo tapped home with five minutes of normal time remaining, following a David Marshall spill, and then Shota Averladze scored a brilliant winner in extra time. Celtic got revenge in the Scottish Cup but not before Rangers defeated them in the league for the first time in two years and repeated the 2-0 scoreline at Parkhead in February, the first win there for six years. It was a victory that left Rangers three points clear, having played a game more but with a far superior goal difference. It was a squad that was clearly able to be kings of Scotland once again.

Able but not quite a vintage Rangers side, there were some late heroics on the road against Hearts and Dundee, but also careless points dropped at home to Inverness Caledonian Thistle and Dundee United. All of this meant that Rangers were two points behind Celtic as the final derby of the season came into view at Ibrox at the end of April. The common consensus was that a win was required if we had any realistic title hopes, a draw would keep it barely alive and a defeat would open up a five-point gap with just four games remaining and leave us dead and buried. Celtic were deserved 2-1 winners, always looking more in control and showing the experience so desperately needed to navigate these final obstacles. Some Celtic fans held aloft a banner that day, on what appeared to be a bed sheet that had seen better days, that proclaimed that they had won the league at Ibrox. McLeish wasn't exactly defiant himself when he said, 'I'm not saying that everything is now lost, but it's difficult to see Celtic losing it now.' The difficulty was more than the simple arithmetic involved. Martin O'Neill's side had won the title three times in the previous four seasons and three other cups to boot. It looked very ominous indeed.

For any Rangers fan looking for positives, the number of times this Celtic side had been successful wouldn't have helped but the *nature* of their triumphs might have. Martin O'Neill's four cup wins (he'd win the Scottish Cup at the end of this season) were all against more provincial opposition, whereas his two Old Firm cup finals in 2002 and 2003 had ended in defeat. The three league titles were won convincingly but all involved an early Rangers implosion. The one time there was a challenge, in 2002/03, they faltered, albeit by the most minuscule of margins. In other words, there were question marks over this side's ability to handle the pressure at the very end of a competition. By the broadest definition imaginable, the heat was still on, but even this Celtic dressing room, packed full of neuroses, surely wouldn't choke from here?

Choke they did. An inexplicable 3-1 defeat by Hibs at Parkhead the following Saturday, the third coming from Scott Brown, gifted Rangers an opportunity to get the deficit back to two points if they could win up at Aberdeen the next day. In the pouring rain and waterlogged pitch, they did exactly that, with goals from Barry Ferguson and dado Pršo underlining a strong and resolute performance that demonstrated a gritty will to keep this challenge going by continually asking questions, bearing in mind that Rangers would play first for the next two weekends. The questions were posed each Saturday but Celtic answered them well enough on the Sunday. It would therefore go down to the wire, with Rangers needing to win at Hibs, who were still chasing European football next season, and hoping that Celtic wouldn't, when they visited a Motherwell side with ostensibly nothing to play for whatsoever.

Despite the placebo mantras of Marvin Andrews, urging us to keep believing, there was in fact little belief amongst Rangers fans on that Sunday morning in May. Again, this wasn't a head-to-head decider or a cup final, where you could back your team to do their job and lift the honours. It wasn't a final day within our own control. Only twice in the post-war history of the Scottish top division had the team in second place on that final day ended up champions by virtue of a result elsewhere. Rangers overhauled Dundee in 1948/49, winning 4-1 at Albion Rovers, whilst the league leaders lost by the same scoreline at Falkirk, and Celtic themselves were the beneficiaries of an untimely Hearts wobble and some generous St Mirren defending at the close of the 1985/86 season. Generally speaking, the side with their noses in front did the business. It wasn't about whether fans, and players, had belief in Rangers, it was about whether they had belief in Motherwell. 'I didn't think that they stood a chance to be honest,' said Adam Thornton, who had made his way to Easter Road that day. 'We had absolutely scudded them the week before (4-1 at Ibrox) and they had nothing to play for, whereas we had a tricky game. Hibs had a good young side at the time and were chasing Europe. We were just hoping for the best really.'

The same could probably be said for the Rangers team in the first half. McLeish was able to name a fairly strong side to give himself the best chance possible of success that day. Ronald Waterreus, the latest in a long line of Rangers goalkeeping signings that worked an absolute treat, took his place between the posts behind a back four of Fernando Ricksen, Marvin Andrews, Sotirios Kyrgiakos and Michael Ball. Barry Ferguson and Alex Rae provided the midfield ballast, whilst Shota Averladze and Thomas Buffel supported Nacho Novo and dado Pršo up front. It was Hibs who looked liveliest in that opening spell, befitting a good season and a group of players full of promise, and they could have easily been in front in the opening ten minutes through Derek Riordan and Garry O'Conner, the latter skimming the crossbar from a glancing header. Rangers responded through Novo, who managed only to hit the post from a tight angle after Simon Brown in the Hibs goal misjudged the bounce on Rae's through ball. It was a fairly feisty first half in the middle of the park, but little else to write home about as the mood had been dented by news of the inevitable Celtic goal coming through from Fir Park on the half-hour mark, Chris Sutton putting them in front. The situation at half-time was exactly as feared and expected.

The away dressing room was understandably flat and it was up to the manager and senior pros to ensure that Rangers at least held up their side of the bargain, just in case. Speaking to *FourFourTwo* in 2019, McLeish said, 'the players came in with hunched shoulders when they heard the Celtic score and I knew I had to pick the guys up again. I had a word in Barry Ferguson's ear and said, "you can't be sitting there with your face tripping you. You've got to be rallying these guys." Then we had big Marvin Andrews telling everyone in the dressing room "keep believing" and gradually the atmosphere changed a bit. I got everyone together and said, "here's the scenario. If we score a goal and Motherwell score a goal you're champions."'

There was a noticeable difference in that opening spell of the second half. Pršo was causing problems and he opened up a glorious chance for Buffel, who was only denied by a perfectly timed Steven Whittaker tackle. The two Rangers attackers were involved again just before the hour mark and this time it did pay off. Buffel's purposeful and energetic running and the Croatian's intelligent flick eventually moved the ball out to Novo on the right-hand side. His low fizzing ball was intended for Pršo but Gary Caldwell got there first, only to deflect the ball into the back of his own net. Hope was re-kindled but Celtic were pressing for a second at Fir Park. 'Every second person seemed to have a radio,' recalls Adam. It was just now a matter of waiting, especially as the two sides appeared to have signed a non-aggression pact. The Hibs' chase for Europe would be determined by goal difference between them and Aberdeen, even if they lost. If they attacked for the point that would guarantee their place, it may have left too much space to be exploited by a Rangers side with their tails up. Losing by three or four could finish their dreams. Losing by one would probably be enough. Tony Mowbray, not known for his prosaic managerial decisions, on this occasion chose to stick with the hand that he currently had and the remaining half an hour was played at a surreal walking pace. 'Our boys were keeping the ball at the back and Hibs were happy to let them do it,' said McLeish. 'Sotirios Kyrgiakos and Marvin Andrews just passed the ball between them. There was one moment when Marvin threatened to go forward and I shouted, "Don't you dare!" I had visions of one of our guys slipping and a Hibs player running in to score, but they stayed back in their own half. We had old heads like Alex Rae and Barry Ferguson who were able to play a clever game and see it out for us.'

'There was no real pressure but [manager] Terry Butcher certainly had us up for the game. He's a big Rangers man, as we all know, and the team-talk was unbelievable. He really wanted to win it,' Richie Foran, who was playing for Motherwell that day, told the BBC years later. They came out strong after the interval, with Didier Agathe having to block a Stephen Craigan header off the line, but it was Celtic who were still the more dominant. John Hartson squandered three opportunities and Craig Bellamy one more, as veteran ex-Celtic goalkeeper Gordon Marshall produced an excellent display. The week before the game I was surprised to detect a degree of tension and concern whenever the topic came up with Celtic supporters whom I knew. I personally, couldn't see any way in which they'd drop points. 'Fitness' was the response I received from more than one. 'We're not fit enough.'

They weren't, as it turned out. The slow and sodden pitch at Motherwell cut up and drained whatever was left in the Celtic legs, with so much nervous energy having been burned already in that first hour. 'Barry Ferguson had asked how long to go,' said Kenny Clark, the referee in Leith that day. 'I said, "four minutes" and he said, "just blow, this is boring".' And then it happened. 'Some of the Celtic players started to argue among themselves and argue with the referee as they started to feel the pressure,' recalled Foran. 'I had a shot and shanked it but it fell to Scott [McDonald] and he absolutely pinged it into the top corner. When I saw that, I ran off the other way. I thought, "there's no way I'm celebrating, I'll be lynched when I go back to Ireland!" I remember a young Celtic fan crying his eyes out afterwards. He called over in an Irish accent, "Richie, what have you done?" That stuck with me. There was such a sadness among the Celtic support.'

'I felt the stand shaking at that equaliser,' remembered Adam. 'It was just completely unexpected. We naturally assumed the worst.' It is a different feeling to any other football experience. Even goals and victories that happen for your team, against the run of play, are enjoyed in a completely different fashion. You can see that game take shape, you are involved in its pattern. You feel very much in the moment. News like that, the dream message you've been waiting for, must be akin to how lottery winners feel. And then, when you now are filled with so much hope, there is an agony for the two or three minutes left to play, at the prospect of Celtic nicking a winner in the cruellest fashion.

There would be another goal at Fir Park but it was simply confirmation that the impossible had become possible. A Motherwell break a minute later found McDonald with another chance to shoot at goal from a tight angle on the right-hand side. The lifelong Celtic fan from Australia hit it low but it deflected off the foot of Stan Varga and up and over the despairing Rab Douglas. Butcher celebrated on the touchline with as much aggression as he had shown up at Pittodrie all those years before. At Easter Road, thousands, including the Rangers manager, assumed the news was the final whistle. 'I didn't realise there was a second goal until hours later,' said Adam.

McLeish's actions to his players indicated that he thought it was full time. It may as well have been. Rangers, incredibly, were champions for the 51st time. 'I've not heard a noise like that at an away ground at the final whistle, especially given how surreal the second half had been. Folk were crying everywhere, hugging strangers. We walked back over the wee bridge after the game and I was just behind Marvin Andrews when he popped out the sunroof and I got a high five! I think every Rangers fan seems to have been there at that specific moment mind you.'

Understandably the two managers had extremely contrasting reactions. 'There was absolutely nothing said in the changing room,' said Craig Beattie. 'Martin sat on the floor for 20–25 minutes and didn't say a word; everyone was just looking at the floor. It was very rare for the manager to be stuck for words.' For McLeish, however, this drama may have even topped 2003. 'Winning the championship in 2003 was, of course, probably the ultimate because I was in charge of a brilliant team and we beat a very strong Celtic team. But the feeling I got at Easter Road that day was like nothing I had ever experienced before or since. Because it was so unexpected, the party we had back at Ibrox was so special. It was all impromptu and I think many of us were sitting there wondering what had just happened. It was amazing.'

Whether you were there, watching at home or jumping out of your car and running around a McDonald's car park like a maniac, if this poll was about the greatest Rangers moments then this may well top the lot. It was the sheer lack of expectancy and detachment from where the real action was taking place that created the kind of scenario that usually only exists in the dreamworld. It is therefore no surprise that it makes this list; however, there is perhaps some curiosity that it squeezes into the top ten, especially ahead of the three immediately behind it. For Rangers could have won by seven or eight and it would not have mattered, had Celtic done their job. The tenth greatest Rangers game was really about a great Motherwell game. It was a gift. A beautiful one that we clearly haven't gotten bored with after a few years, but a present nonetheless.

Alex McLeish was correct, however, in that you need to be waiting to accept gifts, and not fumble that vital moment yourself. And what are great football games in truth, but a collection of moments that evoke strong feelings. There have been very few hours, amongst the thousands watching Rangers, that produced emotions that were quite as visceral as this.

9

Rangers 2 Parma 0

Champions League Third Qualifying Round, First Leg Wednesday 11 August 1999

'He's a reliable player, Vidmar. Maybe doesn't have the subtlety when he finishes off his moves and runs.'
(Archie McPherson, commentary, 28th minute)

For those Rangers fans slowly making their way from Ibrox Stadium on the night of 21 April 1993, most, if not all, would have felt an acute mixture of abject dejection and searing pride. The door to the inaugural Champions League Final in Munich had been left ajar but, despite giving their all, *sans* Mark Hateley in the final two games, that Rangers side couldn't quite force it open. As spring turned to summer, the disappointment dissipated with the glory of the first domestic treble in a generation and fans were left feeling very secure with our place in the game. European football was changing and we were at the forefront of it. We'd surely go one better next season. Or the next again. Or the next …

Five summers later and that security had been shredded. Dick Advocaat was tasked with restoring pride following continuous humiliation on the continent. With a fresh injection of money and new ideas he set about the job immediately in that season's UEFA Cup. With one turn in Leverkusen, it was his young Scottish protégé Barry Ferguson who sparked a famous win against the highly rated German outfit and arguably the first modern football performance by a Rangers team. Advocaat's new side would succumb to the eventual winners Parma, but without disgrace. After a 1-1 draw at Ibrox and a first-half lead at the Stadio Ennio Tardini, Rangers controlled the tie until Sergio Porrini saw both a red mist and a red card. All thoughts in the summer of 1999, following another treble, were of further restoration work. This time back in the Champions League. Much would depend, as ever, on the draw.

It was Parma again. Of the remaining 30 teams left in the hat for the final qualifying round, there were arguably only three ties that would have been on a par with facing the UEFA Cup holders: Chelsea, Valencia and fellow Serie A side Fiorentina. Other potential opponents such as Dynamo Kiev, PSV Eindhoven, Real Mallorca, Galatasaray and Borussia Dortmund would have fallen into the 'tough but beatable' bracket. The rest, given how much this Rangers side were purring at the time, would have been considered a ticket to group stage. It wasn't just this Parma side and the recent defeat that was to be feared, it was what Italian football represented in that decade. Of the 30 European club finals in the 1990s, Italy was represented 21 times. The tone was set from the very start. At the end of season 1989/90 AC Milan won the European Cup, Sampdoria won the European Cup Winners' Cup, Juventus won the UEFA Cup, beating Fiorentina in the final, Maradona's Napoli won the league title and the Inter side of Lothar Matthäus and Jürgen Klinsmann finished third. What Rangers were to Scottish football in the 90s, Serie A was to European football: completely and utterly dominant.

Reservations about the task at hand weren't the only cause of gloom in Glasgow on the day of the match. Britain's first visible solar eclipse since 1927 meant that visibility in the city was only 82 per cent around 1pm. By early evening the clouds had parted and fans could travel to Ibrox with genuine reasons for growing optimism. Firstly, although Advocaat would dismiss this a 'cheap excuse', the Serie A season hadn't yet started and this was Parma's first competitive game of the season, having not been involved in the earlier qualifying rounds. Secondly, as Sergio Porrini had pointed out in the build-up that week, this was not the draw that Parma had wanted either. We had given them both a fright and a fight the previous season and the Italian media certainly viewed it as a bad pairing. This was a world away from the reputational ruins of Gothenburg and Strasbourg just two years before. Finally and most importantly, we were red hot. At the weekend we had travelled to Tynecastle and defeated Hearts 4-0, the biggest margin of victory Rangers had inflicted there in 36 years. Other than the scoreline and the performance of most players, especially the versatile Claudio Reyna who scored two, it was also evident on that day why the manager viewed his new number nine Michael Mols as the final piece of his jigsaw.

In addition to their rustiness, it could also be argued that Parma were under strength in terms of the available personnel compared to the previous tie. Gone, to Lazio, was their main man in midfield Juan Sebastián Verón, whilst fellow Argentinian Hernán Crespo was injured along with his £21m strike partner Amoruso. Parma would have to 'make do' up front with their new £7m forward Marco Di Vaio playing off their new £12m creator Ariel Ortega, the latest holder of the 'new Maradona' tag which was placed on Argentinian *enganches* until Lionel Messi arrived and it suddenly became less relevant. All of this was built upon one of the strongest defensive units you could find at the time. Gianluigi Buffon, Fabio Cannavaro and Lilian Thuram would all have claims to be in World XIs for the era and the experience of Dino Baggio and World Cup winner Alain Boghossian in the midfield cannot be under-rated. This was a football team from the very top level and many felt that it would need Rangers to be at their strongest to match them.

We weren't. Arthur Numan and Andrei Kanchelskis were definitely ruled out through injury and there were doubts about Neil McCann, Claudio Reyna and Giovanni van Bronkhorst, although all three would eventually start. Rangers would line up with Stefan Klos in goal, a back four of Sergio Porrini, Craig Moore, Lorenzo

Amoruso and Tony Vidmar coming in for Numan with Reyna, Barry Ferguson, van Bronkhorst, McCann, Rod Wallace and Mols making up the rest. Newspaper reports had the side down as a 4-4-2; however, it is arguably far more of a 4-3-3, with the latter three names displaying a fluid and intelligent interchanging movement.

Ibrox was very loud. Even in the great 92/93 season there was often a tension and awe at the beginning of a European night and the crowd grew into their role as the game developed. As the decade wore on the support would often project their frustration onto a Rangers side in Europe and, as a result, it was not necessarily an atmosphere conducive to achieving great results. This was a new era, however, as David Edgar explains: 'I can't remember an Ibrox on a midweek game with so many kits on view. There's such a difference between an Ibrox that thinks "we can do this" as opposed to an Ibrox that is thinking "oh shit man, I hope we don't fuck this up!" There is a symbiosis between the fans and the players. As we grow in belief, so do they. People talk about Dynamo Kiev in 1987 and this was up there with that.'

That belief from the outset was matched on the pitch as Rangers should have been 1-0 up inside the first minute when Rod Wallace's effort was saved by Buffon after being sent through by van Bronkhorst. It was an opportunity where it was perhaps better to gamble and take the shot first time, but it was an early reminder that if there was a moment of hesitation, this defence would quickly shut the chance down. The opening 25 minutes were relatively even, with some nice stuff from both sides and an intriguing battle brewing between Ortega and Amoruso. The Argentine tried to arrest the pattern of the game by immediately pressing the Rangers defence following the Wallace chance and then later getting a good cross in for Di Vaio.

Whether or not Parma were trying to combat the perceived, stereotypical physicality of a Scottish team with some kind of pre-emptive strike is unclear; however, Fabio Cannavaro was fortunate not be booked for an early tackle on McCann. He eventually found the book in 15 minutes for an even worse challenge on Wallace and then, incredibly, was shown a second yellow in the 26th minute for a needless foul on the Englishman when Thuram appeared to have total control of the situation. For a team and a support looking for further reasons to believe, this was literally a game-changer.

The pace didn't let up and Rangers had another effort for Buffon to deal with, the first since the opening minute, as Reyna finished a lovely passing move involving van Bronkhorst, McCann, Mols and Wallace, with a decent strike. It would need more than that to beat the world's number one. A moment of sheer magic, or, indeed, fortune. It would come from perhaps the most unlikely of sources. Frustrated at being seen simply as the deputy for the 'trainer's son', Tony Vidmar did all he could to etch his name into Rangers folklore. On 33 minutes, after a nice period of possession, McCann sent a great ball out wide to the Rangers left-back. Minutes after Archie McPherson had criticised the Australian on commentary for being too obvious in his choices, Vidmar tried his luck by cutting inside Luigi Sartor and having a shot on goal. The strike was on target and Buffon would have had a job to keep it out, but the spin off Thuram's lunge gave him no chance whatsoever. Ibrox erupted.

'Tony Vidmar's face is a joy to watch,' remarked David. 'A mixture of delight and "did I just do that?" The place shook. You can see the camera moving because the stadium is moving!' Given the memory of the previous encounter and the fact that no Scottish club had won in Italy at that point in time (Paul Le Guen's Rangers would be the first to do so in a UEFA Cup group game at Livorno in 2006) there was a keen sense around the ground that a second was required and, more importantly, was there for the taking. A Parma side this strong, however, were very unlikely to collapse, and in the 37th minute Alberto Malesani sacrificed his main attacking threat in Ortega and replaced him with a defender, Stefano Torrisi, thus changing to a back four and sending a message that he'd accept the 1-0 defeat and take their chances at home in a fortnight. There were few bigger signs of the new-found respect that Advocaat had managed to resurrect.

Rangers had control of the remainder of the first half but were playing in front of tight lines. The space that the movement of the front three had exploited in Parma's three-man defence had disappeared. Reyna again popped up with a strike from just outside the box right before the whistle, but Buffon was once more equal to it.

The second half started with less composure and fluidity than the first. Very little was created in terms of clear cut opportunities, and after ten minutes Advocaat made an attacking move by removing the goalscorer Vidmar for Jörg Albertz. There was no real need for an extra defender and van Bronkhorst was given the role of a very liberal left-back as Rangers tried to force the issue. It succeeded in opening the game up as van Bronkhorst caused problems from a free kick, which Thuram scrambled to clear. and Paulo Vanoli, later to be a Rangers player, caused problems in behind Porrini, whilst Marco Di Vaio forced a corner. Vanoli and Albertz were both booked, the Italian for a terrible tackle on Ferguson and the German for simulation in the penalty area.

Rangers were in the awkward position, as time ticked by, of wanting a second but knowing that conceding an equaliser would likely be fatal. Despite the jeopardy of the situation, the home crowd, unlike on previous European nights, didn't project anxiety but re-fuelled the players with hope and energy. This continued during a period where it looked more likely that ten-man Parma would get the next goal. Klos, carrying a knock, stood up well to Di Vaio and then Boghossian in the 72nd minute who had a fantastic shot drilled into the ground which then bounced awkwardly towards goal. It was an excellent save, following a terrible Amoruso header and slack marking by Ferguson, which proved to be crucial. Under the cosh, Advocaat looked to his bench once more. Perhaps Gabriel Amato for Mols and Scott Wilson for Moore, who looked like he might have picked up a knock.

They weren't used. Albertz attempted a tired clearance but managed to win the ball back and then Rangers broke free. Wallace ran the ball into the right-hand channel from the halfway line before clipping a cute ball over to McCann. Surrounded by yellow and blue shirts, he laid it back into the path of the on-rushing Reyna, who met it perfectly through the legs of the luckless Thuram and into the net. Buffon looked devastated, lying back on his post. Reyna, meanwhile, looked like Marco Tardelli.

As the Ibrox noise was turned up to 11, chances to kill the tie came thick and fast. Mols, now enjoying a breath of space for the first time that night, started to twist and turn and cause problems. Ferguson and Wallace too had opportunities to put the shaken and depleted rearguard under severe pressure. In injury time Rangers had three huge chances to book their place in the Champions League. Albertz sent Mols clear in the 90th minute but his first touch was uncharacteristically poor. Albertz then created the best opportunity for Wallace by way of a stinging shot that Buffon did well to keep out. Although the Italian narrowed the angle well, Wallace should have scored from the rebound. Van Bronkhorst had the last chance to provide real comfort, but he blasted his shot well over. Perhaps the passion that had driven the team on from the first whistle had overwhelmed the side when they needed cooler heads.

Advocaat will have surely relished such an illustrious scalp, but publicly he maintained the image of the tough, taciturn taskmaster. 'Tonight we played an excellent game but still we had some players who did not bring the performance they can bring to the team.' Buffon, however, who had for some reason worn a Rangers goalkeeper top with the badges swapped, was not for playing poker. 'It will now be impossible for us to reach the Champions League group games,' he said immediately afterwards. 'This Rangers team is so much better than the one we faced last season in the UEFA Cup. To score three goals against them on our own ground will be very, very difficult. That is why I say victory may be beyond our reach.'

It is not difficult to see why this match features so high on the list. Given the context, the pressure to qualify and the standard of opposition, this match is arguably the greatest European result for Rangers post 1986. It wasn't a smash-and-grab display of grit and spirit. There was fortune, of course, but there was quality too. A Rangers team went toe-to-toe with Europe's best and came out on top. There was a belief that we were back in the big time and that enveloped the entire stadium. 'It was an incredible night,' remarked Claudio Reyna later that night. 'The noise level is something I will never forget, from the moment we came out for the warm up to the end of the game.'

Rangers would face a far fitter and sharper Parma side in northern Italy a fortnight later. Their 1-0 victory was not enough, however, as Advocaat's men held on grimly to such a hard-fought advantage. A sizeable continental obstacle had been overcome, the fans now had their team back in the Champions League and with a genuine belief of making an impact for the first time since 1992/93.

Much would depend, as ever, on the draw …

8

Rangers 2 Aberdeen 0

Scottish Premier Division
Saturday 11 May 1991

'Events are called inevitable only after they have occurred.'
(Mason Cooley)

'Reality is a sliding door,' said Emerson, the poet-philosopher not the Brazilian midfielder and 'Soul Glo' enthusiast. Students of history are often warned to beware the lazy trap of inevitability when trying to assess why things happened the way that they did, as if there were no alternative outcomes possible. In Scottish football, the 1990s belonged to Rangers, characterised as they were by 'nine'. With such financial advantage and talent available, it was only a matter of when, and not if, Rangers would wrap up title after title, the whole decade blurring for some into one long, untroubled procession. That may well be true for those middle years, with opposition crushed mentally before they could even consider lasting the pace, but not so for the final two seasons of the run and certainly not at the start. Counterfactual history is an enjoyable exercise for those of us who revel in the academia of 'what ifs'; however, there was nothing theoretical about the situation facing Rangers on the final day of season 1990/91. Failure to beat Aberdeen at Ibrox and there would be no title that year, no nine-in-a-row legacy and possibly an alternative history where Walter Smith was simply a caretaker boss in charge for four games instead of a behemoth that dominates the history of the club.

It was an appropriate conclusion to what had been a turbulent season. Even the first trophy success of the campaign, the ever-reliable Skol League Cup, perfectly encapsulated the heightening tumult within Ibrox. Trevor Steven had scored a wonderful goal, bursting through from the heart of the pitch, to beat Aberdeen in the semi-final and Richard Gough popped up in the box late on to defeat Celtic in the final but by then, incredibly, he was club captain as the two ties sandwiched the surprise departure of Terry Butcher. Short of fitness and form at the start of that season, post Italia '90, he was still regarded as the foundation stone of the team and therefore the decision by Souness to show his ruthless streak once more sent shockwaves through the support. It was a fanbase still trying to deal with the fact that their number-one hero, Ally McCoist, was spending so much time on the bench that he was gaining the nickname 'The Judge'. They unfairly blamed the summer signing Mark Hateley for this situation, even though it was clear that a target man was always in Souness's plan and that it was therefore really Maurice Johnston who was the reason McCoist wasn't getting game time. As had been the case for the previous two seasons, it was Aberdeen who were the main rivals and they had clawed their way back into contention with a win at Pittodrie, which then precipitated back-to-back Old Firm defeats at Parkhead in the league and Scottish Cup, the latter a 2-0 defeat with three Rangers players being sent off. A lead that was once seven points in January, was three by the end of March. Far from harmonious maybe, but Rangers were still in control and already had one cup at the top of the marble staircase.

'April is the cruellest month,' wrote T.S Elliot in his painfully perfect masterpiece *The Waste Land*, and so it felt for Rangers fans everywhere in 1991 when the father of the revolution was sensationally shown the door. Graeme Souness had mentally checked out anyway by the time he told David Murray that he wanted to accept Liverpool's third offer to become manager in the summer. The physical change in his appearance when he left Ibrox, compared to the bright Young Turk who had burst through the door five years earlier, was stark. If he wasn't facing a backlash from the fans about attacking selections, he was arguing with tea ladies in Perth about jugs of orange juice. Half a decade in one of the most pressurised jobs in football was taking its toll, the extent of which was unknown even at the time. Murray, at that moment a dynamic force for good at the helm, was clinically decisive. There would be no long goodbye, the way there would later be for Smith and McLeish, and Souness was told to go there and then.

Fans were left worried and concerned about a season that was quickly spiralling out of control. 'I sometimes struggle to get it across to younger bears how much fans our age adored this guy,' said David Edgar. 'He was our footballing father. He was responsible for the turnaround but by then he looked unhappy. He had found Scottish football too small for him, he felt smothered. I think the Hateley thing had annoyed him, I think he had felt the right to be trusted when it came to decisions about players but if there was a rival for his affections amongst the support then it would be Ally.' Although some big names such as World Cup-winning manager Franz Beckenbauer and the Arsenal manager George Graham (on the way to his second title in England) were strongly linked, the players supported a promotion for the assistant. 'The immediate message from Murray and Gough was that Walter Smith was doing the training anyway and that this wouldn't be much of a transition. The levels of trust at the time were absolutely implicit, so we backed him. However, I was 13 and I won't lie to you, when I saw names like Beckenbauer and Graham and what we got was our assistant manager, I was a little disappointed.'

Handed a two-point lead with four games to go, Smith steadied things with two gritty 1-0 wins, away to St Mirren with a late and brilliant goal from the youngster Sandy Robertson, and at home to Dundee United in a midweek fixture four days later.

On 4 May, the penultimate day of the season, there was a possibility that Rangers could win the title if they were to beat Motherwell at Fir Park and Aberdeen dropped points at home to St Johnstone. It didn't quite go to plan. Not only was the title not secured, Rangers ended that day second in the table. The Scottish Cup finalists (and eventual winners) took the lead on 25 minutes from a John Philliben shot into the roof of the net, after a Davie Cooper corner, but Rangers were handed an opportunity to get back on terms in the second half when Pieter Huistra was sent tumbling in the box by Craig Patterson; however, Mark Walters, usually so reliable from the spot, blazed over the bar. Pushing for an equaliser, Rangers were caught on the counter attack when Dougie Arnott scored a second with only five minutes to go. With Aberdeen having already won 2-1, even the 2-0 defeat would have kept Rangers top by way of the slim virtue of having scored more goals. Despite the advantage, the game wasn't managed well at all as Rangers continued to press and, when Terry Hurlock's bad pass was cut out, Arnott counter-punched once more with a beautiful dink over Woods that went in off his left post. Rangers had led the way at the top of the Scottish Premier Division since November, and now, with only one game remaining, were somehow behind.

'The Motherwell game was a horrible afternoon,' recalls David. 'Sitting in a pub with all the adults and no one was talking. Just the radio blaring. The response was very reactive. "That's what happens when you don't appoint a manager. I told you this would happen." But by the Monday morning I had picked myself up. I was of the opinion that if this Rangers team lost one game, they wouldn't lose two. We were Rangers and this is what the last five years had taught me. I got more nervous as the week went on, however, and you'd read reports in the paper that the Rangers dressing room was essentially a scene from *M*A*S*H*, but I was still sure that it would happen.' Richard Gough was ill in hospital, Trevor Steven was definitely ruled out, whereas McCoist and Durrant made the bench when they would be considered nowhere near fit enough to make a normal match-day squad and John Brown started, despite being told that his Achilles would definitely snap during the afternoon.

For the first time since 1965, the champions of Scotland would be decided on the final day in a direct shoot-out between the only two sides with a chance of taking the crown. The tension was cranked up all week long, and for one player it had started early in the day. 'I went into Ibrox early that day, around 10am,' said the new assistant manager Archie Knox when he spoke to *Heart and Hand* in 2019. 'I heard a shout from the bath and here was Bomber [John Brown] lying in one of the baths shouting, "Let's get into them!" I remember thinking "fucking hell Bomber, it's only 10 o'clock. It's five hours before we get kicked off and you're up for it already."' Future Rangers player David Robertson was making his final appearance for Aberdeen that day, before his move to Ibrox in the summer. 'There was so much hype around it. Rangers had so many injuries so we felt that we would get what we needed: at least a draw. We were in a Portakabin because of the building works going on in the Main Stand at the time

(Rangers were in the away dressing room whilst the temporary hut was assembled for visitors at the tunnel). I remember looking to Paul Mason, because we could hear the Rangers supporters thumping and singing upstairs, and we just looked at each other as if to say "this is going to be pretty difficult here".'

Smith went with the same starting XI that had failed at Motherwell the previous Saturday, which was Chris Woods in goal, a makeshift back four of Gary Stevens (an ever-present that season), Scott Nisbet, John Brown and Tom Cowan, a midfield of Ian Ferguson, who ironically was coming back into fitness and form after a lengthy spell out, Terry Hurlock, captain for the day Nigel Spackman and Mark Walters, with Hateley and Johnston up front. Aberdeen arrived at Ibrox unbeaten against Rangers in the three league meetings that season. A 0-0 draw at Pittodrie was followed up by a 2-2 draw at Ibrox before Christmas when they came back from 2-0 down. The 1-0 victory was at the start of March and was part of an incredible run towards to finish line. Aberdeen had racked up 23 points from the previous 24 available, scoring 25 goals in the process with a fluent and vibrant 4-3-3. Rangers, meanwhile, limped into this game with just 16 points from the last 12 games, and at a scoring rate of just one a game. The momentum was only going one way.

Aberdeen helped change that momentum themselves. Alex Smith, an experienced coach, blinked first and binned the formation that had got him to the summit right at the moment that he needed to plant his flag. Their move back to a more sturdy 4-4-2 was a sure sign of a team who knew that they didn't need to win. It was still a side with a mixture of experience and youth. A young Eoin Jess was partnered with the excellent Hans Gillhaus up front, whilst the young full-backs Stephen Wright and Robertson could be talked through the game by Alex McLeish and Stewart McKimmie. The midfield lacked the dynamism of the previous shape, but in Bobby Connor, Jim Bett, Brian Grant and Peter Van de Ven, it didn't lack know-how.

The weak point, however, was Michael Watt, the rookie replacement for the injured Theo Snelders in the Aberdeen goal, and it was one that didn't go unnoticed by one of the Rangers forwards. 'I had a knack for spotting a weak point in a defence and then drilling and drilling until no one wanted to mark you,' recalled Mark Hateley when he spoke to *Heart and Hand*. 'Their biggest weakness was their goalkeeper and I nailed him in the first ten minutes. I didn't look at team sheets etc as I needed that time in my own head before a game. I remember walking down the tunnel and I saw this young man and thought he was a mascot or something! I thought "here's an opportunity," so I turned to Gary Stevens when we got out on the field and asked him to hang one up in the first ten minutes, not to fire one across, but one where the goalkeeper could come for it. Sure enough he did, the young boy came out and I caught him with a real sore one and the moment he hit the floor the two centre-halves, who would normally be all over me, didn't want to know. They left him on the floor and from that moment I thought, "we cannot lose this game".'

That challenge was in the first minute of a frenetic atmosphere at Ibrox, being re-shaped with the addition of the Club Deck. The early exchanges were mostly physical, with Gillhaus, Stevens and Van de Ven being the most notorious. When the football was eventually played, it was the team on form who made the better openings. Jim Bett and Gillhaus went over the bar from chances of varying degrees of difficulty, but the chance of the season fell to Peter Van de Ven. It originated from a poor clearance from Spackman that was picked up by Stewart McKimmie in the middle of the park. His first touch was heavy and his second would be a foul by today's standards, but it resulted in a through ball to the moustachioed Dutchman, clear of the onrushing Nisbet. The chance was over so quickly but he simply appeared to freeze in the moment, just passing the ball back to Woods with the outside of his boot. No back lift or power, just an apology for a shot on goal.

The early Aberdeen pressure was exacerbated in the 20th minute by the need to replace the injured Tom Cowan, who had effectively been playing with a broken leg for a few minutes. Smith brought on the half-fit Durrant and started a game of defensive musical chairs that wouldn't end there. Somehow, Rangers began to get more of a foothold in the game, with Ian Ferguson going close with some long-range specials, but Aberdeen continued to be a threat on the break. As the interval approached, Aberdeen still held all the cards. 'I remember big Alex [McLeish] saying to me "come on we are nearly halfway there,"' recalled Robertson on *The Time Capsule*. 'Two minutes later big Hateley scored and we were never getting back into the game just because of the support and determination that the Rangers players had.'

The goal was created by Mark Walters, his control, patience and execution remaining sublime even as he slipped on the touchline. The finish from Hateley was world class. 'It was a perfect ball, right in between the penalty spot and the six yard box, but there was still a hell of a lot left for Hateley to do,' said David Edgar. 'First of all he needed to beat this commanding centre-half to the ball, then he needed to get enough power on it, because it dropped out of the sky, and then guide it accurately. He did all of that with such a thundering header. Full credit to Watt for making the despairing dive because it made the goal look even better. Ibrox was just insane, Hateley spun off, going wild, and it was just the perfect time, right before the break. However, it changed little. Like an away goal in Europe, Aberdeen still only needed one to be champions. But my dad was completely serene at half-time. "They've missed their chances son, we have scored ours. Another one and we are home."'

It didn't take long in coming after the re-start and was the result of two Aberdeen mistakes. Bobby Connor had mopped up a Rangers attack and had pressed the ball higher up the field for Scott Booth, a half-time substitute for the injured Jess. Booth chose to immediately go back into the Aberdeen half, but the ball lacked any kind of force behind its confused purpose and Maurice Johnston pounced. His shot was straight at Watt, but he spilled it right into the path of the waiting Hateley, who turned the ball into the empty net. The Rangers scorer is in no doubt that this was a direct result from his original interaction. 'The second goal came directly from that incident. He spilled it because he saw me bearing down on him. His eye was on me. The rest is history and we didn't stop for the next six years.' It is often said that this match was the turning point for Mark Hateley and his relationship with the Rangers support, winning them over in the biggest match of the season. If so then it is more than a little unfair. He scored 15 goals that season, most notably against Celtic at New Year, and the only goal in some tight away games, including a last-minute winner at Tynecastle in January. The adulation was possibly starting to get warm by this stage at any rate, but it was indeed a definitive way to seal the deal.

Alex Smith replaced Van de Ven for Van der Ark, and once Aberdeen returned to their 4-3-3 they immediately looked more at ease, but it was far too late in the day to cause any significant concern. Even John Brown's inevitable tendon injury didn't lead to the necessary capitulation as Spackman and Stevens were now at centre-half, Hurlock at right-back, with Johnston back into midfield. Rangers continued to regroup and see out the danger until the moment when Ian Ferguson asked referee Brian McGinlay how long was left and simply raised his arms aloft at the answer.

It was a famous win that endures as much for its adversity as its importance. When fans relay their tales of this day, they will always include the injuries and the state of the league table after Fir Park. It is a very Rangers quirk, beautifully exemplified by the popular old song 'A Trip To Ibrox', the story of a fictitious Old Firm New Year victory which starts with Celtic going a goal ahead. Even in poetry, Rangers fans would rather come back from trouble than bask in a controlled mauling.

However, the importance of the result should be the reason that it makes it to the top ten. Never was the nine-in-a-row era more threatened by one match than this, and the sliding-door questions around the period are almost endless. Would Souness have continued to preside over that dangerous slump if he was granted his wish to continue on to the end of the season and, with some more time to consider it, would Murray have appointed a bigger name in 1991? Would Aberdeen have played so meek and mild at Ibrox had Rangers shut down the Motherwell game at 2-0, and how would a patched up Rangers have coped? If their Dutchmen had taken one of their early chances, would Rangers have had what it took to come back from behind? Smith would have most probably stayed on even if Aberdeen had snatched the title but, without the quest for the nine in the background, had the next few seasons played out in much the same fashion as they did, would he have been sacked three years later on European grounds, at a time where Rangers could still just about financially compete, before the game left us behind?

None of those doors, of course, were opened. Instead Smith used that win as a catalyst and produced two seasons of absolutely sparkling football, with McCoist and a now fully accepted Hateley finally discovering their alchemy the following term. 'We've been preparing all week for one game. One cup final,' said Hateley immediately after the game. 'And Rangers in a cup final? Who'd bet against us?' The flow of history really isn't inevitable. There really are a myriad of possible twists and turns that can lead to significantly different outcomes, no matter how small they seem at the time. However, in the 1990s, Rangers doing the business when it absolutely mattered most, was as close as dammit.

7

Rangers 6 Dunfermline Athletic 1

Scottish Premier League
Sunday 25 May 2003

'It was turmoil but, at the same time, anyone who hasn't lived through that atmosphere and the emotions is missing something.'
(Alex McLeish, post-match)

It was the kind of afternoon that made you feel sorry for those who don't like sport. The kind who sniff at the emotions invested in professional athletes engaged in real competition but will happily lose themselves emotionally in professional actors pretending to be other people. The sporting conclusions that remove the breath of those already immersed can't be contrived by even the best writers for stage and screen. Imagine not experiencing that gradual increase in belief during the final day of the Ryder Cup at Medinah or complaining that the match-winning innings by Ben Stokes at Headingley, when all looked lost beyond saving, was the first item on the news. Like the end of any great tale, the impact is heightened by the narrative that precedes it. Cup finals and prize fights endure, of course, but they are bite-size stories. Europe's victory in 2012 was special because of the hammering they took for a day and half before some light was opened at the end of the Saturday and the stage for the Sunday was set. Stokes's innings would have been sensational in any setting but the ebb and flow of a test match provided even sharper context for its miraculous brutality. Once again, a football league season, when it goes down to the wire, infuses those final games with so much story and emotional investment. It's not just about the fluctuations of one isolated 90 minutes, it's about fans going through the full gamut on a weekly basis. It is torturous, it can be unbearable, and there's nothing quite like it.

Rangers have won the league championship on the final day of the season six times in the last 50 years and only the 2-0 defeat of Motherwell at Ibrox in 1978 doesn't make it onto this list. By some quirk of beautiful group-think, the *Heart and Hand* listeners have chosen the five that did in perfect order of ascending drama. In Games 46 and 15, we have discussed the 'standard' story of these affairs, the one where the team that starts the day with their noses in front and in control takes care of business and walks away with the title as most expected. Then, in Game 10, we had the 'gift'. The one where favours are required and are duly, albeit so rarely, received. A day when everything is out of your team's control and so with it becomes weary agony and then searing ecstasy. In the last chapter we re-assessed the tension involved in the 'showdown', the result of pure fixture caprice, where the two challengers are able to fight it out directly for the main prize. Finally, here, we have the most dramatic conclusion of them all. Rangers and Celtic were locked on points and goal difference at 3pm that Sunday afternoon. All that separated the two was the fact that Rangers had scored more over the course of the season. With Rangers at home to Dunfermline and Celtic down at Kilmarnock, neither side had destiny fully in their grip as they took to the field. In a beautifully tense combination of the usual scenarios, both sides needed to do their own job but both also needed to know what was happening at either side of the M77. It produced a day that has never been quite matched in Scotland ever since.

Once again, the full story provides the finale with more weight. Season 2002/03 was an exceptional one in itself, before we even get to the twists and turns of its denouement. Rangers fans started the season, Alex McLeish's first full term in charge, with reason to be optimistic. Despite having gone two seasons without winning the title, the first time fans had experienced that since 1986, McLeish had grabbed the two domestic cups of 2001/02, both with memorable defeats of Celtic along the way. He inherited a very talented squad but one that needed to smile again and feel loved, after the scorched earth of the Adovcaat era's conclusion. That feel-good factor continued to sweep into the new season. Despite dropping two points at Kilmarnock on the opening day and taking only four points from 12 against Celtic, Rangers recorded their best points average since the war (2.55 per game and with everything pre 1995/96 adjusted for three points for a win), and to date the only time a Rangers side has averaged over 2.5, with Advocaat's 1999/00 hitting that mark dead on. As with almost all great achievements, these new heights were driven by competition, the incessant accumulation of points being simply necessary against a very strong Celtic side.

Indeed, by the middle of March, the script was being written for this season to be Celtic's year of destiny. Despite Rangers having the better of the first two derby clashes, Celtic won the third and sat three points behind with a game in hand. More than that, they were still in all four competitions as their UEFA Cup quarter-final against Liverpool was finely poised after the first leg. As their run developed, so did the taunts. 'You'll be watching *The Bill* when we're in Seville, it's going to be three in a row!' Apparently, they were going to win the lot! By the end of the month, the scale of that ambition had been halved. Inverness Caledonian Thistle were quickly becoming Celtic's *bête noir* as they were eliminated from the Scottish Cup in the Highlands, but not before Rangers had won the Old Firm League Cup Final at Hampden, a game we almost contrived to throw away. The first hour was magical, a 2-0 lead that should have been more, created by fast, dynamic, interchanging attacking football, the very opposite of the more robust, rudimentary O'Neill approach. Complacency then met brute strength and the lead was eventually cut to one, and then almost eliminated entirely, but John Hartson dragged his penalty wide of the post in the dying minutes.

Celtic's European progress was maintained, however, and qualification for that season's UEFA Cup Final was secured before the final derby showdown of the season at Ibrox in April. A Rangers win would have probably ended the title there and then, as it would have secured an 11-point gap, albeit with Rangers having four games left and Celtic five. There was a general flatness around Ibrox that day. It was pointless to deny it. As good as our domestic season was shaping up, European success, especially for a Scottish club in the 21st century, would have eclipsed it. Celtic rode their wave and were deserving winners. Rangers continued to stumble against fellow Scottish Cup finalists Dundee up at Dens Park the following weekend, with Barry Ferguson missing two penalties in a 2-2 draw. Celtic would defeat the same opponent 6-2 at home in their game in hand, a match moved by the authorities so that they could prepare adequately for the final. There was now no margin for error and for the next two fixtures Celtic got to set the target by playing first. Not only did Rangers have to match their result, we had to score the required amount of goals.

There is so much to admire about this Rangers team during that season. Some of the football was excellent, the team were unbeaten in the league until Boxing Day and they possessed that often crucial championship-winning ability to string together runs of wins (one eight-match run and one seven) but it was the response in this run-in most of all that showed their monumental mental strength. A 4-0 win at home to Kilmarnock and a 2-0 win away to Hearts were bang on the required rate of scoring and it meant that Rangers started the final game with the slimmest of arithmetical advantages. By the time kick-off came, however, they would have the psychological edge too. José Mourinho's Porto had managed the UEFA Cup Final better during the week and saved us all that particular nightmare scenario. The mood around Ibrox was completely different than it had been a month earlier. Fake police hats were in abundance as thousands of relieved fans could now properly respond to songs about television police dramas without any fear of comeuppance. All eyes were now on the task in hand and, with both sides joined together on a goal difference of +68, that was clear: score more goals than Celtic.

McLeish had the luxury of a clear week's preparation and a strong squad available from which to select his starting XI. Stefan Klos was in goal, as he was for every single game that season, and the reliable four of Numan, Amoruso, Moore and Ricksen shaped up in front of him. Barry Ferguson and Mikel Arteta, the summer's big addition, would control midfield, leaving Rangers with a mouth-watering front four of Ronald de Boer, Shota Averladze, Michael Mols and Claudio Caniggia. The start typified the season. The play was patient but with purpose, and controlled passing led to a half-chance for Mols that he somehow managed to squeeze in off the post. It was a dream start after only two minutes and it felt like the Main Stand moved in front of my eyes. Rangers were now +69.

Then, just after ten minutes, the unthinkable happened when Dunfermline, and the experienced Craig Brewster in particular, were given the kind of freedom that a defence not planning on having to play with too much intensity might afford. The ball eventually fell to Jason Dair and he unleashed a brilliant drive into the top left-hand corner. It was a goal that his uncle, Jim Baxter, would have been proud of 40 years before but Dair looked as if he had just scored at the wrong end, which in a way he had. It was a day of mixed emotions for the Dunfermline and Kilmarnock players, some of whom had history with Rangers and Celtic. Dair's goal was a perfect example of a professional doing their job but without too much relish. +68

Rangers didn't hang around to respond, and five minutes later the advantage was restored. Again there was no panicked long ball, instead some composed play, although the final ball down the right flank for Fernando Ricksen was a little overdone and his 'pass' back to Caniggia was effectively a tackle. There was nothing frantic about the Argentine's finish, however, as he coolly swept the ball home. Chris Sutton headed Celtic in front soon after so any further advantage was short-lived. It was Caniggia's seventh goal against the Pars that season as Rangers scored 23 against them in seven games. A perfect opponent then, when you are in the search for goals. There would be one more on the half-hour mark and it came from what appeared to be a lost cause. An Arteta corner was cleared and, after some more patient passing, a speculative ball down the left was sent for Amoruso to chase. Not exactly possessing the frame of a typical winger, it was a bizarre sight to watch this hulk not only chase down the ball, but control and deliver a delightful cross for Averladze to head home. It was not something that Adam Thornton would forget. 'That Amoruso assist is so vivid as it was pretty much right in front of me. It was one of those where he was galloping towards a lost cause and you think, "Just leave it, it's going out of play, it's in their area, there's no danger." And when he got it I was then thinking, "Ok well done, just get it back to Numan and we can build something," but no, no, instead he delivered this incredible cross. But the exhilaration was short lived because news of a Celtic second came through and you knew it was going to be like that all day and that we'd need five or six.'

The situation at half-time was much the same as it was at kick-off, with the two sides tied on goal difference and Rangers still holding that control on the basis of goals scored. All that breathless drama and we were no further forward after 45 minutes. Within ten minutes of the re-start an Alan Thompson penalty put Celtic 3-0 in front and ahead in the title race for the first time that day. Rangers, by contrast, and with the pressure now on, were slower and more timid. Any knots in the stomach at the start of the day were now ballooning. There were chances, none better than an indirect free kick from ten yards after Derek Stillie picked up from a back pass but it didn't go quite to plan. 'Here was the moment to get another breakthrough,' recalls Adam. 'We were expecting Amoruso to hit the top corner, which he did, but it was the top corner of the Copland Rear sadly.' Brewster nearly emulated Dair's effort on 63 minutes but Stefan Klos, such an underrated hero of this free-flowing side, made a brilliant save.

It was perhaps the shot in the arm that was required and a minute later saw the kind of moment that summed up this incredible afternoon. Neil McCann had replaced Caniggia at half-time and had been industrious from the outset. His brilliant cross was met perfectly by de Boer, who ghosted into the danger area from seemingly nowhere and Rangers were back in front. Or were they? The celebrations were halted by the man in front of me who, with a radio earpiece in one ear, shouted, 'Wait … Larsson … No, it's fine, he's hit the post.' At the exact same time as one header flew into the net, another crashed against the woodwork. League championships shouldn't be judged on those moments. Such a view ignores the 37 other games available to secure the flag. The mistakes made, the opportunities lost. Every point is worth the same. Our need for drama and narrative, however, demands that it be crystallised in that way. On the final day of a season crammed full of moments, that was it. +71

If Larsson had scored, the sense of deflation that would have spread around the stadium may well have been critical. Instead Rangers powered on and three minutes later followed up one of their finest goals of the season with the worst, but most important. Again it was McCann causing all of the problems on the left and his cross was eventually bundled home by Steven Thompson, a winter signing from Dundee United. It was Rangers 100th league goal of the season and finally created some breathing space. Celtic would need two now. +72

They'd get their chances. Thompson had another go from the penalty spot but this time he blazed it well over the bar, but Stilian Petrov did manage to get Celtic's fourth with 17 minutes to go as they re-joined Rangers on the same goal difference. Back at Ibrox, Steven Thompson hit the bar with a header and then tried to force a pretty tired shot at goal but it looked like we were spent for the day until Neil McCann wriggled clear of Mark McGarty and was eventually fouled in the box for an injury time penalty. 'All I can remember thinking at the time was "I sincerely hope that Barry Ferguson is nowhere near this fucking penalty!"' said Adam. It would be the young Spaniard, Arteta, who had saved the blushes in Dundee from the spot, who stood up when the moment demanded. Players of far greater experience, like Ronald de Boer, couldn't watch. 'I knew this was a big occasion when I saw Ronald de Boer looking the other way at the penalty. It means a lot to us in this little part of the world but a player of his experience? It just showed you how big a drama this was.'

He needn't have worried. The penalty was stroked home with the utmost class and confidence and, even though he sought to ruin such a moment with the worst celebration in the history of the game, he was responsible for finishing the title race as a contest. Only then, deep into injury time and in the final breath of the season, did we know that it was actually ours. The players looked as exhausted as the supporters felt, strolling around the park, some with face in hands, as we all waited those final seconds for the final whistle to blow at Rugby Park. It was perhaps a moment of drama made more for television, with its split screen views, than for those of us relying on FM stereo. Television, however, can't replicate the live experience of that communal celebration when the news came through, nor the shared celebration when Howard from the Halifax adverts, in a career moment that could only be matched by being in the finale of *The Office*, handed over the Bank of Scotland Scottish Premier League crown to Barry Ferguson. Ticker tape, fireworks and all, there is nothing that matches that roar when your team lifts trophies.

'If you want a happy ending, that depends, of course, on where you stop your story.' said Orson Welles, who knew a thing or two about drama himself. Such is sport that it never really ends. There is always another season. Such was life at 21st-century Rangers, that success could never be enjoyed quite like it was in those sunnier days at the end of the 20th. There was always a spot of grey on the horizon, although the naivety of youth could sometimes ignore that. 'McLeish had won five out of five realistic trophies since coming in halfway through the previous season and, at the time, it felt like the start of something,' said Adam, 18 at the time. 'Which, of course, it wouldn't be. Amoruso and Numan would leave immediately, Ferguson soon after. Downsizing was now going to be the reality for the foreseeable future.'

It is perhaps this context that can somewhat diminish the love for this season and this team. 'Tactically it was a bit of a breakthrough at that time in Scottish football,' said Adam, host of *Tactics Talk* on the *Heart and Hand* network. 'The media were incessant that season that we didn't have this big number nine, an out-and-out striker that we could rely on each week. "You could win a cup but not a title," they would say. Celtic had three of them of course. However, we had four interchangeable attackers on the field at all times.' It was a flexibility that won a treble, which was confirmed at Hampden the following week in the Scottish Cup final. This match at Ibrox was Rangers' season in microcosm with six different scorers making their mark on the day and six different players reaching double figures for a season that brought us 100 goals and ultimately decided the destiny of the league.

So much of this afternoon can't have been good for our health. Grown adults feeling sick with nerves, helpless as we always are to affect anything on the field. But you wouldn't have it any other way. 'What's the point? Why put yourself through it? It's only a game.' Well, because of the ending of course. Like any good drama.

+73

6

Leeds United 1 Rangers 2

European Cup Second Round, Second Leg
Wednesday 4 November 1992

'I fell in love with football as I was later to fall in love with women: suddenly, inexplicably, uncritically, giving no thought to the pain or disruption it would bring with it.'

(Nick Hornby, *Fever Pitch*)

'It would be completely irresponsible of our supporters to turn up,' so said Alister Hood, the Operations Executive at Ibrox in 1992. With it only being three years since the Home International between Scotland and England was abolished due to crowd trouble, the decision to ban both sets of away fans from the 'Battle of Britain' clashes, the matches that would determine the first-ever British entrant into the Champions League, was unanimous. These were to be exclusively the preserve of the home support. Travelling was strictly prohibited.

Fat chance. Such plans were probably never designed to keep *everyone* away, just enough to manage the situation in a controlled fashion. Anyone who believed otherwise, that some fans would simply sit tight and say, 'oh well, it's STV for me then,' doesn't know football fandom at all. For some, it is simply not an option to miss any game, let alone the big ones. Missing big family moments because Rangers happen to be up in Dundee that day is just shrugged off as an occupational hazard for a job that they don't actually have. Annual leave allocation is dependent on European runs. And, when the other kind of love raises its head, decisions have to be made. As one friend put it, 'you just have to be up front about your addiction from the start. Other things can come and go but following the bears isn't negotiable.' And it *is* a genuine addiction for some. Being so close to the heart of the action, the feeling of being enveloped by it and sharing this collective identity with a large group of people, means that testosterone levels can increase and decrease by up to 20 per cent depending on how the game is going, leading to rapidly fluctuating levels of euphoria and stress. It is the psychological impact of this continual chemical change that many believe to be 'the bug'. For some fans, you *have* to be there.

'We were always going to make it,' Barry McNeil told me. 'I was 20 years old at the time and my old man was working with a company that was based down in Leeds so he managed to sort us four tickets. There were actually eight, but four went elsewhere. There was never any dubiety about it happening. There was no hassle either. I was down with my pal Cammy [Gordon Cameron] who is sadly no longer with us, and two other boys that I didn't know too well. We ended up befriending a Leeds fan in a pub in the afternoon and he made sure we were ok near the ground. We were just there to watch our team.'

If there was ever a game that season to sneak your way into, it was this one. Perfectly poised after the first leg at Ibrox (Game 30), it didn't need the inevitable media hype that it got. The English press pack believed the tie to be all but over, with Gary McAllister's sensational away goal the key that they believed Leeds United needed to take away with them. Much of that was famously pinned on the Rangers dressing room wall but any sober analysis should have been able to pierce the hyperbole and bluster. Leeds had already lost four times in the league by this point and had conceded 23 goals, only scoring 25 in reply. Andy Goram's goal, meanwhile, had only been breached 11 times, in contrast to the fireworks at the other end as Ally McCoist was warming up for another Golden Boot-winning season, his hat-trick at home to Motherwell on the Saturday another contribution to the 38 Rangers goals already. Howard Wilkinson remained bullish, however, that his side would be able to do to Rangers what they did to Stuttgart in the last round. 'It's no secret we have been conceding goals this season and it is a problem, but we will certainly score against Rangers and we will win the tie.' Although Walter Smith seemed to shrug, with a confidence that his side would do their talking on the park, Richard Gough met Wilkinson's challenge in his pre-match conversations with the press, which were realistic and eerily prescient. 'I think it looks as though we will have to get a goal to go through and I would love to see how they would handle it if we were to score very early as they did against us at Ibrox.'

'We were there relatively early,' recalls Barry. 'About 20 minutes before kick-off we were in our seats, which were four rows behind the Rangers dugout. The whole game plan was to be as quiet as we could possibly be, but I had enjoyed a few beers and as soon as I saw Archie Knox I shouted, "ARCHIE!" and he looked at us as if to say "what the fuck are you boys doing here?" That brought a wee bit of attention to us, I must admit.' Smith had kept the media, and Wilkinson, guessing about who would replace Trevor Steven, an injury blow from the first leg. In the end he opted for the industry and mobility of Dale Gordon to slot into a very established XI, instead of the flair of Huistra or Mikhailichenko. This was a night for battlers as well as ball players, but the former would have to come first. The Rangers side that night, who were on £20,000 a man to get through, was Goram in goal, McPherson, Gough, Brown and Robertson, Dale Gordon, Ian Ferguson, Stuart McCall and Ian Durrant, with Hateley and McCoist up front. No natural width but a trusted set of players for the biggest night of the season so far. Leeds were without David Batty, who was stretchered off during the 2-2 draw with Coventry City at the weekend. He was replaced by the late

David Rocastle, the only change to the side that lined up at Ibrox. It was a side that included John Lukic, not only under fire for his performance that evening but for his start to the season in general. Despite Gary McAllister's public defence of him – 'We are all right behind John. He makes great saves week in, week out and if it had not been for him we might not have been in the European Cup' – there was no hiding from the fact that he could only point to one clean sheet in 16.

This may have been a step up in terms of tests, but it is always foolish to write off a side that are in a winning groove, and doing so under pressure. This match arrived near the end of a busy 17 days for Rangers, where they faced Leeds United home and away, won the Skol League Cup against Aberdeen, gave an exceptional performance in a convincing 4-2 defeat of Motherwell at Ibrox and would finish on the Saturday with a trademark 1-0 win at Parkhead. It was a side that was firing. It was a side that was ready.

Rangers would rely on their rearguard in this game, but you wouldn't have predicted that from the very first exchange when Leeds could have driven a bus through the backline as Rocastle released Cantona, but Goram stood up well. Brown probably did enough to put off the Frenchman, still considered a bit of a liability in his adopted land, but Gough was nowhere to be seen. It was an inauspicious start but any nerves dissolved straight from Goram's clearance. The long kick upfield was flicked on by Ian Durrant, beating Chris Fairclough to reverse the traditional roles and set up his target man. Hateley let it bounce once and then, bang. Inside two minutes the Leeds away-goal advantage, the platform on which this siege would be based, had disappeared in the most spectacular fashion. 'People were still taking their seats as it was the first few minutes and so even though we stood up, it wasn't really noticed. We didn't bring attention to ourselves thankfully because there was still a lot of milling around.'

If Rangers took on the Leeds role from the first leg, then the hosts responded in a similar fashion too, with much of the first half being an onslaught on the Rangers goal. Within the first ten minutes Andy Goram was demonstrating why he would be such a key part of that night and that season, twice more denying Cantona when he managed to find space in behind the Rangers defence. He would continue to go long when he had the ball, the goal of course coming that way, but all it did was hand the initiative back and the same pattern would repeat itself. Rangers were clearly more comfortable dealing with the creative threat from that Leeds midfield once they had reorganised their shape, rather than be caught on the back foot by trying to play through them. A Strachan free kick caused all sorts of mayhem, but neither Fairclough nor Chapman could guide the ball home. Rangers were 3-1 ahead in the tie but there were clear signs of nerves at only 12 minutes on the clock.

Rangers won their first corner on 18 minutes and therefore the first opportunity to put Lukic under pressure, which Gough duly did but the goalkeeper managed, just, to get his hands on the ball. Rangers gradually looked more comfortable on the counter, Durrant on a bursting run before finding Hateley who couldn't gather cleanly and was eventually smothered out. The Leeds United route was more direct, Cantona getting some space just after the half hour, which Goram did well to stop, and then Stuart McCall heading off the line from a Chris Whyte header, before the siege continued without losing pace. Cantona claimed a David Robertson handball, then saw an over-head kick of his own and a Gary Speed volley blocked, before a Rangers breakaway suggested a sign of things to come as Durrant set up McCoist, whose first-time shot was well saved by Lukic. As the interval approached, it was becoming clear that Eric Cantona and Andy Goram were having their very own personal duel. Goram closed him down after a Dave McPherson calamity allowed more space and then he saved very well from a great effort from outside the box that rounded off a more intricate midfield move from Leeds involving Strachan and McAllister. With a midfield including those two in addition to Speed and Rocastle, it is still surprising that they didn't continue to try to play through the middle more often, instead of the direct cross balls, by which time Gough and Brown were dealing with ease, be they high-floating deliveries or low-fizzing drives. Leeds had responded with the same kind of heart and courage that Rangers had shown in adversity the fortnight prior, they were just missing the goals.

There was no let-up in the pace and intensity once the second half got underway, this British derby ignoring continental mores, regardless of the name on the trophy. Gordon Strachan nearly matched McAllister's famous goal in the opening exchanges but the shot was fired just wide. Rangers perhaps sensed a danger in holding too deep a line and started to force the issue themselves, with Hateley causing John Newsome some issues and Lukic having to get his body behind an Ian Ferguson volley. It was soon time for the Goram v Cantona show to resume when the Frenchman breezed past Brown, after a slip by Gough, but still couldn't beat Scotland's number one. Goram was soon called in to deny Cantona's strike partner, Lee Chapman, whilst Gough suffered a second head knock of the match, the first resulting in him refusing to leave the field after he cut his eye in the first half, the quick clean up on the field perhaps not even meeting the standards of the day.

Leeds United, getting more and more frustrated, tried the intricate route just before the hour mark with some nice triangles between Speed, McAllister and Chapman before John Brown robbed Cantona, fed Ian Ferguson, and so one of the greatest Rangers goals got underway. An exchange between Hateley and Durrant left the Englishman rampaging down the left flank on the break, taking the ball and two Leeds players with him. This left Chris Whyte in no-man's land when Hateley bypassed them all by delivering a sumptuous cross for McCoist, loitering at the back post, to header home. For all the power of Hateley's opener, nothing that happened in either leg could match the beauty of this perfect counter-attacking goal. Voted the fourth greatest Rangers goal in the *Heart and Hand* poll of 2018, the only thing more mesmerising is the fact that McCoist wasn't broken in half when Dale Gordon came rushing in to celebrate when he was already on his knees.

There was a recognition in the home support behind the goal that they had just been knocked out of the European Cup by another piece of Rangers brilliance. In the Main Stand, however, the reception was less gracious. 'By the second goal, we were well-known,' said Barry. 'Cammy and I were chatting to those in the row immediately behind us and they were broadly fine, expect this one big beast of a bloke who was sat directly behind them. When McCoist scored we couldn't help ourselves. Cammy shouted Yes! I then shouted Yes! We stood up and then … bang! This guy booted the boy behind us. Stewards then got involved and, sadly, Cammy got an early bath that night!'

Leeds responded gamely, even though the atmosphere had been sucked out of a stadium already diminished by reconstruction work. Steve Hodge and Rod Wallace were thrown on by Wilkinson and indeed it was Wallace who brought the save of the night from Goram as he reacted well low down to stop a typically instinctive bit of Wallace play following a poor header in the box by Gough. The Rangers game management after that killed enough time to thwart any hope of a comeback, indeed Brown himself nearly grabbed a third with nine minutes to go when he popped up at the back post with a header, but Lukic did well to keep him out. Smith spoke later saying that as he grew more relaxed in the stand perhaps his side did on the field, and eventually Cantona broke through Goram with a low-drilled shot across the Rangers goalkeeper for a consolation. Rangers were very scrappy in the last ten minutes, the effects of the competitive edge disappearing, with Wallace nearly scoring an equaliser that would have spoiled the night a little, but Goram was once again equal to it and then Ian Ferguson picked up a needless booking that would see him suspended for the opening game of the Champions League, one where Walter Smith could have done with him.

Rangers had proven their critics wrong at Elland Road that night, ironically the season in which things were to change significantly in terms of disparity across the border. Andy Goram delivered a world-class performance and, certainly at that time, was the best stopper on these islands. It really was the last line that saved the day in a game which doesn't entirely support the popular narrative that it was a solid defensive unit as a whole that proved ultimately decisive. Wilkinson was his honest self in the aftermath, with a little dry humour too, when he said, 'In virtually every respect, I cannot see how my team could possibly have done better, and after tonight, right now I find it difficult to understand how Scotland ever lose football matches.'

The overall shape might not have been as resolute as we tend to remember it being on this evening but the spirit and confidence most certainly was and, with such quality at either end of the park, it is not hard to understand where it came from. It was, of course, the kind of character that endears a Rangers side to the support in a way that won't be forgotten as long as those who were around to see them shall live. It was the kind of Rangers team that drove some fans to find whatever solutions were available to ensure that they got to see them play.

John Brown summed up that spirit years later: 'Nothing scared us. When you are involved in Old Firm matches and you can play in those games without being overawed then you can play in any game. Leeds United's stadium was like our backyard, it didn't intimidate us at all. They played "Eye of the Tiger", the *Rocky* tune, beforehand and we turned round to see Ian Durrant shadow-boxing their centre-half, Chris Fairclough, in the tunnel. We were laughing because we could see they had fear in their eyes, even in the tunnel at Ibrox. It was something Walter [Smith] and Graeme Souness had said. He said, "stare them out and if they can't hold your gaze then that is half the battle".'

The Battle of Britain was a battle of sorts but it had magic as well as machismo, charm as well as brawn. The kind of things that make people fall in love.

5

Dundee United 0 Rangers 1

Scottish Premier Division
Wednesday 7 May 1997

'I remember going to a fans' event after we'd clinched the eighth title. I walked in the door and everyone was going mental. A big Rangers fan pulled me to one side and said, "Great win big man but you better not fuck it up next season."'
(Richard Gough)

A strange, coincidental quirk of this project is that the average age of the voter, as of May 2019, was exactly the same as me – 38 years and five months.[3] For the average voter in this poll, their childhood imagination would have been ignited by the Souness revolution, their adolescence guided by the fatherly hand of Walter Smith and their entry into adulthood shaped by the swagger of an Advocaat Rangers team. The average voter would have been 17 years old before they experienced a season without winning a trophy. The average voter is a 'nine-er', one whose formative years were caught up in the obsession of matching a particular sequence of league title success. It should be of no surprise, then, that 15 of the fifty games, 30 per cent, come from the period between August 1988 and May 1997. The last of that group, fittingly, was where it all finally ended.

The conclusion of this particular epic was a little more stumble and farce than Tolkien. The key arithmetic had actually been settled more than three weeks before in Kirkcaldy, when Rangers thrashed Raith Rovers 6-0 to ensure that Celtic couldn't possibly achieve more points. They had a game in hand to Rangers three, but the goal difference was a considerable 17 in the champions' favour. It was now a question of where that extra point would be secured and this generation-defining journey would come to a triumphant end. It could have been Tannadice a week earlier, but Dundee United's inability to beat Kilmarnock in their Scottish Cup semi-final meant that the replay would need to take that date where, incidentally, they would repeat that particular failure. Fittingly, then, this meant that the ninth title could be decided at Ibrox on the first May bank holiday Monday, when second-from-bottom Motherwell

---

3 80% of the respondents were asked to confirm their age and the response was very high, meaning that the sample size was over 70% of the entire poll population.

were visiting. Sky Sports were able to sell the ideal title package that day, as Manchester United needed only to beat relegation-bound Middlesbrough at Old Trafford earlier on to be crowned champions of England for the fourth time in five years. The two sides that dominated the decade on either side of the border were due to be coronated, one after the other, with routine home fixtures.

It didn't work out like that. Incredibly, United were 3-1 down with five minutes to go before half-time and, although they would eventually secure the 3-3 draw, it left an uneasy feeling on the way to Ibrox on that gloomy, overcast afternoon, that this wasn't going to be that simple. Rangers were awful, as if they were simply awaiting the point to be handed to them. Owen Coyle's two clinical strikes ensured that the champagne had to be kept on ice, with two tricky away games left – Tannadice and Tynecastle. The goal difference was still healthy, a gap of ten, but a couple of 2-0 defeats and theoretically it would be opened up for Celtic, however unable they were to ever pounce on those kind of opportunities in practice.

The game wasn't live on television so those without tickets on that Wednesday night had to keep up with one of the most iconic moments in Rangers history via teletext or radio, a further complication for those of us who were supposed to be revising for the Higher Maths exam the following morning. Andy McGowan was one of the lucky ones making the trip up to Dundee and it would be a night that he was able to share with someone who meant a lot to him. 'I went up with the Stevenson District Supporters' Club and I somehow had two tickets. I had a pal who had gone most of the season but he wasn't a die-hard, just a passing social interest in Rangers, so I gave my ticket to someone else, a guy called Tommy Reid. Tommy was a gentleman, a local legend, Rangers through and through, but he didn't have a ticket. It gave me a great deal of pleasure to give him the call to tell him that he had one. We were in that main stand corner, overlooking the tunnel.'

The Rangers line-up spoke volumes about the exertions that this saga had taken on Walter Smith's squad. The XI that took to the field on the night that Rangers won nine -in-a-row was Andy Dibble in goal, Alec Cleland and David Robertson at wing-back, a back three of Gordan Petric, Joachim Björklund and the captain for the night Alan McLaren. Craig Moore played in midfield with Charlie Miller and Paul Gascoigne, and Brian Laudrup and Gordon Durie spearheaded the attack. It was Gascoigne's first start since January and, if it wasn't for the mania surrounding the conclusion of this season, cooler observers would have predicted the worst for the rest of his career. Tommy McLean's Dundee United had a mixture of experience in the shape of Dutch goalkeeper Sieb Dijkstra, Jim McInally and Stewart McKimmie, graduates of the Rangers 1992/93 season Steven Pressley and Gary McSwegan and a smattering of Scandinavia with Erik Pedersen, Lars Zetterlund and Kjell Olofsson.

The Rangers urgency from the start was like night and day compared to the Monday, with Laudrup and Durie trying to make things happen immediately, Durie testing Dijkstra on the wet surface from range. However, Dundee United were keen to play their own part when McSwegan, no stranger to a title-winning goal himself, created some space in behind the wing-back system but Dibble sensed the danger early and McLaren made sure he cleared decisively from McKimmie's follow up. Andy Dibble, at Ibrox for less than two months, was merely the last in a long line of cameo appearances stretching back to Mel Sterland, that Souness and then Smith used to perfection throughout the era.

There was a piece of skill in the first ten minutes that was something of an overture for things to come when Laudrup took a pass out of the sky on the edge of the Rangers box, and, with one touch, took control of the ball, as well as taking his marker out of the game. If that was typical of Laudrup's magic touch, what happened soon after was a collector's item. With 11 minutes gone, Rangers had kept the ball well from Gascoigne out on the right all the way to Miller on the left. From an intelligent throw in, David Robertson gave the ball straight back to Miller, enabling him to get away from Olofsson and whip in a first-time cross as the ball rose slightly on his instep. The fizzing pace on the cross was converted perfectly by the head of the onrushing Laudrup and the ball was bulleted into the top corner to give Rangers a much-needed lead. Jock Brown in commentary said it was a 'classic from Laudrup', although I can't think of many that the great man sent home with his dome. 'It was the most un-Laudrup goal that you could imagine!' recalled Andy. 'My recollection was that we were far more nervous than we actually should have been. To get that early goal, however, was exactly what we were looking for.'

It was Brian Laudrup's 20th goal of the season, more than his previous two seasons combined, and, given our calamitous injury list, it was a season when he needed to pull out his best in order to get Rangers over that line. 'What can you say about Brian Laudrup that hasn't been said before?' said Andy. 'He's the greatest player that I've ever seen play for Rangers. It is as simple as that. The guy was absolutely sublime. This season in particular we were going to the well with a few players, flogging them to a degree, and he was one of them. He was a talisman. He could create space, could pass, could link up, could shoot. Everything. I talk a lot about how fond my memories are of watching Rangers at this time and he was probably the main reason.'

Rangers were immediately settled by the early goal and should have extended that lead in the spell that followed. Charlie Miller was desperately unlucky with a volley from a corner that was superbly saved by Dijkstra and he later robbed McKimmie before sending Laudrup clean through for a one-on-one with the United keeper. Dijkstra was rounded with ease before Laudrup's shot was somehow cleared off the line by Pedersen and then again from Durie's rebound. Jock Brown simply assumed that the great Dane would score, perhaps so did Laudrup himself, and the sitter was as exceptional as his header. He was booked later on for persistent fouling, thus completing a trio of unique Brian Laudrup moments in a Rangers jersey. Dundee United weren't passive bystanders in that first half, with Andy McLaren causing the Rangers left a number of problems and Mark Perry should have arguably won a penalty in a tussle with Moore in the Rangers box.

Not long after the restart, the night was nearly capped off with a poetic flourish when Paul Gascoigne picked the ball up 25 yards from goal, tormented Steven Pressley before passing the ball past the stranded Dijkstra but onto the bottom edge of the post, before being cleared away. It would have been greedy of us to seek the perfect night, but a 2-0 win and a goal each for Laudrup and Gascoigne, the twin creative architects of that final phase, would have been beautifully appropriate.

The rest of the game was fairly end-to-end, Moore and Robertson going close for Rangers before Charlie Miller went even closer, rattling the bar from the edge of the box, and McSwegan threatening at the other end. With just a minute remaining, Smith sensed the opportunity to give his two stars the standing ovation that they so richly deserved when he subbed the pair of them for Derek McInnes and Ally McCoist. Soon after, it finally happened. A whistle that thousands of Rangers supporters had been waiting for was eventually blown. 'I was twelve when it started and nearly 21 when the journey finally ended. I had followed this through. I'd dreamt about it, I'd thought about it, I had hoped that it would happen. There were moments when I really didn't know if it would happen and at least one season [1995/96] where it was completely in the balance throughout. By the end, it wasn't a pressure of success, it was a pressure of failure. So when the final whistle went, I remember that it was relief. It was also very much a sense of being part of history as well. Something that wasn't an everyday occurrence following Rangers. I can't recall there being too much emotion in the stands, unlike Aberdeen 1987 where a dam burst. It just felt like something was over, finally.'

For those fans from a generation before Andy's, it perhaps had an even stronger resonance. 'Tommy was the link to the past. He was the guy on the bus who you listened to. He had fantastic stories. You might have heard them more than once but you always listened to them, because they were so good. It gave you a sense of perspective. I'll be telling wee guys on the bus one day about nine in a row. Being able to sit next to him was special because he had gone through it all as a Rangers fan. He knew what this meant.'

There have been wilder title celebrations for a Rangers side, some won from a far more precarious position than this one, but I'm not sure that there were any quite as emotional for the players. 'It wasn't muted,' said Andy. 'It *was* a celebration, it just wasn't a fist-pumping one. The sense of the evening was epitomised by Richard Gough, in his blazer, looking every inch the Rangers captain. He had his arm around every player on the pitch, and, more than that, he had a word for every one of them. He held onto them for longer than normal. And it was the same for Ally McCoist, with all nine medals, as it was for Andy Dibble. When you see a guy like that, an absolute warrior, shedding tears as he lifted the trophy it tells its own story. He wasn't throwing it up in the air and shouting. He did it slowly, almost bringing it back down to give it a kiss and then raising it again. It's a celebration in keeping with the perspective we have now.'

'Each one has their own characteristic,' said Walter Smith immediately afterwards. 'But this one has a great deal more significance as it meant equalling Celtic's record. I had won five championships before that but if I hadn't won that one, I would have been the person who lost nine in a row.' The comments were an accurate reflection of the mood of the time, however unfair it would have been in retrospect. Smith dragged every ounce of effort from a squad that were more than happy to keep going back to their own personal wells for him. It took its toll, however. The players on Rangers books, but not available for Smith's selection that night, included Andy Goram, Trevor Steven, Richard Gough, Stuart McCall, Ian Ferguson, Ian Durrant and Mark Hateley, whilst Jörg Albertz warmed the bench, only half-fit, and Ally McCoist played one minute. Smith's trust in these players was unwavering and based on a solid foundation; however, the need to get nine meant that squad management suffered. During those nine seasons Rangers would roughly average five players in and five players out throughout each season[4] but season 1997/98, the quest for the record-breaking ten, would see ten players coming in and 12 going out the door. Such high turnover is hard to get right and it didn't work. Sergio Porrini would be a decent acquisition overall and Lorenzo Amoruso would be a club legend but would hardly play during that fateful campaign because of injury, the same reason that Thern and Negri were disappointments, so once again Smith had to go back and rely on a group that would ultimately run out of steam at the crucial moment.

Over 20 years later, how do we as a support reflect on nine-in-a-row? There were negative consequences, of course. The corollary to such domestic dominance was a continental drift away from where the real action was happening. It was clear, from around 1994 and the wreckage of AEK Athens[5], that Rangers were starting to look inwardly just at the moment in footballing history when the rest of Europe was looking outwards, to a far greater panorama. We knew what would work in Scotland, even if it didn't in Europe, and the obsession meant that there was no real debate about priorities. A tabloid poll the following season found that a sizeable majority of Rangers fans would have preferred the Scottish title in 1997/98 to winning the Champions League. By the time Rangers were able to put this to bed and re-focus on Europe, it was too late to play catch up, although attempts were still made and to ruinous effect.

There is perhaps a natural tendency to assess the period with a bias towards those who completed the job compared to those who set it up. Laudrup and Gascoigne are

---

4 5.11 players brought in and 5.44 players moved out

5 Rangers were eliminated at the Champions League qualifying stage for the second season in a row, and with some degree of humiliation.

the names that come so readily to mind because they were two key figures who sealed the victory. This perspective can therefore sometimes diminish the service of those who were at Ibrox for the duration such as Richard Gough, Ally McCoist, Ian Ferguson, Ian Durrant and, of course, Water Smith himself. That final day in 1991 and the near perfection of 1992/93 are celebrated with clarity but not so much the quality and excellent balance of that Souness side from 1988–1990, enhanced by the signing of Maurice Johnston, equally significant on the pitch as it was off it. Nor perhaps does Smith's first full season in 1991/92 get the credit it deserves, because of the haul that was to follow the next season. And, of course, there are the under-rated contributions in the first half of the era that should be more widely celebrated such as Ray Wilkins and Nigel Spackman with a similar argument to be made that the likes of Mark Walters, Gary Stevens and Trevor Steven don't get fully recognised as the heroes that they most certainly were. Our recollection of the era is much like this whole Greatest Games project in microcosm, with nearly half of the matches chosen during the period coming in the final 12 months. The broad-brush approach to memory allows only a few chosen moments to shine but, in doing so, loses so much valuable detail.

Ultimately, the importance of equalling this statistical benchmark is something that is very much dependent on generation. For those old enough for the term 'nine-in-a-row' to have negative connotations, the number was significant. It *had* to be equalled at the very least. For those who weren't born at the time, there is a mystical quality associated with the period. Jordan Campbell, the Rangers correspondent for *The Athletic*, is of a generation who only know tight title races when Rangers were mostly the underdog. 'That level of dominance always seems hard to comprehend for me. When I watch the videos back there's just this controlled arrogance about them. It seemed to be a romantic age.'

For my generation, the 'nine-ers', although we can still lament some of the mistakes made, there is an increasingly deep sense of gratitude that we were brought up through it. Following the fortunes of a football team will always keep us in that continual state of emotional flux right up into old age. However, it is during those formative years when the impact is most acute. Before mortgages and marriage, kids and careers. Your team winning on a Saturday was one of life's top priorities, at times it felt like number one, and when your team was Rangers, your life pre-adulthood during that time was basically milk and honey. It seems ridiculous and overwrought to say this, but it is ultimately true: Graeme Souness and Walter Smith were more responsible for our childhood happiness than many family members and friends.

Nine-in-a-row was a richer tapestry than it is often depicted, with plenty of disappointments and missed opportunities contained within those vibrant threads. By its conclusion, the claustrophobic tension was often unpleasant and exhausting. However, time and again, it produced moments that those of us who witnessed them couldn't forget even if we tried. Seventeen times during that spell, a Rangers captain lifted silverware amidst the countless goals, saves and signings that we savoured with our dads, talked about with our friends and dreamt about at night. There has never been a generation of kids who grew up supporting Rangers that were more fortunate than mine. As the end of school approached and the real world beckoned, it was perhaps fitting that our childhood heroes, tiring and ageing as they were but still possessing some magic, lifted their final reward together.

4

Celtic 2 Rangers 3

Scottish Cup Final
Saturday 4 May 2002

'Here now is Neil McCann. Is there going to be a sting in the tail?'
(Ian Crocker, commentary)

By now it should be clear that the definition of a 'great' football game can be very stretched indeed. There are some pretty grim football matches on this list that are there either because of their symbolic importance or due to the fact that they delivered a meaningful reward. Of the games that fall under the more neutral definition – a finely balanced game where there are dramatic swings in momentum and there's something important at stake – we could arguably only count in single figures. One could possibly make an argument for the 'Centenary' Cup Final of 1973 and the 2016 semi-final along with Dynamo Kiev and Parma at Ibrox. Definitely on that list would be the two Skol League Cup finals against Aberdeen in the late 80s, the 3-2 win over PSV in Eindhoven, the victory at Parkhead in November 1996. And this one. The 2002 Scottish Cup Final ticks a lot of boxes. A dramatic late win in an Old Firm cup final that swung back and forth. A game stamped for eternity by iconic imagery and one that had a lasting impact beyond the afternoon itself. Of all the Rangers games that would be considered great by many neutrals in and of themselves, this is the greatest of them all.

There was a buoyancy amongst the Rangers support at Hampden that day that, looking back on paper, would be easy to consider misplaced. Celtic had won the title as early as 6 April and would eventually rack up 103 points and a points average that they hadn't seen since 1968.[6] What's more, Rangers were in flux with a manager change in the winter that many had considered evidence of downsizing following the avarice of Advocaat. Despite a stuttering start, including a 0-0 draw away to Berwick Rangers in the first Scottish Cup tie, Alex McLeish had stopped the rot against Celtic as a run of five defeats in a row was ended in the most spectacular fashion in the CIS Insurance League Cup semi-final at Hampden in February. An extra-time screamer from the very-much maligned Bert Konterman sent Rangers through and loosened a psychological stranglehold immediately. The final two league clashes ended in 1-1

6 All seasons adjusted to three points for a win.

draws so, despite Celtic's strength, there was reason to believe that this final wouldn't be a foregone conclusion.

Rangers had won that League Cup Final, a comfortable 4-0 win over Ayr United, so were trying to rescue the season with a cup double and, by defeating Celtic in the process, set the tone for the following league campaign, something that Ian Crocker made mention of in his commentary before kick-off. This wasn't just about winning the Scottish Cup, it was about laying a marker that would still be seen at the other side of the summer. Unusually, this wasn't the end-of-season showpiece event as was tradition. Because of the climate in Japan and Korea, the 2002 World Cup started early and therefore domestic seasons had to follow suit. With Hampden hosting the Champions League Final ten days later, Zinedine Zidane's outrageous volley and all, it was felt best not to have two cup finals on a brand new pitch and so the Scottish Cup Final was played before the league season had come to an end. In each of the previous four seasons that the national stadium had hosted a European final, Rangers won the Scottish Cup, the kind of gloriously irrelevant statistic that you cling onto like a lifeline on days like these.

Both sides arrived at Hampden with their fair share of bumps and bruises and those would show over the course of the afternoon. Ronald de Boer was taking painkilling injections for a broken toe and Claudio Caniggia, whose Scottish renaissance had incredibly won him a place in Marcelo Bielsa's World Cup squad, was carrying a knee injury. Martin O'Neill was already missing Joos Valgaeren and had to replace him in defence with a half-fit Chris Sutton whilst gambling on Paul Lambert in midfield, despite having some pretty serious ankle trouble. Rangers lined up with Klos in goal, a back four of Numan, Amoruso, Moore and Maurice Ross, a midfield three of Ferguson, Ricksen and de Boer with the pacy trio of McCann, Lovenkrands and Caniggia in attack. Celtic's very familiar 3-5-2 was made up of Douglas, Mjällby, Baldé and Sutton, Alan Thompson and Didier Agathe at wing-back, Lennon, Petrov and Lambert in the middle, with Larsson and Hartson up front.

Rangers started the brightest with some quick and intelligent football, an Amoruso header and a Neil McCann free kick being the best for us to get excited about in the opening exchanges. The clash of styles was immediately stark as Alan Thompson indulged in some Greco-Roman wrestling with Maurice Ross at the corner flag, and then Sutton was even more blatant with a body-check on Caniggia that triggered a recurrence of his injury and forced him off the field for treatment. He'd later have to be replaced by Shota Averladze and, whilst he still made it to Japan, his sole contribution to the tournament was a red card from the bench in the final group game against Sweden.

Rangers were, however, down to ten men until the situation could be assessed, and the lack of organisation was soon apparent. Stefan Klos did well to tip the ball over the bar from a Hartson cross, but the subsequent marking from the corner was a shambles.

Bobo Baldé won the first header, Hartson won the second from the closest of range, and Celtic were 1-0 ahead after 19 minutes. A young Adam Thornton watched on from where the West Stand met the South. 'It was everything I feared really. A perfect example of the height disadvantage we had. Baldé was well above Amoruso and Ricksen was, if we are being kind, trying his best to mark Hartson. It was a real threat that they had. O'Neill's Celtic were undeniably a good team because he set them up perfectly for a side with so many players over 6ft 3in and some star quality in Larsson.'

In the 42 Old Firm clashes previous to this, the team that scored first had never lost. However, there was just something about this game in the build-up that felt different, perhaps the fitness levels would produce a more chaotic afternoon than normal and even I had a bet on Celtic scoring first, but Rangers winning the match in 90 minutes. The response was immediate and was starting to typify the Rangers approach that McLeish was quickly changing. After enjoying 12 or so passes to allow the heart rates to settle down a little, Ferguson chose to go long and sent up a ball for the newly formed defensive unit to deal with. Sutton and Mjällby were like the Keystone Cops as they jumped for the ball, Mjällby's header was a weak one and Lovenkrands pounced. His awareness that he could create an opening was immediate and, with his first touch, although heading back towards his own half, he did so. His second, a turn and drive low to the bottom left of the Celtic goal, was brilliant. Sutton was slow to close him down, Douglas, it would appear, never properly anticipated the speed of the decision, but take nothing away from the young Danish forward who, with his fourth goal in five games against Celtic, was starting to create something of a legend.

The rest of the first half settled into a familiar narrative groove. Rangers tried to exploit Celtic's ponderous and makeshift defence with speed of movement and skill. Lovenkrands tested Douglas with a volley, Numan had an attempt from range that whistled wide and Averladze just failed to connect with a low pacy cross from McCann. Celtic, meanwhile, carried out assaults with impunity, Hartson's forearm smash on Moore the best example, and the fear from their set pieces was visceral. Thankfully for Rangers, Henrik Larsson had a quiet afternoon, the only moment of concern coming just before half-time when he slipped in the box, as he was often prone to do, after some attention from Amoruso. Only a month later *The Sunday Mail* produced the most cringe-worthy front page in Scottish history, a remarkably high bar in this country, by using a picture of Larsson's boot and begging readers to touch it ahead of Sweden's World Cup clash with England that morning. Further proof of the importance of historical studies, lest anyone forget that Scotland was once a key part of The Enlightenment.

Upon re-watching this game, it is clear by the interval that there is one box that it doesn't tick, as is often believed. The overall quality is lacking significantly. These were two sides very much in need of a summer rest, with unfit players littering the playing surface. It has drama in much the same way that a bruising heavyweight clash does and it would continue along that line as the game went on. Adam Thornton was in agreement. 'Nostalgia overrules everything when it comes to this game. The quality was poor and both sides were ragged. I was nervous at half-time because it was Celtic and we still had all the scars of the last 18 months. I remember my dad and I talking at the break and wondering if the League Cup semi was an aberration and purely the result of a freak, wonder goal. Maybe it wasn't a sign of the tide turning after all.'

Paul Lambert's ankle had given way to the pressures of this fixture and he had been replaced by Jackie McNamara, meaning Celtic reverted to a back four, with Mjällby at left-back, and they never looked comfortable for the remainder of the game. Five minutes after the restart, however, they were back in front. Hugh Dallas had begun to show the cards in this half, Hartson with a tackle right in front of the referee that even he couldn't escape without punishment. Minutes later Amoruso followed him into the book when he had his hands all over Larsson about 20 yards from goal on the left-hand side. Worse was to follow from the resulting free kick, as Lennon's cross was met flush by Baldé, who had left the former Rangers captain on the floor. It was a strangely poor performance from Amoruso, always so reliable in big games when he was in form, as this was the season when he had won the Player's Player of the Year award. The tide had turned again. 'I was now starting to fear the worst,' recalls Adam. 'We've shown character before so quickly but can we do it again? Even if we do, the marking at these set plays ...'

The Rangers response lacked the intensity and energy that they showed after the first goal, with most of the initial opportunities going high and handsome from both Numan and Ricksen. Rangers weren't penetrating into the danger areas whereas they were giving up a little more space for Celtic to look ominous, none more so than when John Hartson fell in the box, as one wag on a message board at the time put it, 'under the strength of Arthur Numan's aftershave'. Celtic were relatively comfortable and in control of the final until Barry Ferguson changed the dynamic with a bolt out of the blue from 30 yards that crashed off the post. It was an energy changer and Rangers used to it pile more and more pressure on the Celtic goal, who were now firmly in retreat. Even the Rangers corners now looked threatening, and when one from McCann wasn't cleared properly, it allowed Ricksen to send it back in towards Amoruso with a high looping header. The Italian was cleaned out completely by Baldé, possibly inside the box, but Dallas award a free kick over 20 yards from goal.

There were originally three Rangers men surveying the opportunity, although Amoruso, perhaps sensing that this wasn't his day, left it to Barry Ferguson and Fernando Ricksen to fight it out. In that moment, in that game, there was only going to be one taker. Rab Douglas had offered up a huge space to his right for the young Rangers captain to hit, almost as a dare. Ferguson took him up on it with a brilliant strike that most probably would have taken Douglas out anyway, poor positioning or not, such was the accuracy into the far side of the net. It was a coming-of-age moment for Ferguson. He had the big moments before, of course, Leverkusen being the most iconic, and had set up a thumping 5-1 derby win in November 2000, but this was different. Here he was in a cup final, with Rangers behind the eight-ball in many ways, and he stepped up with some magic to propel his team towards success. It was elation for Adam and the thousands of others jumping around Hampden as Ferguson removed his jersey in excitement. 'It was just the perfect time to get a goal because we were starting to create chances and McCann was getting more and more into the game whilst they were retreating. It was just a brilliant free kick. Douglas's position is horrific, but he still has to get it in a perfect spot. The place went bananas and it felt very much the incentive was ours.'

With 20 minutes to go, the cup was very much up for grabs, although Celtic did respond strongly, forcing more errors from Amoruso and a foul from Moore on the edge of the box; however, Larsson's free kick and subsequent shot from the rebound were appalling. Rangers had the possession but couldn't find the decisive pass as the minutes ticked away. 'I was still slightly nervous,' said Adam, 'and I would have taken extra time with ten minutes to go. My dad, the eternal optimist, was saying, 'we're going to get one,' but he had been saying that for the last two years.' Rangers never looked panicked, however, even when moves broke down and, as the control and stamina started to disintegrate around them, the key chances would fall our way. The best appeared to have fallen at the feet of Ricksen, after a Douglas howler from a McCann cross, but he chose to try and pass the ball into the net and Mjällby managed to clear. De Boer should have had a tap-in soon after but Peter Lovenkrands, with all of the goalscoring confidence, opted to try and prod the ball home instead of attempting to wrap his foot around it for the cut-back. 'That was it there for me,' sighed Adam. 'In retrospect I don't blame him for the decision, but at the time I was furious. I absolutely would have taken another 30 minutes there and then. We just seemed on top and our style and stamina were always likely to be successful if we had to go again.'

Celtic, too, tried to land the knockout punch as these two sluggers neared the bell but their efforts from wide looked insipid and exhausted. Once again a Martin O'Neill side, so firmly based around bullying from set pieces and long balls, were not as conditioned as they should have been. Rangers kept the control and tempo, Ferguson continually trying to dink balls over the top of an immobile Celtic defence, and Lovenkrands should have had a penalty when he was pushed to the ground by Mjällby as he tried to latch onto one of them. Celtic may have escaped a late winner there, but their luck wouldn't last. Amoruso waltzed past an almost stationary Petrov on the half-way line and sent the ball out to Neil McCann on the left wing. Deep into injury time he sensed that this was the last chance to kill the match dead and drove at McNamara and Agathe, who seemed unable to make much effort in closing him down. Despite the ball taking a slight bobble, he was still able to deliver the perfect cross.

The 'Corridor of Uncertainty' is a term more associated with cricket than football, but it is the only way to describe McCann's delivery. He didn't launch it high, to be headed away, or a low fizzer that was more dependent on chaos than craft. Instead it was an impeccable arc that cut out the drained Chris Sutton and was tantalisingly too far away from the dithering Rab Douglas, but one that managed to open up the chance for Lovenkrands to steal in from behind and have one final sight of goal. There was still work left to be done, it needed the perfect cushion down into the ground and away from Douglas; however, Lovenkrands in that form was only ever going to get it spot on and the cup was won. 'I was pre-alcohol at this stage and I've still never celebrated a goal like that in my life,' said Adam. 'I don't know how he saw the cross and trusted Lovenkrands to make the run. You just didn't cross into the Celtic box! These are the goals that, as a young boy, you want to score: diving headers, direct free kicks and overhead kicks. To get two of those goals in this game, with the importance of it and the timing of them, is exactly why they still burn brightly in the memory. It's dreamlike stuff. It was just so final. It was done. You knew it and so did they.'

It was surely the pinnacle of that incredible run of form by Peter Lovenkrands, in the fixture that matters more than others. 'Martin O'Neill liked his big defenders and with my pace I fancied myself to do ok against them because you don't get many players who are really big and really quick too. And ,of course, when you're at Rangers, how you perform in the derby matches is such a big part of whether or not you are perceived as doing your job properly. The expectation for all Rangers players is that you beat Celtic. It might not always happen, but that is always the expectation. And if you're going to be at Rangers, it's something that you have to be able to deal with.'

The Celtic end emptied and Rangers partied hard that evening; however, the impact of this cup final was more enduring than just that. Much had been made of our inability to deal with the physical nature of this Celtic side and much shame was felt about the consistent bullying from the summer of 2000 onwards. Yet, McLeish didn't fight fire with fire immediately and nor in the summer of 2002.[7] He countered brawn with brain, strength with pace and this game was a mighty affirmation that this was the correct path down which to continue. It fed into the next tumultuous season of 2002/03 and it is difficult to believe that if it was Larsson who had popped up at the back post to nod in a winner, the following treble-winning epic would have turned out in the same way. 'I honestly don't think it would have been successful, no,' said Adam in our discussion on this particular 'what-if' on *The Time Capsule*. 'If the opposite happened we could have said that there had been an improvement, but Celtic still did it when it really mattered. Instead, what we got here was a huge wave of optimism and belief in our approach and style. It legitimised that and it can't be underestimated.'

---

7 Despite the signing of Kevin Muscat, a notorious football 'hardman', McLeish never used him in an Old Firm game. Wisely.

This cup final resonates strongly for many reasons, but again it is more evidence of great moments making great games. For the front cover of this book I chose a picture of Lovenkrands celebrating the winner in front of the Rangers support, not only because it is an iconic moment from a game at the high end of our poll, but because, in one supreme shot, it perfectly encapsulates the whole project. The professional footballer, his name crisply printed above the most famous of all footballing numbers, enjoying the kind of moment he will have dreamt of since childhood by blowing kisses to a throng of strangers, for whom that moment at that time meant just as much. Men, women and children are jumping for pure joy. Strangers are hugging, couples are dancing, fists are pumped, arms are stretched triumphantly, kisses are blown back to the conquering hero. Few of the people there know each other and most never will, but for that collection of seconds they are all friends forever. It is a feeling that almost escapes mere words; however, it is what we continue to search for again and again. The freezing winters on the terraces are endured for those hazy spring afternoons. The barren years, where the direction and very existence of your football club is questioned, are forgotten about the next time a captain walks up the steps and collects some silverware. This is what greatness feels like.

3

Fiorentina 0 Rangers 0

(After extra time, Rangers won 4-2 on penalties.)

UEFA Cup Semi-Final, Second Leg
Thursday 1 May 2008

'Manchester, brace yourself ...'
(Peter Drury, commentary)

As is so often the case, sport manages to provide its greatest moments with a neat narrative all by itself. The Rangers European campaign of 2007/08 crossed paths with teams from all five countries that featured in the 1971/72 run, including a Russian opponent in the final, as well as the opportunity for a pilgrimage back to the Camp Nou during the Champions League stage and fixtures that re-united us with old adversaries Sporting Lisbon in the quarter-finals and then Fiorentina, our first-ever European final opponents back in 1961, in the penultimate round. Contrary to popular wisdom, 0-0 is by far the least boring scoreline, as the stress intensifies with each passing minute. Arguably our most dramatic evening, it was given the finest Hollywood treatment that football can provide: a penalty shoot-out.

The vast majority of Rangers fans experienced the unbearable, but unforgettable, tension on television, either at home or in the pub. For many of us, the action was shaped by the increasingly popular ITV4 commentary duo of Peter Drury and former Liverpool and Republic of Ireland full-back Jim Beglin. Such was the antipathy shown both towards and by STV, as evidenced in Game 23, it was a joy to watch those away legs in the company of football men who seemed to marvel at what was developing, nearly as much as we were and, as a result, fans sought out the main national coverage instead of the local one. Drury, such an underrated voice in a progressively busy football media landscape, is so often unsurpassed at coming up with the perfect words to fit the pictures. As if it were possible, he managed to add to the operatic drama in front of him that night in Florence and only matched it years later in Rome, when Barcelona were, incredibly, knocked out of the Champions League when they seemed to be home and hosed. Even for the neutral, Drury ensured that the hairs on your neck were standing.

The vast majority of us know what it was like to watch that game at home through the gaps in our hands, I may have even switched channel when one player stepped up to hit a Rangers penalty; however, only a few thousand know what it was like to be in that corner of the Stadio Artemio Franchi and only 13 know what it was like to wear the badge in one of the biggest games in Rangers history. It made sense, therefore, to ask Steven Campbell, one of the lucky few with a ticket, and Kevin Thomson, a key part of the Rangers midfield, to take us through all the emotions of a quite incredible night.

****

Kevin, let's go back briefly to the night in Lisbon where, for so many of us, it felt like a turning point in the campaign. The prospect of winning the UEFA Cup all of a sudden felt so real. Was that the same for the players?

KT: That team had belief, even when we were in the Champions League stage, it was just the way Walter built his teams; however, the performance that night was as good as we played all season. We rode our luck so often during that season, at home to Barcelona and in Bremen for example, but less so that night. We were so good and, considering that two or three of their players went for in excess of £20 million, to go over there and teach them the lesson as we did in their back yard was a stand-out, so you're probably right in that the wider audience felt that we could actually go on and win it instead of us just producing a couple of away days for the fans.

You had to miss the first leg at Ibrox, how hard was that to watch in the stand?

KT: It wasn't as difficult as you might think! It wasn't pre-planned, but missing the first leg was not a bad thing when it came to picking up yellow cards because it meant that I wouldn't miss the final due to suspension. Listen, watching any game in the stand is hard, whether you're suspended or injured, you wanted to play but I was just desperate for the boys to give us an opportunity for the tie to still be alive.

It was very much alive with a 0-0 home-leg result, something that was becoming part of the formula for this side?

KT: That was the foundations of our success. We did have some luck but that team had some resilience. You don't get from Red Star Belgrade in a qualifier all the way to the UEFA Cup final with just the break of the ball.

Steven, this journey was quite literal for you and many others. How many trips did you do that season?

SC: I didn't go to Greece (against Panathinaikos) but that was the only one that I didn't do. At that point in time I was travelling with the Queen Street True Blues bus, I had done since I was 16, I was travelling to see Rangers all the time and was doing these trips with the same boys. The thing that propelled it was a feeling that you needed to go to the last one. It wasn't really the intention to go on all of them but the last one just kept getting delayed.

Was there a struggle for tickets for Florence?

SC: I've no idea how it happened but I actually didn't get a ticket originally, even through the Travel Club or the usual sources. However, a friend of a friend had a ticket but wasn't going and he said that I could have it on the condition that, if we got to the final, I had to give him my ticket for that. I said 'of course, no bother' and would worry about that later. But I didn't have a hotel room or anything, just a ticket and a flight. There weren't actually that many fans there, I think people were running out of holidays and money. The core guys were there but it wasn't like the bigger trips. I tried to stay with my friends but never got past the front door. My Renfrew patter wasn't enough for the Italian receptionist! We were in the bar having a good night but, as closing time approached, I didn't have anywhere to stay. Thankfully, these bears took pity on me and I literally slept on their floor underneath their supporters' club flag!

Presumably the team had better accommodation Kevin. What was the night before like?

KT: We were in an absolutely beautiful hotel! I remember training on the pitch the night before. I've played on some bowling greens in my time but this pitch was out of this world. It was breathtaking how good it was and it just felt that there was a camaraderie within the team that we could go to these places and do the job.

Given that Rangers seemed to be playing a game every three days at the time, how detailed was the preparation for Fiorentina?

KT: The biggest thing that the manager used to impress upon us was that we had to defend well. We had to get people behind the ball. He used to reiterate that we had to do our individual jobs. The best way that I can describe that Rangers team was that it was a team full of men. We were all different ages, at all different stages, but it didn't matter where you played on the pitch, we had guys who were capable of following instructions and digging in for the team. For example, going down to ten men during extra time naturally wasn't ideal. The odds were stacked against us, but if any team could cope with that situation in such a massive game, and they don't come much bigger, it was us. We just had a way of knowing how to get a job done. It could have gone to 20 penalties each, we still would have got through that night. Walter was really basic in his instructions but emotionally highly demanding. He knew the time to say the right thing or to burst a door down. He was meticulous without being over-complicated.

Was it surreal to find yourself in the stadium where Rangers were in a European semi-final?

SC: Very much so. I spoke to my dad before I left and said, 'take it in son' and I was conscious of that so I took it easy on the day of the game. We enjoyed some nice food in the piazza. It wasn't the normal away trip! Also, word was starting to filter through that Bayern were taking a bit of a hiding in the other semi-final and my thoughts were that the Russians were the easier draw so we should be ok if we got through. We had to get there though! We got into the stadium quite early. It was like a colosseum even though we were fenced in. It was when I was standing and watching the teams warming up that it fully dawned on me why I was here and what I was about to watch.

As outsiders, we hear so much about playing the game and not the occasion. Just how easy is that in practice, when you are a Rangers player walking out on the pitch on such a night?

KT: It's hard to think back and appreciate how much pressure we were under, but I think history shows that the greatest Rangers players never let emotion and pressure get the better of them. I think we had calm heads that night. We were on the cusp of being the most successful Rangers teams ever, but there was still a humility within the squad that ensured that we wouldn't get carried away with ourselves. I know we didn't win the final in the end, but I don't think we let anyone down. We just came up a wee bit short against a right good team. We didn't get the run of the green that we had enjoyed before. It was just one of those nights. I don't think that the approach was wrong or it was because we couldn't handle the occasion. I do think that the SFA were a shambles and didn't help us out, but that's another story.

How nervous was it in the corner?

SC: We were tense! We had our midfield back for this leg which was a big deal. My memories of the Ibrox game were that it was pretty much a non-event. Adrian Mutu had tried to get things happening but couldn't, and we were happy to sit back and take the 0-0. The start of this game was far better. We were more involved in the first 20 minutes in Florence than we were in the 90 at Ibrox. The game itself eventually took a similar pattern from most of the others though. The Italians fancied it and they eventually took more and more control. They seemed as if they expected to get a goal, then another and get on their way to the final. The thing that struck me though, as the game went on, is that they just kept launching high balls in and that was food and drink to Cuellar and Weir as opposed to trying to play through and spinning them. Maybe they lacked the pace that Zenit wouldn't, later on.

When you are up against it and you know that it's going to be much of the same for the entire night, how important is it to have Carlos Cuellar and Davie Weir behind you?

KT: They were different class. The first three signings that the manager made were Weir, Ugo Ehiogu and me. He knew where the problems were and he later brought Cuellar in and then Bougherra after him. He had an eye for a player that would give him a platform to create the type of team that he wanted. I was also the type of player that would complement Baz well, and later Pedro Mendes. Getting the right combinations are what the best teams are built on.

It was a cagey first half, a little scrappy. What was it like in the Rangers dressing room at the interval?

KT: Walter had a go at me at half-time. He said, 'what's up with you?' 'I'm fucking doing Saša's job man! I'm doing two fucking jobs!' He said, 'Son, just keep on fucking running!' That's what it was like. He just knew that there were players who would go to the well for him. So many of us dug really, really deep that night.

There were chances in the second half, Davis should have squared for Whittaker, but there were some close things at the other end too. How was it in the stands?

SC: You watch so many games without your Rangers glasses on and, if it followed the same pattern at this, you'd expect the home team to get the goal eventually. It's a little different when you're so wrapped up in it, but as time went on the momentum changed. They were now getting stressed and concerned that the straightforward night they had in mind wasn't taking shape.

Extra time was much of the same but the game got more stretched. Christian Vieri got away from Cuellar in the box but his effort went wide and then Daniel Cousin had a great shot that deflected off Tomáš Ujfaluši and went very close. And then, just into the second period, Cousin showed the side we all knew was there when he lost his head and used his head in very much the wrong order. How did the team react to that?

KT: You just dig in for each other. You just have a sense. Sometimes words are cheap and growling at each other isn't enough. Actions speak louder. With Daniel going off and Saša tiring late on, I just had to find a way of covering and doing my own job. I remember Baz telling me that he was done, with 15 minutes left against Barcelona at Ibrox, and I just growled at him and told him to lift it. He would do the same often too. But sometimes it just wasn't needed. That team would just get the best out of each other any way that they could. There were no dickheads, no arseholes. A group of players – all different religions and backgrounds – but all they did was do their best for each other. It is such a hard thing to create as there are so many people wanting different things in football, but we had a group that simply wanted the best for Walter Smith and for Rangers.

What about the fans?

SC: Oh it was over! Tatties for us! You just couldn't believe that he had done it. We had got so far and we just couldn't believe that this is how it would end. Everyone around us was deflated. It is a real slog doing that job for Rangers in this type of game. It's the kind of thing that doesn't come over on television but that player, Cousin or Darcheville, has to run their defence ragged. Now they've got the rest of the night off and we really do have to lock in for penalties. We had some chances, they had more, but we were counting down the minutes since the red card.

And so to those penalties, where Rangers of course had enjoyed success twice already in the last two months, with victories in the League Cup Final and Scottish Cup semi-final. There wasn't an England-type neurosis hanging over us. How confident were you?

KT: As I said, I was confident that night regardless if it went to 20 of them, but I don't know how you fans cope! I was a fan for this period of time, not taking any. It's not great. I was never a penalty taker, never a goalscorer. At Hibs I came through an era where there were other players who demanded that, and it was the same at Rangers, so the penalty shoot-out wasn't something that I was that keen on doing myself. I wasn't scared to go but I wouldn't have jumped through hoops to take one. Given that it was me, Davie, Carlos and Kirk Broadfoot left, it would have likely been me next so it was a running joke with the lads that it was just as well wee Nacho scored or else we'd have been out!

SC: First of all, I was happy that we were hitting first. My pal next to me was in no doubt whatsoever. He was convinced that was it, we were going to the final. I wasn't sure. I had just never experienced anything like this in all my years following Rangers. I never thought that I would see my team in a European final so there was so much hanging on it, but I was relieved when I saw that it was Barry stepping up to tuck the first one away!

Not the best start ...

KT: I think Barry could shut his eyes and hit 20 penalties and score 19 of them. He hit his penalty well but you'd rather he hit it shite and it went in the net! There was all of a sudden that sick feeling that you're going to be on the wrong end of this run that is going to be an anti-climax.

SC: It wasn't a bad penalty but you just expected him to score and then the Italians did and Steven Whittaker is next up. I said to my pal Harv, 'Why is he hitting one?' but actually, we didn't have too many obvious ball-striking options.

There was never any doubt that Whittaker would score in my mind. Papac I thought would be ok, but, in all honesty, I nearly had a seizure when I saw Hemdani was strolling towards the spot, but before that Fabio Liverani missed. Relief?

KT: Pure relief. We were back in it and there was just this surge of adrenaline.

SC: I actually didn't see the Hemdani penalty because, after the Alexander save from Liverani, I ended up about two or three rows in front. So in the time that it took to get everyone back up and say sorry to whoever you had knocked over, I had missed the fact that it was him taking it. He just kind of scuffed it in like he was in the back garden. I was struggling to keep tally with the score by this point. There was just so much going on. It took me a while to understand that if they missed next, it was all set up ...

KT: If I was allowed a bet that night, I'd have put my money on Christian Vieri scoring! It was one of those penalties that just shows you. He was a superstar but as he approached the penalty, he had no belief.

SC: I couldn't tell you who hit it! It was just a different level of excitement. It was bedlam when he missed but with penalties, the celebrations are different. Goals in open play produce a sustained mental-ness. These were big but quick. These were our wildest dreams and it was all coming down to one penalty.

Was there anyone associated with Rangers around the world who didn't believe that Novo would score?

SC: It was just so exciting. I said that if he scored, he'd run to Govan Cross. I was delighted when it was him who had the ball.

KT: I've never felt as excited on a football pitch as when the wee man walked up, but also as nervous. The diagonal run from where we were on the right-hand side of the centre circle to where the fans were in the left-hand corner, is one of the best feelings in my life. I had friends from Peebles in the stand and I don't know how they managed to escape injury because every time I looked up there were just bodies rolling on top of each other!

SC: It was like nothing I had ever experienced when that ball hit the back of the net. There were no songs. Just everyone going nuts for so long. Hands down, the next five or ten minutes was the best time I've ever had watching Rangers. It felt like it took an eternity before anyone even broke out in song. To be there with the people I have travelled the continent with watching Rangers was just incredible. I was crying my eyes out.

Did Cousin celebrate?

KT: He did, to be fair to him. I got sent off in a League Cup Final, but if you get the result then it gets forgotten. The regret was two weeks later when he couldn't play in the final because I think that was a big blow for us. He'd have fancied that and we suffered from it.

What did Walter say afterwards?

KT: He was emotional. He started off talking, when the music went off in the dressing room, and then he just kinda laughed a wee bit, almost in disbelief. It was similar when we were 0-0 at half-time at home to Barcelona and he said, 'I can't put into words how exceptional you have been out there. The only bad news is that you have to do it all again for another 45 minutes.' When we got in the dressing room and the music was on, everyone was hugging, but when it went off the dressing room was actually quite subdued. Although we had the belief beforehand, there was this kind of surreal feeling that we had got to the UEFA Cup Final. I remember being empty. I remember grabbing a blue Powerade thinking, 'I just need to get some sugar into my body!' It was a kind of deflation, but I can't tell you how happy I was to look at my phone and walk through the mixed zone, which used to be a pain in the arse, but to walk through there and get on the bus and speak to your mum and dad, your mrs, your pals and read the messages that were pouring in. It was an incredible feeling that no one will ever be able to take away.

We never slept all night. There was a lot of food for us when we got back to the hotel, which was beautiful and at the top of the hill. Some had a few glasses of wine and a beer but, believe it or not, there was a big group of boys who played Mario Kart on the Nintendo DS, so whenever we got a bit of success we used to play for £20 a head. There was no wild party, we had a game at the weekend, but it was as simple as us sitting around the big dinner table trying to whack each other off the track! Whitty and I didn't sleep a wink, how could you? We just stayed up chatting and the phone never stopped going. The high was too high, there was no way of sleeping.

How were the bears enjoying their night?

SC: We were in the stadium for ages. We noticed that there were all of a sudden pockets of bears around the stadium once the Italians had left. We genuinely felt that we were going to win the lot. The wheels had been coming off and there was a tiredness on show, but all of a sudden that wasn't the case. They then shepherded us into these yellow school buses that I had only ever seen in *The Simpsons*! There were rows and rows of these buses and everyone was on them, doing The Bouncy! It was just absolute carnage. We were on an early flight back to London but there was no sleep to be had as we just kept telling each other that we were in a European final. This was the point that I remembered that I now didn't have a ticket for it! I eventually had to spend £1,200 to get two off a Spurs fan on eBay. It was a stupid amount of money but you just couldn't not go.

This game is the third greatest game in the history of Rangers Football Club. There are seven games in total during your time at the club. How does it feel to be a part of something that was so highly thought of?

KT: The character in me wishes I was in the number-one game and, if we had managed to do it in Manchester, I think that might have been the case. However, I think that it's brilliant that my team, my era, will always be remembered and the run to Manchester will be highly regarded by so many fans. It makes me proud, at 22/23 years old, just a lad from the Borders getting brought up playing rugby, that one day I would be playing in a UEFA Cup Final and being a small part of such a special team. The biggest thing for me, except the footballing achievement of getting to the final, knowing what the fans have to endure on these trips, getting shepherded around and treated so badly and the massive expenditure that goes into getting them everywhere, was having that moment in front of them. Just having a sing-song and a jump around. It is hard to put into words how special that was.

2

Celtic 0 Rangers 3

Scottish Premier League
Sunday 2 May 1999

> ***'I can still remember vividly what it was like going in on the bus. There were no nerves among the Rangers players. Just a belief I had never experienced before. We knew what we were going achieve.'***
>
> **(Neil McCann)**

The name Chris Lewis may not be the most famous amongst those that have been woven into the long Old Firm tapestry. An obscure footnote he may be, but his involvement in the aftermath of this particular derby clash speaks volumes about the interminable circus that follows, and too often overshadows, the actual sport. The evening of 2 May 1999 was perfect in many ways. The perfect scenario, the perfect game plan, the perfect result and the perfect encapsulation of what the Old Firm fixture really is. Chris Lewis wasn't an unused substitute or a little-known member of the backroom staff. He wasn't a linesman nor was he one of the Celtic fans who ran onto the pitch or indeed the one who started the match in the upper tier and quickly ended it on the bottom. Chris Lewis is a body language expert who was engaged by Celtic's CEO Allan MacDonald to find evidence of refereeing conspiracy and to excuse the violence that emanated from the stands.

'Was it purely coincidental that shortly after he was seen patting Giovanni van Bronckhorst, a coin came onto the park and struck the referee?' said MacDonald in his report to the SFA and SPL. By any normal reading, this behaviour is unhinged, not to mention the wonderful imagery created whereby a coin, apparently with a mind of its own, was so incensed that it forced its way out of a fan's pocket and hurled itself towards Hugh Dallas at the corner flag. This isn't a normal city nor footballing country; however, in the words of Captain Blackadder, when his plan to fake insanity fails to get him sent home from the front line, 'I mean, who would have noticed another madman around here?'

'What would your ideal Rangers game look like?' This was the question that Iain McColl, his brother and his friends had pondered together for years, travelling the country and beyond watching Rangers. 'The kind of last-kick-of-the-ball drama to win the league, which we would see with the Helicopter Sundays, was brought up but it always came back to winning the league at Parkhead.' The dream scenario had been created at the end of Dick Advocaat's first season as manager, after a few twists and turns in the spring of 1999. What had seemed a very comfortable grip on the title had been shaken. Celtic had been dreadful in the first half of the campaign, dropping 20 points away from home, but their form picked up considerably after the winter break and Rangers began to wilt a little. A home defeat to Dundee United in March was immediately followed by a shocking 3-1 loss away to St Johnstone in April and meant that the gap was only three points when Advocaat's men travelled to Dens Park in the middle of that month. They could only manage a 1-1 draw and so the situation, with five games left to play was that Rangers had a four-point cushion but needed to go to Parkhead for the final Old Firm league game, having not won any of the first three. The two draws at Ibrox were frustrating but the 5-1 defeat in November was humiliating. Rangers left the east end of the city still with a seven-point lead but it was the manner of the scoreline and performance that caused so much concern. Lacking discipline in every way, Rangers had Scott Wilson sent off before chasing the game as if it was an exhibition match. It was a harsh lesson for Advocaat, reinforced in his meeting with Ian Ferguson soon after it, that this wasn't just any other game. He got caught up in the occasion and embarrassed himself and he was keen not to do it again.

If the momentum had swung towards Celtic with St Johnstone's defeat of Rangers at McDermaid Park, then that was where it would swing back. Finishing third and losing out in both League and Scottish Cups only to Rangers, in the final and semi-final respectively, Sandy Clark had moulded a dangerous team up in Perth, and their 1-0 home defeat of Celtic on 24 April handed a tantalising opportunity for Rangers, who were at home to Aberdeen the following day: win and set up the chance to seal the title the following Sunday at Parkhead. A 3-1 win would come, but not without a struggle and some magic from Gabriel Amato. 'The horror on the faces of Celtic regulars I worked with that week told me all I needed to know.' said Iain. 'They were terrified of what could happen and, for once in these games, if we could play like we were capable of, then we would do it. We just simply couldn't let this chance pass by. This was it. This was the dream scenario.'

From the media interviews during the week, Advocaat was different than before. Almost everything he said appeared to be a reference to the unnecessary chaos of the previous visit. 'It's a football game,' he said to Sky. "Hopefully we can do it on a football matter, that's the most important thing.' It was something supported by players at the time and since. Colin Hendry talked in the Rangers monthly magazine about the serene calm as the players had their Sunday morning walk. Neil McCann still talks about the absolute assurance on the team bus. Jörg Albertz said similar when he sat down with me for *Heart and Hand* in 2019. 'That was a positive thing about Advocaat, he could take the pressure off the boys. His team talk was excellent that day. We were so focussed, we knew what we could achieve and he made it very clear that we couldn't throw this away by getting drawn into fighting and that stuff. "Keep calm, do your job!" We knew that we were by far the better team. It's never easy to play against Celtic but we went there with broad shoulders knowing that we could achieve something if we stayed calm. They wouldn't have a chance.' Lorenzo Amoruso described that dressing room as a 'church. So silent. So focussed'.

Iain McColl's Sunday wasn't quite as reverential. 'We were all making plans that week for what we were going to do during the day (it was a 6:05pm kick off) and word had got to us that in the pub league, the guys from the Grapes Bar (a well-known Rangers pub) were playing guys from the Heraghty's Bar (a well-known Celtic pub). The game was played at the red ash pitch next to The Grapes and this mini bus pulled up with a mixture of guys in Celtic away jerseys and green t-shirts. The crowd was growing, the songs were being sung. Their boys were going down the wing and getting tripped up and having the ball taken off them. It was an absolute farce and had to be abandoned at half-time with The Grapes about 11-0 ahead! The mood on the bus to the game was positive. There were no doom and gloom merchants, as is often the norm before a big game, just because of nerves. Everyone was bouncing, fist pumping each other. We were going to do this. My brother and I were sat right at the very back of the very top tier and right on the dividing line between the two sets of supporters. You could reach over and shake one of their fans warmly by the neck if you so wished. I said to my brother that these were either going to be the very best or very worst seats in the house that day.'

Andrei Kanchelskis was a fresh injury blow for Advocaat, with Arthur Numan and Barry Ferguson already established absentees. Stefan Klos took his place in goal behind a back four of Sergio Porrini, Colin Hendry, Lorenzo Amoruso and Tony Vidmar. Claudio Reyna, Giovanni van Bronckhorst and Jörg Albertz were the basis of a midfield three with Gabriel Amato, Neil McCann and Rod Wallace, an ever-present in the league that season and with 26 goals under his belt, working interchangeably. Despite the Celtic injury list (Gould, Burley and McNamara were out and Paul Lambert wasn't 100 per cent) they were still 11-8 favourites, perhaps with a nod to Rangers' poor Old Firm record thus far that season. Dr Joe Vengloš, a Celtic manager against whom you'd struggle to manufacture antipathy, opted for a 3-5-2 with Kerr in goal and Stubbs, Annoni and Marshall in defence. Vidar Riseth and Stéphane Mahé were deployed at wing-back with Morten Weighorst, Paul Lambert and a withdrawn Henrik Larsson behind Harald Brattbakk and Mark Viduka.

As is so often the case with these fixtures, the opening 15 minutes neatly showcased everything that would ultimately define this match. Rangers were quick, McCann's break past Annoni in only two minutes, and very tidy, as exemplified by a brilliant bit of Reyna intelligence when he stopped a Larsson breakaway in its tracks. Celtic were more keen to use the air and find Viduka and Larsson; however, as suspect as Klos could sometimes be from crosses, Hendry and Amoruso ate that up all evening.

In the eighth minute there was a perfect crystallisation of the two approaches when Riseth attempted to shoulder Albertz away and engage in some extras. The German midfielder simply ignored it and walked away. 'Stay calm and play your game.' That attitude reaped early dividend. On the 12th minute Rangers built from Vidmar at the back, who fed Albertz in the middle of the park, who neatly kept the move flowing out to van Bronckhorst on the left. His ball to Rod Wallace in behind the Riseth was perfectly weighted and the danger was now on. As the Celtic defence gravitated towards that ball, McCann was left in acres of space in the middle of the box. No one could get close to Wallace, whose cut-back was good enough to find McCann's outstretched leg and Kerr was well beaten. 'The quick goal was ideal because they wanted a battle,' recalls Iain. 'They wanted it on the pitch and in the stands. And this quick, passing move that carved them open killed that dead. I had a policeman's finger in my face. "Just stay back!" My brother told me to focus, as if we were on the pitch itself.'

Any semblance of control that Celtic had on the game evaporated soon after as Rangers looked dangerous, breaking with speed and precision and the 3-5-2 was being exploited often through Vidmar and McCann. Amoroso v Viduka was a continually intriguing battle but the real chances fell to the likes of Weighorst and Riseth who were almost comical in their execution. It was becoming more evident that Stéphane Mahé was not enjoying his evening as he was twice booked for dissent, the second of which typified a team living on the volcano, as he was effectively complaining and gesticulating in the face of Hugh Dallas after he did his job by blowing for the Rangers foul. Before he could, correctly, book Neil McCann for the foul, Mahé was responding in advance. This, and his elongated exit from the stage, was a crazy display of teenage tantrum at a tense stage of a crucial match, but one that would soon just fade into the bigger picture of absurdity.

With six minutes left before the break Sergio Porrini was fouled by Weighorst down by the far-side corner flag. Van Bronckhorst, in no huge hurry to get the ball, was encouraged by Dallas to get a move on by way of a pat on the lower back, by which point currency was already starting to rain down upon the area. The Dutchman's attempts to take the free kick were further delayed as a Celtic fan ran onto the pitch to try and get at Dallas and then soon after, when one of the coins struck its intended target square on the head. With blood pouring from the match official, there was a legitimate feeling inside the ground that the match could be called to a halt. 'There were surges coming down the stairs, guys were purple across the aisle,' said Iain. 'We worried that they were going to try and get the game abandoned.'

When van Bronckhorst eventually did get his free kick away, it only led to more bedlam. It was a long cross, perhaps longer than intended, and in trying to avert the danger at the back of the box, Vidar Riseth wrestled with Tony Vidmar. It wasn't a stone-waller but it could certainly be justified, and Dallas didn't flinch from his responsibility, despite Paul Lambert making it clear that he only gave it because he had been struck on the head. It was too much for some fans as more made their way onto the pitch and one later fell down from the top tier, such was the outrage. Parkhead was descending into chaos but, thankfully for Rangers, the coolest man in the stadium had the ball on the spot. Chewing his gum, Jörg Albertz looked to blast it but simply passed it into the bottom-left corner and Rangers were now in dreamland at the interval.

The second half was fairly open but, unsurprisingly, it lacked anywhere near the tension and drama of the first. Neil McCann should have done better, with two good opportunities, and Kerr did well to stop, rather than save, a blistering Albertz free kick following his handball outside of the area, whereas at the other end Klos had to be alert to a Bratbakk volley across the face of goal. The atmosphere had turned into a strange lull as those Celtic fans who weren't already at Glasgow Cross defiantly taunted the visitors, perhaps saving themselves for a long night ahead, by singing 'Can you hear the Rangers sing?' As ever, their timing was perfect. With 15 minutes remaining, Jonathan Johansson, a second-half substitute for Amato, opened a gap in the Celtic defence with a neat flick through for Neil McCann from a Colin Hendry ball out of defence. McCann, who had described himself as feeling 'untouchable' that night, turned Scott Marshall and the rest was simple, as he rounded Kerr and stroked the ball home before checking his run, lest he followed straight into the Celtic end. It was just one more goal but, on that day, there felt a huge difference between a 2-0 win and a 3-0 hammering. The same song could be heard again but with one significant word changed.

There was just time left for some silliness. With five minutes left Riseth attempted to clatter Rod Wallace in the middle of the park with a late lunge that the English striker managed to avoid, but took the chance to turn back to let the Norwegian know that he wasn't best pleased. It was a push to the chest that sparked a fracas and, probably because of that, Wallace incredibly saw a straight red. It was an ample opportunity for Dallas to level the playing field but such parity was short-lived. Riseth's desire not to remain on the park at the final whistle manifested itself in a disgraceful tackle on Reyna deep in the Rangers corner and he saw a second yellow. It was the last of any meaningful action as minutes later Tony Vidmar sunk to his knees holding the ball, Derek McInnes lifted van Bronckhorst up in the air and Advocaat took his acclaim on the bench with his staff, Bert van Lingen's tears and all.

All our dreams were made as a Rangers team celebrated a league title at Parkhead. The mock 'huddle', all two seconds of it right in the corner where the Rangers fans were packed, was a welcome salute to a support who felt almost insulted that they had lost their title for a whole year. The fact that it was now back was entirely down to Advocaat's message and his plan. 'Calmness was the secret to that game,' said Albertz. 'They lost the plot, arguing with the ref and with each other in the stands. We didn't get drawn into it. It was incredible, winning the title on your rivals pitch. Simply one of the best things ever.' When Lorenzo Amoruso met with me in 2019 he said, 'we knew our jobs and we deleted them completely from the field.' It was an absolutely perfect turn of phrase. Celtic didn't help themselves but they really were just taken out of the contest by a team with consummate focus. It should have been the story of the season.

Alas, it wasn't. 'OLD FIRM SHAME GAME' screamed the same tabloids that had billed it as the 'PARK DREAD CRUNCH' the previous morning. Sky were quick to moralise on the general behaviour despite practically billing it as a re-enactment of the Battle of the Boyne all week. Quite why Rangers were dragged into this corporate responsibility, thanks to a tame Rod Wallace push and because the kind of people who wait by a tunnel to throw coins at footballers found their celebrations to be 'inflammatory', has never been adequately explained. However, the general approach to covering this fixture hasn't changed. Even now, an Old Firm aftermath is dominated by the amplification of nonsense – feasting over gestures and flicks, tugs and words – instead of explaining the wider patterns of the game itself. Thoughtful footballing theories are ignored for the indulgence of tiresome conspiracy theories. Anyone who thought that the hiring of a body language expert was the apotheosis of such a mindset only had a few weeks to wait until even that was surpassed. In the final minutes of the Scottish Cup final, where Rangers completed a treble with a 1-0 win over Celtic, a ball ricocheted off Lorenzo Amoruso's chest in the box. Celtic pleas for a penalty were dismissed by Hugh Dallas, yet again the man directly in the line of fire. Later on BBC Radio Scotland a Celtic fan phoned in to complain about the decision. 'But it hit his chest,' said the panellist Joe Harper. 'Aye,' said the caller. 'But how did *he* know that?'

Of course the old religious tropes were rolled out as the sole explanation for the 113 arrests and widespread disturbance following a fixture with an evening kick-off on a Sunday directly preceding a Bank Holiday Monday. A sporting fixture that was once very much a manifestation of genuine sectarian division in the West of Scotland is still talked about in the same terms, as if it wasn't now something of a pantomime in an overwhelmingly secular country. It is easier for the columnists to find the same tired angles, and for politicians to create straw men, than for anyone to accept the perhaps more uncomfortable truth that people in Glasgow, as in Milan, Rome, Rotterdam and Buenos Aries, just take their football far too seriously.

Twenty years on, Rangers fans still appreciate all there is to rightly celebrate about this evening. It simply doesn't get better in domestic terms. The pain of the failure to land ten-in-a-row 12 months earlier was cleansed in a fashion that we could only have dreamt of. The kind of opportunity that doesn't present itself often was approached by a Rangers team with relish and ruthless professionalism. It was also a reminder that, despite the farce of the surrounding bazaar, the famous old fixture, in its 477th meeting, can still produce excellent footballing stories.

It was the 100th Rangers victory over Celtic. It was the greatest of them all.

1

Rangers 3 Dynamo Moscow 2

European Cup Winners' Cup Final
Wednesday 24 May 1972

'This is the greatest moment of my career with Rangers. There could never be another club for me.'
(John Greig, post-match)

For all the influence that recency bias has on this list, it is still this night, nearly 50 years on, that remains the daddy of all Rangers games. With 1,316 points in the poll, over 450 more than the match in second place, it is rightly honoured by fans of all ages as the greatest. A European trophy in one of the most famous stadiums in the world, built on attacking football and goals from two cast-iron heroes of the Ibrox faithful. What's not to love? Well, as is often the case with Rangers, it is never, ever that simple. As this vote shows, we are happy to recognise Barcelona '72 amongst ourselves, but when it comes to trumpeting this night to the rest of the footballing world, especially to our city neighbours, there is a definite reticence. Whether it be because the tournament itself is now entirely obsolete or because of the lack of iconic technicolour or what happened immediately afterwards, we tend to use our world record of league titles as the achievement that defines us most of all, which is a shame, because the story of Rangers in the European Cup Winners' Cup 1971/72, with all the major narrative ingredients included, is one of the best in the history of the sport.

The roots of our tale are dark ones of sporting frustration and human tragedy. By the mid-60s Celtic were considered, by the *Daily Mail*, to be 'so far behind Rangers that it is no longer a race.' What happened next was supposed to be our history and most fans inside Hampden, as Rangers won the Old Firm League Cup final 2-1 in October 1964, would have assumed as much. Treble-winners the previous season, Jim Baxter switched his team-mates' positions to counter Celtic at every turn, conducting the action like Toscanini. Two months later, after doing much the same to Rapid Vienna as Rangers cruised through to the quarter-finals of the European Cup, he was hacked down for his impudence. Stuck in the mud, the maestro and his broken leg would be a portent for his club's form for the foreseeable future. Rangers never responded to the injury, neither, in truth, did Baxter himself, and the club's confused decision-making was exposed time and again as Stein's Celtic disappeared over the horizon. 1961 and 1967 had come and gone without continental success, and although Willie Waddell had broken a domestic drought of four years with the League Cup in 1970 it was barely laying a glove. A decade that had started with Rangers leading the British charge to new frontiers had ended with the club stuck well behind the slipstream. Things were grim.

All of that was placed into perspective on 2 January 1971. Around five minutes after the end of a dramatic but good-natured Old Firm New Year fixture at Ibrox, someone slipped on the massive Stairway 13, down which thousands tried to pour out into the gloomy evening. A crush ensued and 66 fans died. The club was plunged into grief but was eventually led out of it by Waddell. 'Mr Rangers' may have had his detractors on the field of play, but he was exactly the kind of statesman that Rangers needed immediately afterwards and in the years to come, as he would go on to lay the foundations for a stadium that would be a lasting memorial. Speaking to *The Scotsman* years later, Waddell said, 'It's strange what comes into your mind, but when I first went to the top of the steps and gazed down on the pile of bodies, my initial thought was of Belsen, because the corpses were entangled as they had been in the pictures which came out of the concentration camps. But my God, it was dreadful: there were bodies in the dressing rooms, in the gymnasium and even in the laundry room. My own training staff and the Celtic boys were working flat out at the job of resuscitation, and we were all trying everything possible to bring breath back to those crushed limbs. Honestly, I will never forget the sight of Bob Rooney, the Celtic physiotherapist, with tears in his eyes giving the kiss of life to innumerable victims. He never stopped, nor did the Rangers doctors, nor the nurses and ambulance staff who flocked to join them, and we will never know how many lives were saved in there in that frenzy of activity.'

Rangers learned the lessons that football didn't but, as Daniel Harris pointed out in his article for *The Guardian* on this campaign, things had to get back to normal. 'In such circumstance, it seems crass to discuss on-pitch woes, yet, at the same time, not crass at all; more than 80,000 people were gathered that afternoon for the specific purpose of enjoying a football match, and subsequent attendances were as usual. People cared about the game before the disaster and people cared about the game after the disaster, because it was, and is, impossible for them not to.' Although it was never really mentioned specifically within a more buttoned-up emotional culture, in season 1971/72 Rangers had to produce something for them. 'Jock Wallace said the only thing you can do to make these people's lives a bit happier is to go out there and win games and win trophies,' said Derek Johnstone on STV's *The Football Years*. 'We wanted to do it for them.'

It wouldn't come in domestic business, which was showing no real signs of improvement whatsoever, but Rangers in Europe under Waddell were a different animal altogether. Stade Rennais were the first, but not the last, continental opposition to complain about 'anti-football' as Rangers pressed them heavily in a 5-3-2 system, with Colin Stein and Willie Johnston leading the smothering operation from the front.

They boasted that they would show Rangers what real football looked like at Ibrox, but a solitary Alex MacDonald goal was enough to relegate the aesthetic conversation to the periphery.

Waddell's preparation in this run is too often understated. Rangers managed to get three 1-1 first-leg draws in France, Italy and West Germany that set up decisive second-leg victories at Ibrox. There was no coincidence there. It was football planning at a time where bally-ho-death-or-glory still seemed to be the order of the day for most British clubs. Arguably the finest example of this *McCatenaccio* was against Serie A leaders Torino in the quarter-final. Waddell's system saw Derek Johnstone come into defence alongside Colin Jackson, with Dave Smith sweeping up behind. Smith, in *To Barcelona And Beyond*, said that he had experienced pressure before but 'nothing like that night in Turin'; however, the system, which was rehearsed and rehearsed in training, limited the Italians to one strike, with Willie Johnston grabbing the Rangers goal. Waddell and Wallace liked to give their players pictures of their opposite numbers, with some details on their strengths and weaknesses on the back. In his autobiography John Greig remembers such a pre-match discussion with Waddell. 'The boss held up a photograph of one of the Torino players and said to me: "John, this is their number one player, Claudio Sala. He is just 19 and he is the new Italian wonder boy. I want you to put him out of the game." I asked: "Just for this one game, boss, or for good?" "I'm serious, John," he rapped and I replied: "So am I, boss, so am I."'

There was one round, however, that strayed far from that tight script. Every good story needs an element of comic farce and the second-round tie with Sporting Lisbon provided just that. Perhaps it was because Rangers played the first leg at home that the conditions for chaos were created which the usual masterplan normally negated. Favourites for the competition, ahead of Bayern Munich, Torino and Liverpool, Sporting were put to the sword in the opening 45 minutes, 3-0 down at half-time with some cleverly worked goals, two from Stein and one from Willie Henderson, a nice reference to the previous glory era, in his final season at Ibrox. The Portuguese managed to find two second-half goals to set up a fascinating second leg. The away plan started well, with Rangers managing to shut down a quiet opening quarter, but the match showcased the adaptability of this Rangers side in a bruising encounter. Stein equalised a minute after Héctor Yazalde's opening goal and, although João Laranjeira gave the home side a lead at the break, Stein equalised again inside the first minute of the restart. They'd have to cope with Ronnie McKinnon's broken leg ('the worst tackle I've ever seen in my life,' according to Greig) and a late third goal that sent the match into extra time. It was Henderson again, however, who brought Rangers back into control and a Fernando Peres fourth with only five minutes remaining could only tie the sides at 6-6, Rangers having the away-goal advantage, except that the Dutch referee Laurens van Ravens wasn't quite *au fait* with the rules and ordered a penalty shoot-out. Shook up by the vociferous atmosphere, Rangers crumbed on the spot, missing three penalties (or four if you include the one Smith missed before being given a reprieve from a re-take). Incredibly it took a *Daily Mail* journalist, John Fairgrieve, to come into the deflated dressing room with his rulebook and a quick and impassioned appeal was made, successfully, to the UEFA rep. Rangers progressed.

They progressed all the way to the final, of course, to be held in the magnificent Camp Nou, Barcelona. 'I had been to the Lisbon, Torino and Bayern games at Ibrox and I was always going to that game, especially because I had missed out on Nuremberg,' recalled Hamish Tindall. 'My dad went in '67 and he wouldn't take me because I was only 11. The Barcelona trip was arranged very quickly. I spoke to the boys who ran the supporters' club (the YMCA Rangers Supporters' Club from Dundee) and, even at 16, it was me who actually organised the transport! I got them a bus from Brechin. It was £20 a head and there were 37 that went over on that bus. It was me who picked the tickets up and that had to be done through the SFA. Given the size of the stadium, tickets weren't an issue. Anyone who was there on the day could get in.' More than 100 planes, more than 200 buses and many more cars carried around 25,000 Rangers fans to Catalonia, mostly organised by Dixon Travel, based in the city's Southside and the official provider into the turn of the century. All who travelled were convinced that it would surely be third time lucky. The Rangers players were secluded from the growing frenzy, being 15 miles from town, acclimatising in their own training camp. Warned by Wallace not to stay out in the sun, there were more than a few strangely red faces at mealtimes, including Sandy Jardine, who could have done more damage had his go-kart trip gone awry on the day before the final.

A £30 trip all in, nearly £400 in 2019 money, was costly but manageable and the distance was within range, although not without its challenges. 'We left on the Sunday, stopped twice and got to Barcelona the night before the game. I didn't sleep in a bed for a week. I slept on the bus, even that night. We could have a shower down at the beach when we went for a swim! On the way back we jumped in a fountain in France just to freshen up!' Apart from an acute fear of missing out, there was another reason why being in Barcelona was worth the hassle. Incredibly, the game could not be shown live on television due to the fact that Scotland were playing Wales at Hampden in a Home International, with England to come at the weekend. Listening on the radio and waiting for the highlights was the only option for those stuck at home and the quality of that was still very grainy black-and-white, Franco's Spain still being behind the curve on the new colour technology that was becoming the norm.

Waddell had some defensive injury worries to contend with. Colin Jackson, pulling out of a tackle with Tommy McLean in training in the final session, had aggravated an old ankle injury and he wouldn't make it. This meant that 18-year-old Derek Johnstone had to reprise his role in defence and more pressure was placed on the Rangers captain to battle through his own injury concerns and make the starting line-up. Greig, with his lucky goatee beard that hadn't been shaved since the Sporting Lisbon home game, could hardly walk but took injections in order to take his place. In all honesty, he was never going to miss it, the resentment of 1967 still fuelling his desire to finally lift a European honour in royal blue. 'Roger Hynd hurled his runners-up medal into the crowd. I bounced mine off every wall in the dressing room.' With this possibly being his last chance, John Greig would need to be chained down in order for him not to lead his team out on that stage once again.

Dynamo Moscow were breaking new ground as the first-ever Russian side in a European club final, although the USSR had won the first-ever European Championship held in Paris in 1960. Given the political climate and the visit to a fascist state, there was perhaps more pressure placed on Konstantin Beskov's men, unused as they were to such high stakes. Tactical discussion had to make way for countless *nakachkas* – Communist ideological diatribes – as they were promised the title Master of Sport if they were to triumph on Franco's soil. Usually an attacking side, although experiencing some domestic difficulty too, the Russian threat was blunted by losing Vladimir Koslov and Anatoly Kozhemyakin to injury before the game, and they switched to a more containment approach in place of their natural flair. It was arguably the most decisive factor in the match.

Rangers were probably most vulnerable in that opening spell, mainly due to the fact that they had missed their warm up because of pitch invasions from a Rangers support who, even that early, were already at fever pitch. The Rangers side that walked out under the new lights at the Camp Nou on that famous night was: Peter McCloy, Sandy Jardine, Willie Mathieson, John Greig, Derek Johnstone, Dave Smith, Tommy McLean, Alfie Conn, Colin Stein, Alex MacDonald and Willie Johnston. John Greig announced himself on Yozhef Sabo with a thumping challenge from behind in the opening seconds, but Rangers were nervy in the first quarter, failing to connect too many passes and find much in the way of rhythm. Dynamo had long-range efforts, as did Tommy McLean; however, a more adventurous Russian start may have changed the course of the night and history itself.

One of the stand-out performers against Bayern at Ibrox was Dave Smith, who started to express himself on this big stage when it mattered most. Reflecting on his career with *The Scotsman* years later, he talked about playing the game 'within the rectangle' and a disdain for hoofing it out of the park under the slightest bit of pressure. Described by Derek Johnstone as 'one of the best talkers in the game', Smith organised the two defenders in front of him but also was able to move the ball out of defence with ease. Although it followed a dubious tackle by Jardine out near the touchline, his long pass for the run of Colin Stein in 23 minutes was inch-perfect. 'Wooft!', screamed Archie Macpherson on the mic. The finish was lightning quick, up into the roof of the net, and Rangers were ahead in a European final for the first time in three attempts. According to Stein in *To Barcelona And Beyond*, the goal was as much down to confidence as anything else. 'If you don't have confidence, one touch can turn into two touches and the chance is gone. It's difficult to coach a striker because so much of it is about instinct. Willie Waddell had Dave Smith playing sweeper before it had been heard of in Scotland, with Colin Jackson and Derek Johnstone there to attack the ball. We built from the back and it worked very well.'

From then on Dyanmo wilted under the pressure of the new experience. Speaking to *The Guardian* in the build-up to the next Rangers European final in 2008, against Russian opposition of course, goalkeeper Vladimir Pilguy said, 'I don't think we were weaker than the famous Scottish club but not having experience of such matches, we were overly worried and as a result froze before our appearance on the pitch. We were affected by the usual atmosphere in Barcelona before the game, and in Moscow before we left there were *nakachkas*. For instance we were spoken to by the vice-president of the Sportkomitet of the USSR who believed that by slogans and appeals he would lift the moral spirit of the team to a new level. We didn't need it. We knew how much was at stake – the honour of Soviet football. For the defeat we have nobody to blame but ourselves. We didn't manage to show over the 90 minutes the sort of football we were capable of playing.'

Just before half-time, the Rangers lead was doubled and again the architect was Smith, with a sumptuous ball from the far side at the end of another run out of defence that seemed to leave the opposition spellbound, such was the lack of aggression in the press. 'I knew where Dave Smith was going to put the ball and I simply got a run on the boy and scored with the header,' said Willie Johnston, one of the smallest players on the pitch rising beautifully between Vladmir Basalayev and Valeri Zykov to meet the cross and provide comfort for any supporters who might have been on edge. Johnston, too, had felt the determined will coursing through his veins before the players had even left Glasgow. 'We knew how hard it was when we had lost before so we were saying to ourselves "in Barcelona, we're not going to get beat".' Surely, not now?

And surely not when he rolled in a third after only four minutes of the second half. If the first two goals were commensurate with the occasion, the quality of the third may be in doubt. From surely the longest punt ever seen by a goalkeeper in a European final, the Russian defenders Oleg Dolmatov and Vladimir Dolbonsov, were statuesque as the ball evaded both of them and Colin Stein, before finding Willie Johnston with all the time in the world to instantly control the ball with his right and then just poke it past Pilguy with his left. 'That's it Bud!' said the captain to his goalscorer, 'we can't lose now.' Even in his commentary position, Macpherson was befriended by Rangers fans who were offering him drinks from their bottle of Fundador!

This is Rangers, however, and there would be no serene cruise towards the party. Dynamo, perhaps shaken out of their stupor, finally discovered their bravery and Beskov threw on Vladmir Eshtrekov with just over 30 minutes left to salvage something. The impact was almost immediate but, typically, it came from a Rangers error. Or, indeed, a collection of them. Neither Derek Johnstone, Willie Mathieson or Sandy Jardine could be particularly proud of their roles in presenting the Russians with a way back into the game, all three passes being weak and complacent, but Gennady Yevriuzhikin pounced on the Rangers left and his low cross was turned in by the substitute.

'I was in the middle tier,' recalled Hamish. 'For the third goal I came down closer to the pitch but I never went on the park. I was just waiting for the presentation. I was young so I was naturally confident about Rangers and it was the first time in my life that I had been drinking, which just added to that. Near the end I wasn't so confident mind you!' There were a couple of counter punches by McLean and Stein, but the Rangers legs had gone. The remaining half hour was a siege on McCloy's goal, with Mikhail Gershkovich, the second Dynamo substitute, looking the most threatening. The play around the Rangers box was intricate as McCloy had to save twice from him and watch another header zip over the bar. Jardine was called upon to frantically hook a ball off the line and he then tested McCloy himself with a mistimed clearance that went straight towards goal. Predictably, with just three minutes to go, Eshtrekov eased away from the tired pursuit of Mathieson in the box to slam home a second.

Rangers fans were now just praying for a whistle. There was a false alarm when the referee blew for offside and hundreds spilled onto the park again. Finally the agony was ended, the fabled European trophy had been delivered and for thousands of Rangers supporters, who had watched other fans take to the field in such moments, including their greatest rivals, it was now their turn. 'I began to panic,' said Hamish. 'I remembered when the Rangers fans first ran on the park I thought, "We could be in trouble" because we had been given a warning after Newcastle for exactly that [in 1969]. The last few minutes were very stressful. I was so nervous. The reaction, however, was joyous. A lot of people don't understand it. Ajax played at Wembley, Celtic played in Lisbon. If you look at the history before it, everybody ran on the park at European finals. Celtic fans had to jump across a moat to get on in Lisbon. It was the common thing. But when the police pulled the batons, that is when it turned nasty and got out of hand.'

The Spanish police force had shown relative ambivalence towards the previous invasions. With only 400 Russians high up in the stands, there was never a question of violent confrontation. This was pure elation, with more than a little sangria mixed in for good measure. Now, however, with the television pictures cut off to the outside world, their approach was very different and a riot ensued on the pitch – bottles, batons and all. The carnage ensured that players and fans alike would be denied the public celebration that they so richly deserved. Instead, John Greig met with UEFA officials in a small room in the Camp Nou basement, was given the trophy and then told to leave. The iconography is therefore limited to dressing-room celebrations, especially the embrace between manager and captain, or on the back of a coal lorry when the players eventually got to Ibrox the following day, and there isn't an image that is truly befitting the moment or the overall achievement. Even as the players, in brilliant royal blue tracksuits, paraded the cup around Ibrox, there were still question marks over whether or not we would even get to keep it. The Russians had made a lot of the mistaken invasion, when there was still some time left on the clock, and even the great Lev Yashin, then a coach at Dynamo, appealed for a replay. 'They had mad faces, with bulging eyes,' said Pilguy in his 2008 interview. 'They had to be cleared from the field and although they didn't really do us any harm, it meant the game was held up, and that was a big advantage for our opponents. They were exhausted by that stage and could hardly drag their legs, and I'm sure in that final four minutes we'd have scored a third.' It was a whole three weeks before UEFA finally upheld the result but banned Rangers from Europe for two seasons, later cut to one after a successful appeal by Waddell.

'It's a regret that I never saw a presentation,' said Hamish. 'The first time that I actually saw the cup was when Rangers played Clydebank in the League on the first day of the next season. We were on the way back when it was paraded at Ibrox. After Barcelona, we totally believed that we would see Rangers win regular European honours after that. My dad was a Rangers fan but he didn't go all the time; however, I started a Rangers supporters' club, the Dundee Loyal. I've been watching Rangers for years and years, I still wear the same scarf I had in 1964 and I desperately want to see them win another European honour. Manchester 2008 was the biggest disappointment for me. I was at every game that season, home and away.'

It is this sense of a lack of fulfilment when discussing the greatest-ever triumph that makes Rangers the club, and the institution, that it truly is. Even forgetting the events that marred the night itself, there's a slight reluctance to celebrate this so publicly, perhaps because there was an expectation that more would follow in that decade, especially the one we wanted more than any other. The whole story of Rangers in Europe is underpinned by frustration and underachievement. There are 17 fantastic European matches in this list, including this winning final, and all of them would make the top 20 in most clubs' history. And that doesn't even take into account the other victories that failed to make the cut, both at Ibrox and from Mönchengladbach to Monaco, Leverkusen to Livorno. It is because of the standards that were set at Rangers from the very outset that there is almost always a 'but' when it comes to discussing our own success.

Yet this night, or really that entire run, is a story that really should be told with gusto and pride. It may not be around anymore, but the European Cup Winner's Cup had a style and prestige to it at the time, and Celtic and Aberdeen, although they enjoyed more glamorous finals when it was their time, couldn't boast the journey to them that this Rangers team had to overcome. In the dressing room afterwards, Willie Waddell said, 'You don't realise what you lads have done tonight. Plenty of great Rangers sides in the past have never done it. You'll be immortalised by Rangers fans forever.' Perhaps that aura needs a little more gleam.

Waddell's place on that pantheon may well need some restoration too. It was his assistant Jock Wallace, promoted that summer as his boss moved upstairs, who would break Stein's stranglehold and open up an era of dominance himself. However, it was Waddell who not only put the club back on the right path but achieved something far greater and more resonant than league titles or even trebles. From the grim reality of carrying dead bodies around a football stadium to ensuring that Rangers were represented at every single funeral, he set about the task of providing some much needed light in the darkness, with genuine love and hard work and then, with the same drive, he went on to help create a lasting memorial well into modernity, with the re-building of Ibrox Stadium.

When the term 'great' is used correctly within sport, it is usually because an event feels transcendent. It applies to nights that are about more than just medals and goals. As a footballing achievement, this match deserves to sit above them all, there really isn't a greater Rangers game. But it was more than that. It was the finale of a story about a Rangers team in turmoil, who were desperate to finally provide something illustrious for those who loyally followed them everywhere and to pay a fitting tribute to those who couldn't. For those who never came home.

Printed in Great Britain
by Amazon

52172805R10163